ECONOMICS OF PUBLIC

01865 843000

44 1865 314 301 Henneman

008

Butterworth Heinemann (4/04)

C/O Elsevier 0208 308 5700

Cust. 01865 474000

Harcourt 01865 310366

Titles of related interest

HARBURY
Workbook in Introductory Economics, 4th edition

ROSEGGER
The Economics of Production & Innovation

Related journals *free specimen copy available on request*

Long Range Planning

World Development .

ECONOMICS OF PUBLIC FINANCE

FOURTH EDITION

*An Economic Analysis of Government
Expenditure and Revenue
in the United Kingdom*

by

CEDRIC SANDFORD
University of Bath, U.K.

PERGAMON PRESS

OXFORD . NEW YORK . SEOUL . TOKYO

UK	Pergamon Press Ltd, Headington Hill Hall, Oxford OX3 0BW, England
USA	Pergamon Press, Inc., 660 White Plains Road, Tarrytown, New York 10591-5153, USA
KOREA	Pergamon Press Korea, KPO Box 315, Seoul 110-603, Korea
JAPAN	Pergamon Press Japan, Tsunashima Building Annex, 3-20-12 Yushima, Bunkyo-ku, Tokyo 113, Japan

First edition 1969; Reprinted with minor revisions 1970
Reprinted 1976
Second edition 1978; Reprinted 1981
Third edition 1984; Reprinted 1987
Fourth edition 1992

British Library Cataloguing in Publication Data
A catalogue record for this book is available from the British Library.

Library of Congress Cataloging-in-Publication Data
Sandford, C. T. (Cedric Thomas), 1924–
Economics of public finance: an economic analysis of government expenditure and revenue in the United Kingdom by Cedric Sandford.—4th ed.
p. cm.
Includes bibliographical references and index.
1. Finance, Public—Great Britain. 2. Fiscal policy—Great Britain. I. Title.
HJ1023.S15 1992 336.41—dc 20 92–13793

ISBN 0 08 037305 4 Hardcover
ISBN 0 08 037306 2 Flexicover

Printed in Great Britain by B.P.C.C. Wheatons Ltd, Exeter

Preface and Acknowledgements to Fourth Edition

The basic structure of the book remains the same as in the Third Edition, but it is a sign of the pace of change in public finance in this country that nearly all the chapters have been largely re-written. Thus the new edition includes an account and critique of the Conservative Government's tax reforms: the restructuring of corporation tax; the dismantling of capital transfer tax and its replacement by inheritance tax; the big reductions in income tax; the special investment and savings incentives and the increase and restructuring of national insurance contributions; the introduction of individual taxation in the income tax and the attempt to widen the base of V.A.T. and the increase in its rates. The latest research on the effects of the income tax cuts is included and that on the compliance costs of taxation — the importance of which is being increasingly recognised.

In local government finance the life and death of the community charge is documented and the changes in the non-domestic rate and the grant system.

The changes on the public expenditure side have hardly been less than on the taxation side, with the search, by the Executive and Parliament for more effective methods of control, as witness the Financial Management Initiative (F.M.I.) and the establishment of the National Audit Office. The principles of the F.M.I. have permeated into the education system and the health service and the latest government developments with economic significance in these fields are outlined, including the student loan scheme, as well as the, as yet, theoretical search for more meaningful ways of allocating resources in the health service.

Whilst the chapter on budgetary policy retains its place, the

v

emphasis on controlling inflation and reducing unemployment has shifted to monetary policy and supply side measures—and this is fully recognised if not considered at length.

The tax and expenditure changes have had their effect on the distribution of income which has become much more unequal since 1979 and they will undoubtedly also affect the distribution of wealth, though this will take far longer to show up in the statistics.

With 1992 looming, progress has been made towards tax harmonisation, or at least tax approximation, in the European Community and the more important developments are considered.

For all this change, there remains much that is unsatisfactory in the United Kingdom tax system and the final chapter looks at possible reforms, including the possibilities for more "green" taxes.

In all these revisions I owe a debt of gratitude to many other authors, not least those of the Institute for Fiscal Studies, which continues to publish high quality monographs on topical issues. I have sought to recognise the contribution of other authors by way of footnotes. To acknowledge all I have gained in a variety of ways from colleagues, students and tax officers would be difficult, if not impossible, but I would specifically like to thank Ann Robinson, formerly of the University of Bath, John Cullis of Bath University and Gordon Keenay of the Statistics Division of Inland Revenue. I need hardly add that I, alone, am responsible for the opinions aired and for any mistakes.

My publishers, in the person of Sammye Haigh, have been particularly tolerant of a long-delayed typescript and I thank them. Finally, my thanks are due to my wife, Christina, who typed many of the changes in the late hours. To her and daughter Anna, I dedicate this book.

October 1991.   CEDRIC SANDFORD

Contents

Introduction

This book is about economics. A common impression is that economics is concerned with conserving candle ends and pinch-penny
saving; indeed, an economist has been irreverently defined as a man
who splits his trousers trying to save shoe leather. This is a misleading impression. As the economist J. B. Say put it, "Economy must
not be confused with parsimony." Economising may mean something very different from cutting back on this or that expenditure.

Economics, in fact, is a scientific study of how man uses, or fails
to use, the resources at his disposal to satisfy his wants. When most
people think of "resources to satisfy wants" they think of money. It
is true that we can reasonably regard our personal economic problems in these terms. Yet to identify economic problems with money
is again to be misled, or at least to be superficial. If national economic problems were simply a question of scarcity of money we could
print more. The government does not do this (except within defined
limits) because, if it did, prices would rise, reflecting a scarcity of
goods and services; hence behind the scarcity of money lies a
scarcity of goods and services. Indeed this is not the end of the trail;
underlying the scarcity of goods and services is a scarcity of the
means to make the goods and services—workers of various skills,
raw materials, plant and equipment. These are the real resources
which economics is about; money is the medium by which they are
exchanged and the common denominator in which their values are
measured; it is true that fluctuations in the quantity and value of
money itself may complicate economic problems, but *the* economic
problem is that of utilising as effectively as possible the scarce *real*
resources. Indeed even personal economic problems can be viewed
in this light. The reason we each have an economic problem of
scarcity of money is that the real resources we have to offer in
exchange for our income are limited—limited to the amount of

property which (through the medium of money) we lend to the economic system and to the amount and quality of the labour we can personally supply.

Because man's wants are almost insatiable and because the resources to satisfy them can be used in different ways the issue of choice permeates economic decision-making. We cannot have all the things we want; we have to choose between them. That being so what we decide to have is at the cost of the alternative sacrificed. As an individual the cost of the washing-machine I have just bought is the fridge I could otherwise have had. As a nation the cost of a new hospital may be two new schools. Besides choices between alternative goods to be enjoyed now, as individuals and nations we have choices to make between the present and the future. We can consume more today if we save less; but then we have less to buttress our future living standards. Similarly as a nation we can choose between consumption and investment; consumption raises current, investment future living standards.

These choices are never absolute. We are never going to decide to have all hospitals and no schools or vice versa; or all consumption expenditure and no investment or vice versa. The difficult decisions are "marginal" ones; how many more hospitals in relation to how many more schools. Airy generalisations, like "Education is first priority" or "Health must come first" get us precisely nowhere.

In *Economics of Public Finance* we are particularly concerned with the satisfaction of *collective* wants. We consider the economic problems which arise in relation to the government or public sector of the economy: how resources are divided *between* the private and public sectors, and *within* the public sector, how resources are allocated to satisfy the various ends of government expenditure. The book thus commences with a consideration of the economic role of government, examines the scope and control of public expenditure and considers particular services in more detail. The main method of diverting resources from private to public use is by taxation—which compulsorily deprives the private citizen of spending power to confer it on the government; hence much of the book is taken up with an account of the so-called principles of taxation and an analysis of the incidence of the main forms of tax. The particular problems of local government expenditure and taxation are then considered.

Government expenditure and taxation, in direction and extent, by deliberate policy or unwittingly, can profoundly influence the distribution of income and capital in the community and this we examine in Chapter 11. Further, government expenditure and revenue vitally affect the overall level of activity in the economy; although Keynesianism may be out of fashion, no book on public finance since Keynes can fail to include an account of the principles and practice of budgetary policy. Inflation has become so prevalent in Western economies and its impact on the tax system is so considerable that a short chapter is devoted wholly to it. Further, membership of the European Community (E.C.) has important tax implications and Chapter 14 on International Perspectives mainly deals with these. The final chapter looks at possible reforms in public expenditure and taxation practice and procedures and seeks to clarify some of the issues facing British governments and people.

Any writer on economics is faced with the need to draw more or less arbitrary demarcation lines. He must include sufficient of the topics on the fringes of his theme for a comprehensible and comprehensive presentation, but not so much that balance, unity and purpose are lost. Perhaps the biggest omission, in a book on government expenditure and revenue, is the very limited treatment of borrowing; or, more generally, national debt and interest rate policy. The chapter on the regulation of the economy, necessarily touches on monetary policy and includes an account of the views of the "monetarists", but the conventional view is taken that anything like a full examination and explanation of monetary policy is best undertaken within a volume on money and banking. Again, consideration of management of the economy leads on to international problems of exchange rates and the balance of payments, and to issues of economic planning—indicative and administrative, national and regional. These topics are touched upon but not explored in depth; to have done so would have taken us well outside our brief. Two further omissions should be mentioned: no attempt has been made to analyse the position and problems of the nationalised industries—a special public sector of the economy which is a study in itself; nor, except in the chapters on control of expenditure and local government finance, have the organs or administrative framework of government been considered other than incidentally.

The procedure of the book is to examine general principles — whether of expenditure, taxation or budgetary policy — but to relate them specifically to the economy of the United Kingdom; indeed to give particular emphasis to issues, like the effect of taxation on incentives, which are a matter of current controversy and concern. By this means it is hoped that the text will be more lively and interesting, for general principles without application are arid.

The economist, as such, should not determine or even seek to determine the objectives of policy. It is not for him to argue that the level of government expenditure is "too high" or "too low"; that more resources should be applied to defence and less to the social services (or the other way round) or more to education and less to health; or that we should, in our government expenditure and revenue, seek to diminish inequalities of income or wealth. In all these questions non-economic considerations enter. The economist's concern is with means rather than ends. He seeks to put issues in a quantitative perspective by demonstrating their order of magnitude. His contribution is to point out implications of policies and inconsistencies between policies; and by so doing he often helps to clarify the ends which are sought, for often in our national policy ends and means are confused. The economist can hope to demonstrate how a particular objective may be achieved at less cost in scarce resources, or more fully achieved at the same cost. Thus, if the economist can show how and how far education and health services are investments, with beneficial effects on future output, this is a useful (though not a sufficient) guide to the resources that should be allocated to them. If he can demonstrate that a particular tax, for an equal yield to the Exchequer and without other "adverse" effects, will bear less heavily on effort and enterprise than an alternative, he has contributed to the efficient use of resources. And even where, as so often, a change of tax or expenditure would further some objectives at the expense of others, at least if the economist can identify and better still quantify the effects, a more rational choice can be made between alternatives. I hope that this book may help to demonstrate the contribution economics can make to social and fiscal policy.

Economics of Public Finance is intended as an introductory text. I hope that it will prove useful to undergraduates in economics and, because of the emphasis on expenditure, to university students of other social sciences, especially sociology, who need to study aspects of economics related to their main discipline. Much of the book is suitable for the good "A"-level student in economics and for those preparing for exams in business studies and professional qualifications in municipal and public administration and in banking. It is also my hope that the book will prove acceptable to intelligent laymen in the professions, business and administration who seek to understand and assess government fiscal policy. No knowledge of economics is assumed on the part of the reader; I have sought to minimise the number of technical economic terms used and to explain those that are introduced. But the book is intended to be intellectually demanding. If the more esoteric techniques are eschewed, no deliberate attempt is made to oversimplify complex issues. In particular, at the risk of tedium, I have felt it necessary to indicate in some detail the basis of the statistics used and to stress their limitations. Experience has impressed me with the wisdom of the adages that "Statistics are like a bikini; what they reveal is interesting but what they conceal is vital"; and that "politicians" (and others) "use statistics as a drunken man uses a lamp post, for support and not illumination". I have therefore been particularly careful to try to avoid adding to the irresponsible propagation of misleading statistics.

Doubtless readers and reviewers will not be slow to indicate how far I have fallen short of these objectives.

CHAPTER 1

The Economic Role of Government

For what reasons and in what ways do governments exercise control over the resources of a nation? These questions lie at the heart of any examination of the "public sector" of an economy. Answers can be sought in various directions. We can adopt the approach of the political philosopher who seeks to explain state action by examining the nature of the state itself. We can follow an historical approach and try to explain the context in which particular governments have, at various times, taken over particular economic roles. To some extent we shall do both of these, but our main method of approach is essentially that of the economist; we will examine the way in which resources would be allocated in a *laissez-faire* economy (where the state's economic activities were minimal) and, by pointing out the deficiencies of this system of allocation indicate the need, the direction and, to a point, the extent of state action. We could have developed an economic approach from the opposite extreme by examining the allocation of resources in a completely centrally planned economy under an economic dictator, demonstrating deficiencies in this allocation procedure and hence the need for creation and development of a "private sector". But this book is written with the "mixed" economies of the Western world in mind and hence to postulate the development of a public sector from a *laissez-faire* economy is more appropriate because it accords more closely with the historical pattern even though it is presented as an approach of logic rather than history.* As our last sentence implies, the various

*The historical movement is not necessarily all one way, as recent developments in the

1

approaches to the economic role of the state are complementary rather than competitive; anything approaching a full understanding requires an appreciation of the social and political scene and historical knowledge; but the logic of resource allocation is an appropriate starting point for a book on economics.

The Price System

How then are resources allocated in a *laissez-faire* economy? The answer is through the workings of the price system, which comprehends not only the prices of consumer goods and services but also the prices of the resources which are used to make them — machines, raw materials, labour. The millions of consumers and the tens of thousands of producers determine the allocation of resources, consumers in purchasing goods and services, producers in securing control over the factors or agents of production to produce the goods and services.

Functions of Price System

The "textbook" functions of the price system are usually taken to be three.

(1) *The price system secures the distribution of goods and services.* Given (a) the volume of goods and services produced and (b) the distribution of income (and capital) the price system secures the distribution of goods and services in such a way that each individual obtains that combination which, *within his budget limitations*, enables him to maximise (expected) satisfactions. This can be contrasted with a system of (physical) rationing, when people who like eggs but not bacon have to take the ration of each and cannot substitute eggs for bacon unless by coincidence they happen to find someone of opposite tastes with whom they can exchange.

(2) *The price system acts as a guide to consumers' wants indicating what*

United Kingdom and many other predominantly capitalist economies indicate; recent moves to "privatisation" have pushed back the frontiers of the state. Where the frontier lies at any particular time is affected by experience, party ideology and even fashion.

should be produced in the future. Suppose, for example, that following the edict of the Roman Catholic Church releasing Catholics from the obligation to eat fish on Fridays, Catholics started to consume more meat instead. Then signals would be sent through the market to the various "factors" concerned with the production of both meat and fish. Meat stocks in the retailers and wholesalers would fall; the scarcity would push up prices; higher prices would make butchering and cattle farming more profitable; existing butchers would seek to expand their businesses and new butchers might set up shops; farmers would seek to expand their production of cattle and take on more cowherds and new farmers might enter the agricultural industry; producers of foodstuffs for cattle would benefit from an increased demand and more resources would be needed to provide foodstuffs; producers of fertilisers for improving the yield of cattle food would feel the benefit and builders of cattle sheds; and a host of others would be affected in greater or lesser degree—slaughterers, importers, breeders, vets. Thus, in various ways, through the opera tion of the price mechanism, by people seeking to gain from higher profits or wages, more resources would be pulled into the production of meat to satisfy the consumer demand. Conversely fish prices and the incomes of those concerned with the catching, curing and marketing of fish would fall. Fewer boats and nets, fishermen and fishmongers would be needed and some would leave the industry. Some fishmongers might turn butchers and some fishermen turn farmers or farm labourers, but it does not follow that resources from a declining industry move directly into an expanding one: the transfer is generally likely to be indirect and involve a complex of inter-related movements.

New products are rarely initiated by consumers, whose role is passive rather than active. Nevertheless, consumers by the exercise of a continuous right of veto, play a major part in determining whether products initiated by producers shall continue to be made and if so in what quantities and at what prices.

(3) *The price system acts as a guide and stimulus to the organisation of production.* Here we are concerned with the prices of the agents or "factors" of production. There are a large number of alternative

ways in which producers can make a particular product (or more accurately, group of products which are close substitutes for each other). Moreover, in pursuit of profits, producers will seek to produce any given output at minimum cost. Given these two facts it follows that if the price of one of the factors of production rises, then producers will seek to substitute other factors for that which has risen in price. This kind of substitution can take many forms; it may be the substitution of one natural raw material for another; or of a synthetic material for a natural material; or of machinery for labour or vice versa; or of one kind of labour (say skilled) for another (unskilled); or of one kind of machine for another machine. Whatever form substitution takes, it is a method of economising scarce resources. The rise in price of a particular factor reflects an increasing scarcity of that factor relatively to the demand for it; the "principle of substitution", which we have just outlined, will ensure that the factor is used where the return on it is highest; it will be used in ways in which the value placed on it by society, as demonstrated by the preferences expressed through the price system, is greatest. If there are other factors which are close substitutes at comparable prices for the factor which has risen in price, they will be used instead of it; the factor which has become more scarce will then continue to be employed for those uses where there are less suitable substitutes or where the substitutes are not available at comparable prices. Similarly, if the price of a factor falls relatively to other factors, because it has become less scarce, then there will be a tendency for this cheaper factor to be substituted for dearer factors. Thus changes in the prices of the factors of production act as signals to producers to rearrange their "in-put mix", in the interests of their own profits; in so doing they are securing a more economic use of resources.

Characteristics of the Price Mechanism

One of the essential characteristics of the price mechanism is the interdependence of prices; it is indeed an economic truism that "everything depends on everything else". A change in the price of one good (e.g. fish) has its effect on prices of related goods (e.g.

meat) and on the prices of the many factors of production used in producing the good in question (e.g. fishmongers' profits, fishermen's wages and boat-builders' profits); and since factor prices are also incomes, this will in turn have some influence (although it may be very small) on the prices of things which fishermen (etc.) buy in so far as they are different from the goods and services which butchers and meat breeders (etc.) buy. This interdependence has an important significance for government policies. If a government intervenes in the free operation of the market mechanism at one point this will have a series of repercussions; if a policy is to be rational it must take those repercussions into account. Thus, suppose, as happened during the 1939–45 war, that faced by rising prices and in the interests of the poorer members of the community, a government imposes rent control over certain classes of unfurnished residential property, and that the controls remain in force for a considerable period of time. The effect is to keep rents (the price of house room) at a level below that which would have been reached in a free market. Certain consequences then follow from the interdependence of markets.

First, as the price is artificially low there are more people who wish to rent a house at the controlled rent than can obtain one; and there are many who would be willing to pay a higher rent if only they could obtain one. This may lead the less scrupulous of the potential tenants and landlords to adopt devices to evade the law, e.g. "key money", the payment by the new tenant of a large undocumented lump sum for the key of a house. Second, the effect will spill over into markets for close substitutes—the renting of furnished property and houses for purchase. Owners of houses will attempt to move into these markets by reletting houses furnished or putting them up for sale; if existing tenants are not to be evicted the government will have to legislate for security of tenancy; then the owners will transfer to the other markets if the tenant leaves. If new houses are built they are likely to be sold or let furnished rather than let unfurnished. Thus the supply of unfurnished houses to let diminishes. On the demand side, potential house renters, frustrated by their inability to obtain unfurnished house-room, swell the demand for furnished house-room or houses to purchase. There may also be a further influence reducing the supply of house-room if the controls are long-lasting during a time of rising prices: landlords may find that it no longer pays to maintain their properties and the quality of rented accommodation deteriorates.

The policy will generate changes in the distribution of income. Tenants will gain at the expense of landlords (which may or may not be the poor gaining at the expense of the rich); also sitting tenants, those fortunate enough to be living in rented property when the controls are introduced, gain relatively to those who are forced to buy houses or rent furnished property at inflated prices. In both cases this redistribution is essentially haphazard and not related to any criterion of social justice.

Moreover, uneconomic use of resources will ensue. Labour mobility is likely to be reduced because people in rent-controlled accommodation will be unwilling to move to a job which would require a change of residence, for then they would lose their rent "subsidy". Also those in rent-controlled houses which have become too big for them may continue to live there, because to leave would involve the loss of their rent advantage.

This illustration serves to show that governments which intervene in the market mechanism must take the inter-relatedness of prices into account. If they do not, then they may be unprepared for the consequences, and may indeed find themselves pursuing policies which act to the detriment of those they most intend to help.

The price system, at its best, is a remarkable mechanism for securing the dispersal of decisions; it achieves a kind of delegation of power. Any society, whatever its socio-economic form, has to find some solution to the economic problem—viz. that the desires of its members are in excess of the resources to meet them so that a choice has to be made about which desires should be met. The decisions might be made by an economic dictator who exercised the choice between alternatives; this would mean a concentration and centralisation of power in decision-making. When the price system is the mechanism for securing the allocation of resources, decisions are decentralised; large numbers of individuals as consumers and producers, exercising their vote in the "ballot box of the market place", to use a somewhat hackneyed expression, by the aggregate effect of their individual decisions determine what shall be produced.

Moreover, again at its best, the price mechanism harmonises the individual and communal interest. Each individual pursuing his own self-interest is, at the same time, *ipso facto*, pursuing the interests of the community. If more meat is wanted, then its price rises, and butchers and farmers and others responding to that price increase in the interests of their own profits or wages provide the additional meat. Or again, if a particular material becomes scarcer, then their self-interest leads producers to modify their organisation of production to economise in the use of this particularly scarce material.

This feature of the price system so impressed Adam Smith, the father of political economy, that he eulogised on the "invisible hand" by whose beneficent influence the interests of the individual and the community were harmonised.

But this, regrettably, is an idealised picture. Since Smith wrote his *Wealth of Nations* in 1776 we have become more conscious of the deficiencies and limitations of the price system. Indeed, by the 1920s the reaction had proceeded so far that the slogan of a particular brand of socialism in Britain was "Production for use and not for profit" as if there were an *inevitable* conflict between the two and what was produced for profit could not also be useful, nor what was useful be profitable to produce. It is time, therefore, to look more closely at the limitations and deficiencies of the price mechanism as an allocator of resources.

Deficiencies and Alleged Deficiencies of the Price System

Where the Benefit is Diffuse or Indiscriminate

The clearest example of services which must be collectively provided is in the maintenance of order internal and external—the police, the courts, the defence forces. Only the very rich could afford to buy their own individual bodyguards and those would be ineffective against enemies acting in concert. For the maintenance of order and defence men have always acted together; the nation state has taken over from the tribe or clan to provide for these collective wants from which all benefit but where the benefit is not precisely allocable.

There is a second category of services where the case for providing collectively for wants is less clear-cut, but is nevertheless very strong; although there is an identifiable individual benefit, to charge the user of the service through the price mechanism would be impossible or inconvenient or disproportionately costly. The provision of most roads and bridges and the lighting and paving of streets are in this category. To finance minor roads with many crossroads by private toll would be difficult if not impossible, while toll charges on rarely used bridges would be easier to collect but not worth the cost of collection. There is a further consideration; the additional cost to the service arising from the individual user (called marginal cost by economists) is nil or negligible; if a toll is charged this will debar some people from using the facility who could have benefited from it, when their use would have added nothing to the cost of providing and maintaining the service. In these circumstances (and the same argument applies to parks and museums) the case for providing the facility from taxation and having no user charge is strong. Even so, for major bridges (like the Forth or Severn) and motorways with few and controlled entry and exit points, if because of government impecuniosity the choice lies between private provision and tolls or no provision, then private provision through the price mechanism may be preferable.

This limitation of the price system, that it is an inappropriate mechanism for the purchase of services which are "indivisible", where the benefit is wholly or largely diffuse, merges imperceptibly into the problem of social benefits, where there is an *element* of diffusion of benefit.

Private and Social Costs and Benefits

Where private producers make a product and private consumers buy it through the price mechanism, the costs (for producers) and the benefits (of consumers) which enter into their calculations are private costs and benefits. As Professor Pigou demonstrated in his

Economics of Welfare early this century, there may be other costs and benefits not taken into account (sometimes called "spillover" effects or "externalities"); there may be a divergence between social costs (which include all costs) and private costs; similarly social benefits may not be identical with private benefit.

The most well-worn example of social costs over and above private costs is the smoke from the factory chimney, which increases laundry bills, blackens buildings and aggravates chest complaints. But there are many other illustrations: slag heaps and pylons which spoil the beauty of the countryside; uncontrolled real property development which becomes an eyesore; the siting of a factory in a congested area, which adds to the congestion, raising travelling costs not only to the new factory, but also to other factories and the general public. In all these examples there are costs generated which have not been taken into account by the private producer. However, it is not only production which has these so-called "externality effects"; consumption also may create social costs over and above private costs. Thus smoking increases the incidence of lung cancer and bronchial complaints and imposes costs on the community's health services; drinking adds to road accidents and also may result in more communal expenditure to maintain law and order; and private motoring pollutes the atmosphere and congests historic towns.

On the benefit side, one of the reasons advanced for the subsidisation of agriculture is that, by and large (and as compared with industry), it improves amenities. Further, as we shall examine in detail in Chapter 4, some expenditure on education and health services provides social benefits over and above private benefits.

Where the private costs of an activity, whether production or consumption, do not cover the full costs, then, in the absence of government action, this form of production (or consumption) is likely to be extended beyond what it would be if the full costs were taken into account. Conversely, activities which give rise to benefits in excess of private benefits are developed less than their real return justifies.

Nevertheless, it does not follow that whenever there is a social cost or benefit not allowed for by private individuals the government should intervene. Almost any human activity gives rise to some cost or benefit to others. If I neglect my garden the weeds blow on to my neighbours' plots; if I look after my garden well, then my neighbours and passers-by enjoy the beauty of my flowers; but it would be absurd to suggest that the state should intervene to penalise bad gardeners and subsidise good ones. Before intervention on these grounds is justifiable the differences between private and social cost, or between private and social benefit, must be substantial. Moreover, the differences may need to be quantifiable before intervention is useful or an over-correction may result—although this depends on the form of government intervention: intervention by regulation may be appropriate without the difference between private cost and social cost having been precisely measured.

Another important consideration is that the borderline of private and non-private costs is continuously shifting. Appropriate regulations may bring within the category of private costs what was formerly outside it. Thus a "clean air" or an anti-pollution regulation pushes the costs of pollution of air or water into the category of private costs; the regulation compels the private producer to incur costs, such as new heating and cleaning equipment and new fuels, to prevent the pollution.

Monopoly

The existence of monopoly elements may prevent the pricing system from working in the ideal way presented in the model. If demand for a good increases, the theory of the price system postulates that the consequential rise in price will lead to an increase of supply of that good; the rise in the price of the product will raise the prices of the resources used to make it, and thus labour seeking higher wages and capital higher profits will flow into that industry. But if there is monopoly in the industry then movement of factors into it may be checked and the higher price may result not in increased production but simply in bigger monopoly profits. The monopoly power may rest on "technical" factors such as the economies of scale* derived

---

*"Economies of scale" summarises the various reasons why a larger scale of operation may bring lower average costs than a smaller scale. For example, many costs (e.g.

from the use of highly sophisticated and expensive equipment; or on the financial power of a concern to buy up or force out of existence new rivals; or it may be a monopoly power of a trade union or professional association controlling and restricting entry into an occupation in the interests of its members. Whatever form it takes monopoly may prevent the efficient use of resources by checking the movement of the factors of production in search of the highest returns. Expressing the same point in a different way, if monopoly elements are present the automatic harmonisation of individual and communal interest, which Adam Smith praised in the price system, may not be achieved.

It follows that control of private monopoly and restrictive practices is a valid field for state action and also the dissemination of knowledge which helps to make competition more effective. It does not follow that the way to deal with private monopoly is necessarily to turn it into public monopoly, for, though public monopolies may be in no danger of making extortionate profits at the expense of the community, because of the lack of competitive pressures, they may waste resources and be equally unresponsive to consumer demand. Moreover, United Kingdom experience with public monopolies suggests that they are almost always subject to political interference by ministers which dilutes responsibility and reduces efficiency.

Loss of Consumers' Sovereignty

Closely linked to the monopoly argument is the contention asserted most forcefully by Professor Galbraith and denied equally forcefully by others that the price system is no longer a guide to consumers' wants; that "consumers' sovereignty" is no more. Galbraith argues that the large corporation, operating under production conditions which require forward planning for many years ahead to secure long runs and a low average cost of product, now dominate the economic scene; that to support this forward planning firms must

interest on money borrowed or site rent) vary with time, regardless of the size of output; if more output can be produced in the same time, say by working equipment more intensively, these "overheads" are spread over a larger number of units of output and are less for each, so that, on this count, average costs (i.e. costs per unit of output) fall.

control demand and that the means to do so are available to them through advertising infused with the black arts of modern psychology; in short that the firm can induce the consumer to accept whatever it produces. His opponents maintain that Galbraith has grossly over-stated his case; that "consumers' sovereignty" was always a misnomer for describing the power of consumers, which in relation to new products has always been passive, but with the fundamental right of veto; that the large corporation and advanced technology are not as dominant in the economy as Galbraith would have us believe; and that many examples can be quoted where the consumer has refused to accept the mass advertised products of the large corporation (notably the failure of the Ford Motor Company to market the Edsel car and I.C.I. to sell Ardil). Moreover, it can be pointed out that the power of the consumer is evident, though exercised through a different medium, in the market research exercises which big firms feel it necessary to conduct at an early stage of product development.*

The Provision of Capital on an Adequate Scale

A further argument, related to monopoly, is sometimes put forward, to the effect that the market mechanism is no longer able to supply the money capital for industries based on advanced technology; that the scale on which such industries require capital is so vast, and possibly the risk factor so large, that the ordinary mechanism of the market cannot meet their needs and the state has to step in with loans or grants. It is clear that governments do financially support advanced technology industries, and this must be recognised in a book which analyses government expenditure and revenue; but it is not clear that these industries *have* to be subsidised. We must distinguish between industries where the government has a direct

*See, for example, J. K. Galbraith, *The New Industrial State*, Hamish Hamilton, 1967 and *The Age of Uncertainty*, B.B.C. Publication/André Deutsch, 1977; G. C. Allen, *Economic Fact and Fantasy*, Occasional Paper 14, Institute of Economic Affairs, 1967; Christina Fulop, *Consumers in the Market*, Research Monograph 13, Institute of Economic Affairs, 1967; S. J. Prais, *The Evolution of Giant Firms in Britain*, Cambridge University Press, 1976; J. Jewkes, *Delusions of Dominance*, Hobart Paper 76, Institute of Economic Affairs, 1977.

defence interest and is a main consumer of the product and industries where this is not so. It is where government is a main consumer of the product, e.g. aircraft and nuclear energy, or where the activity may have defence implications, as in space rocketry, that its financial support has been most marked. Other industries dependent on advanced technology, such as I.C.I. in Britain, have not received special state aid.

A recent example of abnormal risk factors requiring government support has been in respect of nuclear power stations. The United Kingdom Conservative Government under Mrs Thatcher originally planned to privatise nuclear power stations by including them within the larger of two proposed private generating companies. The abnormal risk associated with nuclear power, especially the large and uncertain costs of decommissioning nuclear power stations, raised doubts on whether the public would subscribe to the flotation. In the event, the government felt obliged to retain them in public ownership.

Unemployment

Experience has shown that a *laissez-faire* economy is unstable, that it is subject to successive booms and slumps on a cycle of approximately 10 years. Moreover, the assumption that individual and communal interests are harmonised through the free operation of the price system breaks down in the context of unemployment. Employers employ workers if they expect to be able to sell the goods the workers help to make, the general level of employment therefore depends on aggregate demand for goods and services. If workers fear unemployment, in their own interests they may react by cutting their demands for goods and trying to save for a "rainy day", but if they do this they will create the very unemployment they fear. Similarly, if industrialists fear a slump which will reduce their sales of goods, they may react, in the interests of their profits, by cutting back on their orders for new equipment; but then people will become unemployed in the industries making machinery and these unemployed workers will have less money to buy consumer goods — so unemployment will spread. There is a need for government action to maintain sufficient demand to ensure a high and stable level of employment compatible with other objectives, particularly the control of inflation.

Inequality of Income and Personal Wealth

We indicated that the first function of the price system was to secure the distribution of goods and services *given the distribution of income and capital (or wealth)*. The price system has sometimes been criticised on the grounds that it results in luxuries being produced before necessities; that the rich man can have his caviare when the poor man cannot even obtain the necessities of life. But this is a criticism of the distribution of income rather than of the price system as such— which, functioning as a distributive mechanism for goods and services, simply reflects the distribution of income and wealth. Nevertheless we cannot wholly dismiss this criticism of the price system as beside the point. Differences and changes in prices, and therefore incomes, are necessary to the effective working of the price system if resources are to be re-allocated in accordance with society's changing demands. Governments may wish to reduce the inequality of income and wealth; and much can be done within the framework of the price system to reduce inequality by taxation and cash transfers. But there is a point beyond which those redistributions cannot go without impinging on the efficiency functions of the price system. The functioning of the market mechanism implies a responsiveness to demand through individual reactions to incentives—the prospect of higher profits or bigger wages. Both heavy taxation of the better off and cash subsidies to the poor may have the effect of reducing incentives.

These are the main, although not the only limitations of the price system. Ignorance and inertia of both producers and consumers, whatever their cause, hamper the effective working of the system.

State Intervention in the Economy

The Form

Where these limitations or defects of the price system have been shown to be both valid and significant state intervention, in one form or another, is called for. Intervention may take any or all of three forms—regulation, finance and provision.

Regulation may be positive or negative and affect consumers or producers; thus the state may require school attendance up to the age of 16; it may insist on car drivers having "third party" insurance; it may forbid the sale and purchase of narcotics, prescribe licensing conditions for alcoholic liquors and restrict cigarette advertising. It may endeavour to preserve the social benefits of a locality by imposing planning controls over property developers; prevent the use of certain fuels in "smokeless zones"; and proscribe restrictive practices. It may fix minimum wages by law in certain "sweated industries".

State financing may take the form of a policy of redistribution of income and wealth to ensure that all can afford goods and services that the state considers all should have; this redistribution may be by cash transfers or it could take the form of vouchers for particular services, thus ensuring that spending was on the approved services and goods. The state also may seek to influence the purchase of particular goods and services by subsidising some to encourage their consumption (or conversely imposing on others particularly heavy taxes to discourage purchase).

Finally the state may itself provide services—roads, education, health. These services may be paid for by taxation or by "user charges" or a combination of both. "User-charge" is an expression applied to state-provided services instead of "price" to emphasise the fact that the charge on the user is rarely the full cost; "nil user charge" is a cumbersome expression but less misleading than "free" when applied to goods the cost of which has to be met by taxation or other means.

Several of our most important state services span all three methods. Thus education is governed by regulation—all children must attend school to the age of 16; it is mainly state-provided and state-financed (by taxation) without user-charge, but there are exceptions such as user-charges (fees) for courses at state-provided technical colleges. It is important to realise that state interest in a particular major service like education (perhaps because of the existence of major social benefits over and above private benefits) does not of itself imply state *provision*. It would be possible, for example, for education to be privately provided through the market mechanism at all or any level, and for the state to regulate standards and provide finance either through its general policy of redistributing income or by means of specific grants, loans or vouchers. The number of possible permutations within the range of regulation, finance and provision (with varying user costs) is very large; this is an area of economic and political discussion and decision-making of fundamental importance.

The Characteristics

The process of purchasing "private" goods through the market mechanism has certain distinguishing characteristics from the purchase of "public" goods, i.e. goods provided by the state, paid for by taxation and supplied at nil or nominal user cost, e.g. defence services, roads, education, museums. With private goods no one is compelled to buy what he does not want; ultimate control rests with those immediately concerned with the enjoyment of the good or service; and individual payments are at least proportional to (expected) individual benefits. Provision of public goods, on the contrary, save in the unlikely case of unanimity, involves overriding minorities (or even a majority); there is an irreducible element of coercion—the difference between a price and a tax. Also actual decisions on public goods are taken by ministers or officials; the most the electorate can do is to choose at election time between competing programmes which set out in broad outline the parties' proposals on a whole series of topics; an elector has to accept a package deal and may dislike many of the proposals of the party for which he votes. There is thus no certainty that any particular proposal has majority support for the broad lines of policy proposed, let alone for the details. Moreover, governments do not always carry out election pledges and many decisions on the provision of public goods crop up between elections, so that the electorate is even more limited in its ability to express an opinion on them.

There is, indeed, reason to believe that in public spending governments may have certain predilections which may well accord neither with an efficient use of resources nor the wishes of the majority of the electorate if they appreciated the full implications. In a democracy based on territorial representation producer interests, which tend to be geographically concentrated, are likely to be favoured as against consumer interests which are dispersed (and also less obvious). Thus governments are often tempted to impose tariff or quota restrictions on foreign imports which offer a cheaper product to consumers but threaten domestic industry. Again, governments are often over-tender to prestige expenditure, e.g. on aircraft or other highly expensive products of sophisticated advanced technology, especially where the appropriate experts are in government service, or have the ear of government, and are able to press their views with force and persistence.

It would follow from this analysis of the differences between public and private goods that there is a *prima facie* case for the provision of goods through the price mechanism. As we have seen from our analysis of the limitations and deficiencies of the price mechanism there may be good reasons for over-ruling this *prima facie* case in many instances; but the presumption for provision through the price mechanism holds unless overthrown. Moreover, it also follows that if the state has a particular concern with the way in which resources are allocated and wishes to modify the allocation, there is a *prima facie* case for modifications by means of taxation and cash transfers where possible rather than the provision of goods or services, unless there is some over-riding reason for state provision. Thus, if the government wishes to help the poor, it is generally better to do this by cash transfers than by the provision of "free" or below cost services; that way a direct relationship between individual benefit and expenditure is retained and also a more realistic relationship between price and cost.

Value Judgements

Some people would disagree with the philosophy behind these arguments. The state, they might argue, becomes a "God of the gaps", intervening in the economic system only where the price mechanism is seen to be deficient. They would see the state fulfilling a more positive role. To seek to eliminate poverty and reduce income inequalities by cash transfers would be insufficient. They would argue for state provision of certain services, most notably education and health, on grounds that these important services should be provided to all citizens as a common badge of citizenship; that they should be state-provided and only state-provided.

It is indeed true that both positions represent particular sets of value judgements. The argument for private provision through the price system, unless there are strong over-riding considerations, rests on an individualist philosophy; that the individual and the family are, given an appropriate environment and despite exceptions which do not upset the rule, responsible and capable of exercising responsibility and that there is moral value in freedom of choice and political value in dispersion of economic power. The collectivist argument, on the other hand, reflects doubt about the capacity of individuals to choose wisely and the relevance of the family to modern life and seeks as its objective the transformation of society and the removal of distinctions of social class.*

Not all people fall neatly into the "individualist" or "collectivist" categories, but there is nonetheless a fundamental difference of philosophy as to the objectives of the social services. It is not for the economist, as such, to attempt to decide between moral philosophies; his concern is with means, not ends. But the appropriate means cannot be found unless the end is recognised. It is therefore an economist's function to clarify ends; to help to establish where there are differences of objectives. It is also the task of the economist to indicate the relative costs of achieving alternative ends. His approach should be "scientific" rather than "emotional",

---

*For a discussion of these views see A. T. Peacock, The Political Economy of Social Welfare, *The Three Banks Review*, December 1964.

but he is too often tempted to let his "individualist" or "collectivist" philosophy cloud his scientific reasoning.

Many of the topics touched on in this chapter are considered more fully in the remainder of the book. Our subject is those aspects of government intervention in the economy which require expenditure and the raising of revenue; we shall only incidentally touch on problems where the main method of control is regulation (e.g. monopoly). In the next chapter we look at the historical growth of government expenditure in the United Kingdom. In Chapter 4 we shall be looking at particular areas of government expenditure where collective provision is a necessity, as in defence, and examining the divergence of social and private cost and benefit in education and in health expenditure. Chapters 5 to 9 on taxation include an examination of the effects of taxes on the efficient use of resources. Chapter 11 analyses the distribution of income and capital in the United Kingdom and in Chapter 12 the problems of state intervention in the economy to maintain a high level of employment will be examined. In the final chapter we return to some of the issues raised by the alternative approaches of the "individualist" and the "collectivist" attitudes to welfare expenditure.

CHAPTER 2

The Growth of Public Expenditure

The main purpose of this chapter is to provide an historical perspective by examining the growth of government expenditure in the United Kingdom and the changes in its composition. We then briefly examine some theories of government expenditure as a prelude to analysing the causes of public expenditure growth.

Measuring Government Expenditure

In 1790 government expenditure, taking central and local government together, was £23 million. In 1990, 200 years later, including net lending by central and local government, the corresponding figure was over £200,000 million, approaching 10,000 times the 1790 total. A comparison of money amounts over a long period is almost meaningless; but even if our comparison is restricted to recent years, we must both appreciate the basis on which the statistics are compiled and modify the data in various ways if any comparison is to be meaningful. There are four main sets of problems: defining government expenditure; allowing for changes in the value of money (which varies inversely with the price level); adjusting for population growth; and relating government expenditure to total output.

Definition of Government Expenditure

In defining government or public expenditure we must first decide which spending agencies to include and then which items of their expenditure to take into account. There are four possible spending agencies to consider: central government, local government, the national insurance fund and public corporations of which the most important are the nationalised industries. Clearly the first two must be included. There is also a strong case for including the national insurance fund on the grounds that its disbursements are wholly determined by government policy and its income is derived primarily from levies on employers and employees of a largely compulsory nature and scarcely distinguishable from taxes, together with, for most years, a general exchequer contribution. More difficult to decide is the treatment of public corporations. This book does not examine the policies of nationalised industries nor attempt to assess the total influence of the public sector on the economy, and in the tables which follow the expenditure of nationalised industries has been excluded. We have thus treated them as more or less autonomous bodies whose spending, although influenced by government, is not controlled by it in the same way, or as directly, as the expenditure we have included.

Having decided which spending agencies to include, there remain problems to be resolved and adjustments to be made. Part of local government expenditure is made from grants received from central government; transfers like this between public authorities must be omitted to avoid double counting when we are taking both authorities together. Also there is the question of treatment of government financial transactions on capital account. These include loans to private and nationalised industries. Because the government is really acting as an intermediary between the borrower and the capital market, there is a case for excluding them. On the other hand they add to the total which governments must raise by taxation and borrowing. Another capital account problem is the treatment of the proceeds of government sales, principally privatisations. They reduce the amount the government must cover by taxes and borrowing; but, because they are non-recurring items, the trend in expenditure may be more clearly seen if they are omitted.

Even after these adjustments to obtain a suitable definition there remains an irreducible element of arbitrariness about what constitutes expenditure; it may vary according to the particular organisational arrangements adopted. For example, some government departments receive income from charges on the sale of goods or the provision of services (e.g. museum postcards and prescription charges); the usual procedure is to reckon expenditure net of these charges.

Again, the level of government expenditure is affected by whether a government provides a benefit by means of cash payments or tax concessions. In 1968 the British government increased family allowances and then proceeded to "claw back" the whole of the increase from standard rate income tax payers: even though the net result was the same for the beneficiaries, this method of payment put up the figures of government expenditure much more than if the increase in family allowances had gone only to the poorer families not paying income tax. The effect on public expenditure of adopting a different method of child support was even more pronounced when, from 1977–78 child tax allowances were phased out and replaced by a child benefit paid in cash. Another illustration of the same effect arose in 1966 when the Labour government replaced investment allowances by investment grants; this policy was in turn reversed by the Conservatives; such switches in the method of promoting investment affect the level of government expenditure even if the aggregate financial incentive is unchanged; thus encouraging investment by grants instead of allowing an off-set against profits tax increases government spending, but, of course, also raises tax income. The Americans have aptly coined the name "tax expenditures" for reliefs given through the tax system.

Another form of arbitrariness arises because government trading expenditures which generate some corresponding income may enter into government expenditure if they come directly under ministerial or local government control but not if conducted by a separate public corporation; thus in our figures expenditure on council housing is included, but not that by nationalised industries. The Post Office is included in the earlier figures but not the later; it was run under direct ministerial control until 1969 but then it became a separate public corporation; before that, from April 1961, its accounts had been separated from those of the central government.

Within the total of government expenditure some important distinctions must be recognised. For some purposes we need to separate current expenditure (on services and on goods which will be soon used up) from capital expenditure (on the acquisition of assets like schools, hospitals and roads which we can go on using for many years to come). Assuming no problems of demand management arise,* there is a stronger case for using loans to finance capital expenditure than current expenditure, because capital expenditure benefits the citizens of the future as well as the present and hence they can reasonably be called on to pay extra tax to meet the future interest and repayment charges on the loan.

It is especially important to distinguish between that part of government expenditure which is on goods and services (sometimes termed "exhaustive" expenditure) and expenditure which takes the form of transfer payments—cash payments to individuals such as social security payments, family allowances and interest on government debt—which are not payments for particular economic services. Transfer payments largely leave the control of real resources in the hands of individuals; the recipients determine what shall be purchased and produced; government expenditure on goods and services on the other hand is a direct claim by the government on the community's resources. As we shall see in Chapter 12, this distinction is also important in assessing the effectiveness of alternative measures for regulating the economy.

All these probems of defining government expenditure apply to the present and the recent past. If we seek to survey government expenditure over a series of earlier years, other problems are added; the data are less complete and even the definition of the United Kingdom changes.

In the tables which follow we have used as our basis for government expenditure the measure designated "General Government Expenditure" in the National Accounts and in the Public Expenditure White Papers. This is the measure this government uses to delineate trends and for international comparisons. It consists of the combined spending of central and local government, including both capital and current spending plus net lending. It

*See Chapter 12.

measures the amount the government has to raise by taxation and borrowing. However, in Table 2.1, to show the long-term trend more clearly, we have excluded privatisation proceeds and in Table 2.2 we show the figures with and without the receipts from privatisation.

Changes in the Price Level

Where significant changes in the price level have taken place we can only meaningfully compare one year with another if we can allow for these changes. This adjustment is not simple, especially when, as with government expenditure, we are trying to measure price changes in goods or services, which are not sold in a competitive market. But in principle what we seek to do is to measure the expenditure of all years we are comparing in terms of the prices of one year.

Changes in Population

We should expect government expenditure to rise if the population rose; hence changes per head of population are likely to be more significant than changes in total expenditure. Even this measure obtained by dividing total expenditure by total population is inadequate for some purposes; expenditure may well vary according to the age (and to a less extent the sex) composition of the population; thus a high proportion of old people (and women live longer than men) is likely to put up expenditure—especially on retirement pensions and health—whilst a high proportion of children will put up education costs and child benefit payments.

Government Expenditure and Total Output

It is useful to be able to relate government expenditure to some datum line which takes into account the changing real income of the community; hence it is customary to express expenditure as a percentage of community output or product. This measure has the advantage that it incorporates some automatic (even if imperfect) allowances for changes in population size and in the price level; at the same time it offers an indication of the relative size of the public and private sectors of the economy. It must be stressed, however, that this percentage is not the proportion of total output which government directly controls; if we wish to measure that, we should express government expenditure on goods and services (excluding transfer payments) as a percentage of community output.

To express government expenditure as a percentage of community output does introduce a further source of confusion because of the different measures of community output. National product may be expressed "gross" or "net", the difference being an allowance for capital consumption (or depreciation) which is the value of equipment used up during the course of production. Again "national" product, the total value of the output of goods and services produced by the members of the community, can be distinguished from "domestic" product, which consists of output produced at home, ignoring the value of any net output from overseas property owned by residents in the home country; during the 1970s and 1980s the net property income from abroad of United Kingdom citizens never exceeded 2 per cent of gross product, but earlier in the century the United Kingdom was a big creditor-nation. Finally national or domestic product (and correspondingly, government expenditure) may be valued at "market prices" or "factor cost"; to value in terms of market prices means including in the price any outlay taxes or subsidies, whilst valuing at factor cost excludes such elements and values at the prices paid for the factors, or agents, of production—labour, capital, land—which made the products. If market prices are used the value of national output between one year and the next may change simply because of a change in the structure of taxation; thus, when in 1979 Sir Geoffrey Howe, as Chancellor, reduced income tax and compensated by a substantial rise in V.A.T., the effect was to raise national product at market prices relatively to national product at factor cost; and, following the switch, the ratio of public expenditure to national product at market prices was lower than if the tax structure had not been changed.

If the statistics were perfect and readily available, the measure nearest to the ideal would be public expenditure (net of any elements of subsidy or outlay tax in respect of the goods or services purchased) as a percentage of net national (or domestic) product at factor cost. However, figures of capital consumption are unreliable and a more consistent series is obtained by using gross rather than net figures. Between "national" and "domestic" there is little to choose. The difficulty with using the factor cost measure is that of excluding from government expenditure the element of net taxes on spending.

In the event, the measure used by the government and that followed in international comparisons is to express government expenditure as a percentage of gross domestic product (G.D.P.) at market prices. There is one further complication. Domestic (and national) product can itself be measured in any of three ways—by means of expenditure, output or income. In principle they should give the same result; in practice there are discrepancies. Before 1984 the United Kingdom government used the expenditure measure; since, it has used an average figure, G.D.P.(A), for measuring trends. The difference caused by using G.D.P. rather than G.N.P. is slight—amounting in recent years to only about half a percentage point. However, using market prices rather than factor cost reduces the ratio for recent years by as much as 7 or 8 percentage points (as is shown by a comparison of Tables 2.1 and 2.2).

There is a final implication of expressing public expenditure as a proportion of community output which needs to be borne in mind: the measure is as susceptible to changes in the denominator (national output) as to changes in the numerator (public expenditure). It would be possible for this measure of public expenditure to show an increase even though public expenditure had actually fallen, if national output had fallen relatively more. This is a meaningful (if possibly misleading) outcome; it indicates a rise in the share of the public sector in the total economy.

Where does all this leave us? Public expenditure as a percentage of national output is the most meaningful single measure of the trend in public spending over a period of years, provided a consistent series is used. Even then, however, the student needs to be on the lookout for "statistical quirks" affecting either the public

TABLE 2.1

Government Expenditure in the United Kingdom expressed as a Percentage of G.N.P. at Factor Cost (selected years 1790–1990)

Year	Expenditure as % of G.N.P.	Year	Expenditure as % of G.N.P.
1790	12	1964	38
1840	11	1968	45
1890	8	1972	44
1910	12	1976	50
1932	29	1980	52
1951	40	1984	49½
1961	38	1988	45
		1990	46

Sources: 1790–1961, J. Veverka, The Growth of Government Expenditure in the United Kingdom since 1790, *Scottish Journal of Political Economy*, Vol. X, No. 1, 1963; various *National Income and Expenditure* blue books, subsequently redesignated *National Accounts*, published annually, H.M.S.O.

expenditure figures (like a switch from tax allowances to cash payments) or the national output figures (like an increase in tax on goods and services entering market prices). However, for any analysis other than that of the general trend, a much more detailed breakdown is required, and in particular we need to distinguish between transfer payments and government expenditure on goods and services (exhaustive expenditures).

Table 2.1 takes a very long look at the trend of public expenditure in the United Kingdom since 1790 by expressing total government spending as a percentage of gross national product (G.N.P.) at factor cost to give as consistent a series as possible following the figures produced by Veverka. The years have been chosen to bring out the trend (the periods of major wars being omitted). Over such a long period discrepancies are inevitable, but there is no mistaking the trend. Public expenditure surged upwards in the twentieth century, much of it since 1964. It peaked in the early 1980s.

Table 2.2 looks in more detail at the figures for the period since 1964. The figures are taken from the Statistical Supplement to the Autumn Statement—the successor to the annual Public Expenditure White Papers—and show General Government Expenditure in cash terms, in real terms (i.e. valued at the prices applicable in

TABLE 2.2

General Government Expenditure, United Kingdom, 1963–64 to 1989–90

Year	Real terms* (exclu. privatis- ation proceeds) Total £bn	£bn	As per cent of GDP at market prices Goods and services only	Total	Total (excluding privatisation proceeds)
1963–64	11.3	101.1	20½	36¾	36¾
1965–66	13.6	110.8	21	37¾	37¾
1967–68	17.5	132.6	22¾	43¼	43¼
1969–70	19.3	132.8	21¾	41	41
1971–72	24.4	141.8	22¾	41¾	41¾
1973–74	32.0	160.8	24	43½	43½
1975–76	53.8	180.2	26½	49¼	49¼
1977–78	63.9	167.1	23½	42¾	43¼
1979–80	89.9	181.1	22½	43¼	44
1980–81	108.6	184.3	24	46	46½
1981–82	120.5	187.0	23½	46¼	47¼
1982–83	132.6	192.0	23¾	46½	47½
1983–84	140.4	195.3	23½	45½	46½
1984–85	150.6	200.3	23¾	45½	46¾
1985–86	158.2	200.2	23	43¾	45
1986–87	164.4	203.2	22¾	42¾	44
1987–88	172.8	203.1	22	40½	41¾
1988–89	179.3	198.2	20½	37	39¼
1989–90	189.9	203.0	21¼	38¾	39½

* Cash figures adjusted to 1989–90 price levels by excluding the effect of general inflation. The deflator used is GDP at market prices adjusted to remove the distortion caused by the replacement of domestic rates (treated as an outlay tax) by the community charge (treated as an income tax). The GDP figures for measuring the percentages are likewise adjusted.

Source: Public Expenditure Analyses to 1993–94, Statistical Supplement to 1990 Autumn Statement, Cmnd. 1520.

one year, i.e. 1989–90) and as a percentage of G.D.P. at market prices (both with and without the effect of privatisation proceeds). They also distinguish separately government expenditure on goods and services as a percentage of G.D.P. The years are financial years, ending on April 5.

The main points to note are that government expenditure is twice as high in real terms in 1990 as it was in 1964; as a percentage of G.D.P. the increase is much less because of the growth of G.D.P. — especially when measured in terms of market prices. It is this difference in the G.D.P. measure used which accounts for most of the differences with Table 2.1 (as described above).

After a big increase in the previous four years, public spending was cut back slightly in real terms in 1968–69. There was a substantial real reduction in 1975–76 to 1977–78, which followed negotiations with the International Monetary Fund (I.M.F.) in the latter half of 1976. Public expenditure plans were revised downwards; £500 million of government owned shares in British Petroleum Company were sold in 1977–8 (counting as negative expenditure) and the introduction of cash limits in 1976 (see below, Chapter 3) led to a substantial underspending, so that actual expenditure was about £4 billion below the revised plans of January 1977. After that, government expenditure overall continued to grow but at a slower rate, until roughly stabilising between 1985 and 1990. Even without privatisation proceeds the percentage of public expenditure to G.D.P. has dropped since the mid 1980s, but is rising at the turn of the decade as the effects of recession reduce G.D.P. or slow up its growth, whilst government expenditure increases on unemployment benefit and income support.

A comparison of the growth of expenditure on goods and services with total expenditure makes it clear that transfer payments have risen significantly more than expenditure on goods and services.

Later in this chapter, and in the next, we shall examine more fully the reasons for the huge growth in public spending both over the past century and since the Second World War. For the moment let us take a closer look at the broad changes in the content of public expenditure over time.

Changes in the Content of Expenditure

In Table 2.3 we examine trends in the composition of government expenditure by breaking down the expenditure of various years in percentage terms, first by function, or the nature of the expenditure; second by "economic category", i.e. whether a direct claim by the government on real resources or a cash transfer; third by "level", i.e. whether local or central government.

TABLE 2.3

Government Expenditure by Function, by Economic Category, and by Level

Year	By function					By economic category		As percentage of total expenditure — By level	
	Administration and other	National debt interest	Defence	Social services	Economic and environmental services	Goods and services	Transfers and subsidies	Central governmental	Local governmental
1790	17	39	26	9	9	57	43	83	17
1840	16	42	23	9	9	53	47	78	22
1890	22	15	28	20	15	80	20	59	41
1910	14	7	27	32	20	81	19	50	50
1932	7	25	10	45	14	48	52	65	35
1951	6	11	25	43	15	62	38	77	23
1961	7	10	20	47	16	61	39	73	27
1966	7	11	16	51	14	60	40	68	32
1974	7	10	12	53	17	57	43	67	33
1980	6	11	11	55	17	54	46	70	30
1985	7	11	12	54	15	51	49	73	27
1990	8	9	11	57	15	57	43	69	31

Sources and definitions of public expenditure as Table 2.1.

Note: Percentage figures in columns 2–6 for respective years do not always total to 100 each year because of rounding.

Function

Some of the divisions within this category are a little arbitrary. Social services comprise education, the national health service, social security benefits, various personal social services and housing. The division between economic and environmental services and administration, etc., is the least reliable.

The column "Administration and other" is something of a rag bag, and no conclusions about the total cost or efficiency of administration can be inferred from changes of a point or two. Nevertheless the much lower proportion of government expenditure under this heading for the twentieth century as compared with the nineteenth can reasonably be taken as a reflection of improved methods of administration (perhaps assisted by economies of scale) covering both improved use of labour services and mechanisation in various forms from typewriters to computers.

The changes in the proportion of expenditure taken by debt interest are worthy of note. Despite a phenomenal increase in the national debt, particularly during the two world wars and in the 1970s, interest payments on a debt which in 1990 stood at some £160 billion only amounted in recent years to around 10 per cent of gross government expenditure; and as most of the interest payments are liable to income tax, the net payment is substantially less. This 10 per cent compares with 39 per cent in 1790 and 42 per cent in 1840. Partly, of course, this decline is to be accounted for by the overall growth in government expenditure as the government has extended the range of its activities and by the growth in community income. But also much of the proportional decline is linked with the price increases since 1932. Debt interest is relatively fixed in monetary terms; some forms of government expenditure on debt interest are absolutely fixed, like the payments on Consols;* other interest payments may rise gradually as securities reach maturity and are replaced by new ones carrying higher rates of interest. But the net effect of inflation has been to reduce the real value of debt interest

*Consolidated stock, to give these government bonds their full title; an irredeemable security introduced in the 1880s by Chancellor Goschen, at a rate of interest of 2½ per cent.

payments. In an inflation—at least one which has not been fully anticipated—debtors gain and creditors lose; the debtor pays interest in money which is depreciating in value. The government, which is the biggest debtor in the community, gains most from this process. (Conversely the relative high figure for 1932 reflects the low price level associated with the Great Depression.) The drop of two percentage points between 1985 and 1990 partly reflects Budget surpluses (negative public sector borrowing requirements) in some of those years.

Defence expenditure between 1790 and 1961 is remarkable for its stability; apart from the exceptional year of 1932, defence expenditure varied between 20 and 28 per cent of government spending in these peace-time years. Since 1961 there has been a pronounced downward trend; in real terms defence expenditure has varied little since 1961, but as a proportion of government expenditure it has fallen markedly. There has been some increase in real terms in the late 1970s and into the 1980s but, at a time of growing public expenditure as a whole, not enough to make much difference to the percentage.

The growth in social services is the outstanding feature of the figures of expenditure by function. From the end of the nineteenth century the social services have grown steadily as a proportion of peace-time government expenditure, the abnormally high unemployment expenditure of 1932 interrupting the smoothness of the trend. The figures reflect a fundamental change in the nature of social services. In the late eighteenth century and for most of the nineteenth century "social services" meant poor relief, and the philosophy was that of "relief from destitution within a framework of repression", as the Webbs put it in their monumental history of the Poor Laws. But before the end of the nineteenth century the emphasis was shifting from a punitive to a curative or preventive policy, from mere relief to an attempt to treat the causes of poverty—ignorance, old age, sickness, unemployment. Moreover, a further transformation was taking place by which the social services were not designed only to meet problems of poverty, but were becoming welfare services for the whole of the community.

Expenditure on economic and environmental services tended to increase with the urbanisation of the nineteenth century—roads had to be constructed, paved and lit; urban refuse and sewage disposed of. Perhaps more surprising is the relatively lower rate of this expenditure since 1910, although road building and urban renewal programmes have seen a recent increase. During the Thatcher years there was a decline in financial support for agriculture and industry, the nationalised industries were required to meet financial targets and sometimes to repay borrowing and privatisation proceeds were treated as negative expenditure. These changes account for the lower figure in this sector in the past decade. Over the longer period this component of the total has fluctuated as a result both of changes in policy and in the form of investment incentives.

Analysis of the changes column by column tends to understate the revolution which has taken place in government expenditure. The larger part of the national debt is a product of war as also is some of the "social service" expenditure—on war pensions to veterans and widows. Thus in 1790 at least 65 per cent of government expenditure was "war related" and half of the remainder was administration. At the time of Waterloo the proportion of war related expenditure was even higher. This contrasts markedly with the period from the middle 1960s when social service expenditure has accounted for over half of government spending.

Economic Category

The last year of our table shows a division of government spending between "Goods and services" and "Transfers and subsidies" similar to the first; but, as reference to the analysis by function soon shows, the nature of the expenditure and the transfers is very different. In particular in 1790 about 90 per cent of the transfer expenditure represented interest on the national debt; in 1990 the majority of transfers were social service payments such as pensions, child benefit, unemployment pay and income support.

Level

The nature of the expenditure is closely related to its level, to whether it is central or local. Thus nearly all transfer payments, whether debt interest or social service payments, are made centrally and hence changes in the proportion of central to local government spending reflect changes by economic category. Defence expenditure is almost entirely central; the predominance of defence spending and debt interest account for the overwhelming proportion of central spending in 1790. On the other hand, much environmental expenditure is met from local authority budgets and the two expand together in the nineteenth and early twentieth centuries. But these are not the only influences. The quality, the efficiency and the appropriateness of local government structure influence the willingness of the central government to hand over functions to local authorities. The growing concern in the twentieth century with equality of opportunity has also created a demand for central provision to secure the required uniformity of treatment, although sometimes this has taken the form of central government directives reducing the autonomy of local government which continues to administer the service. Since the early 1950s there has been a significant rise in the proportion of government spending at local level largely reflecting the growth of education expenditure.

Theories of Government Expenditure

Why has government expenditure grown in this way? Beyond what we have already said in Chapter 1 can we provide any theoretical explanation of the timing and of the nature of government expenditure?

One of the earliest attempts to explain the growth of public expenditure was that of Wagner, a German economist writing towards the end of the nineteenth century. He evolved a "law of increasing state activity" — that government expenditure, at least in industrialising countries, must increase at a faster rate than output; the law was based primarily on empirical observation of Western Europe.

Wagner argued that social progress brought increasing state activity which in turn meant more government expenditure. He adduced three reasons for this growth of state activity. First, with economic development and increasing division of labour economic life would grow more complex and therefore the causes of friction would increase; for the state to maintain order and an efficient economy would require more resources on police and legal services. Secondly, new technology would create the need for large amounts of capital in production, which could only be provided by joint stock companies or public corporations; in Wagner's view the public corporation was superior to the joint stock company. In particular the state had an increasing role in production where technical conditions favoured monopoly. Finally, Wagner saw increasing state activity in fields like health and education where the social benefits of the service were not susceptible to economic evaluation.

Wagner's thesis contained important insights. He appreciated some of the market limitations discussed in Chapter 1. But his thesis in part depended on a particular "organic" view of the state, which was not a necessary interpretation of the situation.

Whilst Wagner sought to explain the *trend* of public expenditure, the most useful pioneering work in Britain, that of Professors A. T. Peacock and J. Wiseman,* offered a working hypothesis to explain the *fluctuations* in government expenditure over time.

They start from the basis that decisions about public expenditure are taken politically under the influence of popular opinion expressed through the ballot box and other media. As we pointed out in the first chapter, in the provision of "public goods" there is no direct relationship between payment and benefit to the individual; hence there is also a lack of clear relationship in the citizen's mind between benefit and cost. Thus citizens can have ideas about public expenditure which are different from, and may be incompatible with, their ideas about reasonable burdens of taxation. In settled times the citizens' ideas about "reasonable" tax rates are fairly

---

The Growth of Public Expenditure in the United Kingdom, 1st ed., Oxford, 1961. Introducing a 2nd edition, Allen & Unwin, 1967, the authors were able to refer to several recent studies of government expenditure elsewhere which lent some support to their "working hypothesis".

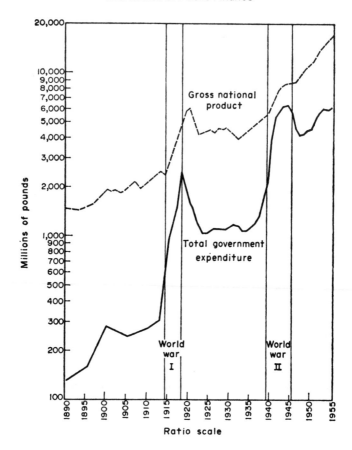

Fig. 2.1 Total government expenditure and gross national product, at current prices, 1890–1955. (Source: A. T. Peacock and J. Wiseman, *The Growth of Public Expenditure in the United Kingdom.*)

stable. Government expenditure can increase without increased tax rates if incomes are growing, but a rise in expenditure of much more than this is unlikely: notions of acceptable tax burdens are more influential than ideas about desirable increases in expenditure in determining the size and rate of increase of public expenditure.

There may thus emerge a divergence between ideas of desirable expenditure on the one hand and tolerable levels of taxation on the other. This divergence is narrowed by large-scale social disturbances such as major wars. These create a *displacement* effect which has two aspects. First it affects the level of *acceptance*; the crisis leads to the acceptance of new tax levels which subsequently persist. Secondly it has an *inspection* effect; wars force to the attention of governments problems of which they were formerly less conscious — thus the Boer War demonstrated the poor physique of many working class volunteers and led Imperialists to join forces with social reformers to inaugurate the welfare state,* whilst evacuation of children from London slums during the Second World War showed up the extent of malnutrition. Moreover, wars impose new obligations on the state, in the shape of increased debt interest and war pensions, which continue when the war itself has ended.

This hypothesis is based on a statistical study which shows government expenditure rising rapidly during war-time and subsequently settling on a "plateau" below the peak of the war years but substantially above pre-war levels of expenditure. This pattern is very pronounced for the two world wars and there is a trace of it for the Boer War, the Great Depression and the Korean War.

The authors of this hypothesis are modest in their claims for it; it is helpful, but it is far from being a final answer. Why "notions about taxation are likely to be more influential than ideas about desirable increases in expenditure" is never explained in a wholly satisfactory way. Moreover, the increases in government expenditure of the sixties and seventies do not fit at all easily into the theory of "social disturbance".

The "working hypothesis" of Peacock and Wiseman is not the only attempt by British economists to provide a theory of public expenditure. The welfare theories of Pigou and Dalton earlier this century treated government expenditure in terms of the logic of choice. They argued that the extent of government expenditure should be that which maximised social welfare, an amount such that the benefit (or social utility) from the expenditure of the "last"

*B. B. Gilbert, *The Evolution of National Insurance in Great Britain*, Michael Joseph, London, 1966.

(or marginal) pound raised in taxation just equalled the cost (or disutility) to the taxpayer. The amount of government expenditure on the various services should be determined by a similar condition, i.e. that expenditure on each service should be pushed to the point at which the benefit (or utility) from the marginal pound on all lines of expenditure was equal; given this situation no rearrangement between private and public expenditure, or between the various forms of public expenditure, could add to social welfare.

The theory is ingenious but hopelessly unrealistic; it rests on a capacity to equate the unmeasurable; it ignores the special characteristics of government expenditure by treating the government as if it were an individual, a single unitary being; it begs, as Professor Lord Robbins has put it, "The great metaphysical question of interpersonal comparisons",* and it is a "normative" statement, one which postulates what ought to be, rather than a "positive" statement which seeks to describe and explain what is.

Much more useful as an explanatory tool than the Pigou/Dalton thesis is the "public choice" approach developed in the U.S.A. during the past two or three decades and associated with economists such as A. Downs (*An Economic Theory of Democracy*), J. M. Buchanan and G. Tullock (*The Calculus of Consent*), A. Breton (*The Economic Theory of Representative Government*) and W. A. Niskanen (*Bureaucracy and Representative Government*). "Public choice" concerns the application of economics to political science. To explain the growth of the public sector has not been a major objective of the public choice literature, but much public choice theory is very relevant to that growth.

We can distinguish two major characteristics of the public choice approach. First, it is based on individual behaviour. There is no question of government being treated (as in the Pigou/Dalton model) as a single unitary being, nor does public choice theory rely on some assumption of the existence of a "common good". Rather it assumes that in their political activities men behave as rational beings seeking to maximise their satisfactions or utilities. This is interpreted to mean that, in a democracy, politicians are vote maxi-

---

*L. C. Robbins, *An Essay on the Nature and Significance of Economic Science*, Macmillan, London, 1932.

misers who wish to stay in power; and citizens cast their votes so as to maximise their real income stream. Bureaucrats (defined as those in charge of bureaux whose finance comes from grants and not from the sale of their output) are motivated by considerations such as salary, power, prestige, promotion and the perquisites of office, for which budget maximisation is a realistic proxy.

Public choice theory is not claimed to be a complete explanation of behaviour, but, like utility-maximising economic man in the market place, it is held by its protagonists to have more explanatory and predictive power than any alternative. Nor is it as cynical as it sounds. Altruism can enter into the utility calculations of individual voters and politicians, and bureaucrats may seek to maximise their budgets because of a dedication to "their service", be it education or defence, which they identify with the national good. Apart from the obvious danger of oversimplification, aspects of this theory suffer in an extreme form from the difficulties affecting other maximisation theories in economics: uncertainty and ignorance of the effects of different measures to achieve the objects of maximisation.

The second characteristic of public choice theory is recognition of the importance of the institutional framework for the way in which individual preferences get translated into public decisions. Such an emphasis on institutions and constitutional practices can help to lead to a better understanding of the reasons for the growth of government spending in the United Kingdom.

Reasons for Growth in Government Spending

Whilst Wagner, Peacock and Wiseman and the public choice economists all provide insights and contributions towards an explanation and understanding of the growth of public spending in the United Kingdom, it can be doubted how far any general theory is capable of providing a satisfactory explanation, especially in relation to the growth since the end of the Second World War. The answer could well be a complex of economic, political, psychological, sociological, institutional and even statistical influences. The following is a more *ad hoc* attempt to explain what has happened over recent decades.

To start with we must recognise the pressures which exist for reduced public spending in time of peace. Professor Galbraith has argued that there is a tendency for the public sector to lag *behind* the private sector because the influences of advertising and emulation (keeping up with the Joneses) apply much less to public sector than to private sector "goods".* If advertising and emulation do work in this way, their influence must have been outweighed by other considerations. More concretely, dislike of rising taxation is a counter to rising public expenditure. The Peacock/Wiseman thesis held that it was because the public took a fairly inflexible view of what were acceptable levels of taxation that public spending remained a more or less constant proportion of G.N.P. in peace-time. In several countries under the weight of growing public expenditure there have been signs of taxpayer revolts in the last decade or so, especially where increases in the tax burden have been swift and severe, as when the impact of inflation on an unindexed income tax has markedly raised tax burdens on particular groups. In the United Kingdom the promise of lower taxes was a potent factor bringing the Conservatives under Margaret Thatcher to power in 1979; but the Conservative Government found it difficult to keep that promise (for most middle and lower income groups cuts in income tax were offset by higher national insurance contributions, higher V.A.T. and the Community Charge) and incurred widespread opposition in its attempt to cut spending. Antipathy to taxation is real, but taking the post war period as a whole, it has been overcome by counteracting influences.

The factors making for increased public spending can be grouped under a number of headings:

(1) *Administrative rearrangements*

We have earlier mentioned the arbitrariness of the public expenditure figures and, in particular, pointed out the differing effect on explicit public spending of providing benefits by tax reliefs on the one hand or cash payments on the other. Whilst (as with

*J. K. Galbraith, *The Affluent Society*, Pelican edition, 1962, p. 213.

investment incentives) there have been changes in both directions, taking the period as a whole the biggest change has been from tax relief to cash payment, notably in the replacement of the child tax allowance by the child benefit and by changes in the form of relief for insurance premiums and mortgage interest payments by home owners. (In the later 1980s, on the other hand, a new set of tax reliefs for savings have been brought in.) Where changes in the ratio of public expenditure to G.D.P. arise because of such administrative rearrangements, they may be regarded as statistical quirks arising from a failure to formulate tax reliefs as a "tax expenditure budget" (see p. 83).

(2) *Technical factors*

An influence highlighted by Peacock and Wiseman and recognised in the Public Expenditure White Papers is the phenomenon of the "relative price effect" or productivity lag. Items which governments buy, notably labour services, tend to rise in price more than the average. As a result, for the public sector to maintain any given share of the total output of the community requires a relative increase in public expenditure. To put the point in a different way. The scope for productivity increases is probably less in the public than in the private sector of the economy, mainly because so large a part of public sector provision takes the form of services where productivity increases are both difficult to achieve and to measure. If wages and salaries in the public sector keep pace with those in the private, the prices of public sector output will rise more than that of private sector output because in the private sector productivity increases mitigate the effect of wage rises on product prices.

(3) *Changes in attitude to public spending*

Whilst it defies precise analysis, the post-war world saw some change in attitude in public spending. The Keynesian analysis demonstrated that general unemployment could be counteracted by increased government spending; moreover, attempts by private individuals to save might result not in increased investment but simply in reduced activity. In these circumstances the Victorian maxim of "leaving money to fructify in the pockets of the people" no longer seemed attractive. Added to the economic argument was a more subtle change in philosophy. Collectivist philosophies gained ground and Galbraith's contrast of "private opulence and public squalor", more relevant in the U.S.A. than in the United Kingdom, yet had more influence in the United Kingdom than in his own country. Under the Conservative governments from 1979 this attitude was reversed and market philosophies predominated; but the collectivist philosophies were a significant factor in expenditure growth in the 1960s and 1970s.

(4) *Changes in the nature of publicly-provided goods*

The change in attitude was both cause and effect of a change in the nature of the goods provided through the state. We stressed, in Chapter 1, that publicly-provided goods are characterised by a separation of cost and benefit. We can also distinguish two kinds of benefit from publicly-provided goods—benefit which is of a diffuse, indivisible kind on the one hand, like that from the defence or police forces; and benefits which are personal and identifiable, such as those from education, health, pensions and social security benefits on the other hand. Over time the balance of expenditure has changed, as late as 1910, a peace time year, over 40 per cent of government expenditure went on administration and defence, services from which the benefit was diffuse. By 1974 defence and administration had dropped to under 20 per cent of total government expenditure and social services exceeded 50 per cent (see Table 2.3). This may help to explain the paradox that the Peacock/Wiseman hypothesis appears to work well up to the mid 1950s but not thereafter. As long as much of public spending was on items which produced no recognisable personal benefits to the individual, the assumption might well be valid that, in settled times, notions of acceptable tax burdens were more influential than ideas about desirable expenditures in determining the level of government spending. However, once government spending was dominated by items bringing concrete personal benefits to individuals, the benefits from expenditure to many if not most citizens might loom larger than the detriments of taxation, especially where the link between tax and expenditure was only imperfectly recognised by, and only imperfectly applied to, any individual. Demographic changes reinforced the point. Retirement pensions are amongst the most direct and personal benefits. In 1911 under 7 per cent of the population of the United Kingdom was of pensionable age (65 for men, 60 for women). By 1991 this figure had risen to over 18 per cent.

Moreover, some of the most important of the services which had become largely state-provided in the post-war period, notably education and health, were services which experience elsewhere suggests are income-elastic, i.e. those on which a higher proportion of income is spent as a community's income rises. The growth of public spending on these services could be regarded as a reflection of the wishes of an increasingly affluent electorate. (It can, indeed, be argued that with less rigid state provision, expenditure on these particular services might have grown more rapidly.)

(5) *The growth of public sector employment*

Along with the growth of services provided by the state has necessarily gone a growth of public sector employment. A large proportion of the working population directly (as with civil servants and local government officers) or indirectly (as with teachers and doctors) has become dependent for jobs, pay and conditions of service on public expenditure. Thus, on the production as on the consumption side, the pressures for increased spending have grown. At the same time the public sector workers have increasingly become unionised (so that a much larger proportion of public sector than of private sector workers are in trades unions) and public sector unions in the 1960s and 1970s became more militant.

It can be plausibly argued that the combined consumer and producer interest give the public sector a built-in tendency to expansion. There are some indications from the public expenditure patterns of O.E.C.D. countries that the countries with the largest public sectors have also been those which, during the decade of the 1970s, saw the highest rates of public sector growth. It is possible that there is a threshold of size; when that is past, growth becomes self-sustaining and can only be contained by exceptional effort.

(6) *The inherent characteristics of politicians and bureaucrats*

These tendencies for growth are fed by the proclivities of ministers, M.P.s and bureaucrats. Heads of the spending ministries make their reputations by new and ambitious schemes. Ability to withstand expenditure cuts is a sign of ministerial virility. The interest of ministers is at one with their civil servants on this issue. Even backbench M.P.s, however much they may call for cuts in expenditure and lower taxes, are to be found on the side of the spenders on concrete issues when cuts threaten a hospital or school in their constituency or the withdrawal of government aid to an ailing firm would increase unemployment amongst their erstwhile supporters.

An Australian economist, Dr. Neville Norman,* has written of a "Political Lower Bound" to expenditure which arises from a series of spending commitments such as on pensions, social security benefits and others which a government does not feel able to cut for political reasons. The margin then left which can be modified is very small and hence the scope for cutting government expenditure is narrowly circumscribed.

(7) *Institutional factors*

It is all very well, however, to say that the heads of the spending departments favour increased public expenditure; what of the Chancellor of the Exchequer and the Treasury and the various devices intended to exert control over public spending? To the issue of control in its various aspects we turn in the next chapter; though we can note at this point that, before 1976, public spending in the United Kingdom grew, in part, as a result of unintended increases arising from deficiencies in the mechanisms of control, particularly in the face of rapid inflation.

*See, for example, N. R. Norman, *Tax Growth in Australia, Why, How and So What?* Committee for Economic Development of Australia, September 1981.

CHAPTER 3

Control of Government Expenditure

The Problem

The growth in government expenditure which has characterised advanced industrial countries this century has increased the need for efficiency in public expenditure whilst at the same time making control of expenditure in some ways more difficult.

The area over which a government can exercise effective control is in practice a good deal smaller than the total of its expenditure. Even over periods of several years a substantial proportion of expenditure is virtually predetermined; in any single year a government can only be in a position to reduce a minority of total expenditure. Interest on the national debt is a contractual obligation and payments on the funded part of the debt at least must be regarded as fixed in the short run. Treaty obligations involving payments are similarly binding commitments. Most governments have commitments on the payment of grants to local authorities or industry or bodies such as the Universities Funding Council in Great Britain which are determined for a period ahead. Retirement or war-service pension rates are only slightly less a committed expenditure as are the maintenance of the real value of other social security benefits; and where a government employs civil servants at agreed salary scales and on conditions of service which prevent dismissal except for misconduct, the maximum reduction on this score is likely to be salary savings resulting from retirement or voluntary departures (less "automatic" incremental increases of staff salaries).

Another aspect of this problem is the extent to which present commitments often imply larger future commitments. Thus if retirement pension rates remained unchanged, advanced countries face rising expenditure on pensions and health services through increasing life expectations.

Again, although some expenditure programmes are entirely central government, like defence, large areas of expenditure are shared between authorities with control by central government being neither direct nor complete. This situation applies in particular to local government services, which represent 30 per cent or more of total expenditure (Table 2.3), and to some extent to health expenditure, which in the United Kingdom is subject to a unique mixture of central and local control. To put the point in another way, with locally administered services, control is shared between local and central government authorities which may have different objectives. (Issues of local government finance are explored in Chapter 10.)

To control expenditure is not the same as to cut it; a rise in government expenditure may represent a controlled increase. Moreover the control of expenditure does not relate only to size. There are really two questions we need to ask about control: by whom and for what purpose?

The most important control is Executive control, exercised through the Treasury, working in conjunction with the spending departments, exercising a management function within the government machine. Parliament and the Committees of Parliament may also exercise control, though much of it is more nominal than real.

Apart from control for purposes of demand management (considered in Chapter 12) four purposes of control can be distinguished:

(1) Control to secure the "right" balance of government expenditure in relation to private expenditure: what Professor Galbraith has referred to as the "social balance". Clearly this is a matter of major policy decision on the overall level of public expenditure.

(2) Control to ensure efficiency in the widest sense, i.e. an effi-

cient allocation of resources as between alternative directions of expenditure in the context of the resources available. This applies both to broad categories of government expenditure such as expenditure on health or transport; and to choices within each category of expenditure, e.g. building a hospital at town A or town B, or a new road at town C or town D.

(3) Control to guard against waste (in the narrower sense) so that once a specific object of expenditure has been agreed it is achieved as cheaply as possible. This implies no unnecessary under-utilisation of labour or equipment; and that a government gets value for money in purchases from outside contractors.

(4) Control to prevent fraud, corruption and unauthorised expenditure.

These four objectives are not wholly separate from each other; in particular the overall total of expenditure is not determined without reference to its components; but it is helpful to distinguish these different aspects of control.

We shall begin with an account of the traditional methods of control as they have been built up within the constitution. Whilst they remain important they have proved inadequate to achieve control in all its aspects and we shall consider methods adopted in the past decade or so to make good their limitations. The Report of the Plowden Committee* in 1961 is something of a watershed.

Traditional Methods of Control

Certain basic constitutional principles have been adopted in Britain which make for a coherent budget and clarify financial responsibilities: the government cannot raise money without the consent of Parliament; within Parliament the power to grant money belongs exclusively to the House of Commons; and the House of Commons can vote money for expenditure, or impose a tax, only on the recommendation of the government.

The main procedures for control have been built up over several

*Control of Public Expenditure, Cmnd. 1432, July 1961.

centuries. One device to check fraud is the requirement that all receipts must be paid into and all expenditure paid out of the Consolidated Fund. Further, there is what is often referred to as the "circle of control" which begins with the Estimates of the spending departments and ends with the examination of the audited accounts.

The individual departments originate the Estimates which are then vetted by and discussed with the Treasury. If no agreement is reached then the ministerial head of the department and Treasury ministers take a hand. Whilst the Chancellor of the Exchequer has the ultimate responsibility, it is now usual for one of his ministerial team, usually the Chief Secretary to the Treasury, who may or may not have a seat in the Cabinet, to have the immediate responsibility for expenditure control. If the minister concerned and the Chief Secretary to the Treasury cannot agree the matter goes to the Cabinet; in recent years any such disagreements have often first gone to a Cabinet Committee (known as the "Star Chamber") and only if agreement cannot be reached there does it go to the Cabinet itself; thus in the last resort, "Treasury control" rests on the standing of the Chancellor in Cabinet.

The Estimates, as agreed between the departments and the Treasury, are then passed by the House of Commons. It was the practice for many years for a selection of the Estimates to be examined in detail by the Estimates Committee which reported to the House of Commons, but the Estimates Committee was abolished and replaced by the Expenditure Committee in 1970, which was, in turn, replaced by a new committee system in 1979 (see below). The House debates the policy behind the Estimates and proceeds to pass Appropriation Acts which authorise expenditure and allocate it to specific heads. The departments spend the money and account for surpluses and deficits. The Comptroller and Auditor-General, with the backing of a large auditing staff (formerly the Exchequer and the Audit Department, since 1983 the National Audit Office (N.A.O.)), scrutinises the accounts and brings any irregularities to the attention of the Public Accounts Committee of the House of Commons.

These traditional methods of control were and are very effective in securing the fourth objective of control, i.e. the prevention of fraud and unauthorised expenditure, which is the purpose for which they were primarily designed. To a less extent the Comptroller and Auditor-General together with the Public Accounts Committee have helped to secure the third objective—to achieve any particular item of expenditure as cheaply as possible; audits in recent years, especially since the formation of the N.A.O. (which we discuss more fully below under Parliamentary Control) have increasingly been concerned with "value for money". But the traditional methods offer no adequate basis to achieve the first two objectives. This is not surprising because they were evolved at a time when the prevailing political philosophy was that government expenditure should be minimised: the government was expected to spend the minimum necessary to provide for defence, secure law and order, service the national debt, give basic poor relief and not much else. Thus the question of the "social balance" and of the relative claims of competing departments hardly arose. The developments, since the Plowden Report have been concerned with methods for the better attainment of the first three objectives.

Plowden and After

The Plowden Committee was set up as a result of a suggestion from the Estimates Committee of the House of Commons. Although its chairman and several members were from outside the Government service it was primarily an internal inquiry and did not take evidence from the public. It made a series of confidential reports to the Chancellor of the Exchequer and a public report which was published in July 1961.

The Committee were concerned that government expenditure decisions (other than investment decisions) were taken piece-meal; the Cabinet might discuss a proposal against the background of the general financial situation, but it did not examine together, as alternatives, the competing expenditure plans of the departments for a series of years nor consider what resources might be available for public expenditure in the future. Hence the first and main recommendation of the Committee was that "Regular surveys should be made of public expenditure as a whole, over a period of years ahead and in relation to prospective resources; decisions involving substantial future expenditure should be taken in the light of these surveys."

This first recommendation was reinforced by a second. "There should be the greatest practicable stability of decisions on public expenditure when taken, so that long-term economy and efficiency throughout the public sector have the best opportunity to develop." The Committee was convinced that "chopping and changing in Government policy is frustrating to efficiency and economy in the running of the public services. It impairs cost-consciousness and financial discipline at all levels."

Thirdly, the Committee recommended improvements "in the tools for measuring and handling public expenditure problems" which should include simplification in the form of the Estimates and the Exchequer accounts and the "more widespread use of quantitative methods".

The Plowden Report was concerned essentially with executive control of public expenditure. In the next section we examine the system of executive control introduced in accordance with the Plowden recommendations and the modifications to which it has been subject in the light of experience.

Executive Control at Macro-Level· P.E.S.C.

The Government lost little time in implementing the first recommendation of the Plowden Committee which was essentially concerned with controlling the total size of public spending and the allocation to programmes (the first two objectives on p. 45). Public expenditure decisions were put on a systematic basis by the establishment of a Public Expenditure Survey Committee (P.E.S.C.) consisting of civil servants, drawn from the spending departments and chaired by a senior treasury official. P.E.S.C. prepared estimates of expenditure over a period of years ahead in the light of the Treasury's medium-term forecast of the likely growth of the economy (the "prospective resources" of the Plowden recommendation). Until the 1979/80 projection the figures of expenditure related to a five-year period, including the year just ended, to provide a firm statistical base—so in effect they "looked forward" about $3\frac{1}{2}$ years. In 1979/80 the five-year period was reduced to 4 years. In 1981 the planning period was further reduced to 3 years.

The figures of expenditure were presented on a "constant price" basis (using "survey prices"—the prices at the time the survey was prepared) which meant that changes in projected expenditure represented changes in volume—real goods and services—in proportion.

The estimates, having been agreed with the Treasury, provided the material on which the ministerial decisions could be based.

Public manifestations of the work of P.E.S.C. were to be found in the three indicative planning documents of the 1960s. The N.E.D.C. study on *The Growth of the British Economy to 1966*, *The National Plan* and *The Task Ahead: Economic Assessment to 1972*, all offered projections of public expenditure in the context of medium term projections of the economy as a whole. Also particular surveys were made of government spending alone, such as *Public Expenditure in 1963–64 and 1967–68* (Cmnd. 2235, December 1963) and *Public Expenditure Planning and Control* (Cmnd. 2915, February 1966). Finally the first Plowden recommendation appeared to be completely fulfilled when in December 1969 the Government published *Public Expenditure 1968–69 to 1973–74*, the first of a continuing series of annual White Papers on Public Expenditure which surveyed the whole of public spending together, with the forward look recommended by Plowden. The introduction of the annual White Papers was preceded by a Green Paper—*Public Expenditure: A New Presentation* (Cmnd. 4017, April 1969), outlining the purpose and proposed format of the annual White Papers, which were to include not only the five-year expenditure projections but also projections of revenue from tax receipts (on the basis of existing rates and allowances) and a functional breakdown of expenditure into exhaustive expenditure, transfers and the purchase of existing assets (like land). This breakdown was particularly useful for demand management purposes.

The new approach was very favourably received. During the

1970s annual White Papers were published some time between November and February; some of the original features were dropped and the format changed somewhat; but the system continued unchanged in essentials until the middle 1970s. By then serious and unforeseen deficiencies had become apparent.

The first difficulty arose over the relationship between the public expenditure projections and the forecasts of G.N.P. Very broadly speaking, the expenditure plans were formulated with the intention of keeping public expenditure rising more or less in line with expected growth of national output. However, when forecasts of economic growth proved optimistic, expenditure invariably rose as a percentage of G.N.P. Thus in the period of the National Plan, 1964–68, G.N.P. was expected to grow at a rate of 3.8 per cent p.a. and public expenditure was planned to rise a bit faster at $4\frac{1}{4}$ per cent p.a. In the event, G.N.P. only rose by 2.2 per cent; public expenditure kept more or less on target with the result that, as a percentage of G.N.P., public spending shot upward. Similarly, the fall in G.N.P. 1973–75 was associated with a large rise in public spending as a porportion of community output. It would appear that the very mechanism for control adopted as a result of the Plowden recommendation had generated an increase in the public sector.

It is easy to say that the remedy lay in improved medium-term forecasting of the economy, but improved forecasting is not easy to achieve. There are always uncertainties which cannot be eliminated. One method of approach is to prepare alternative forecasts — a central forecast with lower and upper possibilities or bounds. This "wedge" approach was adopted in some of the White Papers, but it does not help much. Projections of public expenditure are still based on the "central" forecast and, because of the rigidity of public spending in the short run, any adjustment arising from a shortfall in G.N.P., has to be borne by the private sector. The problem is compounded because, where there are a range of possible outcomes, Ministers will always tend to take the more popular and optimistic one; hence there is a built-in tendency to over-estimation of G.N.P. growth, which likewise means a built-in tendency for public expenditure to grow beyond "prospective resources".

The second difficulty became apparent somewhat later in time, with the acceleration of inflation in the period 1973–75. In this period there was a huge public sector over-spend, much of which arose because of a relative increase in the prices of public sector goods and services. Some increase in relative prices had been allowed for in the projections (because of the recognition of the "relative price effect", p. 41. But the increase in 1973–75, mainly in land and construction prices and public sector salaries, was in excess of the allowance. Moreover, the events revealed two defects in the P.E.S.C. system. (1) Because the P.E.S.C. projections were at "constant survey prices" or in volume terms, there was no requirement or incentive for spending departments to economise in the face of an abnormal price rise. A householder, with given monetary resources, would cut back on those goods which rose most in price. No such necessity imposed itself on departments entitled by the agreed plan to a claim on particular real resources. (2) P.E.S.C. only provided for year-on-year changes in expenditure; there was no early warning system to indicate that something was wrong, Clearly there was a need for a flow of information which would provide a basis for speedy management decisions if spending was going off course.

The Government's reaction to meet the difficulties was to supplement P.E.S.C. with a system of cash limits and a new financial information system (F.I.S.).

Cash limits (dubbed by a former Chairman of P.E.S.C. as "P.E.S.C. Plus") were first imposed on some building contracts in the period 1974–76 and used much more extensively from 1976. Cash limits took the form or specified maximum amounts of cash to be spent on certain services or blocks of services in the coming financial year They covered about two-thirds of central government expenditure, the main exception being "demand-determined" expenditure such as spending on unemployment pay or pensions which (given the rates) depend on the number of claimants. Grants to local authorities were amongst the cash limited programmes and the borrowing of nationalised industries was also made subject to cash limits. The cash limits operated in parallel with the P.E.S.C. constant price projections.

The second development, F.I.S. (dubbed "Inter-P.E.S.C.") was designed to provide regular financial information to the Treasury. Since September 1975 each department has been required to submit returns of expenditure to the Treasury within ten working days of the end of each month. These monthly returns are compared with an expenditure profile for the year, which has been drawn up previously, so that the monthly outflows can be monitored and discrepancies investigated.

A third measure adopted to try to improve the accuracy of the projections of aggregate expenditure has been to increase the size of the contingency allowance, so that it can accommodate both unexpected policy decisions and agreed increases in cash limits.

The two years following the introduction of the full cash limit system showed large shortfalls of expenditure (see above p. 29) at least partly due to the new methods. Whilst this might seem to imply more effective controls, it should be recalled that control and cut are not synonymous terms. A large unintended shortfall in expenditure can be as serious as an overspend because it may upset a government's management of the economy. However, as civil servants became more used to the cash limit system, shortfalls diminished; moreover realistic estimates of shortfall were written into the projections.

More generally, the use of cash limits aids accountability in expenditure at some cost in effective programme planning. The effectiveness of cash limits as a means of controlling expenditure without disrupting programmes too severely depends on the accuracy of the forecasts of price rises in the public sector, complicated by the fact that the cash limits may also partly determine the extent of price increases. A major component of public sector expenditure is wages and salaries. The cash limit system was introduced at a time of strict incomes policy, which made it much easier to forecast the rate of price increase in the public sector. Incomes policies broke down in 1978/9 and in any case the Conservative Government elected in 1979 had repudiated the idea of an incomes policy. Instead, within the public sector, they sought to use cash limits as the way of restricting public sector wage increases. If average wage settlements exceeded the permitted increase in cash limit, one year to the next, economies in manpower would have to be made if the cash limit held.

In 1982 the Chancellor abandoned altogether the use of "survey" prices in the P.E.S.C. planning and presented all the years of the survey in terms of the cash which was considered to be available. Clearly, assumptions about the rate of inflation are crucial in computing the figures. The reduction in the period covered by the surveys (above p. 51) obviously made the move to a cash basis somewhat easier. Inflation rates did not have to be forecast for so far ahead. One advantage of presenting the expenditure plans in cash terms is that they can be more easily related to revenue projections and to the government's monetary policy including the expected size of the Public Sector Borrowing Requirement (P.S.B.R.).

An important addition to the Public Expenditure White Paper should be noted. Starting with the 1979 White Paper (Cmnd. 7439) a table listing direct tax allowances and reliefs, with an estimated cost to the Exchequer where possible, has been included in the White Paper. A tax relief is equivalent to a cash benefit to the beneficiary; to list and value the reliefs in this way is a first step towards a tax expenditure budget.

Since 1969 there have been many changes in the timing and format of the Public Expenditure White Papers, culminating in a major change from 1990. Before the Government introduced, in 1981, an Autumn Statement on the economy, which included data on public expenditure, the Public Expenditure White Paper was generally published in November or December; since 1981, it has generally been published in January. When first introduced it consisted of a single volume (of 81 pages); it eventually divided into two, with the first volume containing the macro-economic data and analytical analyses whilst the second volume contained detailed information on departmental expenditure plans (with the change from a programme to a departmental basis for the chapters occurring in 1986). The volumes expanded over the years and by 1988 had reached some 500 pages. The Treasury and Civil Service Committee (see below p. 76) had proposed in 1984 that departmental reports should be published, which would tie in more closely both with the new committee system that the House of Commons had adopted in 1979 and also with the form of the Estimates, which are on a departmental basis. A report from the National Audit Office* reinforced the case for improving financial information to Parliament and for "an evolving role for departmental reports". In 1987 the Government accepted recommendations from the Treasury and Civil Service Committee to discontinue the Public Expenditure White Paper and instead expand the Autumn Statement the previous November. The format of the 1989 and 1990 editions of the Public Expenditure White Paper represented a transitional stage. The departmental chapters which had been published in volume II were published as separate booklets and statistical material which, until 1988, had been included in volume I was published as a booklet in the series (Chapter 21). As from 1991 it will be published, at the end of January, as a Statistical Supplement to the Autumn Statement and new departmental reports will replace the booklets of the Public Expenditure White Paper.

Hitherto departments have provided the basic information and initial text for the Treasury to produce in the White Paper. Henceforth the departments will be responsible for all stages from the initial draft to the final printing. But the Treasury has laid down certain core material for form and content which must be included in the new reports.† The following components must have a standard format and/or location within the report:

(1) A table of cash plans, at the beginning of each report, covering 5 outturn years, the current year and three plan years (using data provided by the Treasury from the public expenditure survey data base) and distinguishing central government expenditure from grants to local authorities.
(2) The department's overall aims and objectives, quantified where possible.
(3) Running costs and manpower.
(4) Local authority expenditure (where relevant).

A number of essential features are also specified by the Treasury,

*Report by the Comptroller and Auditor-General. *Financial Reporting to Parliament*, National Audit Office, HC 576, July 1986, H.M.S.O.
†*Financial Reporting to Parliament*, Cmnd. 918, 1990, H.M.S.O.

including evaluation, output and performance information, and major initiatives to secure better value for money.

All this is a manifestation of the Financial Management Initiative (F.M.I.) of the Conservative governments under Mrs. Thatcher, which we describe in the next section.

Executive Control-Programmes, Projects and Public Sector Management

The third recommendation of the Plowden Committee had been concerned with improvements in the form of the Estimates and Exchequer accounts and "in the tools for handling public expenditure problems". The years since Plowden have seen various improvements in the form of the accounts and also attempts to increase the efficiency of decision-making in the public sector.

In this section we look in more detail at three such developments: first cost–benefit analysis—in particular an attempt to provide a method of quantitatively evaluating public investment projects; then, at Planning, Programming, Budgeting Systems, otherwise known as Output Budgeting, which had its currency mainly from the late sixties until the mid-seventies; finally we look at the determined attempt under the Conservative governments since 1979 to increase the efficiency and effectiveness of public spending which, in the Financial Management Initiative, provides a more comprehensive and fundamental approach than anything which has gone before.

Cost–Benefit Analysis

Cost–benefit analysis is an attempt to weigh in the balance the social costs of and social benefits from a particular expenditure before deciding whether or not to undertake it. Put in this way it sounds mere common sense and indeed there is nothing new in the theory behind cost–benefit analysis. Industrialists weigh up the costs of purchasing a new piece of equipment against the returns to be expected from its employment (receipts over and above running costs) using more or less sophisticated methods of calculation; and the idea that there are social costs over and above the costs which enter into private calculations, and of which account needs to be taken by society, has been a recognised part of economic theory (to which we have already referred in Chapter 1) since early this century. What is newer is the attempt to carry out the empirical calculations of social cost and benefit and in areas of economic activity where market prices do not apply. Cost–benefit calculations developed in U.S.A. in the 1950s and reached Great Britain about a decade later. The most well-known applications in Britain have been in transport studies: the M1 study (1960); the Victoria Line extension to the London Underground network (1963); and the cost–benefit analysis of four sites to determine which was the most suitable for a Third London Airport (the Roskill Commission Report, 1971). Besides other transport studies, including bridges and ports, the range has widened to include applications to land-use and town planning problems and aspects of health and welfare services, such as *The Costs and Benefits of Family Planning* (1972) and *Care of the Elderly* (1972), a comparative study of domiciliary and residential care and a comparison of the costs and benefits of alternative treatments (e.g. of varicose veins). Besides such particular programmes in the welfare services, in principle cost–benefit appraisals can be applied to whole categories of expenditure, such as health and education, and our consideration of these (Chapter 4) will include some broad attempts to compare costs and benefits on a partial basis (for example the "returns to investment approach" as *one* of the considerations in determining the level of education expenditure). However, in practice, at any rate at the present stage of development, appraisal of particular projects by cost–benefit methods is more likely to lead to helpful results.

We take the M1 Study* as our illustration of cost–benefit analysis. Although it was one of the pioneering studies it remains appropriate because it reveals the methods and problems of cost–benefit analysis in a form of investment which, in principle, should lend itself to cost–benefit appraisal, and because road and motor-

---

*T. M. Coburn, M. E. Beesley and D. J. Reynolds, *The London–Birmingham Motorway, Traffic and Economics*, Road Research Laboratory Technical Paper No. 46, H.M.S.O., 1960.

way building is one of the most important forms of public sector investment.

The Procedure

There are three stages in the assessment; first to list the costs and benefits to be taken into account in physical terms; second to evaluate them; third to reduce them to a form in which total costs and benefits can be realistically compared with each other and with other projects. At each stage in the cost–benefit analysis a number of difficulties are met.

What Costs and What Benefits to Include

In the M1 study against the cost of construction and maintenance were set the following:

(1) Benefits to traffic transferring to the motorway from other roads, including savings in:
    (a) personal time—working and leisure;
    (b) vehicle time (which may result in smaller road fleets);
    (c) fuel consumption, tyre, brake and clutch wear;
    (d) costs of accidents.
(2) Benefits to traffic generated by the motorway.
(3) Benefits to traffic which continues on existing roads (including savings under the same heads as transferred traffic in (1) above).
(4) A trend factor to reflect future savings from the natural growth of traffic.

It will help to emphasise the special features of cost–benefit analysis if we contrast what would have happened had the motorway been built by a private developer as a toll road. Then the private developer would have undertaken a comparison of the same costs with the "benefits" as measured by the expected revenue from toll, i.e. the price charged to users.

The essence of the cost–benefit appraisal is that it takes into account social costs and benefits which are ignored in any private calculation. Thus the M1 study takes account of the gain to the users of the roads from which traffic has been diverted (which would *not* be reflected in the tolls on a privately owned motorway). But there are other social cost and benefit effects not allowed for in the M1 calculation. For example, on the cost side, there is the effect the motorway may have in attracting economic activity to the London and Birmingham urban complexes, which are already regarded as over-congested and where further increase in population is widely considered to be detrimental to the economy in general.

In fact it can be seen that the M1 study only takes account of costs and benefits to transport users (indeed, strictly speaking, only to road users). A full cost–benefit study which takes all direct and indirect benefits into account is indeed an impossibility; but, that being so, which costs and benefits are included is an important matter which is liable to be decided on subjective grounds.

A second difficulty, in the first stage of analysis, is that of obtaining adequate statistical data. Much data collection becomes necessary and some fairly arbitrary assumptions must be made; and, of course, to use the technique for deciding whether to undertake the investment or not, the assessments must be made before the motorway is constructed, and rest on a fairly speculative basis, requiring study of the effect of schemes elsewhere which are as near comparable as possible. (In fact the decision to construct the M1 had been reached before the study was undertaken.)

Problems of Evaluation

Ideally we wish to evaluate all the costs and benefits on the same basis, so that each can be added up in terms of the same unit of account and a meaningful comparison made between them. The obvious answer is to evaluate in money terms, but what "prices" should we use? Theoretically we can say that the relevant price is that which reflects the "social opportunity cost". Opportunity cost is the economist's term to indicate that the cost of A is the alternative which has to be foregone in order to have A. Thus if a particular road-building project A requires the employment of 100 labourers at £200 a week, if the labourers would have been engaged on another project at the same wage, the social opportunity cost of employing them on A is measured by the wage-bill (£20,000 per week). If, on the other hand, the men would have been unemployed but for A, then the opportunity cost of employing them on A is much less and possibly nil. The weekly money cost to the exchequer will be the difference between the wage bill (W) on the one hand, and on the other the saving on social security payments to the unemployed (S) now working on project A, together with the additional tax receipts (T) from their higher incomes $(W-(S+T))$. The social opportunity cost in real terms derives from any detrimental economic effects which may arise from financing this difference from taxation or borrowing. In competitive markets with full employment the market price, the price of the factors of production (e.g. wage, rate of interest) as well as the price of the product, can generally be taken to be a reasonable representation of the valuation in terms of opportunity cost. But this is not true if there are monopoly elements present, and where no price is charged some sort of "shadow" price (i.e. a reasonably appropriate estimate) has to be assigned. The examples below illustrate particular problems.

What valuation should be put on time? A distinction has to be made between working and leisure time. If the M1 reduces driving hours for commercial vehicles, the drivers are available to their firms for other work; the saving in time can be evaluated at the normal wage-rate for drivers. But evaluation of time-saving to the pleasure motorist going on holiday, or to the man journeying to and from work in his own time, is more difficult. Clearly, the opportunity cost will rarely be the usual wage-rate (i.e. it will not normally be open to the man to have worked at his normal wage rate during the saved travelling time); the time has some value, which lies between zero and his normal wage-rate, but just where is almost anyone's guess. In practice the cost–benefit analyst (as in the M1 study) usually takes a conspectus or range of values. But just which value is used may be vital to determining whether the project should be pursued or not.

What value should be put on taxed commodities, e.g. fuel? As we are concerned with social opportunity cost we have to value the saving in fuel at the price less tax. This could mean that it may pay a private motorist (because of fuel saving) to travel on the motorway but there could actually be a social cost of his doing so.

What value should be put on human life? If a new road reduces accidents and deaths, how should these be evaluated? It would be possible to put a monetary value on the reduction of deaths and damage to persons by, for example, considering the compensation which judges award in accidents for which some party was to blame, or by assessing the present value of the expected future earnings of the deceased. Alternatively we could approach the problem in terms of probabilities; a new road might increase by one-thousandth the chance of saving an average human life earning £6,000 per annum with 30 years left to live. Then one-thousandth of the present value of the earnings (rather less than £180) might be regarded as an appropriate valuation. The authors of the M1 study put a "low" valuation on lives saved which "does at least give a minimum monetary weight to savings in accidents".

To some people the whole idea of trying to put a monetary value on human life is revolting. The more the costs and benefits can be reduced to common comparable terms the more the decision maker is assisted, but only if the conversion to money terms is meaningful. M. S. Feldstein* has suggested that for many problems the cost–benefit appraisal may require (i) a statement of costs and benefits which can satisfactorily be evaluated in money terms, (ii) *in*commensurable benefits and costs—where we can evaluate in physical terms (e.g. reduction in deaths or sickness), but not in money terms; and (iii) intangible benefits (or costs) which we cannot measure on any realistic scale but simply list, e.g. the aesthetic effects of a proposed change (e.g. the "cost" of pylons in spoiling scenery).

Comparing Like with Like

To compare costs and benefits the series of annual benefits has to be reduced to present values. For the M1 the procedure was to deduct

*M. S. Feldstein, Cost–Benefit Analysis and Investment in the Public Sector, *Public Administration*, Winter 1964.

from the benefits of each year sums required to cover maintenance and then calculate what rate of discount would make the value of the returns equal to the capital cost. This discounting procedure is, as it were, compound interest in reverse. (Thus at 10 per cent interest £100 today would be worth £110 in 1 year's time and £121 in 2 years; conversely, if 10 per cent is the rate of discount £121 2 years hence has a present value of £100). The rate of discount which equates the present value of the future returns (less running costs) with the capital outlay is the rate of return on the investment. As the M1 study states—"For the construction of the motorway to be worth while, it must be shown that the rate of return obtainable is greater than the current rate of interest and (more rigorously) greater than the rates of return obtainable in other uses of capital (including other road improvements)."

The authors of the M1 study compare the calculated return obtainable on the motorway (between 10 and 15 per cent) with the yield obtainable on Consols (then 5 per cent) representing the cost of government borrowing; their first condition is thus fulfilled by a considerable margin "especially as the motorway can be regarded as a virtually riskless investment". To satisfy the second condition is more difficult because of ignorance about the rate of return on other investments; but, limiting the comparison to other road improvement schemes, the authors concede that because of under-investment in roads many road schemes would yield a return well in excess of the rate of interest and in the short run a number would exceed the return on the motorway; however, with increasing traffic, because of the motorway's reserves of capacity, the comparison would become more favourable to the motorway.

There are problems here. As the relevant consideration is social opportunity cost measured by the alternative use to which the capital might have been put, it can be argued that the relevant interest rate should have been that which a private concern would have had to pay to borrow funds for the same purpose. More serious, to use a rate of return assessed on cost–benefit lines to compare with other rates of return to investments calculated on normal market criteria would be thoroughly misleading. The returns to a private operator are represented by the price charged times the quantity sold—the receipts from tolls in our comparison of the privately owned motor-way. But these receipts will give a yield much less than the sum of the benefits of motorway users as calculated by cost–benefit methods. The price (the toll) will accurately measure the benefits to those who just find it worth while to use the motorway; but there will be other motorway users whose benefits will be in excess of the toll; and others whose benefit would be less than the toll who do not use the toll road but would use a public motorway with no user charge.* Clearly, a rate of return based on cost–benefit appraisals which attempts to evaluate the full benefits to users would be much inflated compared with rates of return calculated on normal accounting criteria.

P.P.B.S.

Output budgeting or planning, programming, budgeting systems (henceforward referred to as P.P.B.S.), like cost–benefit analysis, originated in the U.S.A. and has been more widely applied there than in the U.K. It can be regarded as a move part way towards a cost–benefit analysis for a whole programme of government expenditure, where a full cost–benefit study is not yet possible. Essentially it consists of defining and rearranging "inputs" in rela-tion to "outputs" in the government accounts to promote better decision-making. Traditional accounting has been concerned with the type of resource on which money is spent: staff, buildings, consumables, etc. P.P.B.S. is concerned with the costs of achieving defined objectives.

The most ambitious and comprehensive published scheme for P.P.B.S. in the U.K. has been a feasibility study for its application in education expenditure† and it is convenient to draw on this study by way of illustration. First the total activity of the Depart-ment of Education and Science (D.E.S.) has to be broken down into

---

*Those familiar with the concepts will appreciate that the cost–benefit method includes the whole of "consumers' surplus" at zero price; or the equivalent of the returns to a perfectly discriminating monopolist selling a product of which the marginal cost is zero.
†*Output Budgeting for the Department of Education and Science*, Education Planning Paper No. 1, H.M.S.O., 1970.

major blocks of expenditure or sub-budgets related to broad objectives, which might be:

A. To meet the needs of the community for education (Education);
B. To increase human knowledge (Research);
C. To enrich the quality of cultural and recreational activities (Cultural and Recreational).

Each is then divided into a series of programmes, in which what is relevant is the type and objective of the education (e.g. to degree) rather than the type of institution (e.g. polytechnic or university). The Education block might have the following programmes:

A1 Compulsory Education;
A2 Nursery Education;
A3 Education for the 16-year-old;
A4 Education for the 17-to-19-year-old;
A5 Higher Education (courses not leading to degree or equivalent),
A6 Higher Education (courses leading to degree or equivalent;
A7 Postgraduate Education.

Within these major programmes are sub-programmes; so A1 Compulsory Education might include:

11 Existing pattern and scale of provision
 111 for existing numbers
 112 for population change
 113 for population shift

14 Changes in school organisation
 141 secondary reorganisation
 142 other

15 Changes in standards of accommodation
 151 in Educational Priority Areas (E.P.A.s)
 152 elsewhere.

These components in turn are broken down into a series of more precise and costed programme elements so that, ideally one can say, for example, what it would cost to improve pupil/teacher ratios by X in year Y in E.P.A.s and this can be compared with the cost of improving standards of accommodation in E.P.A.s by defined amounts; or it can be compared with a smaller but national improvement in pupil/teacher ratios . . . and so on. Thus a P.P.B.S. system for education would emerge with hundreds and possibly thousands of costed elements related to defined objectives.

The whole process is designed to enable realistic choice to be made amongst alternatives. Essential to the P.P.B.S. process is the allocation of expenditure to programmes which are as closely identified with objectives as possible; the systematic review of programmes to consider alternative ways of achieving objectives, to assess progress towards objectives and to question the validity of objectives; and special studies to establish the costs of alternatives and to seek better methods of evaluating achievement towards objectives. (Often our evaluation at present rests on a proxy measure, such as an improved pupil/teacher ratio, when our real concern is the quality of the education.)

Attempts to apply P.P.B.S. raise many difficulties. Thus with the D.E.S. we must recognise that it influences education rather than controls it and P.P.B.S. in education would thus be a monitoring and planning rather than a controlling system. There are clearly immense difficulties in identifying educational objectives in terms which lend themselves to quantitative measurement. Also there are problems such as defining costs, allocating costs amongst multiple objectives and identifying marginal costs—the costs associated with small charges in a programme—which are often the most relevant form of cost. Despite its imperfections, P.P.B.S. has the fundamental attraction that it offers a systematic appraisal of government efficiency and a rational framework for choice in public spending.

Developments Since 1979 and the Financial Management Initiative

Policy Reviews

The Conservative Government under Mrs. Thatcher came into office in 1979 determined to reduce taxation and government expenditure. This policy included increasing the efficiency with which government and its agencies utilised resources and one of the first acts of the new government was to appoint Sir Derek (now Lord) Rayner from Marks and Spencer to head a small unit in the Cabinet Office to undertake a series of reviews to identify where savings might be made. Sir Derek had served briefly as an efficiency expert in the Heath Government and the Rayner scrutinies were, in a sense, a continuation of the Programme Analysis and Reviews (P.A.R.s) which had been introduced under the Heath Government but subsequently abandoned. Although the Rayner unit was small, using mainly local officers for each review, its activities were much more focused and benefited from clearer and stronger leadership than the previous P.A.R.s. A report by the National Audit Office, on the progress of the Rayner reviews from 1979 to 1983 identified savings achieved of £171m by 1983/84 (although the scrutinies had identified savings of $2\frac{1}{2}$ times that figure). Whilst small in relation to the total of government expenditure, they were not insignificant. After Sir Derek returned to private industry, the Rayner Unit remained, under the direction of Sir Robin Ibbs, as an efficiency unit now primarily giving advice to departments and agencies undertaking their own internal audits and efficiency studies.

Another feature of the Conservative emphasis on efficiency was an increased use of management consultants, who were brought in by departments especially to help with the problems of financial control of associated bodies.

Besides the small scale Rayner reviews, the Government also set in motion some larger scale reviews of which the most important was the so-called Fowler Review (after the responsible Minister) of social security, in 1983. The Fowler Review was concerned with much more than money saving and was intended as a re-examination of the whole philosophy of welfare provision. This was a very public review, with four teams of ministers and outside advisers; but in the event the philosophy of the welfare state remained largely unchanged as did its cost. One outcome was the modification of a potentially very expensive State Earnings Related Pension Scheme (S.E.R.P.S.).

The Financial Management Initiative

The contributions of the Thatcher years to the process of financial efficiency in government were given a focus in the Financial Management Initiative (F.M.I.). The F.M.I. was formally introduced into government in May 1982 to build on the work already done to improve financial management in departments. The Cabinet Office and the Treasury, through the F.M.I., encouraged the use of new management techniques throughout the Civil Service by assisting departments to develop and implement their own systems, and by monitoring their progress. The principles of F.M.I. were intended not only for central government departments but also for agencies and associated bodies.

The F.M.I. is not a single unified system of management but embodies a set of general rules which are adapted to suit the needs of each department or agency. However, there are certain common basic principles of financial management:

(1) The use of information systems, particularly financial information for accounting purposes and management information to assist managers in making strategic plans.
(2) Clarification of objectives at all levels.
(3) Measurement of performance where possible and the relation of future funding levels to performance indicators.
(4) Devolved responsibility for spending budgets.

These financial and management information systems are closely linked to the annual public expenditure reviews. Each department is also expected to provide clear objectives in presenting its annual financial reports in the public expenditure round.

The implementation of these principles in the field of government is difficult. It is not easy to formulate precise objectives and have meaningful performance indicators for departments like the Treasury. Many government departments, like the Department of Education and Science and the Department of Health have policy-making functions but do not themselves implement policy. The F.M.I. has worked best in functional departments like Inland Revenue and Customs and Excise where it is easier to establish clear objectives, introduce specific targets and monitor them (for example a Customs and Excise target of the 1986/87 plan was "By 31 March 1987 reduce the average amount of V.A.T. outstanding from taxpayers by £60m compared with the position at 31 March 1986"). Budget devolution can also proceed down the line with cost centres being established for units "in the field". Nevertheless, as we shall see when we examine the economics of health and education expenditure in the next chapter, the principles of the F.M.I. have been introduced into schools, universities and health authorities.

In the final section of this chapter, we review all these attempts to improve efficiency in the public sector and make a provisional judgement on the effectiveness of the F.M.I.

Parliamentary Control

In constitutional theory the House of Commons has the authority and power to control government expenditure. Estimates have to be approved by Parliament and governments require the authority of Parliament to raise money. But, save in situations of minority government, those powers of the legislature are never used; to say that Parliament controls government expenditure is about as meaningful as to say that the Queen can refuse royal assent to Bills. The reason for this lack of Parliamentary power is to be found in the fusion of the Executive and Legislative organs of government allied to the strongly disciplined party system.

Even in constitutional theory Parliament has no right to propose *increases* in expenditure; moreover a large proportion of government expenditure, notably expenditure by local government and nationalised industries, is not included in the estimates and is not therefore even subject to formal parliamentary approval.

The Supply debates are in theory about the Government's spending estimates for the coming year, but in practice the Opposition chooses motions to be discussed on the twenty-nine Supply days which enable them to criticise some aspect of Government policy. Thus a motion to reduce a Minister's salary may be the peg on which to hang an attack on the particular policies of that Ministry. Besides the Supply days, other opportunities for Parliamentary debate on spending are provided by new legislation and by adjournment and Private Members' debates. Since 1970 there have been annual debates on the Public Expenditure White Papers. Apart from the latter and debates on the Reports of the Public Accounts Committee (which we discuss more fully below) by and large the debates serve mainly as occasions on which Members can put forward uncoordinated demands for increased expenditure, especially related to their own constituencies. The debates also provide some sort of weather vane for governments on the climate of opinion amongst M.P.s about which directions of spending would be the most popular. At most these occasions may have some influence on the way the government spends: they certainly cannot be regarded as exercising "control" nor as providing any serious analysis of spending alternatives.*

If influence rather than control best describes Parliament's role, that influence is exercised rather more by Committees of the House of Commons than by the House sitting as a whole. On the one hand is the Public Accounts Committee (P.A.C.) which examines the audited accounts of the government. On the other hand are successive committees which have considered the estimates or projections of expenditure—first the Estimates Committee, which was replaced by the Expenditure Committee which has in turn been replaced by departmental committees. It is to a more detailed examination of the work of those committees that we now turn.

---

*See A. Robinson, *Parliament and Public Spending*, Heinemann Educational Books, 1978, especially chapters 2 and 8.

The Public Accounts Committee, the Comptroller and Auditor-General and the National Audit Office

The P.A.C. was formed by Gladstone in 1861 and is the Senior Committee of the House of Commons. It consists of a dozen or so members plus the Financial Secretary to the Treasury who is an ex-officio Member. Like other House of Commons Select Committees it has the power to send for "papers, persons and records" and its proceedings mostly take the form of the examination of witnesses, usually the Permanent Secretaries (who are the Accounting Officers) for each Department.

The main task of the P.A.C. is to scrutinise the way public money has been spent in order (as a former P.A.C. Chairman, Osbert Peake, described in 1948) "first, to ensure that money is spent as Parliament intended; second, to ensure the exercise of due economy; and third, to maintain high standards of public morality in all financial matters." In other words the P.A.C. is not concerned with the first two objectives of control which we listed above (p. 46) — the right overall total and allocation amongst programmes — but it is concerned with the third and fourth — control against waste and fraud.

Unlike other Select Committees the P.A.C. has always enjoyed an expert backing. The Comptroller and Auditor-General (C.A.G.), who has a large staff, is a permanent attender at meetings of the Committee and he brings matters to the attention of the Committee where further investigation is considered desirable. Although the P.A.C. is not formally restricted to investigating expenditures which have been examined by the C.A.G., an analysis for the period 1965–1978 showed that over 90 per cent of the topics covered by the Committee were chosen from issues raised by the C.A.G.*

From the very nature of its investigations the P.A.C. cannot directly prevent wasteful expenditures, but it can highlight them when they happen, examine the causes (such as the inadequacy of Departmental control systems) and suggest ways for improvement.

*See V. Flegmann, *Called to Account*, Gower, 1980.

Moreover the very fact that senior civil servants have to appear before the Committee and answer for any deficiencies generates a healthy concern for financial rectitude and efficiency. A limitation of the work of the Committee has been that the C.A.G.'s audit only covered about 60 per cent of public expenditure excluding expenditure by local authorities, nationalised industries and some other government agencies.

In 1983 some major changes took place which strengthened the financial control of the P.A.C. and of Parliament. By the National Audit Act, 1983, the C.A.G. became an appointee of Parliament (or, strictly speaking, of the Queen on the recommendation of the House of Commons) instead of the government. This change removed any suspicion that he was the agent of the executive. Also the National Audit Office (N.A.O.) was established, replacing the Exchequer and Audit Department. The C.A.G. was head of the N.A.O. which was funded by a separate item in the Supply Estimates and controlled by a newly formed Public Accounts Commission of the House of Commons, consisting of the Leader of the House (a member of the government), the Chairman of the P.A.C. (by convention a member of the opposition) and seven backbench M.P.s. The N.A.O. reported directly to the House of Commons and published its own reports. Under the Act the C.A.G. was given powers to audit some agencies and associated bodies of the central government departments which had previously been outside its terms of reference.

The Act brought about a big improvement but did not go as far as many parliamentarians had wished. They had wanted the N.A.O. (like the General Accounting Office of the U.S.A.) to be able to follow public money wherever it went, whether spent by local government, nationalised industries, bodies receiving grants from public funds and privately owned companies with over 50 per cent of shares publicly owned. The government resisted this pressure. They set up a separate Audit Commission for local authorities; and the nationalised industries' chairmen conducted a successful campaign to keep out of the N.A.O. net.

Before 1983 the P.A.C. and the C.A.G. had important successes to their name. Thus, for example, in 1964 the P.A.C. revealed that, because of accounting weaknesses in the Ministry of Aviation, Ferranti Ltd had made excessive profits from contracts for equipment in respect of the Bloodhouse guided missile system. Their revelations led to the appointment of a special investigating committee (the Lang Committee), the repayment by Ferranti of £4.25m and recommendations to prevent any recurrences. A somewhat similar revelation of overcharging by Bristol-Siddeley Engines led to new rules for non-competitive contracts by which governments would in future have the right to equality of information with the contractor, and to post-cost individual contracts for follow on orders; provision was also made for a review board to which either government or a contractor could refer a contract if the rate of profit fell outside specified limits.

It was the P.A.C. which had first officially proposed that the C.A.G. should be an officer of parliament and that an N.A.O. responsible to parliament and with a wide remit should be established. One advantage of the N.A.O. over the old Exchequer and Audit Department is that because its staff establishment is controlled by parliament through the Public Accounts Commission, more and better staff can be obtained. It has been alleged that the Exchequer and Audit Department was deliberately kept short of high quality staff. The N.A.O. currently (1991) employs just over 900 staff of whom about half are accountants and a further 200 are accountants under training.

The N.A.O. sets out its objectives as follows:

(1) To provide parliament with an assurance that public money has been spent for the purposes parliament intended.
(2) To improve financial control in government departments and other public bodies.
(3) To improve value obtained from the resources made available to parliament.
(4) To improve the techniques and quality of public sector audit.

Before the N.A.O. was established the C.A.G. and his staff had been undertaking value for money audits—to evaluate the economy, efficiency and effectiveness of government's use of resources—as well as financial audits. The move to value for money audits was accentuated with the N.A.O. The line between policy (which is the exclusive province of government) and implementation is often a fine one; but with value for money audits the N.A.O. aims to:

(1) Establish whether a body has sound systems and controls for ensuring economy, efficiency and effectiveness.
(2) Examine how well these systems and controls operate, and whether they provide management with the necessary information satisfactorily to monitor performance.
(3) Assess against predetermined criteria whether value for money is being achieved.
(4) Make recommendations for improvements and work with the body to improve financial control and value for money.

The N.A.O. monitors the changes in procedure made by departments in the light of its work and recommendations and claims that, in 1988 and 1989, savings or economies achieved were around £215m (e.g. £55m saved following legislation to recover invalidity benefit from those who subsequently received civil damages; savings of £73m in the cost of British forces in Germany following the introduction of economy measures and efficiency targets by the Ministry of Defence)*.

Estimates, Expenditure and Departmental Committees

In 1970 the Estimates Committee, which had existed since early in the century and each year had examined in detail a selection of the estimates, was replaced by an Expenditure Committee. Although it did some useful work (including recommending the setting up of the Plowden Committee) the Estimates Committee had always suffered from certain defects most notably in its timetable; the time between the publication of the estimates and their consideration by the House of Commons was too short for it to produce well-informed reports.

The Expenditure Committee was the outcome of proposals of the Procedure Committee in the Report on *The Control of Public*

*N.A.O. *Helping the Nation to Spend Wisely.*

Expenditure and Administration, Session 1968–69. The Report contained two main recommendations:

(1) that a White Paper should be published in November each year, based on the P.E.S.C. exercise; and that it should be debated by the House of Commons for two days;

(2) that an Expenditure Committee should be set up, with a series of sub-committees, which would consider the expenditure proposals of the White Paper in detail.

As we have already seen, the idea of an annual Expenditure White Paper was accepted in 1969; the new Conservative Government of 1970 also accepted the proposal for an Expenditure Committee. The new Committee began work early in 1971 and for almost all of its eight-year life the Expenditure Committee consisted of six sub-committees each of eight members, making a total of forty-eight. These sub-committees were: General; Defence; Trade and Industry; Environment; Social Services and Employment· Education, Arts and the Home Office.

The proponents of an Expenditure Committee had expected that the General sub-committee would coordinate the work of the other sub-committees in a systematic review of the Government's spending plans as laid out in the White Paper. In fact this did not happen; the Chairmen of the sub-committees preferred to go their own way and choose their own subjects and style of investigation, so that the Expenditure Committee functioned rather more as a set of specialist subject Select Committees than as a financial committee. However, in the last three years of its life, some coordination was effected when on two occasions each sub-committee agreed to select one aspect of the White Paper for detailed comment. Moreover the General sub-committee maintained a steady output of reports consisting of an annual examination of the White Paper, critical analyses of the Government's management of the economy and even a foray into taxation by examining *The Financing of Public Expenditure* (1975–76).

As well as seeking to improve the efficiency of decision-making in public-spending and the management of the economy the General sub-committee sought consistently to improve the form and content of the Expenditure White Papers, in order to make public expenditure decisions more responsive to Parliament and public opinion by ensuring that the necessary information was presented in the most meaningful way. Although the Treasury adopted some of its proposals, the sub-committee achieved little success in its aim to secure a more readily comprehensible document.

In 1979 the Expenditure Committee disappeared in a major reorganisation of House of Commons Committees. In 1978, after a long enquiry, the Procedure Committee had recommended the replacement of the existing Select Committee structure by a more coherent system which would enable backbench M.P.s to shadow government departments. The new Conservative Government accepted the recommendation and thirteen Select Committees were set up each with eight to eleven members. One committee monitored the Treasury and Civil Service, others related to Agriculture; Defence; Education, Science and the Arts; Employment; Energy and so on. Expenditure control thus ceased to be the focal point of any individual Select Committee except for the Public Accounts Committee, which remained. Scrutiny of Government expenditure became one of many functions which the new committees could perform if they wished.

Under this new departmental committee system less scrutiny of public spending plans has taken place than in the later days of the Expenditure Committee system. Whilst the departmental committees had the power to explore the spending of the departments they monitored and of the bodies associated with these departments (like the universities with the Department of Education and Science and the Manpower Services Commission with the Department of Employment), the interests of their members, tended to be concentrated on policy issues of a topical nature rather than on a systematic analysis of expenditure. Some of the departmental committees have commented on the related section of the Expenditure White Paper, but the Committees have not joined together for enquiries cutting across departmental lines and only the Treasury and Civil Service Committee has consistently concerned itself with matters of public expenditure. This committee has continued the work of the General Sub-Committee of the Expenditure Committee by making regular comments on the Government's own capacity to control public spending, by calling on the government to improve the timing and documentation of the annual budget and expenditure process and by commenting on the management of the economy. The Treasury and Civil Service Committee has drawn on a wider range of economic advisers than its predecessors and has made a regular practice of calling on the Chancellor of the Exchequer and some of his junior ministers to give evidence in public. Regular probing and judicious questioning by the Treasury and Civil Service Committee has made it a significant instrument for encouraging the Government to accept better machinery for public expenditure management and control and its reports have become the main source of information on changes in government practice on these issues.

It was also the Treasury and Civil Service Committee that first proposed* that there should be departmental reports in place of the functional chapters of the Public Expenditure White Paper and which led, eventually, to the new structure for presenting public expenditure, described above (p. 56) and which came fully into operation in 1991.

Parliamentary Debate on Public Expenditure

The proposals for an Expenditure Committee, and for an annual white paper on public spending which should be annually debated in the House of Commons, had gone hand in hand. Some enthusiasts for the proposals had held that the Expenditure White Paper debates would become the "highlight of the Parliamentary year"; instead they have more often been a flop. A former Chief Secretary to the Treasury described the debate on the 1971 White Paper as "flogging a dead mouse". There are many possible reasons for this outcome: major policy decisions on public expenditure were invariably announced in advance of the white paper which therefore lacked the appeal of headline news; many M.P.s appeared to be

*Second Report of the Treasury and Civil Service Select Committee, Session 1984/85. *The Structure and Form of Financial Documents Presented to Parliament*, HC 110, 1984, H.M.S.O., London.

more interested in the trivia of public expenditure decisions in their own constituencies than in the broad policy decisions of the nation; and the technicalities of the white papers made them hard reading for the professional economist, let alone the layman; and little informed comment has been available to point out the implications of the expenditure choices in a way to bring them alive to M.P.s; further, as we have seen, the work of the Expenditure sub-committees was never coordinated in the way the proponents of the Committee had envisaged.

Since 1979 there has been little change in the form or content of the debates. In 1982 the House of Commons, on the proposal of the Procedure Committee* re-instituted genuine debates on selected Estimates, which has meant, in effect, that the House has debated one of the Select Committee reports; but most of the items debated have been relatively small and insignificant.

If the debates on the Expenditure White Papers have generally been disappointing in quality and attendance, debates held on reports of the P.A.C. have been perhaps even more unsatisfactory. Vilma Flegmann† records the "pretty dismal picture" that, in the period 1966 to 1978, the number of M.P.s who took part in these debates was never higher than 23 and about half were members of the P.A.C. at the time; and five debates attracted ten or less participants.

Assessment of Developments Since Plowden

The thirty years since the initial application of the Plowden recommendations have seen many changes in the system of public expenditure control and not a little disillusionment.

The first recommendation of Plowden was for regular surveys of expenditure over a series of years head. The P.E.S.C. exercise, so widely acclaimed when first introduced, has undergone a series of modifications largely in response to particular crises. The forward "cash" projections of public spending in the 1982 White Paper and

Report from the Select Committee on Procedure (Supply), HC 118, 1980–81.
†The Public Accounts Committee, in *Control of Public Expenditure*, ed. Sandford, Bath University Centre for Fiscal Studies, 1979.

after are very different from the longer forward look in constant price or volume terms of the early P.E.S.C. projections. F.I.S. and cash limits almost certainly improve financial control at some cost in effective resource planning. However, as Sir Leo Pliatzky (the civil servant primarily responsible for introducing cash limits) has written recently "In the long run the workability of operating the public expenditure system entirely in cash terms will depend on progress in coping with inflation".* Even with the P.E.S.C. system in place, it remains doubtful how far the Cabinet really decides, in a considered fashion, on the "social balance" and the broad priorities of public spending. The outcome of the P.E.S.C. round is, in reality, often the result of a series of compromises between a spending minister and the Chief Secretary to the Treasury, rather than a deliberate determination of priorities by the Cabinet. Moreover political expediencies (like the need to mollify irate payers, or non payers of the community charge—see below p. 279) are likely to have the biggest influence on spending decisions.

Plowden's second recommendation, to avoid disruption and waste in the public sector by the greatest practicable stability in public spending decisions once taken, has always been honoured more in the breach than in the observance. Indeed, it carried the implication that adjustments resulting from government management of the economy had to fall almost wholly on the private sector. Yet such changes may cause no less disruption and waste in the private sector than in the public sector, especially in cases such as investment in the motor car industry. It is unlikely that the Committee would have made this second recommendation if it had taken evidence from industry and not just the civil service. In the event under the Conservatives since 1979 there has probably been less crisis cutting of public expenditure than in earlier years, but rather a more sustained pressure on public spending. Similarly, with budgetary "fine tuning" out of fashion (see p. 333) there have been less temporary tax adjustments; but the increased use of interest rates to cope with inflation or balance of payments pressures has not made life any easier for private industry.

*Leo Pliatzky, *Getting and Spending*, Basil Blackwell, 1982.

Perhaps in no aspect has disillusionment been greater than in relation to the third recommendation of Plowden for better tools to deal with public expenditure problems. The techniques of P.A.R., Cost–Benefit analysis and P.P.B.S. have all proved disappointing P.A.R. exercises were internal to departments, were never published as such, were reported to be of very variable quality and the very name P.A.R. has now been abandoned. Cost benefit analysis suffered a set-back with the rejection of the Roskill Commission's recommendations on the third London airport. As for P.P.B.S., following the feasibility study it was tried out briefly in the D.E.S. only to be abandoned. While elements of it would appear to be extant in defence and in the D.H.S.S., no thorough-going application apparently exists in any department of government.

It is clear, in retrospect, that too much was expected of the new techniques. As Wildavsky writes, P.P.B.S. "does not work because it cannot work. Failure is built into its very nature because it demands abilities to perform cognitive operations which are beyond present human (or machine) capacities".* Whilst this may be an over-reaction, there is no doubt that it is particularly difficult to apply P.P.B.S. where objectives can only be defined in the most general way and quantitative measures for assessing the achievement of those objectives do not exist. In this light education, and especially the D.E.S. which is a monitoring and advising rather than a controlling body, was just about the least fertile field for a full-blooded P.P.B.S.

These remarks should not be interpreted to mean that these techniques are useless — only that their limitations must be recognised, expectations from their use correspondingly circumscribed and attempts made to remedy their weaknesses where this can be done. Cost–benefit analysis is a valuable technique if the inevitable element of subjectivity is appreciated. The D.E.S., whilst abandoning P.P.B.S. itself, has encouraged local authorities to use it. If the name P.A.R. has disappeared, policy review exercises have continued to take place.

Moreover, some of the ideas behind P.P.B.S. and P.A.R. have

*Aaron Wildavsky, *Budgeting*, Little Brown, 1975, p. 364.

been subsumed within the F.M.I. As we have already indicated, applying the principle of the F.M.I. is not easy in some central government departments where the actual spending is undertaken by agencies or associated bodies. But the essential differences between the F.M.I. and earlier attempts at efficiency, like P.A.R., is that the F.M.I. is built into the system rather than imposed on top. For that reason it has much more chance of achieving lasting effect. After almost a decade of the F.M.I., attitudes among top civil servants have clearly changed. The permanent secretaries in post have grown up with the changing ideas of the 1980s and are more managerial and financially aware than their predecessors. It is this change of attitudes that offers the hope that the F.M.I. will continue and survive any change of government. The F.M.I. is also more comprehensive than the preceding attempts at executive efficiency in that it has percolated down to the agencies and other bodies associated with departments, such as the universities.

The technological revolution is also on the side of the F M I Effective management in the public services required the amassing, collation and rapid retrieval of vast quantities of information. With computerisation this is a practicable proposition.

The changes which have taken place on the parliamentary side reinforce the F.M.I. The N.A.O. and P.A.C. probe and monitor progress; whilst the new departmental reports, with their standard formats and information and the requirement to specify perform-ance indicators and targets both require departmental officers to think in F.M.I. terms and make that thinking public. The fact that the C.A.G. as head of the N.A.O. is now an officer of Parliament is also a big improvement. All is not perfect. The N.A.O. cannot follow public money wherever it goes; there is not the consistency which many backbenchers desired, by which central government and local government are audited by the same body. But at least the departmental committees can, and do, take evidence from council-lors and local government officers, and a clause inserted into the Act setting up the Audit Commission for local government required the Commission to send to the C.A.G. copies of any of its reports concerned with the implementation of central government guidelines on public spending.

There remains the question whether the timing of the public expenditure data is appropriate. In principle there is much to be said for public expenditure data and tax data being presented at the same time, so that the income and expenditure sides of the budget are visible together and Parliament and the public can see what they are getting for their money. Under the present arrangements the Autumn Statement in November gives much of the data on expenditure; the departmental reports and additional data will appear January–mid February; and the "Budget" normally comes in March. In fact, in 1980, by accident rather than design, because the public expenditure data was delayed by the new government seeking cuts, the two did come together at the time of the March budget. But this proved not to be the happiest of arrangements. The public expenditure data was overshadowed by the tax changes. Moreover, to delay the public expenditure decisions until just before the beginning of the financial year would make life very difficult for individual departments. There would be much more sense in presenting both expenditure and taxation proposals in November to come into effect for the next financial year. This would allow more extended discussion and open debate on tax reform proposals which have often been produced hurriedly in secret and required substantial amendment later. Some components of the Budget, like precise tax rates, might need to be kept secret until the beginning of the financial year to prevent forestalling, but this is less of a problem than is often believed and other countries, like Germany or Sweden, are much more relaxed than the United Kingdom about providing tax details well in advance of their date of implementation.

More progress also needs to be made towards a "tax expenditure budget". As we indicated, since 1979 the annual expenditure white papers have listed, and valued where possible, direct tax reliefs and concessions. These tax concessions should be set in the context of the expenditure programmes, so that, for example, one can see mortgage interest relief to owner occupiers alongside subsidies to council house tenants. Only this way can a comprehensive picture be obtained of the resources provided through the state for particular programmes. Undoubtedly there are problems in this approach, not least that of deciding just what is a "tax expenditure"; but both the U.S.A. and Canadian governments have successfully managed to proceed much further along the path to a tax expenditure budget than the United Kingdom.

CHAPTER 4

Economic Aspects of Government Expenditure

In this chapter we examine four of the major directions of government expenditure in the United Kingdom—defence, interest on the national debt, education and health. With the exception of social security expenditure which amounted to a huge £63 billion in 1990 and consists almost entirely of cash transfers (including pensions, unemployment pay income support and child benefits) these were the four largest individual areas of expenditure in the United Kingdom over the period 1960–90.

Table 4.1 indicates the amount of these four items of expenditure 1960–90 in money terms and as a percentage of G.N.P. Because of price rises, the G.N.P. percentages provide the more meaningful comparisons; even so, it is important to remember that these percentages reflect variations in the rate of growth of G.N.P. as well as in real expenditure on these various services. Also it is necessary to warn the reader that there are discontinuities of coverage and definitions over time, so that significance should not be attached to minor differences.

The table shows the appreciable decline in defence spending as a percentage of G.N.P. during the 1960s, stabilising in the 1970s with a further decline at the end of the period. The big drop in debt interest at the end of the period reflects the effects of large Budget surpluses, leading to debt repayment, in the later 1980s. Education expenditure shows a phenomenal increase during the decade of the 1960s, levelling off in the 1970s as the effect of the falling birth rate after 1964 diminishes the school population and falling as a propor-

TABLE 4.1
Selected Government Expenditures, 1960–90, Compared with G.N.P.
(a)
At Current Prices (£ million)

	1960	1970	1980	1990
Defence	1,612	2,466	11,444	22,875
Debt Interest	1,165	2,025	10,888	18,544
Education	917	2,532	12,762	26,833
Health	861	1,979	11,633	27,671
G.N.P. at F.C.	22,900	44,100	200,835	481,776

(b)
As Percentage of G.N.P. at Factor Cost

	1960	1970	1980	1990
Defence	7.0	5.6	5.7	4.7
Debt Interest	5.1	4.6	5.4	3.8
Education	4.0	5.7	6.4	5.6
Health	3.8	4.5	5.8	5.7

Source: *National Income and Expenditure* Blue Books, and *United Kingdom National Accounts*, 1991.

tion of G.N.P. by 1990. Health spending, which is also affected by demographic changes in the form of increasing numbers of the elderly who require more health care, remains on a steady upward trend 1960 to 1980, but then levels off as a percentage of G.N.P. However, because G.N.P. is growing, health expenditure in the 1980s continued to rise in real terms.

It is not our purpose to examine the details of expenditure under each heading but rather to consider broad economic factors which, whilst we have related them specifically to the circumstances of the United Kingdom, are nevertheless applicable elsewhere.

Defence

Military defence is a "collective good" *par excellence*, wholly provided by the government and where user charges are inapplicable. For a variety of reasons market prices may provide no valid criteria for assessing costs. The government is the only purchaser of defence services in the domestic market, although other governments may purchase some of the products of the defence industries such as military aircraft. The market mechanism for securing manpower for the Armed Forces may be superseded by conscription which provides a supply of labour irrespective of the price (the serviceman's pay and allowances) offered. Further, normal investment criteria of rates of return cannot readily be applied to defence expenditures. These are not the only problems met in attempting to appraise defence spending according to economic criteria: the objectives of defence expenditure are related to foreign policy and may turn on an evaluation of developments in a particular distant part of the world which few people are competent to undertake; the strategy and tactics of defence are the province of experts; the complex technology of modern defence "hardware" defeats the layman; and even those outside government service who seek to inform themselves are denied information for security reasons.

Yet defence takes such a significant proportion of total resources that it cannot be omitted from economic appraisal. The cost and complexity of weapons increase the importance of the "right" decisions being taken. The application of what is essentially cost–benefit analysis to military planning originated in the "operational research" of the Second World War. Operational research was developed then to use military resources more effectively by, for example, selecting routes and schedules minimising risks in shipping, seeking to determine the optimum size of convoys and choosing between alternative designs of military equipment. Subsequently the Americans have developed specialist agencies for military operational research which has become a highly developed science. In Britain a similar specialised unit was created following the proposal in the Defence White Paper of 1965.*

It is perhaps not surprising in view of the problems, the security needs and the relatively late attempts to apply economic criteria that little has been published on the economic aspects of defence expenditure in Britain. But one study by a visiting American, R. N.

Statement on the Defence Estimates, Cmnd. 2592, H.M.S.O., 1965.

McKean,* outlines some of the problems and attempts, in general terms, to show how cost–benefit analysis might be applied to British defence expenditure.

McKean shows that the efficient allocation of resources in defence raises familiar cost–benefit problems in the form of "spillover" effects or "externalities". Thus tactical weapons designed to support ground troops can bring additional benefit by adding to strategic potential. Conversely, siting a base near to large towns can add to the difficulty and cost of civil defence operations by increasing the likelihood of attack. Since the main object of the defence forces is to prevent major war, the "spillover" effects on disarmament negotiations must be taken into account; two alternative retaliatory forces may provide an equally effective deterrent, but possibly one only of them may make it easier to reach mutually advantageous agreements on weapons control. Defence is also an area of expenditure in which are very prominent the problems of time series (i.e. payments and benefits spread over many years) of intangibles and incommonourables, discussed in the previous chapter.

In possible applications of cost–benefit analysis to British defence expenditure, McKean suggests three broad categories. First, the comparison of alternative allocations of resources amongst major activities; secondly the comparison of alternative "weapon systems" to attain the object of each major activity; thirdly, comparison of alternative research and development (R. and D.) programmes.

The first category involves major crucial issues such as the relative amounts to be spent on capabilities for a limited war as against a nuclear deterrent force. Here the scope for applying cost–benefit analysis is limited; it can help a little by spelling out more clearly the costs and benefits of incremental additions or deductions to each area of activity, but in the main this is an area of "heroic judgement", to use McKean's words.

Cost–benefit analysis can give more help when we are choosing among alternative equipment, modes of operation or systems for carrying out the main activities. For instance, a British decision to

*Cost–Benefit Analysis and Defence Expenditure, from *Public Expenditure Appraisal and Control*, A. T. Peacock and D. J. Robertson (eds.), Oliver & Boyd, 1963.

have an independent nuclear deterrent necessitates a systematic study of the many possible alternatives to produce the greatest deterrent power from the amount budgeted. Some elements in the situation are given—e.g. geography, and possibly foreign policy. But a wide range of delivery systems must be considered—manned aircraft; air-launched missiles; land-based missiles purchased abroad; land-based missiles developed at home; ship-launched missiles; submarine-launched missiles; possibly missiles launched from mobile trucks or underwater platforms. For each possible method there would be ancillary equipment, bases, personnel, protective measures, fuel locations, supply systems, radar installations, communications command and control arrangements.

Finally cost–benefit analysis can play a limited role in choice amongst alternative research and development expenditures. Although by its very nature the outcome of a research project is unknown and its cost speculative, by cost–benefit analysis we can attempt to assess the prospective worth of various innovations if successfully developed; this is some guide to the allocation of resources amongst the alternatives.

Application of economic principles to defence expenditure raises many difficulties; nevertheless, to quote McKean, "At this stage . . . the case for more extensive use of cost–benefit analysis may rest mainly on the following point: weighing the costs and gains of alternative actions is *the correct way to look at problems of choice*. It is the right way to approach such problems even if it turns out in particular instances that no quantitative estimates are possible."

The National Debt

The main purpose of this section is to dispel any misunderstandings about the nature and significance of a national debt. What is officially known as the "National Debt" in the United Kingdom amounted, in March 1990, in round terms to £186 billion in sterling plus £7 billion in foreign currency debt. However, some £33 billion was held in government departments or agencies—which amounted to the government owing itself money. If we exclude this sum, we arrive at a figure for "market holdings" of debt of some £160 billion.

However, this does not represent the full figure of public sector borrowings. It relates only to central government debt. Local authorities also have large debts. Of the local government debts of £53 billion in 1990, £47 billion was owed to central government; in effect this will be included in the National Debt as the central government will have had to increase its borrowings in order to lend to local government. Similarly with the debts of public corporations, the bulk of which is owed to central government.*

A vital distinction is that between internal and external debt. Of the central government debt in 1990, some £28 billion, or about 15 per cent, was held abroad.

To set against the debt are certain "real" assets, like roads, schools, hospitals and council houses and certain financial assets like government shareholdings in British Telecom. Some of these assets produce a money income which can be set against debt interest, hence it is often useful to distinguish "net" from "gross" interest (above, p. 21). In the year 1990 the gross interest in the General Government account was £18½ billion, rather more than half of which was matched by rent, interest and dividends. A large part of the debt, however, is not matched by tangible assets. It may have arisen because the government allowed current expenditure to exceed non-loan revenue to sustain demand as part of its policy for managing the economy or it may be the outcome of emergencies, notably wars. Indeed, much of the debt (as measured in real terms) was incurred in fighting two major wars in the 20th century. Where there were tangible assets to set against the debt they consisted of planes, tanks and ships, long since destroyed or obsolescent; the only asset now to be set against this war-created debt is the intangible one of national freedom.

If a *person* has incurred a large debt with no tangible assets to set against it, his position is serious. He must provide, from his income, the interest charges on the debt (and ultimately repayment of capital) and his own living standard is lowered in consequence.

However, the national debt of a country is only analogous to a personal debt in so far as the national debt is external. Payment of

---

*For a detailed analysis of government financial liabilities, see *Financial Statistics* No. 347, March 1991, H.M.S.O.

interest on an external debt can be expected to reduce the living standard of members of the community and the existence of the debt is a genuine deduction from the real wealth or capital of the community, just as, when the loan was acquired, it provided additional real resources for the country to utilise.

An internal debt on the other hand represents a series of claims of members of the same country against each other, which, as such, neither add to nor deduct from either the wealth or the income of the community. People and institutions who hold the national debt, holders of government bonds, national savings certificates and short-term securities (Treasury bills) and other forms of government securities, receive interest on their holdings which is paid by the body of taxpayers; to some extent they are paying themselves interest. The "service" of the national debt (the interest paid on it) is thus essentially a transfer of purchasing power within the community. A large national debt, in so far as it is internally held, is thus a much less serious matter than might be thought.

However, as Professor Lerner has neatly put it, to conclude from this that the growth of public debt is of no importance "must be understood in the same sense as when a man who finds that rumour has converted a twisted ankle into a broken neck tells his friends that he is perfectly all right".*

There are three main ways related to the theme of this book in which the existence of a large internal debt is significant. First, it affects the distribution of income and personal wealth. Payment of interest on the debt is a payment from taxpayer to debt holder; only by sheer coincidence for any particular bond holder do the additional tax payments he is required to make exactly equal his interest receipts; in general this is not so and the existence of the national debt alters the distribution of income in the community. Second, as a result of the debt, taxes need to be higher than would otherwise have been the case. This brings costs in two ways: there is the cost of collecting the additional taxes (and of managing the debt and distributing the interest); more important, if the additional taxes are "imposed" on top of already high tax rates they may distort the

---

*A. P. Lerner, The Burden of the National Debt, *Income, Employment and Public Policy* (essays in honour of Alvin Hansen), Norton, New York, 1948, p. 256.

allocation of resources, for example by reducing incentives to effort and risk-taking and encouraging people (and their financial advisers) to spend their time searching for methods of tax avoidance. We shall be examining these aspects of high taxation in successive chapters. Thirdly, a large internal debt affects the government's management or regulation of the economy. The short-term debt is a substantial part of the stock of liquid assets and an important medium for the exercise of monetary policy. The debt, and in particular additions to it, may have the effect of raising interest rates to the detriment of private sector investment. Furthermore, those who hold the debt as assets feel better off, and may therefore be inclined to consume a larger proportion of their income (a so-called "wealth effect") whilst because no individuals take account of the liability, there is no offsetting effect, as with private debtors. As a consequence the debt acts as an inflationary influence in the economy.

Education

The economics of education is a subject which has developed greatly in recent decades with the lead, as so often in this field, coming from the U.S.A. We shall confine ourselves to three main topics: first, the social benefit element in education expenditure; second, education as investment in human capital; third, aspects of the finance of education.

The Social Benefits of Education

Although in England and Wales (Scotland is an honourable exception) compulsory education and state provision are a product of the latter part of the 19th century, from early in that century the state had shown its interest in education expenditure by making funds available for the assistance of the voluntary school bodies and requiring employers of pauper apprentices to provide them with the rudiments of education.

At least a part of this interest arose from a belief that education provided a social benefit over and above the private benefit to the individual; and at least four directions of this "spillover" effect have been suggested.

First, a certain minimum degree of general literacy is essential if a sophisticated market economy is to work properly. Consumers must be able to read the advertisements for new products and producers the advertisements for jobs. Hence, the provision of this minimum education provides benefits for all in assisting a smooth-working and rapidly adjusting economy.

Second, the political argument: education, it is alleged, makes for more efficient and stable government; in particular, it is an essential for an effective democracy. It is significant that the English Education Act of 1870 which made provision for "board schools" and compulsory education followed the Second Reform Act of 1867, which gave the vote to working men; the cry went up from the politicians: "We must educate our masters."

A third and more doubtful argument has been and sometimes still is presented—that increased education brings social benefits from a reduction in crime. Unfortunately statistics lend no support to this contention. In general in recent years juvenile delinquency has risen along with expenditure per head on education. Moreover, there has been a phenomenon of particular interest referred to by the Crowther Committee;* viz. that the last year of compulsory education was also the heaviest year for juvenile delinquency and that when a boy went to work the tendency to crime was reversed. Not only was this phenomenon of long standing but the raising of the school-leaving age in 1947 brought "An immediate change-over in the delinquency record of the 13-year-olds (who until then had been the most troublesome age group) and the 14-year-olds, who took their place in 1948 and have held it consistently ever since" (para. 63).

Much care needs to be exercised in interpreting statistics; a correlation does not necessarily imply a causal relationship; but at least these facts demonstrate that there is no obviously beneficial effect of education on crime.

A fourth and much more convincing social benefit effect comes

*Report of the Central Advisory Council for Education—England, 15 to 18, H.M.S.O., 1959.

from the conferment of knowledge that has a national and international currency: the research benefit of education. Thus increased understanding of the economic system and of how to cope with unemployment or inflation provides a contribution to knowledge the world over which may benefit countless millions of people.

These are not the only arguments used to suggest social benefits from education. It is, for example, argued that education can promote social cohesion; that particular kinds of education can reduce class differences; and clearly education can be used to inculcate a particular set of values or prejudices of which rulers approve. But with these issues we move into a disputed area of value judgements.

These last apart, in so far as there are significant social benefits of education (and the first and fourth arguments seem to me to provide strong grounds for believing that education confers benefits over and above private benefits) a valid argument exists for state intervention in the market economy to ensure "adequate" educational provision. However, this leaves open the question whether state intervention should take the form of regulation, finance or provision or indeed what combination of the three.

Education as Investment in Human Capital

Education expenditure has both a "consumption" and an "investment" content. On the one hand we hope that the formal process of education is congenial to the child or young person receiving it and further that he or she will derive future personal enjoyment from the fuller life education opens up in the use of leisure. This might be regarded as the consumption element in education expenditure (although the future enjoyment of leisure could equally well be thought of as an investment expenditure yielding a non-monetary return, like the enjoyment from investment in a work of art or expenditure on jewellery). The investment content of education expenditure can be thought of as the increased contribution to production, measured by the higher earnings which education confers on its beneficiary.

This investment element of education expenditure lends itself to measurement. We can attempt to assess the return to education just as we would assess the return to a particular expenditure on physical investment. Let us take as our example expenditure on higher (university) education. Ideally we seek to compare two matched samples of the population identical in all relevant respects (notably intelligence, family background and secondary schooling) save that one group has "enjoyed" three more years of education than the other. Our concern is to compare the profile of their expected lifetime earnings. To assess the *private* return to higher education we calculate the differential between the two sets of average earnings net of tax; against this return we have to set the private costs of education which consist of both private outlay on higher education (if any) plus earnings forgone. The private *rate* of return to higher education is then found by calculating the rate of discount which will make the present values of the expected future returns to higher education just equal to the present value of the private costs of education. (To demonstrate the principle of the calculation of rates of return to education, a highly simplified illustration for one person is given in Table 4.2.)

We can similarly assess the "social rate of return" to education; the social return to education consists of the earnings differential from higher education *gross* of tax; this has to be set against private costs, outlay plus income forgone, together with state expenditure on education. Returns and costs can then be discounted, as before, to obtain the social rate of return to higher education.

Whilst the principle is relatively simple, in practice there are many practical and conceptual difficulties of which the following are amongst the most important.

The elimination of related influences. In practice we cannot obtain matched samples in this convenient way, nor can we assess expected life-time earnings in the simple manner suggested. The procedure generally followed to obtain the return to education has therefore been to observe different age cohorts of the population for the same year, calculate the average net earnings differentials associated with different amounts of formal education and adjust for factors other than education which generate differences in earnings

TABLE 4.2
Assessment of Private Return to Education

Age	Earnings p.a. less tax (without higher education) (£)	Earnings p.a. less tax (with higher education) (£)	Differential return to higher education (£)	Present value of return discounted at 5 per cent (£)	Cost of education (£)	Present value of return discounted to equate with cost (£)
59–60	1200	1500	300	184	—	38
58–59	1200	1500	300	193	—	47
57–58	1200	1500	300	203	—	58
56–57	1200	1500	300	213	—	71
55–56	1200	1500	300	224	—	88
54–55	1200	1500	300	235	—	108
53–54	1200	1500	300	247	—	132
52–53	1100	1400	300	259	—	162
51–52	1100	1300	200	182	—	133
50–51	1000	1200	200	190	—	163
49–50	1000	NIL	—		1000	
				2130	1000	1000

The example is designed to demonstrate the principle of the calculations by reducing the problem to its simplest proportions, viz. one person only, who undertakes a 12 months' education course at age 49–50, with 10 years of working life to follow. No fees are paid by the student for the course but he is responsible for his own maintenance; hence the private cost of education is represented by earnings forgone, set at £1,000 for simplicity.

Two procedures may be followed to assess the return to this education expenditure. The earnings differential can be discounted by the market rate of interest (say 5 per cent after tax) to see if the sum of the present value of returns (in this case £2,130) is higher than the cost (in this case £1,000). Or the annual differential can be discounted by that rate of discount which will equate the sum of the present values of the education differential with the cost (£1,000). In his case the rate of discount is 22.7 per cent. This rate can then be compared with rates of return to alternative investments.

(intelligence, family background, etc.) by reducing the earnings differentials by an appropriate proportion.

The crucial question is, of course, what is an "appropriate" adjustment to obtain the "pure" education differential? Here we have to resort mainly to American data. A large number of American studies* (including a study of the incomes of brothers with different amounts of education) for various scatters of "ability" and "social class origins" all suggest that college education is the main determinant of the extra life-time earnings of college graduates. By a statistical technique, multi-variate analysis, by which we can attempt to allow for all the various factors that influence the level of personal income, the conclusion has emerged that up to 40 per cent of the earnings differential is attributable to these other factors.

Non-monetary earnings. Calculations so far made of the returns to education have only considered the monetary returns to employment. It seems likely that the kinds of employment which graduates enter are those with relatively high non-monetary advantages— longer holidays, fewer restrictions, "perquisites" of various kinds, higher status. If this is so, then the real returns to education may be significantly higher than the calculations of monetary returns suggest. In principle there is no reason why an equivalent money value should not be put on those benefits to calculate the private rate of return. In so far as they are benefits solely of status (of a kind which does not cost the employer anything) it is appropriate to include them in the private rate of return to education but not in the social rate of return.

Extrapolation from the past. An important practical difficulty is that our calculations of the rates of return to education are based on *average* returns in the *past*. Both for personal decisions and government policy the question we really want to answer is: if we spend an additional sum on education *now*, what would be the return to this increment of expenditure? In other words we want to know future marginal returns. Lacking any direct way of estimating the marginal rate of return on current outlays we are forced to draw on

*See especially G. S. Becker, *Human Capital. A Theoretical and Empirical Analysis with special reference to Education*, Princeton, 1964.

past evidence as at least better than inspired (or uninspired) guesses and this can be supplemented by some general considerations. American evidence suggests that earnings differentials between high school and college graduates have remained fairly constant since 1939. Evidence from the United Kingdom labour market about the persistence of earnings differentials over a working life would seem to support this view. There would appear to be two main factors to distinguish: on the one hand the diffusion of additional education to successive age cohorts, other factors remaining the same, tends to narrow earnings differentials at any age level; on the other hand as the quality of education improves earnings differentials may be expected to widen at each age level.

A number of studies have taken place in recent years in the United Kingdom, particularly since fuller data became available from questions included in population censuses. We will simply refer to one of the most recent, the results of which were included in the Government's White Paper, *Top Up Loans for Students,* Cmnd. 520, 1988.

The White Paper contains the estimate of the rates of return to higher education, based on comparisons between graduates and non-graduates with "A" level. Using the average of a series of studies for the period 1981 to 1985, it was estimated that, for male graduates, the social rate of return to higher education in the United Kingdom is of the order 5.5 to 8 per cent, (depending on how much of the earnings differential is attributable to education alone) and the private rate of return was between 22 and 27.5 per cent. This private rate of return is rather higher than for comparable estimates in the United States, but in the United Kingdom the cost of tuition expenditure was not a private cost because the state met the fees and maintenance grants provided by the state were an offset to earnings forgone. The United Kingdom studies also revealed that both the private and the social rates of return to social science, engineering and science students were very much higher than the returns to arts graduates.

The Appendix to the White Paper rightly stresses the limitation to rates of return analyses: we cannot be sure that past patterns will hold in the future, especially where there have been major changes in the education structure or the labour market; the comparison with non-graduate "A" level students may overstate the earnings differential of graduates because those "A" level students who did not go on to university may have been at the lower end of the ability range of "A" level students; the use of life-time earnings ignores other subsequent education and training of graduates and "A" level students and gives no weight to work experience and maturity. Finally, there is the uncertainty of how much of the differential is due to education alone and how much to innate ability. The best that rates of return analyses can do is to give a broad indication of the economic returns to higher education—and these purely economic aspects of education are not necessarily the most important.

To re-state the argument to avoid confusion; three kinds of benefits from education can be distinguished: a social benefit* over and above private benefit (for example from the spread of knowledge or stability of government); a consumption benefit in terms of present and future enjoyment from participation in and results of education; an investment benefit measured in terms of the earnings differential from education (which is some measure, however imperfect, of the contribution of education to output). Calculations of rates of return to education are attempts to measure the "investment benefit" *only*. As such, even if all the conceptual and practical difficulties were resolved, the results should not be the sole determiners of education expenditure; they provide simply a *minimum* estimate of the benefit of education. It is possible that we may be able to make some progress in measuring the other benefits of education; and we must carefully avoid the trap of assuming that because they are not readily quantifiable they are not important. But it is some help in the determination of the extent and direction of government expenditure on education if we can assess quantitatively the investment return.

---

*The accepted terminology is somewhat unfortunate: the social rate of return to education is the return (without deducting income tax) measured against the combined private and governmental costs; it is *not* an assessment of the social benefit or spillover effects.

Finance and Management of Education

The rates of return analyses have a distinct bearing on the appropriateness of methods of financing education.

In the United Kingdom, universities and other institutions of higher education receive the bulk of their income from the state. Partly this comes in the form of student tuition fees and partly as a block grant which, for the universities, is currently siphoned through the Universities Funding Council (U.F.C.) — formerly through the University Grants Committee.

All home-based (as distinct from overseas) students who are on courses which qualify for a mandatory award (which includes all full-time first degree courses) have their tuition fees paid in full and are eligible for a maintenance grant which is, however, means-tested. In most cases the means test is of the parents. If the parental income is below a certain level the students receive a full grant; for incomes above that level the amount is tapered so that the children of better off parents receive no maintenance grant. Where the student receives less than a full grant, parents are expected to make up the amount by means of a parental contribution. Until 1990 the full maintenance grant was intended to be sufficient to maintain the student. In practice, however, the real value of the grant had fallen significantly in recent years and many students have added to their income by claiming social security benefits: income support, unemployment benefit or housing benefit. Whilst the policy is determined by central government, the grants are locally administered.

This system of state support for students has been very generous by international standards, but it has had its drawbacks and its critics. Because the number of students in higher education has grown rapidly, (from about 7 per cent of the relevant age group in 1960 to 15 per cent by the late 1980s) the grant system has become very expensive and it is partly for this reason that the real value of the maintenance grant has been allowed to fall. Also some students find themselves poverty-stricken because their parents cannot or will not make the full parental contribution. The use of the social security system for financing education is inappropriate. It is also argued that the system makes for dependency by students — on the state and on their parents where the latter are contributing to maintenance. Above all, however, there is the issue of principle, which is highlighted by the rate of returns analysis, of how far it is right for the taxpayer to contribute to higher education.

The *private* rate of return to education to first degree level is high especially if non-monetary earnings are included. To this must be added the consumption benefit of education to the individual. Those who receive higher education are moreover naturally fortunate in their intellectual endowment; and where the demand from qualified applicants exceeds the number of university places, there is an element of arbitrariness in the selection process which determines who gains the higher education differential. All this adds up to a powerful case for a larger proportion of the cost of higher education being met by the main beneficiaries when they are able so to do—which implies a system of student loans. A student loan scheme is not free from difficulties, but practicable schemes have for many years applied abroad and various schemes have been suggested for Britain.* Income-contingent or income-related loan schemes—where the ex-student repays the loan if and when his income rises above a specified level—overcome the main danger of imposing a millstone of debt round the neck of a young graduate (who may not *necessarily* become a high earner). If run directly by the state, a loans scheme would not immediately release additional real resources. But as time passed and revenue was collected from the loan repayments, resources would be freed for use in education or indeed elsewhere.

In the event, the government introduced, as from the 1990–91 academic year, a scheme for "Top-up" loans, which it claimed would meet the objections to the current system listed above. At the same time, students ceased to be eligible for social security benefits.

---

*See especially A. R. Prest, *Financing University Education*, Occasional Paper 12, Institute of Economic Affairs, 1966; Alan Lewis, Cedric Sandford and Norman Thomson, *Grants or Loans*, Institute for Economic Affairs, 1980; evidence presented to the Education, Science and Arts Committee of the House of Commons by Alan Maynard, Maureen Woodhall and Cedric Sandford, published as Minutes of Evidence to the Committee's Report on *The Funding and Organisation of Courses in Higher Education*, H.M.S.O., 1980; Maureen Woodhall, *Student Loans: Lessons from Recent International Experience*, Policy Studies Institute, 1982.

The essence of the new scheme is that a loan facility is made available to all first degree students of an amount which, together with a full maintenance grant, will restore the former value of the grant. The maintenance grant itself will be kept at the same money level as 1990–91 and the loan facility gradually increased each year to retain the total real value of grant plus loan, until the loan is equal in total to the grant. Thus the significance of the parental contribution will diminish. The loan carries no interest, but the sum to be repaid is increased in line with inflation to keep it the same in real terms. Repayment will normally start the April following the end of the period of study and spread over 5 years, but if the ex-student's salary is less than 85 per cent of national average income, repayment is deferred and the period extended.

The government had intended that the scheme would be administered by the clearing banks, but they declined to take part. The government therefore set up a Student Loans Company. Colleges and universities certify eligibility and students must have a bank or building society account into which the funds can be paid.

As expected, the retreat from a wholly grant aided system (subject to means test) generated much opposition from the National Union of Students and there was also genuine concern that the removal of social security benefits would adversely affect some students who, for example, had previously received housing benefit to help with high rents and who would not be sufficiently compensated under the new scheme. It was also maintained that the administrative costs of the scheme would be so high that, even in the long run, it would generate no extra resources for education.

It is too early to assess the success or otherwise of the scheme, but the first report of the Student Loans Company, issued in October 1991, indicated that 28 per cent of students had applied for loans and 180,000 loans totalling £70m had been made. The start-up costs of the Company had been £9m and the annual cost £13m. The director of the Company anticipated that the number of students taking up loans in 1991–92 would be very much higher and, with expansion, the cost per student loan would fall.

The Conservative Government has also been notable for other reforms in university and school education which, in so far as they

relate to economic issues (apart from matters like the national cur-
riculum) can be thought of as applications of the principles of the
F.M.I. discussed in Chapter 3. There has been a devolving of
management and financial responsibility through the introduction
of local management of schools. In respect of universities, a larger
proportion of state money has been channelled through student fees
and less through block grants. For home-based students fees remain
well below the average costs of tuition, but have become much
closer to the marginal costs, thus encouraging universities to take
more students even if, in the short term, they receive no additional
block grant for so doing. Within universities the F.M.I. principles
have been applied, with departments becoming cost centres.

The topics considered in this section are by no means the only
economic aspects of education expenditure; for example, economists
ought to be able to say something about the most efficient size of
units, periods of work and "mix" of subjects for schools of all levels,
colleges and universities; but as yet this remains almost virgin
research territory.

Health Expenditures

There is much in common between an economic analysis of health
and of education expenditure. Health expenditure includes the
three aspects of benefit which we distinguished in our analysis of
education—social benefit over and above private benefit (thus making at any rate some aspects of health expenditure a particular
matter of concern to the state); a consumption benefit in that the
prevention and cure of illness give men a greater enjoyment of life;
and an investment-type benefit in that health expenditures by
reducing mortality and sickness may increase individual earnings
and output. Also predominance of state provision in health services
in Britain with nil or low user charges, as with education, raises
financial questions.

The Social Benefit Element in Health Expenditure

The initial concern of the state with health expenditures in Britain
arose from the realisation of the social benefit which resulted from

certain kinds of health expenditure and the social cost from lack of care about health. Diseases contracted and neglected in the East End of London could spread to the West End. The whole community benefited from the elimination of epidemic diseases or suffered if they were allowed to rampage. Health expenditure on Mr. A also benefits Mr. B because A no longer carries diseases he might pass on to B.

But not all health expenditures are of this kind, e.g. a broken leg. With the virtual elimination of many of the more virulent epidemic diseases of the past (e.g. plague, typhus, smallpox) it seems likely that in Britain a much smaller proportion of expenditure on health today is of the kind to produce indiscriminate benefit and that the majority produces private and personal benefits.

The Investment Element in Health Expenditure

How far health expenditure is an investment expenditure as well as a consumption expenditure is an important consideration in determining what proportion of national resources should be devoted to it. In so far as it is an investment expenditure yielding a return in earnings and output it is, to quote the Guillebaud Committee, "wealth producing as well as health producing"; it can create the resources to pay for itself.

Although attempts have been made to establish a rate of return to particular health programmes aimed at the eradication of specific diseases, we cannot attempt to quantify a rate of return to health expenditures in the same way as to education expenditure. We can, however, examine three ways in which health expenditures might result in increased production or productivity.

First the general argument that increased health expenditure, by reducing death rates, promotes economic growth. This was doubtless true in the late 18th and during the 19th century. Many factors assisted the decline in mortality, but improved medicine and medical care were prominent among them. The precise relationship between population growth and industrialisation is complex rather than simple; but the growth in population, resulting primarily from a decline in mortality rates, helped to stimulate a demand for goods and services leading to increased capital formation and economies of scale. At the same time the reduction in death rates, much of which took the form of a fall in infant and child mortality rates, had the effect of increasing the size of the working population both absolutely and proportionately and increasing the mobility of labour. Further, in the 19th century much of the decline in female mortality was of women in the child-bearing ages, making for a self-sustaining growth of population.

Today the position is different. Expectation of life is much higher than a century ago. In Britain in the mid-19th century the average expectation of life of a male (at birth) was 40, of a female 42; by 1990 the respective figures were 72 and 78. In the mid-19th century infant mortality rates were 145 per 1,000 live births; today they are under 10. Again, in 1901 only 7 per cent of the population was over 60; in 1990 the figure was over 20 per cent. Similarly, in 1901, 12 per cent of the female population was aged 45–59; in 1990 the percentage was over 20. Even as far back as 1949 the *Report of the Royal Commission on Population* could say, "Most of the wastage of human life has now been cut out. Only among the old could further reductions in mortality have really considerable effects on numbers."

Thus, the present position in Britain is almost a complete reversal of that of the 19th century. Health services are likely to make greater demands on resources in the future (and contribute less to output) because of their past success. the elderly are likely to be more vulnerable to illness and require more care and treatment; it would also appear that as the more elementary "diseases" are overcome the human body becomes susceptible to more sophisticated diseases (cancers, cardiac conditions and mental disorders) which are more expensive in their demands on the health service.

A second possible way in which health expenditure may benefit production is by a reduction in hours of work lost through sickness.

We lack satisfactory data on loss of output through illnes. Whilst there are figures of certified absences from work as a result of sickness by those eligible for sickness benefit under the national insurance provisions, they do not provide a complete story. For example they exclude uncertified absences (normally absences of 3 days and under) and absences by those not covered by national insurance (e.g. many part-time workers.) On the other hand, about 30 per cent of the recorded certified absences are attributable to people not in employment at all, and never likely to be, who are entitled to claim sickness or invalidity benefit because of chronic illness up to the age of retirement. Nevertheless, it is clear that, in total, we are talking of several hundred million days of work lost. This information, limited though it is, might appear to offer the prospect that further expenditure on health care might effect a worthwhile reduction of output lost through sickness, especially when the results of the General Household Survey (a survey of a sample of householders throughout Britain) suggest that the number of days of "restricted activity" as a result of sickness are approximately double the number of days wholly lost.

In particular, limited, aspects, there may still be economic gains to be had. Thus some recent research has suggested that the cost to the economy of people missing work due to migraine may be over £200m, against only £23m currently spent by the N H S on migraine sufferers. Overall, however the reality is less promising. The trend of days lost through sickness has tended to be upward despite the increase in N.H.S. expenditure. As long ago as 1972, the Director of the Office of Health Economics (set up in 1962), after a survey of the research studies of the O.H.E., concluded that "the pay off for most medical care comes in personal and social benefits for the individual and his family. Those cases where there has also been a substantial economic benefit for the community as a whole are an exception. The economic savings in these cases are a bonus in addition to the personal benefits of medical care; they cannot be expected to justify expenditure on the health services as a whole "*

Finally it is possible that the productivity of labour (output per man-hour) might be raised through the effect of health expenditures on the "quality" of the labour force. This is a concept extremely difficult to measure. By general consent the vast majority of the working population in Britain today is, in some sense, "fit". It seems at least doubtful if further improvements in "fitness" would provide any considerable aid to output.

*G. Teeling-Smith, A Cost Benefit Approach to Medical Care, *The Economics of Medical Care* (ed. M. M. Hauser), George Allen & Unwin, 1972.

In many poorer countries it is possible, even likely, that appropriate health expenditures would provide a substantial "payoff" in terms of output, adding to demand and a mobile labour force and significantly increasing the productivity of labour. But in Britain, in relation to further health expenditure, the choice is health *or* wealth rather than health and wealth. The investment potential of health expenditures in Britain is largely exhausted; expenditure on the health service must be classed almost entirely as consumption expenditure.

Finance and Management of Health Services

Apart from a small contribution from service charges (for prescriptions, dental and optical services) the cost of health services in the United Kingdom is met overwhelmingly from taxation. A small proportion of the population continues to receive private treatment outside the N.H.S. and a rather larger proportion has taken out insurance to provide supplementary benefits to the Health Service; but British expenditure on health is dominated by government expenditure.

International comparison of 23 O.E.C.D. countries for 1984* shows the United Kingdom as the third highest country in terms of the proportion of public expenditure to total health expenditure, at 89 per cent. It also shows that, for total health expenditure as a percentage of G.D.P., the United Kingdom was fourth from the bottom. The highest expenditure was that of the United States at 10.7 per cent of G.D.P. — and the United States had by far the lowest expenditure from public funds; Greece was bottom of the league at 4.6 per cent; and the United Kingdom was 19th at 5.9 per cent. International comparisons can be misleading. We have earlier considered the limitations of G.D.P. as a denominator and the statistics may hide differences, especially in population composition, which affect health needs. But the O.E.C.D. study shows the United Kingdom as very much in line with the O.E.C.D. average on measures such as infant mortality and life expectancy and much

*Financing and Delivering Health Care, A Comparative Analysis of O.E.C.D. Countries, O.E.C.D., Paris, 1987.

on a par with the United States. It would therefore appear that the United Kingdom National Health Service is a relatively cost effective system of delivering health care.

The prime reason for this cost effectiveness would appear to be that (with a few partial exceptions which do not affect the principle) patients do not pay directly for the treatment they receive nor does the pay of doctors and consultants depend on what they prescribe. Thus there is little pressure to over-prescribe or recommend unnecessary operations. Where, as in many health care systems, people pay by means of insurance premiums, there is a particular tendency for costs to be inflated; doctors' pay is related to the treatments they prescribe and, because payment does not come directly from patients' pockets, doctors are even more inclined to push up their charges. An N.H.S. cash-limited hospital and community service is a very effective way of restraining costs.

Of course this does not mean that there is no scope for economies and there is a particular need for them because the health service requires an increasing input of resources simply to maintain the same general level of service. This is partly because of the ageing population, which makes increasing demands on the service; partly because of the "relative price effect" (see above p. 41): the prices of inputs into the health service, particularly drugs, tend to rise more rapidly than prices in general. In addition advances in technology absorb additional resources, which represent a real improvement for the beneficiaries of high tech development, but do nothing to improve the care of the majority. Moreover, where price does not act as a rationing agent, demand will always tend to outstrip supply and waiting lists to grow.

The Conservative governments have taken a series of measures to try to improve efficiency, which we can only briefly touch on here. They include the introduction of general management into hospitals and health authorities; the requirement that certain services (like laundry, cleaning and catering) previously carried out in-house, should be put out to tender; measures to re-allocate health care resources to secure more nearly equal access to health care throughout the country; and the encouragement of income generation methods.

The biggest shake-up of the service, however, arises from the implementation of the proposals in the Government's White Paper of January 1989, _Working for Patients_, Cmnd. 555, which are in process of implementation at the time of writing. The district health authorities, instead of being providers of health services become the purchasers, on behalf of their population; local hospitals and other health units sell their services and can apply for self-governing trust status; general practitioners with large practices can opt to become budget holders and buy hospital and other services on behalf of their patients. Whilst health authorities will normally make contracts of supply with units within their district, they can purchase services from outside their boundaries and will do so if they are offered better terms.

Thus an internal market has been created within the health service. Hospitals and other units will compete with each other for funds. Because money will follow the patients, measures which increase efficiency by increasing patient through-put will not be stifled as they previously were. It is hoped that competition will increase efficiency. The devolving of decision-making and financial control to cost centres is in line with the principles of F.M.I. Moreover, the need for hospitals to earn their income, by supplying what the purse holders—the G.P. budget holding practices and the district health authorities—want, will reduce the power of consultants to do what they most like rather than what is most needed.

It is far too early to know whether the claimed advantages will be attained. There remain doubts about whether the establishment of many separate self governing units may not lead to an escalation of administrative costs; about whether some patients will lose out (e.g. those whose G.P.s are not budget holders) compared with others; about whether quality will suffer. Above all, there must be doubts about whether a competitive model is the right one for a health service. Competition can be wasteful as well as generating efficiency. No one would recommend that electricity distributing companies should compete in the same street, because of the waste of capital by duplicating power lines. Whilst the parallel is not exact, in a similar way, competing hospitals may be in danger of each purchasing highly expensive high tech equipment which then is much less than fully utilised. Judgement must wait on events.

There are many other economic aspects of health services; for example consideration of the best size of hospitals; and the optimum labour combination of the most highly skilled (e.g. physicians) with the less skilled (e.g. nurses). There is also much scope for cost benefit and cost effectiveness analysis with regard to alternative types of treatment (e.g. renal dialysis or renal transplant) place of treatment (e.g. centralised or decentralised Clinics for out-patients) and time of treatment: preventive medicine (e.g. vaccination) early diagnosis (e.g. screening) or treatment only when the patient reports sick. A different issue is the effects of charges like prescription charges on the demand for treatment, e.g. do patients waste doctors' time if there are nil or only nominal charges? (cotton wool and aspirin visits). Another important problem is that of making the service responsive to consumer wishes when there is no price system to reflect them: so far little or nothing has been done within the National Health Service to develop new techniques of consumer research.

There is an even more crucial and transcending area. Where price does not ration demand, the demand for health care will always outstrip resources. Thus fundamental choices have to be made on where resources should be put: how much should go into hip replacements compared with how much for heart transplants? These decisions have always had to be made, but hitherto the outcome has emerged from a complex web of decision-making in which the professional providers have played a big part. With the separation of purchasing from providing, it becomes the task of the purchasers to decide on behalf of their populations. In recent years economists have sought to develop a concept to clarify this kind of decision-making—the so-called Q.A.L.Y. or quality-adjusted life year, which seeks to take account of the effect of treatment both on improving the quality of life and on extending its length, combining these two characteristics into one measure. Different patient conditions are given both a distress and a disability rating by assigning to them a number between 0 (dead) and 1 (perfectly healthy). The Q.A.L.Y.s from alternative forms of treatment—the effect of the treatment in moving patients between different health states—can then be compared with the costs.

There are clearly serious problems to be overcome in applying Q.A.L.Y.s, most importantly that of how to obtain an acceptable ordering of the conditions: whose valuations apply? Hitherto, the literature on the concept has mainly drawn on the pioneering work of Rachel Rosser who acquired valuations from 70 respondents; but others, notably Professor Williams of York University, have built on Rosser's work and also experimented to obtain ratings from a wider community.

This brief account fails to do justice to the subtleties of the research into the possible use of Q.A.L.Y.s in decision-making nor to all the difficulties. The Q.A.L.Y. has a long way to go before it is widely usable or widely acceptable. Its attraction and its superiority to cost benefit and cost effectiveness analysis is that it offers an overall indicator and that it makes people's values explicit. The Q.A.L.Y. is in its infancy but it has much potential.*

The economics of health is a relatively new field.† It has developed rapidly since the mid 1960s but there remains much to be done, often in the form of detailed and painstaking empirical work.

*For further reading see Paul Kind, Rachel Rosser and Alan Williams, Valuation of Life: Some Psychometric Evidence, in *The Value of Life and Safety*, ed. M. W. Jones-Lee, North Holland, 1982; Alan Williams, The Economies of Coronary Artery Bypass Grafting, *British Medical Journal*, 3 August 1985; Chapters 3, 4 and 5 in Alistair McGuire, Paul Fenn and Kenneth Mayhew (eds), *Providing Health Care: the Economies of Alternative Systems of Delivery*, O.U.P., 1991.

†For comprehensive introduction to the subject see John G. Cullis and Peter A. West, *The Economics of Health*, Martin Robertson, 1979.

CHAPTER 5

Taxation—Principles, Classification and Analysis

Purposes and Principles

If the man in the street were asked why a government levied taxation he would almost certainly reply "To raise revenue". He would see taxation as the instrument to pay for the goods and services provided collectively through the state.

Up to a point this is a valid answer, but it raises a further question. As the government controls the supply of money why does it need to raise revenue by taxation? Putting it crudely, why doesn't the government simply print more money to pay for collective goods and services? The short answer is that, to print more money (or to borrow from the Bank of England, which amounts to much the same thing) would be likely to generate inflation. In that case we might say that the main reason a government levies taxation is to provide for collective wants without creating inflation.

Subject to this general purpose, taxes may have a series of subsidiary objectives. Thus a tax may be an instrument of social policy to discourage the consumption of a commodity like tobacco, which is damaging to health; to protect home industry import taxes on particular goods might be imposed at prohibitive levels; as we shall see in our examination of capital taxes in Chapter 9, a heavy death duty is really irrelevant to the normal purpose of taxation but is concerned with the distribution of wealth in the community. Taxes have an important influence on both the total amount and the distribution of the national income and output and a government might choose one combination of taxes rather than another as part of a policy of reducing inequalities in the distribution of income.

These considerations are closely related to the so-called principles of taxation. It is impossible to postulate entirely satisfactory principles. Public finance is very much a part of *political* economy and political and ethical judgements cannot be wholly excluded from any statement of tax principles. Moreover, the principles themselves do not comprise a single mutually consistent system; they conflict with each other. Any tax system represents some sort of practical compromise. But, for what they are worth, here are a number of guiding principles of taxation.

Equity. The term equity can be given more than one meaning; it can be a value judgement on the different amounts which taxpayers of different taxable capacity should pay (sometimes called "vertical equity" which we consider under the heading of "ability to pay"), or it can be a rather more objective concept, as we use it here, to mean the equal treatment of taxpayers of similar taxable capacity (sometimes called "horizontal" equity). Thus a death duty which is widely avoided and paid mainly by the heirs of the peculiarly unfortunate or unsophisticated offends against the principle of equity. Again the main argument for a capital gains tax is to meet the inequity which results when some people can transpose taxable income into untaxed capital gains.

Ability to pay. It is widely argued that taxes should be levied according to ability to pay—but what is ability to pay? Is it taxation of the rich more than the poor but not proportionately more (regressive taxation)? Is it proportional taxation, by which rich and poor pay the same proportion of their income or wealth in taxation? Or is it progressive taxation, by which the rich pay at a proportionately higher rate than the poor? We are here concerned with a value judgement, with equity in its subjective sense. Some economists (the Pigou/Dalton school referred to in Chapter 2) produced a plausible theory to support progressive taxation:* as we acquire

---

*Strictly speaking, and quite apart from the other objections to it, the theory only "proves" that the rich should pay more tax than the poor, not that they must pay

more of a commodity so we put less value on additional increments of it (the law of diminishing marginal utility); and, applying this to money, it was argued that therefore a pound to a poor man was worth more than a pound to a rich man; hence, for equality of sacrifice, the rich man should pay a higher marginal rate of tax than the poor. But this begs all the questions of interpersonal comparisons; and even if it were accepted as valid it would still leave open the question of how *much* more the rich should be taxed. As Goschen, a former Chancellor of the Exchequer, expressed it in the House of Commons' debate on Harcourt's estate duty of 1894, the first tax in Britain to be boldly and openly progressive: "When you embark on this system of graduation there are no stages, no landmarks, nothing whatever to guide you. There is no principle of justice—no principle where you can say you ought to stop; no principle of prudence—no principle whatever. . . . Equality of sacrifice will not find correspondence in the geometrical progression of taxation. . . . You have attempted an impossibility if you attempt to reach what is real equality of sacrifice." To use the terminology of a notable study,* the case for progressive taxation is "uneasy". It rests not on spurious scientific proof but on moral judgements—the case for reducing inequalities of income and wealth. That the tax system should be used to reduce inequalities is common ground amongst the main political parties in Britain, but with differences on how far the process should be pushed. In our subsequent analysis, as a convenient shorthand, we shall refer to this principle of taxation as *equality*, by which we mean reducing inequalities, not advocating equality in any absolute sense.

Efficiency. A third principle can be conveniently summed up under the label "efficiency", but the meaning requires clarification and a value judgement is implied though one which would receive wide acceptance: the judgement that *in general* a tax system is inefficient

proportionately more, which is the meaning of progressive taxation. How much more they should pay (and hence whether the tax should be regressive, proportional or progressive) depends on the rate at which the utility of additional increments of income falls.

*W. J. Blum and H. Kalven, *The Uneasy Case for Progressive Taxation*, Phoenix Books, University of Chicago Press, 1953.

in so far as it distorts the free choices of the individual. A tax which reduces the supply of labour because it distorts the choice between work and leisure is inefficient in this sense; or a commodity tax which distorts the pattern of consumption. This is the principle of *least price distortion*: that tax A is more efficient than tax B, for an equal revenue to the Exchequer, it involves less loss of satisfaction to the taxpayer. It should be remembered, however, that free market prices only reflect private costs and the production and consumption of some goods entail social costs over and above private. A tax on such goods may bring market prices nearer to marginal social cost and thus help to correct rather than create a distortion.

Simplicity and Costs of Operation. In principle a tax system should be sufficiently simple, both in content and in terminology, for a tax-payer of average intelligence to comprehend at least its main principles.

Simplicity is closely related to the costs of collection or, more comprehensively, of tax operation. Tax operating costs consist of administrative costs—the official costs of the revenue authorities and compliance costs—the costs incurred by taxpayers and third parties, notably businesses, in meeting the requirements of the tax laws. Three categories of compliance costs on individual taxpayers can be distinguished: (1) Money costs, like the fees of a tax adviser (e.g. an accountant or banker) and miscellaneous costs like postage, travel to the tax office and do it yourself tax guides. (2) Time costs which include completing tax returns, filing necessary tax data, visiting the tax office, (which can be converted into money costs). (3) Psychic or psychological costs, which comprise stress and anxiety often occasioned by incomprehension of tax returns and obligations. Psychic costs can be a serious matter for retired, widowed or divorced persons who have never been used to completing their own tax returns and can ill afford to pay a tax adviser. (Psychic costs cannot easily be converted into money terms and have been omitted from the estimates of the costs of compliance below.) Businesses may incur very considerable expenses and also considerable costs in the time of proprietors and their families, in acting as unpaid tax collectors in respect of taxes levied on their products, their profits and the income of their employees, from which they are required to deduct tax at source. They may, however, get some offsetting benefits. Thus they may obtain a cash flow benefit from tax collected which they can legitimately hold for a period before transmission to the revenue authorities; and small firms, who, to satisfy the tax authorities, are compelled to keep better records than otherwise they would, may be able to use them to improve their business management.

Recent research,* mainly taking the form of sample surveys of individual taxpayers and businesses, has shed light on what has been a neglected area. It has shown that total tax operating costs are very substantial, in the United Kingdom amounting, in 1986–87, to over $1\frac{1}{2}$ per cent of G.N.P. (against 1.8 per cent for agriculture, fishing and forestry combined). For the main central government taxes, income tax including national insurance contributions, corporation tax and V.A.T,, the compliance costs are several times the administrative costs. Moreover, compliance costs are often regressive in their incidence and fall with disproportionate severity on small firms. Table 5.1 shows the compliance and administrative costs of United Kingdom taxes, in 1986–87, expressed as a proportion of tax revenue. Whilst this formulation is a useful "input–output" relationship, it must be stressed that the percentages for individual taxes may vary very much between years especially because of changes in tax rates and thresholds.

These are not the only principles to be borne in mind. *Flexibility* is important in view of the use of taxation as a means of regulating the economy. *Compatibility* with the tax systems of the E.C. matters for a country which, like Britain, is a member of the Community. The principle of taxing according to *benefit or "benefit of service"* to the taxpayer has no general applicability to the British tax structure but in a diluted form creeps in here and there. For example, the benefit principle in a modified form enters into our system of national insurance, for which all beneficiaries pay; the cost of a TV and radio

*Cedric Sandford, Michael Godwin and Peter Hardwick, *Administrative and Compliance Costs of Taxation*, Fiscal Publications, Bath, 1989.

TABLE 5.1
Tax Operating Costs, United Kingdom, 1986–87

	Revenue	Administrative Costs	Compliance Costs	Operating Costs
Income tax, capital gains tax	£bn	%	%	%
and Nat. Ins. contributions	65.1	1.53	3.40	4.93
V.A.T.	21.4	1.03	3.69	4.72
Corporation tax	13.5	0.52	2.22	2.74
Petroleum revenue tax	1.2	0.12	0.44	0.56
Excise duties	16.5	0.25	0.20	0.45
Other taxes	4.6	0.85	1.48	2.33
Overall Central Government	122.3	1.12	2.79	3.91
Local rates	15.5	1.52	0.37	1.89
Total Government	137.8	1.16	2.52	3.68

Source: Sandford, Godwin and Hardwick, op. cit.

licence is related to the amount the B.B.C. has to spend on broadcasting; and although in general the amount spent on roads is entirely independent of (and much less than) the tax raised from the motorist in licence fees and petrol duties, at least the higher licence fees for heavy lorries are intended to reflect cost and corresponding benefit. With the benefit principle one is really trying to get as near to user cost as circumstances will permit. *Certainty* is a principle in the tax system which we are apt to take for granted: that the individual's tax liability should not be arbitrary and should be calculable in advance; retrospective legislation may infringe this principle. Besides the general considerations for national taxation, there are particular criteria for local taxes (which we shall discuss in detail in Chapter 10) and, as we have already suggested, there may be special social reasons for taxing particular commodities (see Chapter 8).

None of these so-called principles is absolute. The possibility of conflict of objectives in the tax structure has already been mentioned and is likely to arise in particular between simplicity and equity, and between equality and efficiency. Simplicity and equity exist in tortuous interdependence; many of the complications of tax systems spring from exemptions and provisions for special treatment which seek to remove inequities; yet their very existence not only reduces simplicity but often creates the inequities for those whose circumstances place them just the wrong side of the special provisions. An underlying and fundamental conflict also exists between equality and efficiency. There is some point beyond which you cannot push rates of income taxation without reducing willingness to work and take risks; clearly attempts to impose marginal rates of income taxation of 100 per cent would soon reduce the amount of income coming into existence; people would not try to earn income taxed at this rate and if their income was from property, they would change the form of their wealth so that they received less monetary income but more non-monetary satisfactions (for example selling shares and buying pictures or jewellery instead). But at what rate below 100 per cent do disincentives become important? The answer is disputed; we shall examine some of the evidence in our next chapter. If these are the most important areas of conflict they are not the only ones: frequent changes in taxation associated with flexibility create inequities and a change in tax structure to harmonise with the E.C. might constitute a move away from equality

Assessment of any particular tax against these various criteria must be in the context of the tax system as a whole and indeed of expenditure as well. There is no need for every tax to be progressive; what matters is the overall effect of taxation on the distribution of income after the benefits of government expenditure have been taken into account.

Tax Classification

As Lady Hicks pointed out many years ago,* considerable confusion exists in the terminology both of tax classification and tax analysis. The distinction most frequently made is between "direct" and "indirect" taxation, a direct tax being assessed *or* levied directly on the ultimate taxpayer, an indirect tax being levied through some third party (such as a retailer). Thus income tax, which is assessed on the income receivers (but for most people in Britain levied

*U. K. Hicks, The Terminology and Methods of Tax Analysis, *Economic Journal*, March 1946.

indirectly) counts as a direct tax, whilst value-added tax, beer, tobacco or petrol duties are all indirect taxes collected from the consumers of the taxed commodities through some third party. This distinction is in essence administrative; it does not make good economic sense. The economist is concerned to know whether a tax is levied on income, capital (wealth) or outlay (expenditure). In practice the direct/indirect classification has been made to serve both the administrative purposes and the income/outlay distinction, because the two frequently coincide; but they differ in some instances. Thus in Britain a motor vehicle licence is a direct tax (paid to the taxing authorities by the car owner and not "passed on" to anyone else) but essentially a tax on outlay, akin to a sales tax in that it is a necessary payment for the enjoyment of a good or service, i.e. motoring. Local domestic rates were assessed directly on the house occupier, sometimes paid indirectly with the rent, but in essence an outlay tax on the enjoyment of house room. Analysis of the incidence of the road licence tax and local rates needs to follow lines similar to those of an outlay tax.

Our practice in this book has been to confine the direct/indirect terminology to the administrative distinction and to classify taxes as income, outlay (or expenditure) and capital. Corporation profits taxes are included under income because profits on which corporation taxes are levied are in principle income of the shareholders. Further, outlay taxes on final consumer goods and services are distinguished from outlay taxes on the factors (or agents) of production, i.e. charges incurred by producers for employing certain materials, land, machines or workers; in Britain the most important is the employers' national insurance contribution.

Table 5.2 summarises tax revenues in 1990–91 and indicates the proportional contribution of the various taxes to tax revenue. There are certain problems of interpretation and classification. Government statistics do not treat revenue from broadcast receiving licences as taxation, although motor vehicle licence revenue is so treated; we have treated stamp duties as a tax on expenditure, although they are sometimes included with capital taxes. In taking central government tax we have omitted social security receipts, i.e. national insurance contributions, although a strong case could be

TABLE 5.2
Summary of Revenue from Taxation, U.K. 1990–91

	£ bn		Percentage of tax receipts Central Government		Total
Taxes on Income and Capital					
Income tax	55.5		38.7		27.6
Corporation tax	21.6		15.1		10.8
Petroleum revenue tax	0.9	81.2	0.7	56.7	0.4
Capital gains tax	1.9		1.2		0.9
Inheritance tax	1.3		0.9		0.6
Taxes on Outlay/Expenditure					
Stamp duties	1.7		1.2		0.8
Value added tax	30.8		21.5		15.3
Petrol, derv, etc	9.6		6.7		4.8
Tobacco	5.6	62.1	3.9	43.3	2.8
Alcohol	4.9		3.4		2.4
Vehicle excise duties	3.0		2.1		1.5
Other taxes and royalties	6.5		4.5		3.2
TOTAL CENTRAL GOVERNMENT TAXES AND ROYALTY RECEIPTS (excluding social security receipts and national non-domestic rates)	143.3		100.0		
Social security receipts	34.9				17.4
Rates	12.2				6.1
Community charge receipts	10.4				5.2
TOTAL TAX AND ROYALTY RECEIPTS	200.8				100.0

Source: "Latest estimate" figures from Financial Statement and Budget Report 1991–92.
Notes: Customs duties and agricultural levies, which count as E.C. "own resources" are excluded; broadcast receiving licences are not included as a tax. Some columns do not exactly add up because of rounding.

made for treating them as a central government tax. If one wishes to separate taxes on income from taxes on capital, the capital gains tax could be put in either category, "though perhaps the strongest case is to include it with income" (see Chapter 9).

If we look at central government taxation excluding national insurance contributions and the national non-domestic rate, then 57 per cent of central government tax revenue came from taxes on income and capital (of which the contribution from capital taxes was almost negligible, however one classifies capital gains tax) against 43 per cent from outlay (or expenditure) taxes.

The employee's national insurance contributions and those of the self-employed are clearly income taxation. The employer's contribution is formally an outlay tax on a factor of production, but as it is part of his wage and salaries bill, it is likely that the long-term effect is to reduce wage payments below what they otherwise would have been, and hence the whole of national insurance contributions can reasonably be treated as an income tax.

Domestic rates were abolished in Scotland in 1989 and in England and Wales the year after. Therefore the figure of rates in the table, apart from delayed payments of domestic rates, refers to national non-domestic rates—a tax on the annual value of non-domestic property which, since 1990, has been at a nationally fixed rate with the revenue re-distributed to local authorities according to their adult population, in effect a hypothecated national tax—i.e. a national tax the revenue from which is solely applied to a specified purpose (see Chapter 10). The community charge or poll tax, which replaced domestic rates, is set to disappear, in its turn to be replaced by the Council Tax (see below), and in 1991–92 will represent a lower percentage of tax revenue than in 1990–91, because in the 1991 Budget the Chancellor raised value added tax (V.A.T.) from 15 per cent to 17½ per cent in order to use the money to reduce the level of community charge by £140.

Confining our attention to central government taxes without national insurance contributions and the national non-domestic rate, the proportions of income and capital taxes to outlay taxes have been subject to some significant changes. At the end of the 19th century more than half of central government revenue came from outlay taxes. The 20th century witnessed a reversal of this pattern and in the 1920s income and capital taxes combined rose to over 65 per cent of tax revenue. Their contribution remained at well over 60 per cent during the Second World War, thereafter it underwent a fluctuating decline. In 1969–70, for example, the contribution of income and capital taxes combined had fallen to 55 per cent.

There followed a very sharp rise in the proportion of revenue from income taxes, mainly because of a failure to adjust real tax burdens to take account of inflation (see Chapter 13). The situation was reversed by the first budget of the 1979 Conservative Government when the Chancellor compensated the Revenue for substantial cuts in income tax by raising the standard rate of V.A.T. from 8 to 15 per cent.

Tax Analysis

"Impact", "effects", "incidence" and "burden" have all been used to describe the consequences of the imposition of a tax. We follow the suggestions of Lady Hicks and employ the terms "formal" and "effective" incidence.

The Incidence of Taxation

Formal incidence is the immediate answer to the question "Who pays the tax?" It does not take us far with our economic analysis, but is useful in a social accounting sense; the allocation of tax payments in our attempt to assess the effects of taxation on income distribution, Chapter 11, rests on social accounting concepts. Thus the formal incidence of income taxation is on the income receiver, that of a tobacco tax on the smoker. Outlay taxes on factors of production are somewhat more complex, but should also be regarded as a tax the formal incidence of which rests on the consumers of the product. Thus, for outlay taxes, formal incidence represents the difference between the market price of a product and its factor cost (i.e. the payments, including profit, to the factors of production which combined to produce the good or service).

Effective incidence includes the taxpayers' reaction to the tax and its consequences. Thus analysis of the effective incidence of income tax takes account of the results of the tax of consumption, saving and investment and the supply of the factors of production. The effective incidence of a tobacco tax takes account of the (possible) effect that some resources move out of tobacco growing, manufacturing and distributing and that some consumers substitute other goods (e.g.

sweets) for cigarettes. In assessing effective incidence we seek to unravel all the consequences of the imposition of the tax; to compare two economic situations (one of them hypothetical), one with the tax in force, the other without it.

In our analysis of effective incidence we employ the distinctions, widely used in economics between *general* (or macro) and *partial* (or micro) analysis. In general analysis we look at the economic system as a whole; we are thus concerned with income levels, consumption, saving and investment; with interest rates and the price level in general; with the total supply of the factors of production. In partial or micro-economic analysis we examine the effects in a particular sector of the economy, in a particular industry and immediately related industries. Clearly income tax must be analysed primarily on general lines, whilst an excise tax on a particular commodity may most usefully be analysed on partial lines; but the distinction is never absolute. Even a light outlay tax has some influence on the general level of consumption, investment and prices and analysis of a heavy outlay tax on a good of widespread consumption must include consideration of its "macro" consequences. Similarly, an income tax may have results which affect some markets or industries more than others, e.g. by putting a "premium" on the purchase of consumer durables (like pictures or foreign stamps) which yield no money income but offer prospect of capital gain; thus in analysing income taxation we may need to examine more closely some particular sectors of the economy.

Evasion and Avoidance

As effective incidence includes all the consequences of a tax imposition it necessarily embraces "evasion" and "avoidance". These are terms of the tax lawyers who define evasion as illegal tax dodging, for example when the taxpayer fails to declare all taxable income in his tax return, and avoidance as so arranging one's affairs legally that less tax liability is incurred. This definition of avoidance is not satisfactory for the economist; it takes no account of motive or, more important, of the end result. Thus, as the definition stands, a smoker who switches to eating sweets has "avoided" tobacco tax and almost any reaction to a tax imposition becomes "avoidance". It is more helpful to confine the term to action deliberately taken by the prospective taxpayer to achieve an end result substantially that which he had in view before the tax was imposed. Thus, if as a result of a death duty (see Chapter 9) a wealthy man spends much of his fortune on a trip round the world instead of leaving it to his children, this is part of the effective incidence of the death duty but not avoidance. If, however, he makes gifts to his children in such a way that they are not subject to tax (e.g. by a series of gifts in amounts and at times which escape liability—see Chapter 9), then this is avoidance; he largely achieves his original aim.

Incidence and the Price Level

Where there are substantial changes in the price level both the formal and the effective incidence of taxation may change considerably over a period of time. For example, an outlay tax, levied as a percentage of the wholesale or retail price, automatically increases (in money terms) if the price of the product rises On the other hand an outlay tax fixed by reference to a physical characteristic, e.g. weight or number, as with most excise duties, will fall in real terms and as a percentage of the price, in times of inflation. The most significant effects of changes in the price level on incidence almost certainly occur when progressive taxes are being levied in times of rapidly changing prices and money incomes. The same rates of income tax or death duties become increasingly heavy in real terms during periods of rising prices which push the same real income or estate into higher tax brackets. This has been an important influence on the distribution of incomes, which we shall consider in Chapter 11, and the weight of death duty and of capital gains tax. We examine the question of inflation and the public finances in more detail in Chapter 13.

CHAPTER 6

Taxation of Personal Income

The Tax Base

In all developed countries personal income tax is one, if not the, major source of government revenue. Income has generally been held to be the best *single* criterion of ability to pay; and, by means of allowances and rates, an income tax can be a flexible instrument with scope for adjustment to reflect prevailing conceptions of equity.

However, this view, that income tax is the best single criterion of ability to pay, has not gone unchallenged, especially in recent years. Thus, an eminent Australian tax specialist* has argued that in his country tax avoidance and evasion, especially by the self-employed, had reached such a pitch that the tax no longer reflected ability to pay and that a combination of a proportional V A T with a judicious choice of wealth taxation would better serve the cause both of horizontal and vertical equity. A related but broader-based attack has come from those who have argued for an expenditure tax in place of income tax. The origins of an expenditure tax go back to John Stuart Mill. Professor Lord Kaldor was the first in more recent times to present the case.† By an expenditure tax is meant a direct tax, based on the aggregate consumption expenditure of a taxpayer and which could be given any desired degree of progression in

---

*Professor R. Mathews, *The Structure of Taxation*, Reprint Series No. 34, Centre for Research on Federal Financial Relations, Australian National University (reprinted from Proceedings of the Australian Institute of Political Science Summer School on *The Politics of Taxation*, Canberra 26–28 January, 1980).
†N. Kaldor, *An Expenditure Tax*, Allen & Unwin, 1955.

relation to expenditure. The taxpayer would be required to furnish a tax return on which consumption expenditure would be derived by deducting saving from annual income and adding any spending out of capital. An expenditure tax of this kind has also been advocated in influential reports in the U.S.A., in Sweden and in Ireland (see below p. 370). In Britain it was advocated by the unofficial Meade Report (1978).* Except for a brief period in Indian and Sri Lanka under Kaldor's influence, no country has in practice adopted an expenditure tax. However, let us examine the arguments for it more closely.

Income or Consumption Expenditure

One argument used to justify an expenditure tax is that of equity. It is maintained that, in principle, it is fairer to tax consumption than income. A consumption tax taxes what people take out of the productive system; an income tax taxes the value of what they put in. If they save and reinvest income then they are adding to the size of the cake and should not be penalised. Moreover an income tax fails to catch expenditure from capital (and inadequately taxes capital gains unless they are treated on a par with income) but spending from capital or capital gains attracts the full rate of expenditure tax. There is a counter argument that to tax consumption is less equitable than taxing income because the rich are those who do most saving—and therefore an expenditure tax will accentuate inequalities of wealth (with the inequalities of security, opportunity, influence and power which wealth implies). In reply the advocates of expenditure tax would argue that the wealthy do not get off scot free. When they consume their wealth they are taxed and when they part with their wealth by gift or at death, these disposals can be treated as consumption, and taxed according to expenditure tax, or, alternatively, can be made the subject of a stiff capital transfer tax.

There is a further equity argument. One of the disadvantages of income tax is that it relates to annual income and, if income fluctuates and tax is progressive, then the taxpayer pays more in tax than

---

*The Structure and Reform of Direct Taxation, Report of a Committee chaired by Professor J. E. Meade, Institute for Fiscal Studies/George Allen & Unwin, 1978.

if the income flow had been even. To take an extreme example; if the average rate of tax is 30 per cent on an income of £5,000 and 50 per cent on an income of £10,000, a man whose income one year is £10,000 and the next is zero pays 66⅔ per cent more tax than if the income had been evenly spaced over the 2 years. Admittedly an income tax may contain special averaging provisions for big discrepancies—but the basic defect remains. An expenditure tax, it is argued, would be fairer on this score because the taxpayer is better able to even out his expenditures than his income. There is something in this argument, but its truth depends very much on the details of the expenditure tax and how "lumpy" expenditures like the purchase of motor cars and especially housing, are treated under the tax. We must therefore put something of a question mark against this argument. Whether an expenditure tax is more equitable than an income tax depends, with respect to the first issue, on a value judgement; and with respect to the second issue, on the details of the two taxes. It is generally accepted that an expenditure tax, even more than an income tax, needs to be supported by wealth taxes, either in the form of wealth transfer taxes or annual wealth taxes or both.

A second argument used in favour of an expenditure tax is that of economic efficiency: that it will promote saving and hence investment and growth. As, under an expenditure tax, saving does not attract tax, at first sight this outcome may seem self evident, but it cannot be taken for granted that an expenditure tax will necessarily promote saving. First, with an expenditure tax instead of income tax, the gross (pre-tax) return on saving may well be lower. Further, as saving is tax exempt, people saving for a given future income will not need to save as much. Thus, this argument must be regarded as non proven.

More substantial is a further argument on efficiency grounds. An expenditure tax will lead to less investment distortion. With an expenditure tax the rate of return on a physical asset will equal the rate of return which the investor receives. It will not be distorted by intervening tax provisions as with income tax. This point gains added weight because of the way in which income taxes including that of the United Kingdom, as we shall shortly see, provide tax reliefs for some kinds of saving and investment but not others. The result is a massive distortion in the capital market with saving in forms such as pension funds and housing being favoured, to the detriment of other forms of investment like personal holdings of ordinary shares. In recent years there has been an attempt to reduce this disadvantage in the United Kingdom by a tax concession for Personal Equity Plans (P.E.P.s)—see below p. 142.

Another clear advantage of an expenditure tax arises in an inflationary world. We examine the general problems of adjusting taxes for inflation in Chapter 13. As we shall see there, one of the biggest problems is the capital/income relationships. One of the accepted economic definitions of income is the amount which an individual could consume in a year whilst leaving himself with as much wealth at the end of the year as he had at the beginning. A man with £100 in a savings account may receive 10 per cent interest during a year in which the rate of inflation was 10 per cent. At the end of the year he needs £110 for his real wealth to remain intact. He has in fact gained no income from his investment, but he will be charged income tax on the £10 interest. To apply an adjustment under an income tax to allow for this aspect of inflation would not be impossible, but complicated. In practice such an adjustment has rarely been made; so, in effect, part of an individual's capital has been taxed as though it were income. However, the problem does not arise with an expenditure tax. All consumption expenditure is taxed whether it is expenditure from income or capital. No distinction is required between income and capital. Uprating allowances and widening brackets (which is required with income tax anyway) fully takes care of the effect of inflation in respect of an expenditure tax.

Because an expenditure tax does not require a distinction to be made between income and capital it is also argued that it generates other advantages, notably scope for simplifying the tax system; in particular, there is little need for a special tax on capital gains under an expenditure tax regime. Capital gains, when spent, will attract expenditure tax on the same basis as consumption expenditures out of income, so no special taxation is required.

On the other side of the scale, the administration of an expenditure tax would be more complicated than an income tax.

Each individual subject to the tax would be required to complete a more detailed tax return to enable changes in his wealth to be calculated. Moreover if a country changed from an income tax to an expenditure tax regime there would be difficult problems of transition. Thus, in the absence of special provisions, it would be unfair to those who had saved for retirement out of taxed income only to find that, when they came to spend the savings, they were taxed on their expenditure. Again, there would be difficulties about international double taxation treaties, which are designed to prevent double taxation of income, but make no allowance for expenditure taxes. Further, if some countries employed an expenditure tax whilst others continued with an income tax, there could be problems with international migration. People might choose to spend their working life in a country with an expenditure tax regime and then retire (to spend their savings) in a country with an income tax regime. These problems are not insuperable especially where the proposals is for an expenditure surtax rather than a complete replacement of income tax; but they have been enough to discourage governments from effecting such a transformation.

We shall have more to say about an expenditure tax when we come to look at possible reforms of the U.K. tax system in Chapter 13. For the remainder of this chapter we concentrate on income tax.

The Definition of Income

One of the fundamental problems with income taxation is to provide a satisfactory definition of the tax base, income. Indeed, in the United Kingdom no comprehensive definition has been attempted in the tax statutes; rather a series of classes or sources of income is covered by a series of tax schedules. Some of the main issues and difficulties are as follows.

Comprehensive or Narrow Base

A number of economists have argued for a comprehensive definition of income as "additions to spending power over a period of time". On this definition not only wages, salaries, interest, profit and rent would count as income, but also capital gains, gifts and legacies. Receipts in kind would also be included. Capital depreciation would count as a deduction. No country has adopted a fully comprehensive tax base, but the Carter Commission in Canada made such a proposal.* Problems arise with irregular receipts, like legacies; it would be unfair to tax them to the full progressive income tax in the year they are received, for the recipients would then pay much more tax than if they had been more evenly spread over time. Carter proposed to deal with this inequity partly by averaging provisions and partly by restricting the maximum rate of income tax to 50 per cent. But the Canadian government never implemented the Commission's recommendations. More recently the Irish Tax Commission† has proposed a comprehensive income base and has neatly avoided the problem posed by the undue taxation of irregular receipts by proposing a flat percentage rate of income tax; progression is to be introduced into the system as a whole partly by government expenditures at the lower end and and by a progressive expenditure tax at the upper end. No Irish government has yet shown any sign of implementing these proposals.

Even if, as in the United Kingdom, a narrow definition of income is adopted which excludes legacies and gifts, a series of definitional problems remain to be solved.

Income in kind. In principle all income in kind which confers a money-equivalent benefit — whether concessionary coal for miners or houses for directors — ought to be included as taxable income; but the difficulties of assessment would be enormous. Where benefits are inconvertible (i.e. cannot be sold by the recipient) such as a rent-free house for an employee on the firm's premises, the money income equivalent is not clear; the benefit has a money value but less than the market value if freely acquired.

Similarly, it is very difficult to put a precise value on the benefit obtained from perhaps the most widespread and contentious perquisite — the regular or occasional use of the company car for private purposes. United Kingdom tax law seeks to avoid the abuse

*Report of the Royal Commission on Taxation, Ottawa, 1966.
†First Report of the Commission on Taxation; Direct Taxation, Dublin, 1982.

of payments in kind and over recent years various attempts have been made to tighten up—but with only limited success. Perquisites tend to proliferate especially when income tax rates are high and in periods of incomes policies as a means by which government-imposed income constraints can be circumvented. The existence of perquisites which are untaxed, or not taxed to the full extent of the benefit, creates inequities between taxpayers.

One form of income in kind which is not usually claimed as taxable income is that part of a producer's output which he consumes himself—a farmer consuming his own food or a decorator painting his own house.

A particularly important form of income in kind is the "income" a person may obtain from living in his own property rather than renting it to someone else. Many European countries impute an income as a rent equivalent for an owner occupied house and this was the practice in the United Kingdom (under a "schedule A assessment") until abolished in 1963.

The particular method of calculating imputed income under the U.K. scheme was cumbersome; the amount was based on anachronistic rateable values; and, as repairs and maintenance payments could be set against the imputed income, the more sophisticated taxpayers were able, wholly or partly, to offset the liability. For these reasons there was a strong case for abolishing the schedule A assessment on owner-occupiers in the form in which it had existed. But, in principle, to impute an income for tax purposes to an owner-occupied house is in accordance with equity. An example may make this clear. Consider Mr. X and Mr. Y, with the same amount of earned income and identical allowances. Each has £40,000 capital. Mr. X buys a house with his £40,000 and, because no income is imputed to it, pays no income tax on the "returns" to his investment. Mr. Y buys £40,000 of government securities yielding, say £4,000; on this sum he pays income tax, even though he has to pay an annual rental of £5,000* on a house similar to that owned by X.

---

*A landlord letting a house would expect a net return on his capital at least equal to that obtainable from government securities; the gross return would need to be higher to cover repairs and maintenance, depreciation and management charges.

Expenses of incurring income. In principle, expenses which are properly incurred in gaining an income should be deductible from that income for tax purposes. However the borderlines are fuzzy. In the United Kingdom expenses "wholly and exclusively" laid out in the course of pursuing a trade, vocation or profession are deductible for tax purposes and some expenses incurred by employees in the course of their employment are deductible. Thus the employee who needs protective clothing in his work or who has to join a professional society, can claim all or part of these expenses against tax. But the employee is fairly tightly circumscribed; he cannot, for example, claim travelling expenses from his home to his regular place of work; the Revenue authorities take the view that it is open to him to live near his work place. In general the self employed (taxed under schedule D) have much more scope for claiming expenses deductions than employees (taxed under schedule E). Expenses of employees must be "necessarily" as well as "wholly and exclusively" incurred in obtaining the income if they are to be allowable.

A convincing argument can be presented that expenses incurred in acquiring and maintaining professional skills should be tax exempt. We have already pointed out the similarity between investment in physical capital and investment in human capital and it can be argued that expenditure on education and training should count in a similar way to depreciation allowances as an offset to tax. It is not normally so treated in the United Kingdom. In practice often such training is paid for by the state or by an employer. In other ways, too, the case is partly met. Income tax allowances for children and child benefits when these superseded the allowances, continue to be paid as long as the children continue in full-time education. Further the tax differentiation between income from work ("earned income") and income from property ("unearned income") which was a feature of the U.K. income tax and may become so again (see below) has been justified historically because the former was held to be more precarious and of more limited life than income from property.

Another issue, sometimes raised in discussion, is whether working housewives ought to be able to claim expenditure on domestic help as an expense of employment. In fact no such allowance is granted in the United Kingdom. However, until 1990 there was a special tax free amount for working wives (and there remains a personal allowance which a working wife can claim, but which a non-working wife cannot take advantage of unless she has investment income). Whilst this could be regarded as some sort of equivalent it did not apply to single women who had a home to maintain as well as working. This "married women's earned income relief" was really a somewhat illogical survival of war-time provisions introduced to encourage wives to take up paid work.

Finally an anomaly arising from the deduction of expenses might be noted. In the United Kingdom interest on money borrowed by landlords to purchase houses to let is tax deductible. When a rent was imputed to an owner-occupier for tax purposes it was logical that the owner-occupier should be allowed mortgage interest as a tax deduction to set against the imputed income. However, when the provision for taxing owner-occupiers under schedule A was abolished, the tax concession on mortgage interest remained. No government has been prepared to remove it though Mr. Healey, as Chancellor, in 1974 limited it to a mortgage of £25,000; this limit was raised to £30,000 in 1983, but the increase was less than the rise in prices, so the real value of the relief had fallen and there have been no further increases to the time of writing (1991). Moreover, in the 1991 Budget, Mr. Lamont, as Chancellor of the Exchequer, restricted the benefit of the relief to the basic rate of tax.

The time period of income. In considering a comprehensive income tax we spoke of the problem of including irregular receipts like gifts and legacies. A similar, if less acute, problem arises with a narrow-based income tax. Income is normally assessed to tax on an annual basis; where allowances provide a minimum exemption limit and where there is a series of progressive steps in the rates of tax, people whose income fluctuates are taxed more heavily than if the same income had been more evenly spread over the years. This has prompted a suggestion for the averaging of income tax payments over a life-time or a series of years. Not only would this proposal create serious administrative problems but it would also mean that in a year in which income fell, tax, as a proportion of income, would be higher; one or two American states which attempted this method of income taxation in the inter-war period were forced to abandon it in the Great Depression. A more practical proposition to deal with the extremes of fluctuation that may occur in a business or in a few professions such as those of writer and artist is that of the Royal Commission on Income Tax, which recommended that a fall in total income from one year to the next of at least 50 per cent should entitle the recipient to relief by averaging.* This recommendation has not be implemented in precisely that form; but it has been provided in the United Kingdom that income received from a book or artistic work in the year of completion can, if the work took more than a year to produce, be spread backwards over the years of its production.

Capital gains. Because they add to spending power there are strong reasons, even under a narrow-based income tax, for treating capital gains — an appreciation in the value of assets — as income, except where such gains are simply a product of inflation. Conversely capital loss should be regarded as a deduction from income. The case for so doing is strengthened where people are in a position to convert income into capital gain. However, few countries subject capital gains to the full rigour of a progressive income tax.† There are considerable problems in so doing. First, if capital gains were to be treated as ordinary income it would be desirable to tax gains each year as they accrued. But this would mean an annual valuation of all capital, which would be an enormous administrative burden. Further, it might create serious cash flow problems for the taxpayer who would have to pay income tax on the capital appreciation without the gain generating funds from which to pay the tax. For these reasons, in practice, governments have chosen to tax capital gains on a "realisation" rather than an accrual basis. Most

---

Royal Commission on the Taxation of Profits and Income, Final Report, Cmnd. 9474, 1955, para. 203.

†The number of countries so doing has increased with the big reductions in income tax rates in many countries in the 1980s; they include Australia and the United States — though in both countries the capital gains tax is under fire and the equal treatment with income may not last (1991).

realisations take the form of sale, thus giving rise to both a valuation and a flow of funds. Thus capital gains taxes, in practice, are levied on the difference between the value of an asset at acquisition and the value at disposal. This means that the gain has often accrued over many years. We then have a problem analogous to that of the taxation of irregular receipts to income tax. It is inequitable to tax to a progressive income tax in one year gains which have accrued over many years. If the gains had been taxed in each year that they had accrued, the total tax bill would have been less.

There are two further reasons why there are problems about taxing capital gains to the full rates of a progressive income tax. As the Minority Report to the *Royal Commission on the Taxation of Profits and Income* (1955) pointed out, rewards for enterprise often occur in the form of capital gains and to tax them to full income tax rates might stifle enterprise. Further, if capital gains are treated precisely on a par with other income, capital losses should, in justice, be treated as a deduction from other income. This could give rise to a situation that politicians might find embarrassing, i.e. that, in the year of a stock exchange slump, a millionaire might be relieved of all income tax payments!

Many countries, e.g. Canada, tax capital gains under the income tax code, but at reduced rates and with losses being allowed only as an offset to gains, not to ordinary income. In the United Kingdom capital gains are taxed separately from income tax and it is convenient (for reasons explained in Chapter 9) to treat them along with capital or wealth taxes. However, when capital gains taxes were introduced into the United Kingdom, there was a link with income tax and, since 1988, they have been linked again.

Chancellor Selwyn Lloyd first introduced a short-term capital gains tax in the United Kingdom in 1962 by which gains from certain assets held for a limited period (under 6 months for securities, up to 3 years for property) were taxed as income. In 1965, when Chancellor Callaghan introduced a long-term capital gains tax at a rate of 30 per cent, the short-term gains tax was amended so that income tax rates applied to gains realised within 12 months of the acquisition of the asset. To simplify the system and to remove the arbitrary distinction between the treatment of assets held for

364 days and those held for 366 days, the short-term gains tax was abolished in 1971, gains from assets held for under 12 months hence forward being subject to tax on the same basis as long-term gains. Since 1988, when the top rate of income tax was reduced to 40 per cent the top marginal rate of an individual also applies to his capital gains. However, there is a separate annual threshold for capital gains tax which, in 1991–92 was £5,500.

The Tax Unit

In principle there are three possible units as the basis for income taxation (1) the family: husband, wife, children and possibly also other dependants; (2) the married couple—husband and wife; (3) the individual, regardless of whether single or married.

Under U.K. income tax the second of these possibilities was adopted until 1980. Husband and wife were treated as one for tax purposes, the husband being responsible to the Inland Revenue for their joint income. A husband received a married man's allowance (equivalent to just over 1½ times a single person's allowance) and a working wife received a married woman's earned income allowance, which was equal to a single allowance. Thus a married couple, both working, received personal allowances amounting to some 2½ times the single person's allowance.

At levels of income at which higher rate applied, the aggregation of earnings often means higher tax payments than if each partner were taxed on their earnings as single individuals. In 1972 it was therefore provided that a married couple could elect to have the wife taxed as a single person on her earnings, provided that the husband received the single instead of the married allowance against the rest of their joint income. (An election was thus worthwhile if the additional tax paid as a result of aggregating earned income exceeded the difference between the married and single allowances.) A husband or wife could also claim separate assessment. This made no difference to the total tax paid by the couple—the tax bill was shared between them with the available reliefs being divided in proportion to their incomes—but each had independent dealings with the Revenue in his or her tax affairs.

Whilst all three types of unit are to be found in the income tax systems of different countries, the international trend has been in the direction of individual taxation, reflecting changed economic conditions (more wives working) and changed social attitudes (towards marriage and sexual equality). The United Kingdom has followed this trend.

In response to growing criticism, in December 1980 the U.K. government published a green paper,* a discussion document which outlined the present system, considered criticisms of it, and looked at possible alternatives. Public comment was invited, but, no action ensued. A second green paper† was issued in 1986. Then, in the 1988 Budget, Chancellor of the Exchequer Nigel Lawson introduced a reform to come into effect in the 1990–91 financial year.

The 1980 green paper suggested four criteria by which any system should be judged: fairness, simplicity, sex equality and privacy. To these might be added neutrality in relation to marriage and non-marriage, and with respect to the financial arrangements within a marriage. On these criteria the pre 1990 U.K. system came out badly. To give just a few illustrations.

Fairness relates primarily to the relativities between married and single people, between one-earner and two-earner couples and between men and women. To take one example: it could be argued that the two-earner married couple was in too favourable a position as compared with single persons; and that, if the wife was benefiting from the married women's earned income allowance, the husband should not also get the married man's allowance which was based on the assumption that the wife was financially dependent on him.

Simplicity should be an objective of all aspects of a tax structure, as we saw in Chapter 5. The pre-1990 system in relation to the tax unit was not too bad on this criterion, but the options for separate taxation of husband and wife and separate assessment added complications.

The principle of sex equality was violated by the pre-1990 system. The income tax acts deemed the wife's income to be her husband's for tax purposes. Some changes in practice (like the options) had

*The Taxation of Husband and Wife, Cmnd. 8093, H.M.S.O., 1980.
†The Reform of Personal Taxation, Cmnd. 9956, H.M.S.O., 1986.

alleviated the situation somewhat, but the basic principle was unchanged. Moreover the marriage allowance, except where the wife was the sole bread-winner, was only given to married men.

With respect to privacy, it was almost impossible under the pre-1990 system for the wife to keep her income and tax affairs confidential from her husband.

Finally the tax system was far from neutral in relation to social arrangements. Thus, for example, there was a financial incentive for two persons, both working, to marry if their combined income was less than the threshold of higher rate tax; but to stay single if their combined income exceeded that figure and they had substantial investment income (which continued to be aggregated even if they elected that the wife's earned income should be separately taxed).

The basic problem of any attempt to reform the system was how to reconcile two widely accepted but conflicting principles: equal treatment for all individuals irrespective of sex and marital status on the one hand; and, on the other, the recognition that the overall financial circumstances of a household are relevant to the ability to pay tax. Labour incentive effects further complicate the picture; the way allowances are structured affect whether married women have an incentive to engage in paid work or stay at home to look after the family. In times of labour shortage governments favour the first; when unemployment is high they favour the second.

The reform introduced as from 6 April 1990 provided for independent taxation; a husband and wife's income are no longer aggregated and each has an allowance which can be set against income from any source. The reform also provided for a new allowance, called the married couple's allowance (M.C.A.), which is equal to the difference between the old married man's allowance (M.M.A.), now abolished, and the single person's allowance. The M.C.A. is transferable, so that, where the wife's earnings are bigger than her allowance and the husband's are not, it can be transferred to her.

Table 6.1 shows how the changes affect a couple according to whether they are single or married; their income levels; whether they have investment income and, if so, how it is distributed. For most married couples (those where both earn, but their combined earnings did not bring them into higher rate tax; and those where the husband only earns and they have no investment income—situations 1 and 3 in the table) the position remains precisely the same as before the change. The gainers are the two earner families on high incomes who had previously exercised the wife's earnings election and thus had not benefited from the M.M.A. (situation 2); and those where the wife had not earned but had investment income which previously had been aggregated with her husband's income, but can be set against her own allowance (situation 5). If the investment income in situation 5 is equal to or more than the personal allowance, the minimum gain will be equal to the personal allowance times the basic rate of tax (at 1991–92 rates and allowances, £3,295*×25/100=£823.75). However, it is likely that the gain will be more than this as the disaggregation is likely to save tax at higher rate (the maximum benefit in 1991–92 could be £3,295×40/100=£1,318). Thus the better off received a handsome annual bonus as a result of the changes. It will also be observed that the tax benefit for a married couple with investment income depends on how this income is distributed between them. Most notably, if a wife is not working and investment income is in the name of the husband, the wife's allowance goes to waste (situation 4). In this situation there is a tax incentive to transfer earning assets from the husband to the wife. The transfer must be genuine and those who don't wholly trust their spouses will be reluctant to do so. If the wife appreciates the position there is plenty of scope for marital disharmony!

In proposing these changes to the tax unit in 1988, Mr Lawson stated that his two main objectives were: (1) to give married women the same privacy and independence in their affairs as everyone else; and (2) to end the ways in which the tax system could penalise marriage. His proposals achieve these objectives. A glance at the final column of Table 6.1 shows that in all five situations the couple are better off married than single (which was not the case under situations 2 and 5 of the pre-1990 system). Also the married woman

---

*There is higher personal allowance and M.C.A.s for those born before 6 April 1927; they are dependent on income and are reduced by £1 for every £2 by which income exceeds £13,500, but cannot fall below the basic allowance.

TABLE 6.1
Some Effects of the Change in the Tax Unit:
Comparison of Some Situations pre and post 5 April, 1990

				Effective Allowances	
Income of Couples				Pre	Post
1	A earns⎱ basic		S	2	2
	B earns⎰ rate		M	2.5	2.5
2	A earns⎫ into		S	2	2
	⎬ higher				
	B earns⎭ rates		M	2	2.5*
				(WEE)	
3	A earns		S	1	1
	B doesn't earn		M	1.5	1.5
	no investment income				
4	A earns		S	1	1
	B doesn't earn		M	1.5	1.5
	A large investment income				
5	A earns		S	2*	?
	B doesn't earn		M	1.5	2.5*
	B large investment income				

* Likely to benefit not only from more allowances but from lower tax rates (because of non-aggregation).
A=Andy (the man)
B=Barbara (the woman)
S=single
M=married
WEE=wife's earnings election

does gain her privacy, or in the language of the 1980 Green Paper, there is sex equality. However, looking at the other criteria we listed on p. 136, the outcome is not so satisfactory. Simplicity is achieved; but the system is not neutral as between marriage and non-marriage (the Chancellor deliberately set out to favour marriage) nor is it neutral with respect to the financial arrangements within a marriage. Most seriously, however, it falls down on fairness as between married and single persons and, to quote a recent article "the tax allowances to married couples constitutes a substantial tax expenditure which is poorly targeted".* Those who most need help

*Bill Robinson and Graham Stark, The Tax Treatment of Marriage: What has the Chancellor Really Achieved? *Fiscal Studies*, Vol. 9, No. 2, May 1988.

are low income families where the wife is at home looking after young children. They do not benefit. The beneficiaries are the wealthy.

Personal Income Tax in the United Kingdom

As we saw in the previous chapter, the personal income tax is the biggest revenue-yielder in the United Kingdom with national insurance contributions, another form of income tax, coming next. Together they accounted for 45 per cent of total tax revenue in 1990–91.

Structure and Rates

The present structure of income taxation (leaving aside national insurance contributions for the moment) dates from 1973. Before then income was subject to two taxes: income tax and surtax. Income tax applied to all taxable income at the so-called "standard" rate or at one or more "reduced" rates. Surtax was a highly progressive tax imposed on top of income tax, levied on higher incomes and administered from a separate office. Differentiation between earned and investment income was effected by means of an earned income relief.

Anthony Barber, as Chancellor, unified the two taxes, but without making any substantial change in the essential rate struc ture. A wide band of income was charged to tax at what was now called "basic" rate, with the highest income subject to "higher rate" tax. Differentiation between earned and investment income was secured by means of an investment income surcharge.

The Conservative governments which came to power under Mrs. Thatcher in 1979 proceeded to reduce the high marginal rates of income tax which they inherited from their Labour predecessor and to whittle down and then, in 1984, to abolish the investment income surcharge. The first big reduction in income tax rates, in 1979, was associated with an increase in V.A.T. (see p. 209). The top rate of income tax on earned income was cut from 83 to 60 per cent and the basic rate from 33 to 30 per cent. Between 1979 and 1988 several

TABLE 6.2
Income Tax Rates and Taxable Income 1987–88, 1988–89 and 1991–92

	1987–88		1988–89		1991–92	
	Rates (%)	Taxable Income (£)	Rates (%)	Taxable Income (£)	Rates (%)	Taxable Income (£)
Basic rate	27	1–17,900	25	1–19,300	25	1–23,700
Higher rate(s)	40	17,901–20,400	40	Over 19,300	40	Over 23,700
	45	20,401–25,400				
	50	25,401–33,300				
	55	33,301–41,200				
	60	over 41,200				

percentage points were knocked off the basic rate, but the next major cut came in 1988 when Chancellor of the Exchequer Nigel Lawson abolished all the higher rates above 40 per cent and reduced the basic rate to 25 per cent. These are the rates applying in 1991–92, though with increased thresholds. Table 6.2 shows the income tax rates and bands before and after the 1988 Budget and for 1991–92.

Allowances. The first portion of a person's income is exempted from tax by the operation of a series of reliefs or allowances, the actual amount depending on the taxpayer's circumstances. We have already referred to the main personal allowances when discussing the tax unit. For 1991–92 the basic personal allowance was £3,295 and married couple's allowance, £1,720. There are somewhat higher allowances for persons over 65, but they are dependent on income and reduce back to the basic allowances by £1 for every £2 by which income exceeds a certain figure (£13,500 in 1991–92). Additional allowances are also given for particular circumstances, notably a further personal allowance for a single parent responsible for a child under 16 or in full time education (£1,720), a widow's bereavement allowance (£1,720 in the year of the husband's death and the subsequent year unless she remarries before the start of the year) and a blind person's allowance (£1,080). There was formerly a child allowance, but this (and the former family allowance) was gradually replaced during the 1970s by a child benefit, paid in cash to the mother via the Post Office. The child benefit is not taxable. A cash grant has the advantage over a tax relief that the same benefit goes to all who qualify, whereas a tax allowance fails to give benefit, or at least full benefit, to the poorest whose incomes may not be large enough to take full advantage of the allowance; and the tax allowance benefits taxpayer's according to their marginal rate of tax (the tax rate on the top £1 of their income) so that the better off derive more benefit than the less well off.

Besides these allowances various other tax concessions are granted of which the most important are for superannuation and retirement annuity contributions and mortgage interest on the first £30,000 (since 1983) of a mortgage on a principal owner-occupied home.

Premiums on life insurance policies received tax relief before 1984, but from that date the relief was abolished on new contracts, but not on existing policies. Whilst the Conservative Chancellors since 1979 have in some respects sought to reduce tax expenditures e.g. by restricting the relief on insurance policies, by allowing the real value of the mortgage interest relief on owner occupied houses to fall, by increasing the charges on company cars and reducing investment allowances, they have added to tax expenditures in ways intended to increase equity and risk investments and small savings. Thus they introduced a Business Expansion Scheme in 1983, to encourage investment in new and existing unquoted trading companies, by granting tax relief to individuals for investments up to £40,000 per annum. A scheme of Personal Equity Plans (P.E.P.s) allows (as at 1991–92) up to £6,000 per person per annum to be invested in an approved scheme of qualifying equity investments of United Kingdom companies, with tax relief on dividends and no capital gains tax liability. Tax concessions have also been given in respect of employee share options and investment in certain areas designated Enterprise Zones. The latest of such concessions is the provision of tax exempt special savings accounts (T.E.S.S.A.s) introduced in 1990 by Mr. Major as Chancellor of the Exchequer, to come into effect in January 1991. All commercial banks or building societies can offer special accounts under which interest on capital is entirely free of tax provided that the capital is left undisturbed for 5 years. There is an annual limit of £1,800 or £9,000 over the 5-year period, but those who so wish can put in £3,000 in the first year, subject to the same overall limit. The particular attraction to small savers is that they can withdraw interest each year up the net of tax level and at the end of the 5 years still receive a bonus representing the money that would otherwise have gone in tax, provided that the capital is left intact in the account. Tax reliefs for savings and investments have not been the only new tax expenditures. Thus for those over 60, premium payments for private health insurance benefit from tax relief.

Unusual Features of the United Kingdom Income Tax

Although a characteristic of the world-wide tax reform movement of the 1980s was a reduction both in marginal rates of income tax and in the number of tax brackets, few countries have reduced the number of tax rates to as low as two. Even before this reduction to two rates, the United Kingdom income tax was characterised by the very wide band of income at basic rate tax—a feature probably unique amongst national income taxes. In 1991–92 a taxpayer with minimum allowances (personal allowance only) and no benefit from any other tax reliefs, would still require an income of over £26,995 to be paying tax at a marginal rate other than 25 per cent.

Well over 90 per cent of taxpayers pay tax at basic rate. This wide band at a constant rate of tax simplifies administration; but the simplification is bought at the cost of limiting the progression in the income tax. Progression still exists over this band because, as Table 6.3 illustrates, people with higher incomes but otherwise similar circumstances pay a larger proportion of their income in tax; the allowances constitute a diminishing proportion of income as income rises; but the degree of progression diminishes as income rises until the start of higher rate tax is reached.

Investment income surcharge. Although the investment income surcharge has been abolished, it is worth saying something more about

TABLE 6.3
Illustration of Income Tax Progression

Income £	Tax allowances £	Taxable income £	Marginal rate of tax %	Tax paid £	Average rate of tax %
5,500	5015	485	25	121	2.2
10,000	5015	4,985	25	1246	12.5
15,000	5015	9,985	25	2496	16.6
20,000	5015	14,985	25	3746	18.7
25,000	5015	19,985	25	4996	20.0

Assumptions: 1991–92 tax and allowances; each taxpayer has personal allowance and M.C.A. only; tax paid rounded to nearest £; average tax rate rounded to first decimal place.

it because it could well be reintroduced if the Labour Party won a General Election. Discrimination in the income tax in favour of earned as against investment income goes back to the beginning of the 20th century. It was argued that income from property was more permanent than that from wages and salaries, which would cease on illness, unemployment or retirement. This argument perhaps both over-stresses the permanence of investment income and the precariousness of earned income in modern conditions; with social security providing sickness, unemployment and retirement benefits some of the force has gone out of it. But a general case remains either for taxing the capital itself or for taxing income from capital more heavily than earned income. The possession of capital gives its owner advantages over and above any income derived from it and hence confers additional taxable capacity. Moreover the receipt of investment income, unlike earned income, does not entail the sacrifice of leisure. Further, because of the payment of national insurance contributions (which we discuss more fully below) earned income currently bears more tax than investment income.

Adjustment for inflation. Until 1977 any adjustment of allowances and rate bands to offset the effect of inflation (discussed in Chapter 13) had been solely at the discretion of the Chancellor and, in general, the value of allowances in the early 1970s had not been maintained; still less had the rate bands been extended in proportion to the price-rise so as to retain the same real value. In 1977, however, the Finance Bill Committee, against the wishes of the Chancellor, Mr. Healey, passed the Rooker-Wise amendment, so-called after the two rebel Labour members who supported it. This provided for the annual up-rating of the main personal allowances in line with the retail price index. It remained open to the Chancellor to over-rule this provision in any budget, but he had to do so explicitly. No longer would the real value of the allowances be cut by stealth. Sir Geoffrey Howe, as Chancellor, continued the indexation of the income tax by undertaking to maintain the real value of the tax bands.

Social Security Contributions and Benefits

We cannot leave this account of income tax rates and structure without some reference to the interaction with social security contributions and benefits.

National insurance benefits are primarily financed by contributions from employers, employees and the self-employed but there may also be a general Exchequer contribution. The effective incidence of the employer's contribution is disputable (and more is said about it in Chapter 15). But the employee's contribution is very much akin to income tax—a compulsory levy deducted from the employee's pay. It is therefore appropriate in looking at the formal incidence of income tax to consider with it the formal incidence of the employee's N.I. contribution.

When the national insurance scheme was first introduced in 1948 it was based on the principles of the Beveridge Report of 1942— which entailed that above a minimum level of income, all employees below retirement age should pay a flat rate contribution, irrespective of means, to qualify for identical benefits; all, rich and poor, would pay the same contribution for the same security. It was thus a genuine insurance scheme and the receipt of benefits depended on a sufficient number of contributions. However, as the levels of benefits were raised, the corresponding rise in the level of contributions was felt to bear too heavily on the lowest income groups and the principle of a uniform contribution was gradually abandoned in favour of an earnings-related component with a ceiling limit; in 1975, the employee's flat rate contribution was finally abolished.

In addition to the employee contribution a payment is made by the employer; and the self-employed also pay a fixed weekly amount above a lower limit of earnings, together with a percentage of self-employment profits between an upper and lower limit.

We shall concentrate on the contributions of employees and employers (known as Class 1 contributions) which generate by far the bulk of the social security revenue. These have been subject to considerable increases in recent years. In 1975 the standard Class I employee rate (for someone who did not contract out of the State Earnings Related Pension Scheme—S.E.R.P.S.—in favour of an occupational pension scheme) was 5.5 per cent; the employer rate was 8.5 per cent. By 1985 these rates had been increased to 9 per cent and 10.4 per cent respectively, which is their current (1991–92) level.

Since 1985 there have been some important changes in the system. No payments are required by employer or employee below the lower earnings limit, but once the limit is passed contributions become payable by both employee and employer on the whole of earnings. Thus, pre-1985, the receipt of £.01 of earnings above the limit generated a significant fall in the net income of the employee and a substantial rise in costs for the employer. There tended to be a bunching of incomes just below the lower limit.* The 1985 reform was designed both to reduce any disincentive effect to paying higher wages and to benefit the lower paid workers. A series of lower rates were introduced for both employers and employees so that they moved more gradually to the standard rate. At the same time, to pay for these reforms, the ceiling on the employer's contribution (but not that of the employees') was removed.

The 1985 reform, whilst an improvement, still left a series of jumps in liability, even if they were less pronounced than that of the starting point of liability before 1985. On the employee's side the process of removing the steps was taken further by a reform in 1989, which provided for employees to pay 2 per cent of the lower earn-

*See Andrew Dilnot and Steven Webb, Reforming National Insurance Contributions: A Progress Report, *Fiscal Studies*, Vol. 10, No. 2, May 1989.

ings limit (£43.00 in 1989) once they reached the limit and 9 per cent on all excess earnings up to the level of the upper earnings limit (£325 in 1989). In effect this amounted, at 1989 rates, to a single rate of 9 per cent, with an allowance of £43.00, plus a charge of 86p (2 per cent of £43.00) on entering the system. The reform, however, left untouched the jumps in the liability for the employers' contributions.

Meanwhile the removal of the limit on the employers' liability in 1985 generated a new problem; whereas payments in kind, such as car benefits, were subject to income tax, they were not subject to national insurance contributions (N.I.C.). Thus employers who paid workers in kind rather than cash, avoided the employers' contribution. The 1991 Finance Act therefore included a provision by which employers would pay contributions on the benefit of cars provided for the private use of employees based on the scale charges for income tax; and similarly on free fuel provided by employers for private use in company cars.

When N.I.C.s and income tax are taken together for the employee paying Class I (not contracted out) contributions, tax, in the form of national insurance contributions, begins at a level below the minimum income tax threshold (the personal allowance); when the employee starts paying income tax, the marginal rate of tax (N.I.C. and basic rate combined) at 1991–92 rates is 34 per cent; at an annual income of £20,280, the marginal rate drops to 25 per cent before it rises to 40 per cent when higher rate tax begins at £23,700 of *taxable* income. Thus, not only does the long basic rate band of income tax limit the degree of progression at its upper end, but, when N.I.C.s are taken into account, there is a pronounced regress-ive kink before higher rate starts to apply. The marginal and average rates of tax at different income levels, assuming a taxpayer with personal allowance, M.C.A. and standard Class I N.I.C.s is shown in Figures 6.1. and 6.2

The effect of social security benefits at the bottom end of the income scale is also very important. The benefits financed by N.I.C.s under the national insurance scheme—principally state retirement pensions, sickness and unemployment benefits—are payable as of right to those with sufficient contributions. But they

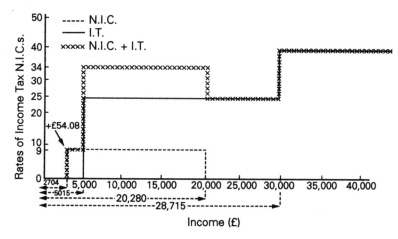

FIG. 6.1 Marginal rates of income tax and of employees' standard National Insurance contributions, 1991–92, for employees not contracted out with personal allowance and married couples' allowance only.

Note: the 2% N.I.C. paid on the first £2,704 if income exceeds £2,704 p.a. (i.e. £54.08) is best thought of as a charge for entering the system and is not shown on the graph.

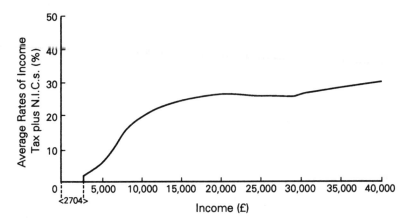

FIG. 6.2 Average rates of income tax and employees' standard National Insurance contributions (combined) 1991–92, for employees not contracted out and with personal allowance and married couples' allowance only.

are neither comprehensive enough nor at a sufficiently high rate, to meet all cases of need. There are therefore a series of other benefits under the social security provisions which are means tested e.g. currently, income support for low income families, family credit and housing benefit. The essence of a means tested benefit is that, as income increases, so the benefit is reduced: in effect there is what is often termed an implicit tax rate. Because for perfectly good reasons, the thresholds of income tax, N.I.C.s and the eligibility levels for means-tested benefits do not coincide, someone on means-tested benefits who obtains an increase in earnings is likely to pay increased explicit tax (income tax and N.I. contributions) and also be subject to implicit tax (i.e. lose benefits). Before 1988, in a few extreme cases, the result was that an increase in earnings actually led to a reduction in disposable income; in other words the combined explicit and implicit marginal rates of tax exceeded 100 per cent. This extreme situation was alleviated by the Fowler reforms of social security in 1988 but there remain many cases where the combined explicit and implicit tax rate are over 70 per cent and a small minority where the rate is close to 100 per cent. This situation has become known as the "poverty trap" or "poverty surtax". The poor caught in the trap find it almost impossible to drag themselves out of poverty and there is a clear disincentive to work.

Administration

Several features of the administration of income tax are worthy of note. One is collection at source, whenever possible. As every schoolboy knows, Pitt introduced the income tax in 1799; but it is to Addington, who re-introduced it after the Peace of Amiens, that we owe the principle of collection at source. Its beneficial effect was immediately apparent in the much improved yield of the tax. Today its main applications are the deductions of employees' income tax by the employer and deduction of income tax at the basic rate from dividend and interest payments made by companies to shareholders and on much of the interest on government stock and on accounts held by financial institutions.

An unusual feature of U.K. income tax administration is the cumulative deduction under pay-as-you-earn (P.A.Y.E.). P.A.Y.E.

TABLE 6.4

Illustration of the Operation of Cumulative P.A.Y.E. — Hypothetical Figures

Week	Weekly income (£)	Cumu- lative income (£)	Cumulative allowances (£)	Cumu- lative taxable income (£)	Rate of tax (%)	Cumu- lative tax due (£)	Tax paid each week (£)
1	50	50	10	40	30	12	12
2	50	100	20	80	30	24	12
3	80	180	30	150	30	45	21
4	20	200	40	160	30	48	3
5	0	200	50	150	30	45	−3 (rebate)
6	100	300	60	240	30	72	27

was introduced during the Second World War when many millions of workers were brought within the ambit of income tax for the first time. Many countries operate a P.A.Y.E. scheme but no other except the Republic of Ireland operates a cumulative scheme by which tax payments are kept in line with liability throughout the year so that, at the end of the tax year, no end year adjustments are necessary for the large majority of employees; just the right amount of tax has been paid. Each employee is given a code number representing his income tax allowances and the employer deducts tax from his wage or salary by reference to the code number and the official tax tables.

The principle of the scheme can be shown by reference to an over-simplified example. Let us assume, to keep the mathematics simple, that a taxpayer's annual allowances are £520. These allowances are then divided into weekly allowances of £10. Tax is deducted as in Table 6.4. As can be seen, tax payments are maintained in line with liability throughout the year.

As a result of this system the majority of employee taxpayers are only required to complete a tax return every 5 years, although they are expected to report to the Inland Revenue any change in their circumstances affecting their allowances and any income they may receive other than from their employer.

From the self-employed income tax is collected in arrears, so that liability can be determined by reference to their trading accounts for the year. This gives them a distinct advantage over P.A.Y.E. tax-payers, especially in times of inflation.

The Effective Incidence of Income Tax

Personal income tax, applying to a large proportion of income receivers, and comprehending income both from work and from property, affects the level of incomes, consumption, savings and investment and must be analysed primarily on general or macro lines. The formal incidence of income tax is on the income receiver—the difference between gross and net income; the effective incidence covers much wider considerations, in particular effects on the supply and mobility of the factors of production. The questions we seek to answer, therefore, are, how far does income tax distort the choice between work and leisure? Does it lead to more or less work being undertaken? Does it increase or reduce the incentive to save and take risks? Does it affect the supply of labour to different occupations? How far is income taxation responsible for emigration and immigration? We shall concentrate on the effects of income tax on the supply and mobility of labour, examining first the theoretical arguments and then the empirical data relating to the United Kingdom. Subsequently we shall examine possible distorting effects of income tax amongst different occupations and then, more briefly, examine the effects of personal income tax on saving, investment and enterprise.

On the Supply of Labour in General

The theoretical analysis. Of the several ways of analysing the problem perhaps the simplest and most useful is to examine the effect of income tax on the demand for leisure. Time can be thought of as divided between work and leisure; an increase in the demand for leisure constitutes a reduction in willingness to work and vice versa.

If a tax is imposed on income from work (or an existing tax increased) the income receiver will be worse off;* he will feel that he

---

*Strictly if the taxpayer benefits from additional government expenditure to the extent of the additional tax his real income has not fallen; but it will still be true that he can afford less of those goods he was previously buying unless the government expenditure is so directed as to enable him to obtain them more cheaply.

can afford less of most things, including leisure; that is to say, he will tend to do more work. However, there is another influence: the substitution effect; the tax has changed the terms on which leisure can be acquired; an increase in tax means that the enjoyment of an hour's leisure costs less than before; less income (and hence less of the things which can be bought with it) is sacrificed if an hour less is worked. On this count, the cost of leisure having fallen, there is a tendency for more leisure to be taken, i.e. for less work to be done.

Economic theory thus demonstrates that the imposition of a tax, altering the terms on which leisure can be acquired, sets up two tendencies, the income and substitution effects, working in opposite directions; it does not tell us which of the two tendencies will be the stronger, but it at least demonstrates that there is no *a priori* reason for believing that taxation *must reduce* the amount of work done.

However, theory can take us further than this. The income effect of the imposition of a tax, tending to increase willingness to work, operates through the change in aggregate income. The substitution effect is essentially concerned with the terms on which an hour more or less of leisure can be acquired, i.e. the rate of substitution between income and leisure at the margin of income. We can say, then, that the greater the marginal effect relatively to aggregate, the greater will be the disincentive (or the less the incentive) effect of a tax increase. The more highly progressive a tax, the greater the marginal effects relatively to aggregate. Thus an individual paying the same amount of tax by either a flat rate or a progressive tax would experience more disincentive (or less incentive) effect as a result of the progressive tax. Even so, the analysis only indicates that, for the same revenue to the exchequer, a progressive tax is less favourable to incentive than a flat rate or less progressive tax; it does not enable us to say that there *is a positive* net disincentive effect. This we can only establish by empirical investigation.

Practical considerations. For incentive or disincentives to effort to be relevant, workers must be able to alter the amount of paid work they undertake. In the short run many workers may be unable to alter their work effort; but there are a number of ways in which workers may possibly have some control over the amount of labour they supply: working more or less overtime where overtime is voluntary; varying absenteeism (the scope for which is greater the less the fear of disciplinary action, which is likely to vary inversely with the level of employment); acceptance or refusal of part-time work. Further, workers on piece rates can alter their supply of labour by altering the effort they put into work within working hours. In the long run workers can react to tax changes by influencing the policy of their trade union on the importance accorded to reduced working hours in negotiations with employers on wages and conditions of work.

Clearly, professional men, solicitors, university dons, accountants, have more control over the amount of work they do than the factory or office worker. Many are self-employed and can choose to accept more or less work and vary the intensity with which they seek out work. They have more scope for undertaking part-time work in consulting, lecturing or writing.

Income taxation might also reduce or increase the supply of labour by affecting the age of retirement; and by the effect on those (principally married women) who, having other means of support, are not obliged to work, but who may decide to take part-time or full-time employment.

Finally, the supply of labour in a given country may be influenced by income taxation in encouraging or discouraging immigration and emigration; but this we shall examine under the heading of the mobility of labour.

Empirical evidence. Over the last 40 years in the United Kingdom there have been a number of studies of the effect of income taxation on effort sufficiently scientific in method to warrant serious attention. Because of the importance and topicality of this subject the evidence is considered at some length.

In 1952 the Government Social Survey undertook an investigation for the Royal Commission on the Taxation of Profits and Income.* The study took the form of structured interviews of a sample of just under 1,500 workers (1,203 male, 226 female) which

---

*Appendix I, *Second Report of the Royal Commission on the Taxation of Profits and Income*, Cmnd. 9105, 1954.

comprised members of a nationally representative sample of 4,000 workers who were in manual, operative and supervisory grades in industry and who were "(a) paid according to some incentive scheme including normal piece rates and/or—(b) were working, or could work, overtime". None of these workers was paying tax above the so-called standard rate, then, effectively, 38 per cent.

The conclusions reached by the Survey were summarised as follows:

> Few productive workers had any detailed knowledge of the way they were affected by income tax.
>
> There was no evidence from this enquiry of productive effort being inhibited by the income tax structure within its present limits.
>
> An attitude towards income tax was a slight factor in productive effort as assessed by hours of work. Those having strong anti-income tax views tended slightly more often than others to work less than average hours, but this attitude was not associated with facts.

A survey of considerable importance was undertaken in 1956 by Professor G. F. Break.* This study was based on interviews with 306 self-employed solicitors and accountants (selected by random means) who were thus relatively free to adjust their supply of labour, nearly two thirds of whom were subject to surtax (1956) and who could be expected to be highly knowledgeable of the rates of income taxation and its effects on their earnings. Of these 306, 128 said that they were or might be affected by taxation, more than half reporting an *incentive* influence (especially in the form of postponement of retirement). If the numbers are reduced to remove the more questionable cases (e.g. those who were very vague, or who suggested they would be affected in the distant future or in certain hypothetical circumstances) we are left with some 34 per cent of the sample. Of these slightly less than half (31 or 10 per cent of the sample) were impelled by taxation to work harder (by postponing retirement or working harder on a day-to-day basis) and rather more than half (40 or 13 per cent) deterred by high tax rates from

*Effects of Taxation on Incentives, *British Tax Review*, June 1957.

working as hard as they might have done (declining work or being less active in seeking new clients or reducing their work load by shifting it to other partners or additional staff hired for the purpose). If the standards of admissible evidence are further raised (e.g. by excluding those for whom taxation was simply one among several motivating factors) the gross effect falls below 15 per cent with slightly more incentive cases remaining than disincentive ones. Thus the figures which result depend on an interpretation of the evidence, and even if this could be agreed it would still not be possible to measure quantitatively the net effect (how much the supply of labour was increased or reduced and the value of the services gained or lost). Professor Break concluded: "Most certainly, however, this net effect, be it disincentive or incentive, is not large enough to be of great economic or sociological significance."

Several subsidiary conclusions from Break's study are of particular interest. Postponement of retirement was the incentive influence most frequently mentioned (because taxation prevented the saving of enough money to provide for future support); moreover not one respondent said that because of high tax rates he expected to retire earlier than he otherwise would have done. Secondly, respondents who paid tax at a marginal rate of 70 per cent or more were considerably more subject to tax disincentives than those facing lower tax rates. Thirdly, tax disincentives seemed to be less frequent amongst London respondents than amongst those in rural areas.

Although out of chronological order, it is convenient at this point to consider a study by D. B. Fields and W. T. Stanbury* because it is a "replication" of Break's study some 12 years later. The sample was chosen from amongst practising accountants and solicitors in the same way as Break's; there was a response from 285 of a final sample size of 319; Break's questionnaire was followed with some small changes and additions and the replies were analysed in the same way.

Of the 285 respondents, 46 per cent claimed to experience some sort of tax influence, divided in the ratio of 22 per cent incentive and

*Incentives, Disincentives and the Income Tax, Further Empirical Evidence, *Public Finance*, No. 3, 1970.

24 per cent disincentive. When the responses were adjusted to remove doubtful cases the result was 11 per cent incentive and 19 per cent disincentive. This is a significant increase in the proportion experiencing disincentive effects compared with Break's survey where the corresponding figures were 10 per cent and 13 per cent. The difference may owe something to the way the interviews were conducted. Although Fields and Stanbury claimed to have repeated Break's approach, in fact they introduced reference to taxation into their questioning at a much earlier stage than Break and this may have somewhat conditioned the interviewees when they were asked what were the influences on the amount of work they did.*

Fields and Stanbury, like Break, found that the proportion of respondents experiencing disincentives increased as income increased; and also that the proportion experiencing disincentive was significantly higher in the counties than in London.

A smaller and more limited study by L. Buck and S. Shimmin† set out to test the theory that high marginal rates of tax deter workers from accepting the opportunity to work overtime. It has a particular interest as this study was *not* based on the social survey methods of interview or questionnaire. The behaviour of 43 day workers from an engineering shop, in which overtime working was a matter of individual choice, was examined from the income, tax and overtime records of the previous year. If the hypothesis was valid, one would have expected to find that workers paying at the standard rate would be less inclined to do overtime, those paying at the lower rates more inclined to work overtime, other things being equal. In fact the data showed little or no relation between an operative's taxable income and the amount of overtime. Overtime was worked in response to financial needs irrespective of whether the rate of taxation was high or low. The authors accepted the limited value of their analysis; if more "other things" could have been held equal, it is possible that some support for the deterrent hypothesis might have been found. But, to put it at its most cautious, this study lent no support to the hypothesis.

*For details see C. V. Brown and P. M. Jackson, *Public Sector Economics*, 4th edition, 1990, pp. 445–46.
†Is Taxation a Deterrent? *Westminster Bank Review*, August 1959.

On another of the ways in which income tax might adversely affect the supply of labour, not considered in the previous studies, some light is thrown by a survey undertaken by a working party of the Federation of University Women.* A postal questionnaire, answered by over 1,500 women graduates, contained a list of possible difficulties about a return to work, asking respondents to indicate by which they were affected. The eleven mentioned included "lack of adequate financial benefit", which subsumes the effect of taxation. When the eleven possible difficulties are arranged in the order of frequency with which they are mentioned by women willing to work but not actually working, "lack of adequate financial benefit" ranked seventh, with "preference for home life and social commitments" and "difficulty in obtaining domestic help" ranking first and second respectively; moreover there is a distinct break in numbers after the fifth difficulty listed. Especially when we allow for the inclusion of other considerations than tax in "lack of adequate financial benefit", income tax does not emerge as a factor affecting significantly the large majority of women graduates contemplating employment in paid work.

An unpublished study† by D. J. Iles of 93 lecturers in Further Education (selected for convenience rather than randomness) examined, by interview, their reaction to an extended college year and to voluntary overtime. Very few of the respondents were in the surtax bracket. The main conclusion was that income tax was unimportant as a motive for work effort in this group.

The most extensive recent research in the United Kingdom has been undertaken by Professor C. V. Brown and associates. A study in 1971 covered a national sample of weekly wage earners, over 2,000 of whom were interviewed. The interviews attempted to elucidate the effect of income tax on overtime hours worked. A very large proportion of the sample claimed that taxation made them work neither more nor less overtime. If those not free to vary the overtime they worked or not regular taxpayers are eliminated, there remained over 60 per cent of the men claiming that tax had no effect

Graduate Women at Work, ed. Constance E. Arregger, Oriel Press Ltd., 1966.
†*The Disincentive Effects of Income Taxation on Work Effort*, 1973, an unpublished thesis available from the University of Bath Library.

on their overtime. Of those that did claim to be affected, the proportion of men claiming that tax made them work more is larger than the proportion claiming that tax made them work less overtime and this feature is accentuated when replies of low plausibility are eliminated.

The ratio of "more" to "less" claims was greater among married men with children than it was for married men without children, which in turn was greater than the proportion for single people.

The number of hours of overtime actually worked in the previous week was consistent with the claims made.

The authors conclude: "The evidence clearly suggests, therefore, that the aggregate effect of tax on overtime is small; it may perhaps add about 1 per cent to the total hours worked, since on balance tax has made people work more rather than less overtime." They point out, however, that the number of women claiming to work less is greater than the number claiming to work more.*

As well as the study on low income earners, Professor Brown was also the initiator of a study on high income earners.† The 1988 Budget, by which the basic rate of income tax was cut from 27 to 25 per cent and, more significantly, the top rate was reduced from 60 to 40 per cent, offered a unique opportunity for a case study on the incentive/disincentive effects of a major change in income tax rates on the behaviour of high income earners.

The Brown/Sandford study owed much to the earlier study of Break, but was not intended as a precise replication. Whereas Break had interviewed both solicitors and accountants, the Brown/Sandford study was restricted to accountants; whilst most of the questions were directed to the behaviour of the accountants themselves, respondents were also asked about the reactions of clients. This part of the evidence is necessarily second-hand; but, on some important issues, such as changes in attitudes to tax avoidance and investment (to which we refer later), accountants' perceptions of their clients'

---

*C. V. Brown and E. Levin, The Effects of Income Tax on Overtime: the Results of a National Survey, *Economic Journal*, December 1974.
†C. V. Brown and C. T. Sandford, *Taxes and Incentives, The Effects of the 1988 Cuts in the Higher Rates of Income Tax*, Economic Study No. 7, Institute for Public Policy Research, 1991.

reactions should be reliable because the accountant is often the agent with whom such matters are discussed and through whom changes are implemented. The Brown/Sandford study was also broader than that of Break. Besides questions on hours worked, holidays taken, changes in work outside the practice, retirement plans, which Break had asked, the Brown/Sandford study also sought to gather information on enterprise, avoidance, international migration and revenue effects. There was also a difference in methodology: Break's interviews related to a static tax situation; the Brown/Sandford study took place after a major change in the tax rate and respondents were asked about changes in behaviour between fiscal year 1987–88 and 1988–89.

The sample for the Brown/Sandford study was drawn from the membership lists of the Chartered Institutes in England and Wales and in Scotland and covered accountants in three geographical areas—London, the South West of England and Eastern Wales and central Scotland; it thus offered a geographical spread covering the City of London, big provincial towns and country areas. All the interviews were conducted by one or other of the authors and those interviewed were either partners or sole practitioners. The findings were based on 316 interviews (a response rate of 69 per cent). Of the interviewees, 179 (or 57 per cent) had paid tax at 45 per cent or more in 1987–88 and thus had benefited from a reduction in their marginal tax rate of at least 5 per cent.

Respondents were first asked about changes in respect of hours worked etc. and, where there were changes, were then asked to give reasons. Only towards the end of the interview were questions specifically asked about how the tax changes had affected them and their clients.

Of the 179 accountants who had paid tax at 45 per cent in 1987–88, as between the year before and after the Budget, 72 per cent had not changed the number of hours they normally worked, 80 per cent had not changed the amount of holiday, and well over 90 per cent had not changed the amount of work turned down or work taken on outside the firm (which, in any case, was negligible). Where there were changes the balance was strongly towards more hours worked, more holidays and more work turned down. Of the

TABLE 6.5
Incentive and Disincentive Effects on Labour Supply of the Tax Reduction, U.K., 1988

Incentive	Disincentive
Longer hours 2/179 (3/316)	Shorter hours 1/179
	Longer holidays 1/179
	Earlier retirement 2/80

80 accountants out of the 179 who were 45 years or over, 10 per cent said that they planned to retire earlier and 2 per cent had planned to retire later.

The crucial question, of course, is how far the changes were a reaction to the income tax change. Taxation was cited as a reason in only a small minority of cases. Two respondents gave the reduction in marginal rates as a reason for working longer (the overwhelming reason was "more pressure of work") and "better off as a result of the tax cuts" was given by one respondent as a reason for working less and another as a reason for taking more holiday. No respondent gave the lower taxes as a reason for postponing retirement; two gave it as a reason for retiring early.

Although respondents with tax rates of 45 per cent or over in 1987–88 are most likely to have been affected by the 1988 tax reductions, it is possible that those on 40 per cent or paying standard rate in 1987–88 might have been affected; some may have been inhibited from income generation by the existence of higher rates. Analysing the responses of the remainder of the 316 accountants brings in one more respondent who experienced an incentive effect as a result of the cut in income tax rates. The evidence on the effect on labour supply is summarised in Table 6.5.

Thus seven respondents out of 316 (or 2.2 per cent) were affected by incentive or disincentive effects as a result of the tax changes. If analysis is confined to those paying at marginal rates of 45 per cent or over in 1987–88, then the figure becomes 6/179 or 3.4 per cent. The tax effects worked in both directions with the biggest disincentive from the reduction in higher rates being the bringing forward of retirement (just as Break had found the biggest incentive of the high rates in the 1950s—then a maximum of 92.5 per cent—was the postponement of retirement). The overall effects on labour supply, however, were very small; the big reduction in higher rate tax from 60 to 40 per cent would appear not to have had any significant effect in increasing work effort; it may even have had a marginally negative effect.

Besides the evidence we have already considered, largely based on surveys, during the past two decades there has been a growth of econometric studies. Whilst many of these have been on American data, some have been on British data, most notably work by C. V. Brown's team using the data base of the 1971 study.

The econometric approach uses cross sectional data—data on the wages, hours worked and tax paid of different people at the same time—allowing for extraneous factors, as far as may be, by the use of regression techniques. From differences between individuals at a point in time inferences are drawn about how individuals might be expected to behave over a period of time. Thus, as C. V. Brown puts it: "Suppose there are two people: A with a wage of W who worked H hours and B with a wage of 2W who worked 1.5 H hours. The inference would be that if a 50 per cent tax was put on B that he would reduce his hours to H."* One of the attractions of the econometric approach is that it not only attempts to specify the direction of work change following a tax imposition but also to measure the extent and, indeed, to measure the strength of both the income and substitution effects. Brown's book summarises the more important of the econometric studies and shows them increasing in sophistication, with the later results broadly in conformity with the survey data.

Evaluating the evidence. This empirical evidence has clear limitations. Only two of the surveys were large-scale, the 1952 study by the Social Survey and C. V. Brown's; but both were restricted to weekly paid workers at the lower tax levels; further, the 1952 study had methodological defects† and relates to a situation of 40 years ago and the interviews in Brown's study relate only to overtime.

*C. V. Brown, *Taxation and the Incentive to Work*, Oxford University Press, 1980, p. 45.
†Outlined in C. V. Brown, Misconceptions about Income Tax and Incentives, *Scottish Journal of Political Economy*, Vol. XV, February 1968.

Only three smaller surveys, those of Break, Stanbury and Fields and Brown and Sandford, include a significant number of people in the higher tax brackets; Break's study is rather old, the Stanbury and Fields study had methodological defects and all three studies were confined to one or two occupational groups. The study by Iles was small, non-random and restricted to teachers; the investigation by Buck and Shimmin was similarly small and restricted in its scope; and that of women graduates was only incidentally concerned with taxation. As for the econometric studies, the earlier ones produced contradictory results and, although considerable methodological progress has been made, the later studies are far from producing reliable results. Nonetheless, there is a consistency about the cumulative weight of the evidence which is impressive. The tentative conclusions on the effect of income tax on work effort can be summarised as follows:

(1) The majority of workers seem not to be subject either to incentive or disincentive effects;

(2) A minority of workers are conscious of an incentive or a disincentive effect, but the overall net effect one way or another does not appear to be large;

(3) At rates of tax of 40 per cent or less, if anything, there would appear to be a slight incentive effect;

(4) At higher rates of tax of 70 per cent or more there is some evidence (notably from the Break survey and that of Stanbury and Fields) of a net disincentive effect.

Two other conclusions of interest emerge incidentally from many of the surveys. First, there is widespread ignorance about the rates of tax which people are themselves paying. Second, there is a common tendency to assume that taxation is a disincentive until it is pointed out how it may act as an incentive (the income effect); people then reassess their own experience in the light of this realisation.

How do these tentative conclusions match up with the theoretical economic analysis? If the results of the surveys are valid they must mean that for many, indeed most, taxpayers the substitution effect of high income taxation (leading to the substitution of leisure for work at the margin, because the cost of leisure in terms of income has fallen) is either small or/and balanced (or outweighed) by the income effect. The substitution effect would be small where income was only one and not the most important of the motives for undertaking work. Alternatively, the substitution effect might be small if, for some taxpayers, income and leisure were complementary "goods"—i.e. that more leisure without more income is felt not to have much value. The studies by Break and Stanbury and Fields lend some little support to this hypothesis; the postponement of retirement could be attributed to this motive, as also the finding that the *incentive* effects of income taxation were more marked amongst those respondents who practised in London than those in country towns. Professor Break hazards the suggestion that "Quite possibly the pressures—or pleasures—of urban life tend to offset the incentive-inhibiting effects of high tax rates."

Our final point must be to stress that the issue is not the simple one it is commonly supposed to be. The nature of income, the supply of effort and the nature of incentives are all complex. Income needs to be interpreted broadly to include all the monetary returns and special concessions of a non-monetary kind over the lifetime of a worker. Thus, for example, a worker or manager may not be deterred by tax from seeking extra income in the later years of his life because salary levels affect pension provisions. As we pointed out on page 152, the supply of effort is, in Professor Peston's terms, "multi-dimensional".* Moreover the basic theory assumes a choice between work and leisure, in which leisure is assumed to be pleasurable but not work—which is over-simplified; and the theory and all the English studies assume individual decisions on this choice, whereas it may be that often the choice is a joint husband and wife decision relating to their combined effort in paid work. Some little evidence in the United Kingdom, and rather more from America, suggests that the reactions of married women to an increase in tax rates may well be different from that of men and the relative strength of the income and substitution effects is related to the

*M. Peston, Incentives, Distortion and the System of Taxation, in *Taxation Policy*, Crick and Robson (eds.), Pelican, 1973.

income of the husband—the higher the husband's income the stronger the substitution effect for the wife.

Individuals clearly differ from each other in their reaction to income tax, but the position is more subtle than this; the same individual at different times in his life may respond differently to the same tax stimulus. Thus a single man might be more affected by disincentive than incentive effects. For the same man, with a wife and young children, a mortgage and a weight of hire purchase commitments, the incentive effects of income tax might predominate. Twenty years further on, with his house paid for and his children no longer dependent, he might prefer leisure to income in the face of an increase in his marginal tax rate. Because of income tax he might postpone retirement (an incentive effect) but, working after retirement age, he might respond to an increase in his marginal tax by reducing the amount of his day-to-day work effort (a disincentive effect).

Moreover the nature of the tax change may significantly affect the outcome. Thus a tax reduction in the form of a rise in the tax threshold may have different results from a cut in tax rates; and people at or near the margin of the threshold or of different rate bands may react differently from those not liable to be moved onto another rate band by the tax change.

Economic analysis has proved its value in this field at least in a negative way. Extreme views about the effects of tax on work incentives have been shown to be clearly wrong.

We turn now to some related influences—the influence of income tax on choice of job and its location; the effect on do-it-yourself work undertaken in the home and the relationship of taxation and incentives and disincentives to evasion and avoidance.

On the Mobility of Labour

Internal. The general argument is that income taxation reduces both the geographical and occupational mobility of labour within a country; in other words, as a result of the tax, income earners are less willing to move to a job which requires them to change their residence or to incur the costs (in money and leisure) of improving their qualifications to enable them to take a different and better paid job. If this is so, then the effect is to leave people in jobs in which they are making a less valuable contribution to total output than they would have made but for the tax; income tax has distorted their choice of jobs. To put the point in another way, if for any particular post the number of applicants is reduced because some potential applicants are deterred by income tax considerations, the choice of candidates is restricted and there is less chance that the best of the potential applicants will be appointed.

There is *some* higher remuneration at which it is worthwhile for a man to incur the expenses, inconvenience and social costs of removal. Suppose that an additional £1,000 per annum of net income would be such a sum; then if the man in question were paying tax at the 1991–92 basic rate (of 25 per cent) he would need approximately £1,333 gross to make the move worthwhile. If the tax rate was 50 per cent, then £2,000 gross would be necessary. There are thus some posts which would offer the necessary remuneration if there were no tax or if the tax were low but for which it would not be worth his while to apply if there were income tax or if he were paying at a high marginal rate. Similar considerations apply to the costs of improving qualifications or retraining.

The argument is formally valid; but an "income effect" can also be postulated: that if men seek a particular net income, the existence of income tax makes them more willing to accept moves to enable them to climb further up the promotion ladder to reach the desired net of tax salary. There are also considerations such as pension entitlements. As with the effect of income tax on effort, much will depend on individual inclination and motivation. There is no survey evidence to suggest that income tax is a significant deterrent to mobility.

External. The argument here is that high taxation encourages emigration; to be specific, that the existence of high income taxation in Britain has promoted the emigration of well-qualified people, the so-called "Brain Drain". *The Brain Drain—Report of the Working Group in Migration*, 1967* (restricted in its terms of reference to

*Cmnd. 3417.

qualified engineers, technologists and scientists) indicated that most of the emigrants were in the age range 25 to 35 and that higher salaries and better research facilities loomed large in decisions to emigrate. International comparisons of tax levels can be misleading where no account is taken of the nature and benefits of government expenditure; nevertheless it is interesting that a comparison of engineering salaries at three grade and salary points (minimum, mid and maximum) between the U.K. and the U.S.A., showing the effects of tax at the time of the Report, illustrated that the difference in net of tax salaries was in each case significantly less than the difference in gross salaries; and that "the percentage of salary deducted for tax in the U.K. was less at the lowest level but more at the higher levels".

The majority of emigrants would be near minimum salary points, and tax would be unlikely to affect their decision to emigrate; but, as the Report pointed out: "The influence of taxation upon a decision to emigrate is greater in just those cases, comparatively small in numbers though they be, where the effects of emigration cause the greatest loss to the U.K.'s potential for economic growth." The big reduction in the top rates of income tax in 1979 and since has significantly reduced the incentive for top salary earners to emigrate. The Brown/Sandford study referred to above (pp. 158–161) included a question on the emigration and immigration of staff of all levels in the interviewees' firms. The amount of international migration, both ways, was considerable, but primarily for work experience. In only one case was tax mentioned as a cause of emigration and even then the emigrant was said to have left these shores only "partly" for tax reasons.

On the Supply of Labour to Different Occupations

A particular application of the argument that income tax reduces labour mobility was forcefully presented by Merrett and Monk.* They maintained that executive talent was being inefficiently used in the British economy because of the high and progressive income

*A. J. Merrett and D. A. G. Monk, *Inflation, Taxation and Executive Remuneration*, Hallam Press Ltd., 1967.

taxation. They argued that executives (defined as all those in a position in the public or private sectors of the economy to exercise an important influence on the efficiency with which national economic resources are used) were attracted to jobs by a combination of salary and "job environment", i.e. the non-pecuniary advantages such as congeniality of employment, security, freedom from anxiety, geographical location, holidays. At the one extreme the authors saw government service, which they considered to have a highly favourable job environment, and at the other extreme an industry in serious economic difficulties which they considered to offer an unfavourable job environment. In a perfectly competitive market differences in job environment would generate compensating salary differences; but because of the standardised salaries in the public sector there is no free market and because of progressive income taxation it is difficult or impossible for net salary differentials to offer the necessary compensation. To take their example using tax and salary levels appropriate to the mid-1960s: an individual with a gross of tax income of £8,000, who required £2,000 net of tax to provide an incentive to move and compensation for a difference of job environment, would require, at income and surtax rates then ruling, an increase of £7,100 gross of tax. It would be worthwhile for a company to employ him if he added to company profits as much as (or more than) his salary. The £8,000 p.a. man would have to add £15,000; if deemed likely only to add £14,000 he would not be employed and there would be a loss to the community. Thus, "progressive taxation must tend to weaken the efficiency and effectiveness of the price mechanism as regards the allocation of managerial abilities". For similar reasons they argued that the favourable job environment in the public sector probably lead to the recruitment of an inefficiently larger share of the non-industrial graduate talent into public service.

This argument is a useful reminder that the effect of income taxation is to give a disproportionate significance to the nonpecuniary advantages of an occupation. But the authors' demonstration of the job advantages of the public sector rests on nothing more than casual empiricism. The same kind of argument could be presented leading to the precisely opposite conclusion: that the public sector executives suffer job disadvantages;* they are overworked, hamstrung, bound by rigid rules and more stringent financial controls; and, in particular, they do not generally enjoy the non-taxed perquisites of the business executive—meals, phones, cars, trips abroad, top hat pensions, loans at below market interest rates and golden handshakes. On the other hand, the civil servant's inflation-proofed pension has acquired an especial value in recent years, which private industry cannot always match. We need more solid evidence to establish just which are the occupations with the non-taxed advantages which attract a disproportionately large amount of talent as a result of heavy progressive income tax.

Whilst it may not be possible to generalise about this issue as between the private and public sectors of the economy, there may be occupations which, with high tax rates, are relatively attractive because they lend themselves to evasion or avoidance (which we discuss more generally below). Various forms of self-employment may come into this category and occupations in which the producer consumes his own product—which is not usually counted as taxable income, e.g. farmers' consumption of home produced food.

A progressive income tax also militates against occupations with fluctuating earnings, like those of writers, and occupations which carry a high income for a relatively short number of years such as those of athletes or professional boxers; unless the tax includes very comprehensive provisions for averaging, the progressive element in the tax means that the recipients of fluctuating incomes pay more in tax than if their incomes were evenly spread over their lifetime.

These last examples indicate the need for some partial analysis of the effective incidence of income tax to supplement general analysis.

On Do-it-yourself Work and the Division of Labour

Income tax can lead to some break-up of the division of labour and hence to some loss of the advantages associated with division of

---

*For example, the incidental comments in Muddling Up the Mandarins? *The Economist*, 11 May, 1968: "A bright young man does now tend to reach the top earlier in business than in Whitehall . . . the common vice, among good civil servants today, of working far too hard."

labour. As a result of tax, income not spent is worth more than income earned. It thus may pay a person to undertake many tasks for himself which he would prefer to pay someone else to do, and which he would have paid them to do, but for the tax. For example, it may cost £100 to pay a professional decorator to decorate a taxpayer's lounge. If his marginal tax rate is 50 per cent he needs to earn £200 to have £100 after tax for this purpose; if his tax rate is 75 per cent he needs to earn £400—for times as much. A man may find it worthwhile to decorate his lounge himself if the net of tax earnings he could have made in the time it took him to do his own decorating would have been less than £100—even though the gross income would have been much more. Doing his own decorating for these reasons occasions a social loss in that the value of the contribution he would have made to the national output if he had undertaken the extra paid work is more than the value of the decorating.

This same argument applies to a variety of do-it-yourself activities—e.g. joinery, plumbing, bricklaying, car maintenance and growing one's own vegetables.

On Avoidance and Evasion

The higher the marginal rate of tax, the more the advantages which accrue from tax avoidance and the more worthwhile it is for the individual to spend time and money on those activities. Similarly the higher the rates of income tax the more the search for tax-free "perks", and the more resources move into the "tax advising" industry. The issue of tax avoidance is closely linked to that of investment (below).

Avoidance may be closely linked with the disincentive effects of taxation. Given avoidance opportunities, an increase in tax rates may increase avoidance rather than reduce work effort. If the avoidance loopholes are closed, then the response to a higher tax rate may be a reduction in work effort.

Similar considerations apply to tax evasion, which will also be influenced by the likelihood of detection, the level of penalties and moral attitudes. If the tax is perceived by the taxpayer as "unfair", the moral reluctance to evade is reduced.

On Savings, Investment and Enterprise

Heavy income tax reduces the capacity of the taxpayer to save, but whether it reduces his incentive to save is a more open question. As with effort there are two opposing effects. A high income tax makes saving for future income less worthwhile since the income is taxed; the higher the income tax the less the net future income from current saving. On the other hand, anyone saving for a given net future income (say in retirement) will have to save more to achieve his object.

It *is* clear, however, that high income taxation stimulates methods of saving and investment which avoid income tax or reduce tax liability. Income tax concessions for home owner-occupiers and reliefs for pension contributions and savings in special tax free accounts like P.E.P.s and T.E.S.S.A.s (see above p. 142) encourage saving in these forms. Investment which brings capital gains rather than high income yield may be favoured where such gains are untaxed or taxed less heavily than income, as in growth shares and even "investments" yielding no money income but an untaxed income of satisfaction and the possibility of capital gain, e.g. pictures, antiques, foreign stamps.

The Brown/Sandford study (above) also casts some light on the interaction of taxation, avoidance and investment. Their survey generated some evidence to suggest that, as a result of the reduction in income tax rates in the 1988 Budget, on balance, accountants were doing, or expected to do, less tax avoidance work. As always in the real world the situation was complicated rather than simple. At the same time as making tax avoidance less worthwhile by reducing the gains from it, the reduction in tax rates had had a kind of income effect. Because the tax reduction had made some people substantially better off, they now had income to invest and were coming to accountants to seek advice on investing it in a tax efficient way. Also some accountants indicated that they had more tax avoidance work in 1988–89 than in 1987–88 as a temporary situation, because, in the light of the changes (including that to capital gains tax) the portfolios of their clients needed to be re-examined. But, perhaps most significant, as many as 30 per cent of accountants considered that, following the tax reduction, their clients took investment decisions more on their economic merit and less on their tax-saving potential; their approach to investment had undergone a change. As this is a field in which accountants would often have a direct involvement the fact that it was second-hand evidence should not undermine its validity; and, if true, it could mean that lower tax rates mean a significant long-term benefit to an economy in the form of more efficient investment.

We should expect heavy marginal income taxation to act as a deterrent to risk-taking and enterprise. Risk-taking is associated with fluctuating incomes on which, as we have seen, a progressive income tax impinges more heavily than on incomes evenly distributed. The small "entrepreneur" may well feel that the scales are weighted against him; whilst a large business can offset failures against successes because its risks are spread amongst various enterprises and products the small man cannot. At this point it is appropriate to consider more widely the taxation of business incomes, the subject of our next chapter.

Postscript

In the 1992 Budget, confirmed by the result of the General Election, the Chancellor, Mr. Lamont, introduced a new 20 per cent income tax band for the first £2,000 of taxable income. The starting point for higher rate tax, 1992–93, remained at taxable income of £23,700 and the M.C.A. was unchanged at £1,700; the personal allowance was increased in line with inflation to £3,445.

CHAPTER 7

Taxation of Business Income

Where business income is earned by sole traders or by partners in an enterprise it is subject to personal income tax. Where a business is incorporated a special tax regime applies. In the first part of this chapter we examine the taxation of corporate income. We next look at the significance of capital allowances and stock relief in the determination of business income and the incidence of tax on business. Finally we consider the taxation of the income from North Sea oil and gas, in particular the petroleum revenue tax.

Taxation of Corporate Income

A company is a legal entity by means of which a group of shareholders acting in concert, and through a board of directors, can do certain things in common. The income of a company, therefore, is really the income of its shareholders. If distributed in the form of dividends it becomes the shareholders' income without restriction; if undistributed it is still the income of the shareholders, and they may be expected to benefit from the re-investment of it, but individual shareholders cannot freely dispose of it; it is their income only in a technical and restricted sense. Taxes on company profits are therefore a form of income taxation; they may be more or less closely related to the structure of personal income tax. The main issues raised by the taxation of company profits are thrown into relief by the changes in methods of profits taxation in the U.K.

There have been three different structures for company taxation since 1965, each embodying rather different principles. Under the pre-1966 system (in operation from 1937) income tax at the standard rate together with profits tax was paid on both distributed and undistributed profits; but on distributed profits the income tax payment was simply a device for collection at source: if the shareholder was *not* a standard rate income tax payer he claimed a rebate or paid surtax according to his personal circumstances. Thus, essentially, under this system, both distributed and undistributed profits were charged to profits tax; undistributed profits were charged to income tax at the standard rate; distributed profits paid income tax according to the personal circumstances of the shareholders. At the time the profits tax was replaced in 1966, the rate of tax on distributed profits and retentions was the same, at 15 per cent; but there had been periods in which the rate of profits tax on distributed and undistributed profits had differed.

In 1966 a new "corporation tax" was introduced. Under its provisions all corporate profits paid corporation tax (at a rate of 40 per cent when first introduced) whether distributed or not. No further tax was paid on undistributed profits. Income tax was paid on distributed profits according to the personal circumstances of the shareholder (but deducted at the standard rate by the company as a method of collection at source). A corporation tax of this kind, completely separate from income tax (save that the firm was used as a collecting agency) is sometimes referred to as the "classical" system.

In 1973 corporation tax was substantially changed. The rate was increased (to 50 per cent initially) but a proportion of corporation tax was "imputed" to the shareholder on distributions. The imputed corporation tax was equivalent to the basic rate of income tax (30 per cent in 1973) and this counted as a tax credit in the hands of the shareholder. If he was a basic rate taxpayer, no income tax was required of him; if he was in the higher rate bracket he paid additionally; if his income was below the tax threshold, he could claim a rebate.

Thus it can be seen that the classical system of corporation tax completely broke the link with income tax which had existed before 1966, collection of standard rate income tax on dividends remaining only as an administrative device; further, whatever the rates of corporation tax, the 1966 system differentiated in favour of undistributed profits, for distributed profits not only bore the same charges to corporation tax as undistributed, but in addition were subject to income tax (which no longer applied to undistributed profits). The changes in 1973 represented a partial move back towards the 1965 position. A corporation tax separate from income tax was retained, but the discrimination in favour of undistributed profits was removed by allowing a credit on dividends against income tax.

The manner in which the current (1991–92) imputation system of corporation tax works, using 1991–92 rates of corporation tax and income tax, is set out in more detail in Table 7.1. Corporation tax is paid in two stages. When a dividend is paid out to shareholders the

TABLE 7.1
Operation of U.K. Corporation Tax, Imputation System, 1991–92 Rates

Assume			
a. Profit	100		
b. Dividend	30		
Then			
POSITION OF COMPANY			
c. Corporation tax on company:			
i. ACT of ⅓rd of b	(10)		
ii. Mainstream after ACT set off	(23)		
Total (33% of a.)	(33)		
d. Post tax income of company	67		
POSITION OF SHAREHOLDER			
paying tax at:	zero	25%	40%
	(exempt)		
e. Taxable income:			
i. dividend	30	30	30
ii. *plus* tax credit (equal to			
ACT at line c(i))	10	10	10
iii. total taxable income	40	40	40
f. Income tax:			
i. at marginal rate on e(iii)	—	(10)	(16)
ii. less tax credit (e(ii))	10	10	10
iii. net Total of f(i) and f(ii)	10	—	(6)
g. Shareholder's net income after tax			
(e(i) plus f(iii))	40	30	24

company is required to make an advance payment of corporation tax (A.C.T.) which, assuming a 25 per cent basic rate of income tax, is at a rate of $\frac{1}{3}$ (25/75ths) of the dividend paid to the shareholder. This A.C.T. can then be set off against "mainstream" corporation tax, which is paid on all profits, distributed or undistributed, after the end of the accounting period. The shareholder, on his part, will receive a dividend of stated amount which carries with it a tax credit. The credit must be included in his income for tax purposes, but as it will correspond to $\frac{1}{3}$ of the dividend it will satisfy the income tax charge of 25 per cent on the total of dividend plus credit. Thus, the basic rate shareholder has nothing further to pay. A shareholder below the tax threshold can claim payment of the credit. If the shareholder is liable to tax at the higher rate the credit must be included in his total income to assess his liability. For example, if the company had declared and paid a dividend of £75, this would carry a tax credit of £25; liability to higher rates of tax would be on the aggregate of £75 plus £25—£100

Under the corporation tax post 1973 small companies or, strictly speaking, companies with small profits, are given favourable treatment. If profits are below a specified figure, which has been regularly increased over the years, a lower rate of tax is charged. The rate in 1991–92 was 25 per cent (equal to the basic rate of income tax) and the profit limit was £250,000, with marginal relief so that the full average rate of profits tax was not paid until a profit level of £1.25m was reached.

It should be noted that, in the computation of taxable profits, interest payments are treated as a cost, deductible before profits are calculated.

Principles of Profits Taxation

It is clear that two main questions are raised by a consideration of these alternative ways of taxing profits: should there be a link between the taxation of profits and personal income taxation? And should there be a differentiation in favour of undistributed profits?

Should profits tax be linked with income tax? There are really two issues here, the first relating to undistributed profits. As undistributed profits are income of the shareholders, should not they bear income tax? Does not equity demand that undistributed profits should bear the same tax as if they had been distributed? There are two snags to this proposition, one conceptual, one practical. Undistributed profits are *not* equivalent to distributed profits for shareholders, since they cannot freely use them; this would seem to provide some justification for a lower rate of tax on undistributed profits (especially if there is a capital gains tax). Further, it would be very difficult to apply the proposition because shareholders do not all pay the same rate of tax; it would be possible to impute retained profits to shareholders in proportion to their holdings and tax them on the imputed profits at the appropriate personal rates—but this would run counter to the previous argument and would raise a host of practical problems. In the light of these considerations supporters of corporation tax can claim that the best procedure is to abandon the link with income tax and obtain the flexibility which comes from the separation, which allows freedom to adjust income tax without at the same time changing the tax on company profits. Supporters of the old system, while admitting that relating personal income tax to tax on undistributed profits is at best a matter of rough justice, maintain that at least the two should not be too widely divorced.

The second issue relates particularly to distributed profits. If personal income tax is paid on dividends, why should dividends *also* be subject to a heavy corporation profits tax? Is not this a discrimination against a particular source of unearned income? A light profits tax can be considered a payment by the shareholders for the benefits of limited liability (although there is no reason why the contribution should vary with the level of profit). A heavy profits tax is likely to be inequitable as between owners of different forms of property, in particular between the so-called "rentier" (the person who receives fixed interest payments) and the ordinary shareholders who bear the brunt of the profits tax. Moreover, a heavy corporation profits tax infringes the principle of efficiency by distorting the pattern of capital holding through its influence on the relative returns from different forms of capital. One aspect of this distortion is the effect on the "gearing" of companies. Companies can finance activities by debenture stocks (which carry a fixed rate of interest as a contractual obligation to be met before profits are calculated) or by share capital (preference shares, whose holders have first claim to the profits but a fixed maximum, and ordinary shares, whose holders receive the residue of distributed profits if any). A heavy profits tax in addition to income tax leads companies to finance by debentures rather than by ordinary shares. Further, a heavy corporation tax affects the relative attractiveness of unincorporated as against incorporated businesses and may lead to the adoption of the unincorporated form even where it is less suited to the particular kind of enterprise.

Should profits taxation differentiate in favour of undistributed profits? The main argument for the classical corporation tax system, introduced by the Labour government in 1966, was that differentiation in favour of undistributed profits promoted investment in private industry. But it is not *certain* that differentiation will result in more retention and reinvestment of profit, nor, if this happens, is it necessarily *desirable*. It is not certain because company chairmen may pursue a distribution policy aimed at maintaining net of tax dividends; this would mean less retention, not more, but also more payment in tax; the net result on the *total* and *kind* of investment would then depend on how the government used the extra revenue. If there *were* more retention the quality of investment might be adversely affected. Increased retention would be likely to mean a reduced flow of new funds coming into the capital market, with the possibility that growth firms, almost by definition those seeking to expand more rapidly than their own retained profits would permit, might be starved of capital. At the same time differentiation in favour of retained profits might encourage firms to reinvest even when the prospects of return were only moderate. "The survival of the fattest" was how Mr. Heath vividly encapsulated the objections to Labour's 1966 corporation tax.

The changes to corporation tax made by the Conservatives in 1973 were expressly intended to eliminate the advantage of retention and thus encourage distributions. This policy allows more freedom (and more consumption) to the shareholders and may result in a more efficient allocation of resources.

Empirical evidence. The two issues, whether discrimination in favour of undistributed profits results in more investment by firms and, if so, whether reinvestment is of a relatively unprofitable kind, are issues which lend themselves to empirical testing and various attempts have been made to test them in recent years. Professor Whittington concludes from a review of the literature:*

> Fiscal discrimination against dividends probably succeeds in increasing the savings available for investment by companies. The additional retentions are possibly worse allocated between companies (in terms of the profitability of their use) than would be the case if they were allocated through the capital market. However, the empirical evidence offers no grounds for strongly held views on the subject of differential dividend taxation: the issue involves quantitative margins which are too narrow for our present data and techniques to deal with. Nevertheless, strongly held views on the subject will persist, because it arouses prejudices arising from fundamental value judgements concerning the virtues or evils of a free market system.

The Effective Incidence of the Corporation Profits Tax

Answers to many of the queries we have raised depend on how far the effective and the formal incidence of a corporation profits tax coincide. The formal incidence rests on the shareholders. How far, if at all, the corporation profits tax can be passed on to the consumer in the form of higher prices is disputed. The older argument was that, as firms were maximising profits before the tax, they could not improve their profitability by any adjustment of price or output after the tax. Profits were a residual and profits tax could not therefore be passed on to the consumer. Today economists are much less ready to accept that firms generally succeed in maximising their profits or even that they generally seek to maximise them; if a firm's price level was below that at which profits were max-

*Geoffrey Whittington, *Company Taxation and Dividends*, Institute for Fiscal Studies, Lecture Series No. 1, 1974.

imised, it could increase its net of tax profits by raising prices and thus passing part of the tax on to the consumer.

Empirical studies have attempted to determine whether corporation tax is shifted into prices, but the methods have not been free from defects and the results have been contradictory and inconclusive.

What cannot be gainsaid is that major changes have taken place in recent years in the formal weight and distribution of the tax. Although between 1966–67 and 1981–82 the yield of corporation tax trebled in nominal terms, as a proportion of the tax revenues of central government, excluding North Sea oil and gas, it declined over the same period from 15 to 5 per cent. The Green Paper (1982)* estimated that in any one year only about 40 per cent of all companies were currently earning sufficient profits to pay mainstream corporation tax and one third rarely or never paid corporation tax. Partly this situation was due to a major decline in company profits; the average net rate of return on capital employed in industrial and commercial companies fell from about 11 per cent in 1965 to 3 per cent in 1980. Partly it was a product of the reliefs and allowances that had been introduced. However, a reform of 1984 reversed the trend of the previous 30 years of offering major tax or grant incentives for investment. Provision was made for the drastic reduction of capital allowances and the abolition of stock relief. Although, in parallel, the rate of corporation tax was cut to 35 per cent (and since reduced to 33 per cent) the changes, allied to an improvement in profitability, had raised the proportion of corporation tax in central government revenue by the late 1980s to the level of two decades earlier. In the next section we consider capital allowances and stock relief in more detail.

Capital Allowances and Stock Relief

In order to arrive at a proper figure for a firm's profits we need to deduct depreciation or wear and tear allowances. Just how much should be deducted is therefore part of the problem of the definition

Corporation Tax, Cmnd. 8456, January 1982.

of income. In the past, British practice has been to allow depreciation usually on a reducing balance basis (so that, if the permitted rate is 10 per cent of the value of a particular kind of machine, then on a capital asset of £1,000, £100 is written off in the first year, £90, i.e. 10 per cent of £900, in the second, and so on). An alternative method of calculation, used for some purposes in the United Kingdom, is the "straight line" basis by which the asset is depreciated in equal amounts each year (e.g. £1,000 depreciated over 10 years at £100 p.a.).

Depreciation provisions are, however, closely linked with special incentives for investment and vitally affected by inflation. As with the method of taxing companies, there has been no consistency in the provision of investment incentives. In 1945 *Initial Allowances* were introduced, which permitted a larger percentage of the cost of a capital asset to be written off in the year of acquisition. Subsequently, in 1954, *Investment Allowances* were brought in; these were a special allowance in the year of acquisition which were additional to the normal wear and tear allowance (so that in total more than 100 per cent of the value of an asset could be set against profits over the lifetime of the asset).

A major change took place in 1966 when investment allowances were replaced by investment grants—a straight investment subsidy. In making the change the Labour government argued* that grants were more readily taken into account by firms in making investment decisions; that they provided help for new enterprises which had not yet started to earn profits; that they would (after a transition period) mean a speedier reimbursement for firms; and that, as their value did not depend on future tax rates, they provided a greater certainty of benefit. The new measures were associated with increased selectivity. In manufacturing and extractive industries investment grants (of 20 per cent) replaced investment allowances for plant and machinery and special treatment was accorded to ships and computers. Initial allowances were available on plant and equipment not qualifying for grants and on industrial buildings. There were various special provisions for development areas.

Investment Incentives, Cmnd. 2874, 1966.

Where investment grants were given, depreciation allowance was the capital cost minus the amount of grant.

In 1971, after the change of government the previous year, the situation again altered and there was a reversion to allowances. The main arguments used in favour of allowances were that they did not involve the subsidisation of unprofitable firms (which could happen with grants); and that they could be administered by the Inland Revenue as part of the tax system. The investment grants scheme had been administered by the department responsible for industry and had required the setting up and staffing of a number of regional offices. In 1972 grants were reintroduced, but only for development areas. (In contrast to 1966, these grants did not reduce the base for annual depreciation allowances.)

Before the reform of 1984, the position on the main capital allowances was that first year or initial allowances of 100 per cent were given for plant, machinery and new ships. Industrial buildings received a 75 per cent initial allowance with 4 per cent annual writing down allowances (straight line basis). In addition there was a wide variety of provision for other specified forms of investment.

Where depreciation or capital allowances are based on historic cost, the allowance over the lifetime of the asset is insufficient to replace it when prices are rising. Thus an effect of inflation is to exaggerate the real profit position of the firm. The larger the proportion of an asset that can be written off in the first year the less will be this distorting effect of inflation, for more of the allowance is given in currency equal, or nearly equal, in value to that with which the asset was bought. Another problem generated by inflation relates to stocks. In any trading period a firm can reduce its excess of revenue over costs by building up its stocks of materials. Hence changes in the value of stocks are taken into account in calculating taxable profits. But stocks may appreciate either because of an increase in physical volume or because of a rise in the price of the stocked items. Following a period of particularly rapid inflation a special scheme of stock relief was introduced in 1975 to ease the liquidity position of firms. The 1975 scheme, introduced as a temporary measure, based relief on the difference between the closing and opening stocks of a business, reduced by a percentage of profits. If the value of business stocks fell, relief previously given was withdrawn by way of a tax charge (the "clawback"). The measure was deficient in that it failed to distinguish that part of the stock appreciation resulting from price rises and that from a bigger volume of stocks. Moreover, with the onset of recession and heavy de-stocking by industry, the clawback posed serious problems for firms. Thus, after the issue of a consultative document, the 1981 Finance Act provided for a new scheme of relief, to apply as from November, 1980. Broadly speaking, it was based on the opening value of stocks (less £2,000) and was computed by applying to this value the percentage increase in a special all-stocks index which reflected only price changes. No clawback applied except where a business ceased or came close to cessation.

One problem arising from this measure and the generous capital allowances granted has been the accumulation of a huge sum of unused allowances and relief. A company which incurs a loss in its trading may set the loss against previous income of an immediately preceding period of equal length or against future profits; where 100 per cent first year allowances have contributed to the loss, the value of the unused allowances may be carried back and set against income of the previous 3 years. Losses not used in this way may be carried forward for use against the trading profits of the company in future years, subject to the limitation that losses due to the 1975 form of stock relief cannot be carried forward for more than 6 years. Hence the situation, described in the 1982 Green Paper and outlined above by which only a minority of companies were regularly paying mainstream corporation tax.

All this changed with the reform of 1984, which had two related components. The 100 per cent capital allowances and 75 per cent initial allowances were to be phased out and replaced by 25 per cent reducing balance depreciation allowances for plant and machinery and 4 per cent straight line allowances for industrial buildings; and stock relief was abolished. At the same time the rate of corporation tax was to be reduced in stages so that from 52 per cent in 1984 it fell to 35 per cent in 1986.

The changes owed much to the view that the high capital allowances had led to much investment of poor quality. The new allowances were much closer to true economic depreciation and brought the tax system closer to economic neutrality in respect of different forms of investment. On the other hand the total incentive for investment was reduced and, with the abolition of stock relief and initial allowances, businesses were much more vulnerable to inflation.

In Chapter 13 we have more to say about the effect of inflation on business in the context of inflation and the tax system generally.

Taxation of North Sea Oil and Gas

The exclusive right to search for and extract petroleum in Britain, under its territorial sea and outside territorial waters where the United Kingdom has rights by international agreement, was granted to the British Crown by Acts of 1934 and 1964. The Secretary of State for Energy exercises the discretion to grant licences for exploration and production and to determine the conditions attaching to those licences. The first "round" of production licences took place in 1964 and there have been a succession of rounds since then, with varying terms. The provisions for oil also apply to mineral and natural gas except for gas sold to the British Gas Corporation under a contract pre June 30, 1975.

The problem with the North Sea oil fields is to devise a financial structure which encourages exploration and production, including production in marginal fields, whilst at the same time ensuring a "reasonable" take for the state. The reconciliation of these objectives has been attempted by means of four levies on the oil companies:

(1) Royalty payments
(2) Petroleum Revenue Tax (P.R.T.)
(3) Corporation Tax
(4) Supplementary Petroleum Duty (S.P.D.).

Royalty payments. Up to 1982 a royalty payment was levied on the sale of all oil from the North Sea. The royalty was paid every 6 months at the rate of $12\frac{1}{2}$ per cent. A royalty constitutes a basic payment irrespective of the size or profitability of the oil field. The danger with such a levy is that it may restrict exploration and production, especially in less promising fields. Because of concern on this count, the 1983 Budget provided that royalties for fields licensed after April 1982 should be abolished.

Petroleum Revenue Tax. P.R.T. came into operation in 1975, following the huge rise in oil prices in 1973 and the beginning of 1974, which was expected to generate windfall profits for the off shore oil producers. P.R.T. was originally introduced at a rate of 45 per cent; it applied to profits in each field, treated separately. In order to encourage production in small marginal fields it was enacted that, for each field, irrespective of size, 1 million tons per annum should be free of P.R.T. subject to a maximum aggregate of 10 million tons. This allowance was divided amongst the producers exploiting the field in proportion to their output.

The P.R.T. also included a "safeguard" provision limiting the proportion of profits (calculated in a specific way) which might be taken in tax.

A number of features distinguish the base of P.R.T. from that of corporation tax. It is calculated six monthly. Both income and expenditure are computed according to carefully prescribed rules to define the part of the company's activities which relate to its exploration and extraction operations and thus the resulting figures have no direct linkage to company accounts. P.R.T. ignores the distinction between capital and revenue account vital in computing corporation tax liability. As already mentioned P.R.T. is on a "field by field" basis; each company having an interest in a particular field is assessed separately in relation to its operations in that field; thus any company engaged in operations in different fields will have as many assessments as the number of fields it engages in. Subject to limited exceptions, a company cannot offset losses in one field against profits in another. In computing allowable cost there is a special provision by which, broadly speaking, capital expenditure on a field qualifies for "uplift", an addition to qualifying expenditure originally set at 75 per cent; thus a firm could offset 175 per cent of its capital expenditure against taxable profits.

P.R.T. is a prior charge over corporation tax—it is calculated without reference to corporation tax; royalty payments are deductible as a cost.

Since its introduction P.R.T. has been the subject of numerous changes. As from January 1, 1979 the rate of tax was raised to 60 per cent. At the same time the rate of "uplift" on capital expenditure was reduced from 75 to 35 per cent and the oil allowance was halved. As from January 1, 1980 the rate of P.R.T. was further increased to 70 per cent. In his 1982 budget the Chancellor of the Exchequer provided that when Supplementary Petroleum Duty (below) ceased at the end of 1982, the rate of P.R.T. would rise to 75 per cent. The Finance Act 1980 provided for advance payments on account of P.R.T. at the rate of 15 per cent of the tax calculated to be due for the previous payment period. Further advance payments, representing an acceleration of existing tax, were provided for on the abolition of S.P.D. and, as from mid-1983, payments of P.R.T. were to be made on a monthly instalment basis to ensure a more even flow of revenue into the Exchequer. The 1983 Budget eased the position for companies by providing for the earlier phasing out of advanced P.R.T. restoring the oil allowance for new fields to its previous level and giving additional relief for expenditure on searching for and appraising new fields allowing it to be offset against P.R.T. on existing fields. In 1987 the field by field principle was further breached when a new "cross field" allowance was introduced. The 1987 Budget also permitted *general* expenditure on research and development to be offset against P.R.T. after a three year delay period.

Corporation Tax. The profits of the oil producing companies are subject to the ordinary corporate profits tax, which is calculated after deduction of royalties, if any, P.R.T. and S.P.D. when applicable. The main qualification is the adoption of what is known as the "ring fence" approach by which profits gained in the extraction and exploitation of oil cannot be used to offset losses from other trading activities; trading losses (including capital allowances) in respect of ring fence activities may be offset against profits from non-ring fence activities according to normal corporation tax rules.

Supplementary Petroleum Duty. Between April 1981 and the end of

1982 a Supplementary Petroleum Duty was charged at the rate of 20 per cent on the total value of oil produced after deduction of the P.R.T. exemption limit. The S.P.D. was regarded as a temporary measure pending a review of the workings of P.R.T.

It will be seen from this account that the system of taxing North Sea oil has been subject to manifold changes since its inception. From 1975 until 1982 taxation became heavier and more complex. Then the process was put into reverse, so that new fields licensed after April 1982 were subject only to P.R.T. and Corporation tax and have benefited from a series of easements in the rules. The changes represented in part a striving to obtain the maximum oil revenues for the state compatible with the discovery and exploitation of the oil fields, especially the smaller, marginal fields. But they owe as much to expediency as to principle—with governments responding to their own revenue needs, to pressures from the oil companies and to fluctuations in international oil prices.

The yield of P.R.T. has been subject to rapid change. From 1978–79, when the first revenue was obtained, together with S.P.D., it rose quickly to reach a peak of £7.2bn in 1984–85 (8.1 per cent of central government revenue excluding national insurance contributions). By 1986–87 it had slumped to £1.21bn (1.2 per cent). The estimated return for 1990–91 (*Financial Statement and Budget Report*) is £0.9bn (0.7 per cent).

CHAPTER 8

Outlay or Expenditure Taxation

An outlay (or expenditure) tax is levied on the purchase, use or enjoyment of a particular good or service. It may be assessed on the capital value of a good, e.g. purchase tax or value added tax (V.A.T.) or on the annual value, e.g. the local rate assessed on the annual value of real property. The amount of the tax may vary directly with the capital value of the good, as with V.A.T which is *ad valorem* (proportional to price); or tax may be "specific"—a sum fixed according to the quantity or weight of a particular good (e.g. excise duty on petrol) or group of related goods (e.g. motor vehicle licences on private cars at the same rate per car). Outlay taxes may be levied on single-use goods, which once used are all used up; the bulk of central government revenue from outlay taxation comes from this variety, notably tobacco, alcoholic drinks and petrol; or outlay taxes may be on durable-use goods, which can go on being used for a considerable period of time, e.g. V.A.T. on cars, refrigerators or cameras

An important analytical distinction is between outlay taxes on consumers' goods and outlay taxes on producers' "goods", i.e. the resources, including labour, which help to make the consumers' goods. We shall examine each separately, though it is possible for particular taxed goods to be either according to their use; thus petrol for private motoring is a consumers' good, whilst petrol for a lorry is a producers' good.

Outlay Taxes on Consumers' Goods

A tax on a particular good or service will have effects on the general level of prices, consumption and saving; but its most pronounced effect is likely to be on the production and consumption of the taxed good and related goods. Hence we will first examine the incidence of outlay taxes by means of partial or micro analysis.

Incidence—Micro Analysis

The formal incidence of an outlay tax is on the consumer of the taxed product and is the difference between the market price paid by the consumer and the factor cost. Factor cost is the payment to the factors of production (broadly, wages, salaries, interest, rent and profit) which have combined to put the good into the hands of the consumer. However, the formal incidence tells us only a small part of the story. A tax will usually alter both market price and factor cost; as a result of the tax consumers may substitute other goods for the taxed commodity and resources engaged in producing the taxed good may transfer to other lines of production. The extent of these adjustments is measured by the elasticity of demand and supply.

Elasticity is the response of demand (or supply) to a change in price. We can measure it numerically for small changes in price* by the simple relationship:

$$\frac{\text{percentage change in amount demanded}}{\text{percentage change in price}}$$

If the percentage change in amount demanded is greater than the percentage change in price, demand is said to be *elastic* (numerically, greater than one). If the percentage change in amount demanded is less than the percentage change in price, demand is *inelastic* (less than one). If a percentage change in price gives rise to the same percentage change in amount demanded, elasticity is *unity*. If the amount demanded is unchanged following a change in price

---

*Elasticity normally varies throughout the length of a curve; hence this measure of elasticity is only meaningful for *small* price changes.

demand is *absolutely inelastic* (zero elasticity). Similarly with supply, which is elastic, inelastic or of unity elasticity if a small change in price gives rise to a greater, smaller or the same proportional change respectively; if there is no change in supply following a change in price supply is absolutely inelastic.

Elasticity of demand depends mainly on the availability of close substitutes; elasticity of supply measures the ease with which resources can be transferred elsewhere.

The effect of a tax on commodities with different elasticities of demand and supply can best be shown diagrammatically with demand and supply curves. A demand curve shows the amounts of a commodity which would be bought in a given period of time at various prices; a supply curve, the amounts which producers would supply at various prices. It is assumed that market conditions are "perfectly competitive", which implies a large number of producers of identical products.*

Figure 8.1 shows a demand curve (*D-D*) and a supply curve (*S-S*) for a commodity; both demand and supply curves have an elasticity of around unity *at the current price level*. *OM* is the amount being bought and sold at *P* the market price. *Q* is the equilibrium point given by the intersection of the demand and supply curves. A specific tax (*VT*) is imposed on each unit of the commodity. This can be shown by raising the supply curve vertically by *VT*. A new equilibrium is now reached at *V*, giving price *P¹* at which *OM¹* will be bought and sold. *P¹* is above *P* but not to the full extent of the tax. Some customers have moved elsewhere, some resources have left the industry. Rectangle *OP¹VM¹* represents the total amount paid for the goods after tax, of which *ORTM¹* is the amount going as payment to the factors of production and *RP¹VT* the revenue going to the exchequer.

The higher the elasticity of demand the more the reduction in amount purchased and the less the rise in price following the tax

---

*The effective incidence of an outlay tax can be shown diagrammatically for other market conditions, but the theory is more complicated, e.g. readers with some knowledge of economics will appreciate that under monopoly the marginal cost curve (the equivalent of the supply curve) is raised by the amount of tax per unit; the resulting output and price are determined by the intersection of the marginal cost and marginal revenue curves, assuming that the monopolist is maximising profits.

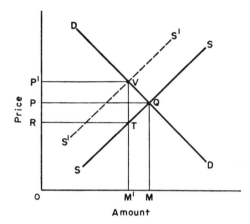

FIG. 8.1 Perfect competition.

imposition (given the elasticity of supply) because the high elasticity of demand implies the existence of close substitutes to which consumers turn. At the other extreme, if demand is absolutely inelastic (a vertical demand curve) there are no close substitutes, price rises by the full extent of the tax and output remains unchanged.

Given the demand curve, the more elastic is supply the more price will rise, because the factors of production can readily transfer elsewhere. If the factors are "specific" to the industry (e.g. specialised equipment which cannot be used elsewhere) supply will be relatively inelastic and price will rise little, supply contract little. Situations for different elasticities of demand and supply are illustrated in Figs. 8.2–8.5.

Elasticity of demand and supply varies according to the time allowed to adjust to a change in price. Demand and supply curves as usually drawn represent the situation after full adjustment; but we can draw curves to show the situation of only partial adjustment.* In general the longer the time allowed for readjustment the

---

*Readers familiar with the Marshallian period analysis will appreciate that we can in theory distinguish the impact, short period, quasi-long period and long period situations with their differing elasticities.

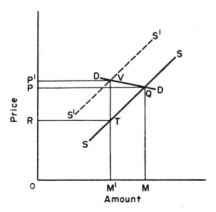

Fɪɢ. 8.2 Elastic demand. Small price rise—large reduction in supply.

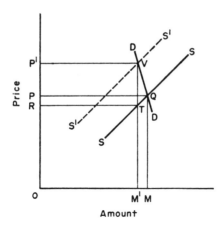

Fɪɢ. 8.3 Inelastic demand. Large price rise—small reduction in supply.

more elastic will be both the demand and the supply curves. On the demand side the longer people have to look around the more likely they are to find substitutes for the taxed good. On the supply side the longer the time period the more resources can be transferred elsewhere because as specific equipment wears out it need not be

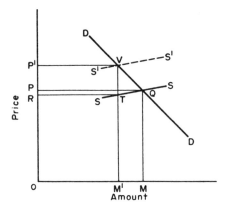

FIG. 8.4 Elastic supply. Large price rise—large reduction in supply.

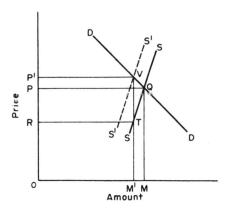

FIG. 8.5 Inelastic supply. Small price rise—small reduction in supply.

replaced by the same kind of equipment. There can be exceptions to the rule that elasticity of demand is larger the longer the time allowed for readjustment. It is possible that a big increase in the tax on a commodity, say tobacco, might lead many consumers to vow to give up smoking. They might cut their purchases initially, but after unsuccessfully searching for a substitute break their vow and return to their earlier level of consumption or something near it. This kind of extreme and often unsustained reaction to a tax has been called a "demonstration" effect.

The situation for an *ad valorem* tax can be similarly demonstrated diagrammatically. As the tax is proportional to price the S^1-S^1 curve diverges from the S-S curve as the supply curve rises; otherwise the analysis is identical.

Implications of the Micro Analysis

It is clear from the above analysis that the imposition of an outlay tax on consumers' goods may have a number of possible results on price and output. Only if all commodities had either supply curves that were infinitely elastic (horizontal) in the long run or demand curves that were absolutely inelastic (vertical) would price always rise by the full amount of the tax; and these conditions are far from being universal.

A further conclusion follows: that (save in the case of absolutely inelastic demand) taxes on outlay goods involve a loss of satisfaction to the consumer by the distortion of consumer choice, over and above the gain to the exchequer. Given the contribution to be made to the revenue, an outlay tax on a good the demand for which is not absolutely inelastic involves an excess loss of satisfaction as compared with a lump sum tax which had no distorting effect on choice. If, however, outlay tax is levied on a good of absolutely inelastic demand, there is no such excess loss. This can be demonstrated as follows: suppose in situation I there is an outlay tax on A, a commodity of absolutely inelastic demand. Then, situation II, the tax is transferred to B, a commodity of elastic demand, and imposed at that level which maintains the yield to the exchequer. Then in situation II purchases of A remain unchanged and purchases of B fall, more of commodities X, Y, Z being purchased by consumers. But it was open to consumers to buy less of B and more of X, Y, Z in situation I and they did not do so. Therefore II must represent a less preferred situation to I.

Similarly on the production side; if demand is absolutely inelastic resources do not have to move out of the industry. The object of taxation is to release resources from private for public use, so that any tax imposition must be expected to lead to a transfer of factors of production; but where additional taxation is concentrated on a commodity the demand for which is elastic, the redeployment is disproportionately concentrated on one industry and cannot be met by marginal changes which do not seriously affect any single industry (including redirection of the flow of new resources into the economic system). Where the tax is on a commodity the supply of which is perfectly elastic, although resources move from the industry, they can move with such ease that no losses are incurred by the producers.*

However, there are circumstances in which it may be desirable to concentrate effects on one commodity or a group of related commodities. First consider the situation outlined in Chapter 1, where the production of a good gives rise to social costs over and above the private costs, which in the absence of government action would result in an extension of the output of that industry beyond the level justified by the benefits derived. The effect of an outlay tax may then be to bring private costs nearer to the social costs and curtail output to nearer the appropriate level.†

Second, outlay taxation can be used as an instrument of economic regulation, where *particular* resources need to be transferred elsewhere. Thus if a threat to national security led to the need for rapid rearmament, then additional outlay taxes on, say, consumer durables using iron and steel, like motor cars and washing machines, would release appropriate resources quickly. Similarly, an export drive might be stimulated if taxes were imposed in the home market on goods for which there was a large export potential.

Finally, it must be recognised that our analysis of the effective incidence of outlay taxes rested on the somewhat unreal assumptions of perfect competition. Where markets differ in their degrees of

---

*Students familiar with the analysis will appreciate that the losses to consumers and producers can be measured by changes in the consumer and producer surpluses.
†The reverse argument can, of course, also apply; that where there are social benefits over and above private benefits, subsidisation may be appropriate. As we pointed out in Chapter 1, identifying and quantifying the social costs and benefits is difficult.

competitiveness of where employers are producing at price and output levels which do not maximise profits, outlay taxes could promote price and output levels in a particular industry which were nearer the optimum. But such industries would be difficult if not impossible to identify.

Incidence—Macro Analysis

Outlay taxes also affect the general level of prices, consumption, saving and incomes. In Chapters 11 and 12 we examine the outlay taxes of the United Kingdom in relation to the distribution of incomes and to budgetary policy to maintain employment and avoid inflation. If, indeed, outlay taxes are levied on goods of absolutely inelastic demand then their economic significance derives solely from their effect on the economy as a whole, including the supply of the factors of production; we shall examine these effects subsequently when we compare income and outlay taxes.

Outlay Taxes on Factors of Production

An outlay tax on a factor of production raises the supply price of consumers' goods which use that factor and thus affects the price and output of consumers' goods in ways similar to those of a tax on the product, varying with the elasticity of demand and supply. But there are additional considerations. A tax on a factor of production also raises the price of the factor relatively to other factors and promotes factor substitution. Thus, if a tax is imposed on one sort of fuel and not on others, this encourages the substitution of other fuels for the taxed fuel. Similarly, a tax on labour will promote the substitution of capital for labour. The more readily substitution can take place, the less will be the rise in price of the factor and of the product.

In general there is a presumption against the taxation of factors of production. Both the formal and effective incidence of such taxes is difficult to unravel and hence, if factors are taxed, the government may have more difficulty in pursuing a clear fiscal strategy for regulating the economy and certainly will find it harder to follow a consistent policy on income distribution. Moreover, taxes on factors of production, entering into industrial costs, can be less easily rebated on exports than taxes on final products and hence exports may suffer.

However, some goods, like petrol, are both consumers' and producers' goods and are taxed whichever way they are used; to try to distinguish, say, petrol bought by a travel salesman as part of his work and petrol for private motoring would create administrative difficulties and invite evasion except in so far as the tax was part of a value added tax in which all tax on business inputs can be offset against output tax (see below). Moreover, the general presumption against taxes on factors of production has not inhibited governments, at any rate in recent years, from taxing the use of labour. National health and national insurance contributions paid by employees or the self-employed can be regarded as a particular form of income tax, but employers' contributions are an outlay tax on a factor of production even though, in the long run, the effect may be to reduce employee's incomes and hence can be thought of as a form of income tax on the employee. It can be disputed how far these insurance payments should be regarded as taxes. In Britain the national insurance fund is administered by the Department of Health and Social Security, the accounts are kept separate from the ordinary estimates and appropriation accounts and the insurance principle relates payment and benefit for the employee if not for the employer. However, the levies are compulsory (except for the additional payments under the graduated contribution scheme) and their incidence is similar to that of a corresponding tax. Indeed, in 1977 Mr. Healey, as Chancellor, imposed a surcharge of 2 percentage points on the employers' contributions which was specifically intended as a tax to contribute to general government revenue. Further, whatever view is taken of the national insurance contributions there is no doubt that the Selective Employment Tax (S.E.T.) 1966–73 which used the national insurance administrative procedure for payment was an outlay tax on the use of labour. We shall return to the question of national insurance contributions in Chapter 15.

Where an outlay tax applies to a factor of production used in a very limited industrial sector, much of the analysis of its incidence will appropriately be partial or micro, concerned with its effects on a small group of industries. Where the tax applies to a factor of production of widespread use, partial analysis gives precedence to general; and where the factor is universally used, as with labour on which national insurance contributions are paid, general or macro analysis is the order of the day.

U.K. Outlay Taxes

Our programme in this section, therefore, is first to examine the continuing big revenue yielders oil, alcohol and tobacco; then to concentrate on V.A.T., explaining how it works and the arguments for and against it as compared with the taxes it replaced and a possible alternative, a retail sales tax.

Drink, Tobacco and Oil

Table 5.2 (p. 119) shows that in 1990–91 the excise duties on tobacco and on alcoholic drinks each yielded around £5bn. Some idea of the significance of their contribution to revenue can be gained from the realisation that each of them yielded about 50 per cent more than the combined revenue from death duties and capital gains tax. The excise tax on the consumption of hydrocarbon oils yielded almost £10bn, 6.7 per cent of central government tax revenue (excluding national insurance contributions). Indeed, these figures understate the contribution of duties on oil, alcoholic drinks and tobacco to revenue, because they are also subject to V.A.T.

The weight of tax on tobacco, petrol and alcoholic drinks poses the question whether it is right that the government should rely so heavily upon these three. It can be argued that their incidence is unequal amongst different consumer-taxpayers; they penalise consumers according to the particular nature of their pleasures. On the other hand, on two of the criteria suggested they come out well. The evidence suggests that the demand for these commodities is very inelastic; consumption has held up well against successive tax increases. A decline in beer consumption reflects a change in tastes rather than a response to tax, for it has been counterbalanced by an increase in wine consumption; and recent falls in tobacco sales probably owe more to health campaigns than to tax.

Then, for all of them, it can be argued that there are social costs of consumption over and above what is paid to the producers. The evidence strongly suggests that smoking helps to cause lung cancer and other chest and heart complaints; and these throw a burden on the community (apart from the victim and his family) through increased health service and dependency charges. Similarly alcoholic drinking may increase the incidence of some illnesses and cause social costs in the form of increased road accidents (which may result from drunken pedestrians and cyclists as well as drunken drivers who can be more readily convicted since the introduction of breathalyser tests). Also both smoking and drunkenness in public places can cause less tangible unpleasantness to other persons. It would be incorrect to suggest that these factors were responsible for the introduction of heavy taxes on drink and tobacco; but in a very general way (for there has been no attempt to quantify these social costs) they are some justification for their continuance.* Motoring also brings its social costs in the form of air pollution, noise and additional hazards; the need to develop and maintain an extensive and elaborate road network; and redevelopment in towns to accommodate the motor car. There have induced been various suggestions and even some abortive attempts to apply in the past a benefit of service principle by which revenue from the motorist is matched up with expenditure on the roads. But to do so would not cover all the social costs; nor is there any reason why the motorist should not be taxed over and above the revenue required for road building and maintenance. Currently by means of petrol tax, vehicle licences, car tax and V.A.T. motorists pay much more in tax than the total of expenditure on roads.

Another more serious ground on which the emphasis on these

---

*For a fuller consideration of the arguments for and against special taxation of alcoholic drinks and tobacco products, see J. W. O'Hagan, The Rationale for Special Taxes on Alcohol: A Critique, *British Tax Review*, 1983, No. 6 and J. W. O'Hagan and K. M. Carey, The Proposal for Upward Alignment of Tobacco Taxes in the European Community, *British Tax Review*, 1988, No. 8.

three taxes can be criticised is that of ability to pay. Evidence from the government's Family Expenditure Survey* suggests that tobacco tax is clearly regressive; overall, taxes on alcoholic drinks are slightly regressive (with beer taxes definitely regressive, taxes on spirits proportional and taxes on wines mildly progressive); taxes on oil are mildly progressive. However, individual taxes ought not to be condemned for regressiveness; what matters is the distribution of the tax burden as a whole.

Value Added Tax

Value added tax in the United Kingdom was introduced on April 1, 1973. It replaced purchase tax and Selective Employment Tax (S.E.T.). Purchase Tax was introduced during the Second World War and levied at the wholesale stage on a wide range of goods, but with exceptions including most food, drink, essential drugs, newspapers and books, and products already covered by excises. It was levied at several rates; whilst the number and level had varied at different times since its inception in 1940, in 1970 there were four rates ranging from 13¾ per cent to 55 per cent.

S.E.T. was an innovation of Mr. Callaghan, as Labour Chancellor of the Exchequer. As introduced in 1966 it was, in essence, a capitation tax paid in respect of each employee by employers in the construction, distribution and service industries; but the method of administration was that all employees paid the tax along with the national insurance contribution and it was then refunded to all except those in the construction, distribution and service industries. There were differential rates of tax for men, women, boys and girls. It was, from the first, a highly controversial tax which aroused strong opposition and the Conservatives in Opposition had pledged themselves to repeal it.

The Conservative government wished to join the European Economic Community and entry carried with it the obligation to introduce a V.A.T., which had become the general sales tax of the Community; but Conservative ministers maintained that they

*See Chapter 11.

would have wished to introduce a V.A.T. anyway as a superior form of general expenditure tax.

V.A.T. is, in essence, a single tax on the value of goods and services consumed in the home market, but it takes on a complicated appearance because its collection is multi-stage. Tax is collected at every stage of production and distribution on the "value added" by each firm; value added is the difference between the prices (net of tax) at which the firm sells its products and the prices (net of tax) which it paid for the raw materials, electricity, equipment, specialised services and products, which it bought from other firms. The combined value added by all firms is the price (net of tax) paid by the final consumer. There are, in principle, several alternative methods of calculating and taxing value added, but the one almost invariably used, and that employed in the United Kingdom and throughout the European Community, is the credit or invoice method. A business registered for V.A.T. pays tax on the value of its inputs/purchases and charges tax on the value of its outputs/sales. Each producer is credited with tax paid then passes to the Customs & Excise the difference between output tax and input tax. Imports are assessed to the V.A.T. at the borders, export sales are not liable to tax (i.e. are zero-rated).

As introduced in Britain in 1973, V.A.T. had a standard rate of 10 per cent on all goods and services except for those products which were zero-rated or exempt.

When a product is zero-rated, input tax is paid but no output tax; the supplier is then entitled to recover from the Customs and Excise the full amount of input tax. Foodstuffs, books and newspapers, fuel and power, new construction, transport and exports were all zero-rated in 1973; also children's clothing, footwear, and a limited range of foodstuffs (like confectionery, ice-creams and crisps) which had previously carried purchase tax were added to the zero-rated goods at the last minute.

Certain goods and services were exempted and small traders with a turnover below a specified annual limit were also exempt. Exempt suppliers pay tax on inputs but do not have to account to the Customs and Excise for tax on their output; they cannot therefore invoice tax on their output although they may attempt to pass on input tax in the price of the products they sell. Exemption is not always an advantage. For example, if an exempt trader of a good normally liable at standard rate sells to a final consumer, then the exemption is an advantage; he can pass on input tax and have a competitive edge over the non-exempt supplier of the same good. But if he wishes to sell to another registered trader, then he is at a disadvantage since that trader will prefer to be invoiced for V.A.T. which he can then offset as input tax against his output tax payments to Customs and Excise. Exempt goods include rent, insurance, postal services provided by the Post Office, banking, education, health, burials and cremations.

When V.A.T. was introduced, certain other adjustments were made. The Chancellor did not wish to forego any of the large revenue from purchase tax on cars, and therefore introduced a special car tax of 10 per cent at the wholesale stage so that this tax and V.A.T. together would continue to bring in much the same revenue on cars as before. Customs and Excise duty on tobacco and alcoholic drinks was reduced when V.A.T. was introduced in order to offset the effect of it on these products.

Table 8.1 presents a somewhat over-simplified example of the operation of V.A.T. and attempts to bring out the differences between standard rating, zero-rating and exempt products. Because it is over-simplified, three warnings must be given about interpreting it. Firstly, the example assumes that the various suppliers at the first stage of production themselves have no input tax — and this would not be true. Secondly, the example may give the impression that it is necessary under V.A.T. to follow through the history of particular purchased goods. This is not so. Total tax paid on inputs is deducted from total tax collected on sale of outputs on an overall basis. Whenever goods are sold the invoices must indicate separately the value of the goods and the V.A.T. These invoices are then the basis of the claim to tax credit by the purchaser. Returns are normally submitted quarterly. Firms which are regularly entitled to rebates (because of zero-rating) are allowed to submit monthly.

Thirdly, the example might appear to suggest that prices must necessarily rise by the extent of tax, i.e. that each supplier is able to

TABLE 8.1
Simplified Example of Operation of V.A.T.

	Input price	Value added	Output price	Paid to Revenue	Tax
STANDARD RATING					
S supplies M	—	200	220	by S	20
M buys from S	220	400	660	by M	40
W buys from M	660	100	770	by W	10
R buys from W	770	300	1,100	by R	30
C buys from R	1,100	—	—	—	—
ZERO RATING at retail stage					
R buys from W	770	300	1,000	paid to R	(70)
C buys from R	1,000				
EXEMPTION at retail stage					
R buys from W	770	300	1,070*	by R	0
C buys from R	1,070*				

Note: In practice a standard-rate trader deducts input tax on all purchases from output tax on all purchases for each V.A.T. period (3 months in the U.K.) As an expository device to show inter-relationships, this example follows particular goods through the production/distribution stages.

Assumptions: "S" has no inputs; tax is wholly passed forward; one-standard V.A.T. rate of 10%.

S=supplier of raw materials, M=manufacturer, W=wholesaler, R=retailer, C=consumer.

* Assumes R passes all input tax forward to C in the price. (It cannot be specified as tax and any trading purchaser cannot deduct it as input tax.)

pass forward to the consumer the full amount of tax and that no burden falls on the supplier. This is true in terms of the formal incidence; the tax as the difference between market price and factor cost is always met by the ultimate consumer. But if we look at the effective incidence of the tax, then we have to recognise that its imposition may have altered factor cost, e.g. by reducing profitability in the short-run. What happens will depend on the elasticity of demand and supply of the good as indicated earlier in this chapter for outlay taxes in general.

Three main advantages have been claimed for V.A.T. as compared with purchase tax and S.E.T., and compared also to other general sales taxes at the wholesale or manufacturing levels. V.A.T. is a very efficient mechanism to prevent the spill-over of tax on business inputs into costs and prices. V.A.T. paid on all component goods and services bought in by firms is automatically deducted from the tax they hand over to Customs and Excise which they have collected on the sale of their goods and services. This avoids the double tax element which occurred under purchase tax and S.E.T. by which, for example, tax may be paid on purchases by a firm (e.g. purchase tax on stationery) and also paid on the final product. (This element of tax on tax was even more significant under the cascade turnover taxes in operation in most of the original E.E.C. countries before V.A.T. was introduced.) It means also that there is no taxation of investment; tax payments on purchases of investment goods are credited against tax receipts from sales; if a firm buys more investment goods its credits rise relatively to its tax receipts; only as new investment makes its contribution to output does tax become payable on the products. There is also the benefit to exports and import substitution. Exports are zero-rated, which means that no V.A.T. is charged, but input tax is recovered by the exporter; V.A.T. does not subsidise exports but it removes any tax disadvantage which might arise from a general sales tax. Although there was no purchase tax on final products exported, there might be a spill-over of S.E.T. and purchase tax on inputs which could not be rebated. Similarly there is an advantage in terms of import substitution; the spill-over of taxes into the costs of goods sold in the home market is rebated with V.A.T., putting them on equal terms with imports on which V.A.T. is levied at the entry point.

In retrospect, the argument that V.A.T. has balance of payments advantages compared with purchase tax and S.E.T. appears formally valid, save for one minor exception, but is not very important. It is not important because the balance of payments benefit is small.* The minor exception is that where exempt services are exported or exempt traders export directly or sell to exporters, there *is* an element of V.A.T. which finds its way into export prices. More

---

*Just before the introduction of V.A.T. a calculation of the *National Institute Economic & Social Review* suggested that the benefit to the balance of payments might be some £20 million.

significant, however, is the general point, especially important for trade between members of the E.E.C., that the comparative accuracy with which input tax is excluded from business costs under V.A.T. removes any suspicion that some countries are gaining trade advantages by subsidising exports through over-generous rebates in respect of sales taxes.

The second advantage claimed for V.A.T. is that, levied over a broad base and at a uniform rate, it has less distorting effects on production and consumption than the multi-rate purchase tax and S.E.T. and other sales taxes at the wholesale or manufacturing stage. Of course, it would have been possible to levy purchase tax at a single rate; but, all wholesale or manufacturers taxes have inherent disadvantages compared with a tax at the retail level. First, even a single rate tax at the wholesale or manufacturing stage creates distortion because, as a result of different mark-ups, the effective rates at the retail stage are different for different goods. Secondly, a tax at a level prior to the retail stage causes distortion by encouraging producers to avoid tax by pushing some activities (like advertising and transport) beyond the taxable stage. Thirdly, a tax imposed at the wholesale stage cannot apply to services. The introduction of S.E.T. was a not very satisfactory attempt to make good this limitation. V.A.T. undoubtedly had the big advantage over the taxes it superseded that it taxed both goods and services on a uniform basis. But the exemptions and widespread zero-rating meant that distortion remained, particularly between zero-rated and standard rated goods. (During the period of higher rate tax — see below — the neutrality argument was undetermined still more.)

This second advantage links with the third. V.A.T. is more effective as a regulator of demand than the taxes it superseded. The narrower the range of products taxed the more the danger that if tax rates are raised, consumers will switch to other products; to ensure a given demand effect from the narrower range, tax rates may have to be raised substantially. This has a more distorting effect on consumers' choice and the pattern of production than raising the required revenue by smaller tax increases over a wide range of products. It follows, too, that V.A.T. would provide a much surer base for future tax increases, including scope for a switch from direct to indirect taxation, than the more restricted base of purchase tax and S.E.T.

One of the concerns expressed before the introduction of V.A.T. was that it would be more regressive than the taxes it replaced. Whereas purchase tax had a structure of rates which sought to tax "luxuries" more than "necessities", V.A.T. had no such differentiation except for exemptions and zero-rating.

In the event the wide range of zero-rating under V.A.T. ensured that the change did not have a regressive effect. Indeed the reverse has been the case. A study* at the time of the changeover suggested that the change to V.A.T. might prove mildly progressive and Family Expenditure Survey data has since confirmed this view. Zero-rated goods are more prominent in the budgets of the poor than of the better off. There is here a trade-off between efficiency and equity considerations. The zero-rating makes V.A.T. less neutral but promotes distributional equity.

Another objection to V.A.T. was that it would have high operating costs, both administrative and compliance costs, and certainly higher than the taxes it superseded. One of the merits of S.E.T. was that it was easy and inexpensive to operate. Purchase tax, collected from some 70,000 wholesalers, was not unduly costly. V.A.T., on the other hand, had a million and a quarter of collecting points when introduced, and currently (1991–92) has a million and a half. Many more Customs and Excise officers were needed to collect it; when introduced the administrative costs as a proportion of revenue were officially estimated at more than twice those of purchase tax and four times those for S.E.T. This still left V.A.T. administrative costs in line with the average for the tax system. More significant are the compliance costs of firms, many of whom have to keep much more extensive accounts than hitherto in order to comply with V.A.T. regulations.

A study,† based on a national survey of V.A.T. registered traders, estimated that total compliance costs amounted to £392m

---

*P. M. Jackson and J. W. McGilvray, *The Impact of Tax Changes on Income Distribution: the 1973 Budget*, Institute for Fiscal Studies, October 1973.
†Cedric Sandford, Michael Godwin, Peter Hardwick and Ian Butterworth, *Costs and Benefits of VAT*, Heinemann Educational Books, 1981.

in 1977–78, representing over 9 per cent of revenue from V.A.T.; however, a more recent study by the same research team* estimated compliance costs at under 4 per cent of tax revenue in 1986–87. This reduction is mainly due to the rise in revenue from V.A.T. following increases in rates (a single standard rate of 15 per cent in 1986–87 compared with a standard rate of 8 per cent and an additional $12\frac{1}{2}$ per cent rate in 1977–78), growth in national consumption and some extension in the V.A.T. coverage. But there had also been a reduction in the costs of compliance in real terms, probably due to increased experience of operating the tax and general improvements in productivity (e.g. word processors instead of typewriters); the reversion to a single positive rate of tax; the removal of some difficult borderlines, notably in the construction industry; and a series of measures by Customs and Excise aimed at simplifying V.A.T. compliance, especially for small traders (e.g. simplified forms and accounting procedures). Thus in 1986–87 V.A.T. compliance costs, measured as a percentage of tax revenue, were only a little above the compliance costs of income tax, capital gains tax and national insurance contributions (taken together) and the operation costs (compliance costs plus administrative costs) were less. (See above Table 5.1).

The most serious aspect of the compliance costs of V.A.T. is that they are extremely regressive, falling much more heavily, relatively, on small firms than on large. Thus, for example, in 1986–87 it cost businesses in the £20,000–£50,000 turnover range (the lowest range for compulsory registration) on average, £7.80 for every £1,000 of goods sold; for businesses over £10m turnover the corresponding figure for £1,000 of sales was only 3p.

This is not the whole story; there are some offsets. Thus, the fuller and more accurate accounts which V.A.T. has required of smaller firms has furnished data which some have been able to use as managerial aids to improve their running of the business. Moreover, most firms obtain an important cash flow benefit. Unless they are repayment traders (selling a large proportion of zero-rated goods) over the three months collection period they receive more

---

*Cedric Sandford, Michael Godwin and Peter Hardwick, *Administrative and Compliance Costs of Taxation*, Fiscal Publications, Bath, 1989.

V.A.T. from their customers than they have to pay to their suppliers. Then at the end of each collection period they are allowed one month's grace before they have to hand over the money to Customs and Excise. Important though it is to firms, it should be remembered that (unlike any managerial benefits) the cash flow benefit is only a transfer. There is a corresponding cost to the Exchequer which is, in effect, making an interest free loan to traders. The compliance costs on the other hand, are real resource costs.

The net effect of the differential incidence of compliance costs and benefits is that many larger firms finish up with negative net compliance costs (the value of the benefits exceeded the costs) whereas the smaller firms have substantial positive net costs. Thus V.A.T. puts smaller firms at a significant competitive disadvantage.

Several other minor points might be noted. V.A.T. has the advantage over purchase tax (levied at the wholesale stage) that if rates are reduced retailers are not left holding stock which has paid the higher rates. Similarly, if some stock is destroyed, the retailer under V.A.T. (unlike purchase tax) can recover (or will already have recovered) the tax paid.

Under V.A.T. as under purchase tax "regulator" powers are available; the Chancellor initially allowed himself the right to vary rates of V.A.T. by up to 20 per cent of the existing V.A.T. rates without prior recourse to Parliament.

Why No Retail Sales Tax?

V.A.T., as we have seen, involves the collection of tax from traders at each stage of production and distribution and, generates high compliance costs. As V.A.T. is essentially a tax on the final consumer, the obvious question is, why not simply collect tax at the retail stage? To this there are two main answers; first, it is multi-stage collection which enables tax which spills over into costs to be rebated. Secondly, multi-stage collection comprises a self-checking system and reduces the amount of tax which has to be collected from the retailer. Until the retail stage is reached, the output tax collected by one supplier is the input tax paid by another; and as the input tax is rebated, the purchaser has an interest in ensuring that it is accurately invoiced and properly accounted for. The most difficult stage to police is the retail stage because of the multiplicity of suppliers and customers; but under V.A.T. as against a straight retail tax, only a relatively small proportion of the total tax is collected at that stage; the incentive to evade and the potential for evasion are both, therefore, much reduced.*

Experience of other countries suggests that if only a low general sales tax is required then a retail sales tax is to be preferred. But if a general sales tax is to be levied at a high rate, on grounds of minimising evasion, there is a strong case for V.A.T.

Changes in V.A.T. since its Introduction

The Labour Party had been very critical of V.A.T. before its introduction, mainly on the grounds of its alleged adverse effects on income distribution. In 1974, Mr. Healey became Chancellor of the Exchequer, and made a number of changes during his period of office. As from April 1, 1974 V.A.T. at standard rate was applied to chocolates, sweets, confectionery, soft drinks, ice-cream and potato crisps, items which had borne purchase tax but had been zero-rated when V.A.T. was introduced. V.A.T. was also applied to petrol (without a corresponding reduction in excise duty). In an autumn budget in 1974, in an attempt to give a mild stimulus to the economy and check the rapid rise in prices, the standard rate of V.A.T. was reduced to 8 per cent. A new higher rate of 25 per cent was applied to petrol in November, 1974 and in May, 1975 the 25 per cent rate was applied to most electrically operated appliances (other than cookers, space and water heaters), e.g. radios, television sets, tape-recorders and electronic musical instruments; also to mowers (electric or motor), boats, caravans, cameras and other cine equipment, fur clothing and jewellery. At the same time the "regulator" provision was changed to enable the Treasury, by Order, to alter V.A.T. rates by up to 25 per cent. Then, in the April, 1976

---

*For a fuller comparison of the respective merits of V.A.T. and a retail sales tax, see *Taxing Consumption*, O.E.C.D., Paris 1988, chapter 6.

budget, because the higher rate was considered to be adversely affecting employment in particular industries, notably the manufacture of electrical goods, the higher rate was reduced to 12½ per cent.

Thus, the position in 1979, when the Conservatives again took office, was that the standard rate of V.A.T. stood at 8 per cent with a higher rate of 12½ per cent. In his first budget, Sir Geoffrey Howe returned to the single positive rate and at the same time increased the standard rate as part of a major switch from income tax (see p. 140). As from June 18, 1979 all goods previously chargeable at 8 per cent or 12½ per cent carried a levy of 15 per cent.

The main changes in V.A.T. made by Sir Geoffrey's successor at the Treasury, Mr. Nigel Lawson, were to standard rate certain goods previously zero-rated, most notably building extensions and alterations, hot take-away food and newspaper advertisements. Following a ruling of the European Court, new commercial buildings also became standard rated. In his first Budget in 1991, Mr. Lamont raised the standard rate of V.A.T. to 17½ per cent to provide the additional revenue to allow a reduction in the community charge in 1991–92.

Several other changes should be noted. When V.A.T. was introduced in 1973 the exemption limit was set at £5,000. Since then it has been raised regularly more or less in line with the retail price index until 1990–91, when it stood at £24,500. In the 1991 Budget Mr. Lamont gave a much bigger than usual increase to lift the threshold to £35,000. This increase was designed to relieve the compliance burden on some of the smallest businesses. Other measures with the same objective of reducing compliance costs on small firms (in addition to those already referred to which help to account for the decline in compliance costs between 1977–78 and 1986–87 (p. 206) have also been taken, of which the two most important have probably been the provision of a cash accounting option for small firms (introduced 1987) and an annual accounting option as from the summer of 1988. However, those adopting annual accounting have to make a series of direct debit payments during the year, so that they derive no cash flow benefit from adopting the scheme. On the other hand, following the recommendations of the Keith Report* a much stricter regime, involving automatic penalties for late returns and for serious misdeclarations was introduced from the mid 1980s and this may well have pushed small traders towards making greater use of accountants to ensure that they avoid the penalties—and this will have raised compliance costs since the 1986–87 study referred to above (p. 206).

Comparison of Income and Outlay Taxes

Let us conclude this chapter by comparing the effects of income and outlay taxation. Leaving apart the special considerations attaching to outlay taxes on labour, and the particular disadvantages of outlay taxes on producers' goods, what are the comparative merits of income taxation and outlay taxes on consumers' goods?

Whilst we must beware of the sweeping generalisation, outlay taxes infringe our criteria of equality in that they tend to be regressive or, at the least, less progressive than income and capital taxes; it is possible to devise a structure of outlay taxes by which the purchases of the rich are taxed proportionately more than those of the poor, but there can be no close adjustment of tax to the consumers' ability to pay. Within any particular income group, outlay taxes, unless levied at the same proportional rate on all purchases, fall unequally on consumers according to the particular nature of their pleasures and the content of their expenditure. We have seen too, that, unless levied on goods of absolutely inelastic demand, they infringe our efficiency principle by distorting consumers' preferences and imposing an excess burden on the taxpayer over and above the gain to the revenue. At the same time selective outlay taxes impose disproportionate burdens of adjustment on particular producers. Why then have outlay taxes at all? Why not concentrate taxation on income and capital so that tax payments can be closely adjusted to prevailing conceptions of ability to pay?

There are several valid answers to this question, but first let us dispose of a piece of sophistry. Outlay taxes are sometimes preferred to income tax on the grounds that they leave the tax-payer with a

Report of the Committee on Enforcement Powers of the Revenue Departments, Volume 2, H.M.S.O., 1983.

choice. Under income tax it is assumed he must pay; under outlay taxes he can please himself for he can avoid the consumption of the taxed commodities. However, any comparison between two forms of tax must be on the basis of an equal yield to the exchequer (unless we can demonstrate that the one which yields less will result in a compensating increase in saving). Whilst individuals can choose to avoid outlay tax by reducing their purchases of the taxed commodities, the community as a whole cannot avoid the tax; to maintain an equivalent yield from outlay taxation the Chancellor would have to extend its range or/and increase its weight if many tried to exercise this "choice".

An argument which offers some dubious justification for outlay taxes is that taxpayers do not realise the extent to which they pay taxes on expenditure but are more conscious of income tax payments; hence there is less psychological resistance to outlay taxation. It can, however, be argued that it is a sound principle in a democracy that taxpayers *should* be aware of what they pay. Only then can they rationally assess proposals for increasing government expenditure.

More convincing are the arguments that there may be good reasons for taxing particular commodities because their production and/or consumption results in social costs. Further, that outlay taxes are often easier and cheaper to administer than income and capital taxes—a particularly important consideration for emerging countries lacking an efficient civil service. Again, that a wide spread of taxation helps to reduce evasion and avoidance—or rather that although in total these may not be less, at least the gains from avoidance and evasion will be less *concentrated* and no-one is likely to be able to dodge tax altogether. A further advantage of outlay taxation is that it catches spending out of capital which income tax misses—although a wealth tax would partly and a direct expenditure tax wholly repair this deficiency. Again, outlay taxation for regulating the economy (see Chapter 12) carries the advantage of speed of action; an increase in outlay taxation brings in revenue immediately, whilst a reduction can quickly put money into the hands of the consumer when the need is to increase demand.

There remains one final and important issue in this comparison.

It is often accepted as axiomatic that outlay taxation has less disincentive effects than income taxation—or, more generally, that it has less distorting effect on the taxpayers' choice between work and leisure. The basis of this contention needs to be carefully examined. We saw in Chapter 6 that income tax gave rise to two effects on the demand for leisure; an income effect tending to increase the amount of work done and a substitution effect which tended to reduce it; whilst the theoretical analysis did not make it possible to say which was the stronger, we could say that the higher the marginal rate relative to the aggregate, the greater the substitution effect relative to the income effect. Hence the more progressive a tax, the greater the disincentive (or the less the incentive) effect. In practice outlay taxes tend to be regressive; this is the fundamental reason why we should expect outlay taxes to have fewer restrictive effects on the supply of the factors of production than income tax.

But outlay taxes do not need to be regressive, nor income taxes progressive. If we are concerned with income and outlay taxes *as such*, we should compare the two on the basis of the same degree of progression. Then, leaving aside for the moment the question of saving, if people were perfectly rational and were faced with the prospect of paying the same revenue to the exchequer by income or outlay tax, there is no reason why the outlay tax should have less disincentive (or more incentive) effects. People (apart from collectors of coins) want money for what it can buy. Just as there is an income and substitution effect with income tax, so there is with outlay taxation. If tax is imposed on the goods I wish to buy, I may either work harder to increase my income in order to buy them despite the tax (the income effect) or decide that the effort is not worth it, work less hard and enjoy more leisure (the substitution effect).

However, people are *not* always rational. As we have already mentioned, income tax impinges more noticeably than outlay tax on the taxpayer. Moreover, this psychological effect is accentuated where the income receiver is not identical with the income spender; a man may be deterred from effort by a tax on his earnings, but not from a tax on his wife's spending out of his earnings.

To allow for saving is more complicated. Ostensibly outlay taxes may be less discouraging to saving: but as most saving has in mind future spending, the conclusion that outlay taxation will be less of a deterrent to saving than income taxation does not necessarily follow.

To sum up a complicated argument. Outlay taxation, with the same degree of progression as income taxation, for psychological reasons may reduce incentive to effort less (or increase incentive more) than income taxation. But the main reason for adopting outlay taxation in an attempt to reduce disincentive effects is that it is likely to reduce the progression of the tax system; that may be politically easier than reducing the progression of income tax.

Postscript

In the 1992 Budget, the Chancellor, Mr Lamont, reduced the rate of car tax from 10 to 5 per cent

CHAPTER 9

Taxation of Capital or Wealth

Meaning and Forms of Capital Taxation

By taxes on capital or wealth we mean taxes *assessed* on the capital value of property but not necessarily paid out of capital or wealth, that is to say, not necessarily having to be met by a disposal of assets. We exclude taxes on the annual value of capital, such as the local rate, and taxes (like a motor vehicle licence) necessary to secure the use of a capital good, but not directly levied on its capital value; these are more appropriately considered as outlay taxes. Further, they lack the generality (i.e. the applicability to all forms of capital, save for some limited and specific exclusions) which is usually taken to characterise wealth or capital taxes. We also exclude stamp duties, which consist of a motley variety of duties levied on the gross value of various properties at the time of transfer, and are also more akin to taxes on outlay than taxes on capital.

Strictly speaking a capital gains tax does not fall within the scope of our definition. It is assessed not on the capital value of property but rather on an incremental increase in it—the appreciation in its value between two dates. Indeed, there are strong reasons for treating capital gains as income: if income is defined broadly to consist of the total available for consumption over a period of time whilst maintaining the value of capital intact, then a real capital gain (not just one which was a product of inflation) can reasonably be regarded as income. The matter is not quite as simple as this; the implications of a capital gain vary according to the source of the gain.* However, without entering more deeply into the theoretical

*See, for example, C. T. Sandford, *Taxing Personal Wealth*, George Allen & Unwin, 1971, chapter 7.

214

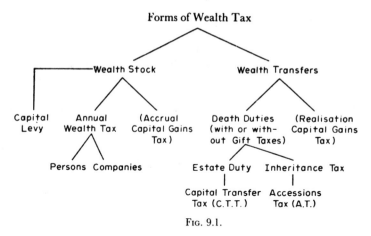

Fig. 9.1.

issue here, it is certainly convenient to treat capital gains taxes along with capital taxes because of a similarity of objectives and of administrative problems. Hence this chapter contains our main treatment of capital gains taxes, although we also refer to them in Chapter 6, on income taxes.

Figure 9.1 summarises the main forms of taxes on capital or wealth. They can be classified as either on wealth stock or wealth transfers. The principal form of tax on wealth stock is the annual wealth tax, usually referred to simply as "a wealth tax". An annual wealth tax is usually levied only on persons, but it may be levied only on companies or on both companies and persons (as in Germany).

Taxes on wealth transfers consist primarily of death duties, and gift taxes which in practice are usually closely integrated with death duties. There is an important distinction between estate duties, levied on the aggregated total of property left at death (with any supporting gift tax levied on the donor) and inheritance taxes, where duty is levied on the shares of the property in the hands of the beneficiaries* (and any supporting gift tax is on the donee). A

---

*When Mr. Nigel Lawson radically amended the U.K. Capital Transfer Tax in 1986 and re-named it Inheritance Tax, he was disregarding accepted usage and effectively re-introducing the former estate duty (see below).

capital transfer tax (C.T.T.) and an accessions tax (A.T.) are more sophisticated versions of an estate duty and an inheritance tax respectively, which we shall consider more fully later in the chapter.

In the diagram a capital gains tax is bracketed because it is doubtfully regarded as a capital tax; we can distinguish between an "accrual" gains tax, where the appreciation in assets is taxed each year whether or not the appreciation is realised, and a "realisation" gains tax, where the gain is only taxed when the asset is disposed of.

A capital levy is a tax on wealth stock. We shall not be considering a capital levy, but the problems it raises and its economic effects are very similar to a very heavy annual wealth tax, with the vital difference that a capital levy is an exceptional measure intended for use once only, whereas a wealth tax is a regular component of the tax system.

In terms of our tax criteria the case for capital taxes rests on three main considerations—equity, equality and efficiency: any particular tax on wealth may have one or more of these objectives. The equity (or horizontal equity) argument is that taxes on wealth are needed to supplement income tax if taxation is to be in line with taxable capacity. The equality argument is based on the value judgement that it is a proper objective of taxation to seek to diminish inequalities of both income and wealth, and a tax policy which ignored wealth could make little headway in achieving that object. The efficiency argument rests on the assumption that capital taxes are less distorting in their effects than equivalent income taxes. The big disadvantage of all forms of capital taxation is administrative, especially the problems of valuing certain assets such as land, closely owned businesses and personal chattels. The other drawback is that a tax on wealth may have unfortunate economic effects: notably, it may discourage saving and adversely affect private businesses including agricultural enterprises.

How far these advantages and disadvantages apply depends on the form of tax on wealth, the weight and structure of the tax and its relationship with other taxes. We shall examine the arguments more fully for different forms of tax on wealth, looking in turn at an annual personal wealth tax (hereafter referred to simply as a wealth tax), capital gains taxes, and death duties (including gift taxes).

At the time of writing (1991) the United Kingdom has a death duty with a very limited provision for taxing gifts and a capital gains tax. There is no annual wealth tax, but the Labour government of 1974–79 came very close to introducing one and, until very recently, the Labour Party remained committed to it. We shall start by examining the wealth tax as the most obvious and direct way of taxing capital.

Wealth Tax

A wealth tax is an annual charge on the aggregate net value (assets minus liabilities) of a person's possessions including stocks and shares, bank balances, unincorporated businesses, land and other consumer durables, like houses, cars, jewellery. It includes all assets save those that are specifically exempted and applies to persons whose wealth exceeds some specified threshold.

The most important distinction with a wealth tax is whether, taken in conjunction with income tax, it is at such a level that the taxpayer can only meet it by disposing of assets; or whether it is possible for taxpayers to meet both income tax and wealth tax from income. As a convenient shorthand the first can be termed an "additive" wealth tax, the second a "substitutive" tax. The distinction is not absolutely clear-cut; for example, whether both taxes can be met from income partly depends on what yield the property-owner is getting from his wealth—the higher the yield, the more the chance that he can pay income tax and wealth tax without disposing of assets; also a tax may be additive (i.e. unable to be met from income) for some taxpayers, say the millionaires, but not for those with substantial but less wealth, say those with £250,000 and below. Despite this imprecision, the distinction is significant both in relation to the purpose of a wealth tax and its effective incidence.

Let us spell out in more detail the way in which a wealth tax may promote the objectives of equity, equality and efficiency and how the objectives relate to the substitutive or additive distinction.

Arguments For and Against a Wealth Tax

Of all forms of tax on wealth an annual wealth tax, because of its regularity, is most capable of serving the objective of equity or horizontal equity—the equal treatment of taxpayers of similar taxable capacity.

Wealth, it is argued, gives its possessor advantages of, for example, opportunity, security and independence. These are advantages over and above income derived from wealth. If a tax system is to be equitable, then income tax needs to be supported by a wealth tax. Although discrimination in income taxation between income from earnings and income from property is intended to serve this purpose of taxing the additional advantages of wealth, it does so imperfectly as compared with a wealth tax, for it takes no account of wealth which yields no income which, nonetheless, carries the advantages we have listed and it only taxes lightly wealth with a low yield. The point was vividly put in an example first given by Professor Lord Kaldor in a study on the Indian tax system. Imagine a maharaja and a beggar; the maharaja has no income but a large stock of gold and jewels, the beggar has no income and no gold and jewels. If you tax them to income tax alone then they will both pay the same— zero. But the maharaja clearly has a higher taxable capacity than the beggar and hence to take this into account income tax needs to be supplemented by a wealth tax. A wealth tax for this purpose would be a substitutive one, intended to be met from income. In the United Kingdom a wealth tax with this purpose would logically take the place of any investment income surcharge and possibly also substitute for higher rates of income tax. Equity is the prime purpose of the wealth taxes in the ten or so countries of Continental Europe which have them. Unlike the United Kingdom these countries did not have an investment income surcharge and the intention that wealth tax should be met from income is made plain by the existence of "ceiling" provisions, which specify a maximum proportion of income (varying from 70 per cent to 90 per cent in different countries) which may be taken in wealth tax and income tax combined.

The use of a wealth tax for reducing inequality of wealth is open to different meanings. The objective may be a limited one to use a wealth tax in a similar way to a progressive income tax; thus a wealth tax would serve to check the accumulation of wealth by the rich and in particular to catch those wealthy persons who avoided progressive income tax by holding their wealth in forms which yielded capital gain rather than income. For this limited objective a substitutive wealth tax would be appropriate. The more radical, and perhaps more obvious way of using a wealth tax to reduce inequality of wealth is to have an additive tax, that is to say, to set the rates of income tax and wealth tax so high that the wealthy cannot meet them without disposing of assets. Thus each year the wealth of the wealthy would be reduced and the cause of reducing inequality directly promoted. A particular development of the inequality argument is the view that a wealth tax to reduce inequality is necessary in order to create a more favourable social climate in which other policies, e g incomes policy, have more chance of success.

The efficiency argument rests particularly on a comparison of income tax and wealth tax and is essentially concerned with the substitution of wealth tax for income tax. The argument has both a negative and a positive aspect. Wealth tax base is related to past and not present effort, hence a wealth tax will restrict the supply of labour and enterprise less than an equivalent income tax. A wealth tax will not deter a man from engaging in additional work effort and enterprise where the object of the activity is increased income for consumption, whereas an income tax might deter him. Where the object of these endeavours is capital accumulation, i e saving, then the position is more complicated and we examine that below. The more positive argument is that because a wealth tax imposes a charge on wealth irrespective of the income from it, the tax encourages people to use wealth more productively, to transfer from nil-yielding to income-yielding assets or from low to high yielding assets. This inducement gains strength the bigger the income tax reduction accompanying an increase of wealth tax. For example, a wealth tax will discourage a private businessman from holding idle money or stock, because tax has to be paid on them even though they generate little or no income. Again if a man possesses some uncultivated land, if there is an income tax alone he pays no tax on it; but if there is a wealth tax he will have to pay tax whether the land yields an income or not. The existence of the wealth tax may therefore encourage him either to cultivate it himself, or to develop it, or to sell it to someone who will cultivate it or develop it.

The arguments against the wealth tax are mainly twofold: the practical difficulties associated with it and possible economic disadvantages. A main argument against a wealth tax, which applies both to a substitutive and an additive tax, is that the advantages claimed are theoretical rather than actual; that they take insufficient account of the realities of the real world. In practice, because of administrative difficulties, the advantages claimed for a wealth tax are only imperfectly realised. The principal practical problems are the administrative difficulties relating to disclosure of assets and valuation. Some assets, like jewellery and personal chattels kept in the home, are difficult for the tax authorities to discover; the authorities have to take the tax-payers' statements about these assets very much on trust. Moreover valuation problems with such chattels and with the value of land and of private businesses are very marked. In practice, in order to reduce such problems to manageable proportions, most Continental countries with wealth taxes employ standardised methods of valuation and undertake the valuation of particular forms of property at wider intervals than 12 months. Consequently, in a particular year, the valuation of some forms of property differs very substantially from the open market valuation of that property.

Conceptual problems merge with the practical problems. We shall be examining in Chapter 11, when we look at the distribution of wealth, some of the conceptual problems of deciding what should be included in wealth and we shall see that if the value of pension rights is included there is a marked reduction in the inequality in the distribution of wealth in Britain. Similarly, we have to decide whether the value of pension rights ought to be included within the base of the wealth tax. If, as is the general practice in European wealth taxes, the value of pension rights is excluded, then the civil servant with a non-contributory inflation-proof pension gains markedly as compared with the businessman who makes no specific provision for a pension, relying for his income in retirement on the sale proceeds of his business assets. Such a person pays wealth tax both on the business assets during his working life and on the investments which he buys from the sale of the proceeds to provide him with retirement income. On the other hand to tax the civil servant on the full value of the pension rights would also be unfair since they are rights which he cannot sell at any time and which, if he dies before retirement, he will not enjoy at all and which he cannot pass on to his heirs.

As a consequence of these difficulties, in fact, an annual wealth tax generates horizontal inequities, between the honest and the less honest in returning details and valuations of personal chattels; between the owners of quoted shares who always pay wealth tax at the market value and the owners of, say, land or houses subject to a cadastral value which frequently falls well below market value; between the businessman and the civil servant.

Similarly the efficiency argument is less powerful in practice than in theory. The differences in valuation which we have already described may create investment distortions. Further, the argument assumes that efficiency is equatable with high yield and implies that resources are infinitely mobile. But low yield is not necessarily a sign of inefficiency. For example, a new business, however good its prospects, can hardly be expected to yield profits in the first year or so of its existence; in these years, because it yields no profit, there is no income generated to give a liability to income tax or profits tax; but a wealth tax has to be paid in these early years whether the business is yielding income or not. Thus a wealth tax may act as a deterrent to the establishment of new enterprise. Similarly the owners of an unincorporated or closely owned long established business may find a wealth tax a serious handicap to adjusting the business when it goes through a bad patch, perhaps because of the loss of export markets for political reasons which have nothing to do with the efficiency of the firm. The outstanding case of low yield unconnected with inefficiency is that of agriculture, where income yields in general are low because of a high demand for land for other purposes than agricultural output; for example, for amenity value, for potential development value, or as a hedge against inflation.

Even if the situation exists that assets in a particular business are yielding a low return for other than temporary reasons, say because of a long-term decline in the demand for the product, where it would be desirable in principle for the assets to be employed elsewhere to yield a higher return, in practice, if the assets are specific, their redeployment will not be possible until such time as they wear out and replacement is required.

Besides reducing the equity and efficiency advantages of an annual wealth tax, the practical problems bring some specific disadvantages with them. Thus a wealth tax is associated with high administrative and compliance costs as a proportion of the yield. Further, because the taxing authorities cannot readily corroborate the statements of the taxpayer about some forms of asset, there is a serious danger of stimulating evasion of taxation and undermining taxpayer morality.

What of the economic disadvantages of a wealth tax? Some adverse economic effects have already been mentioned applying both to an additive and a substitutive wealth tax, for example the discouragement to new private enterprise. The most serious economic disadvantages follow, however, from an additive tax. These are of two main kinds: a possible disincentive to saving and a serious handicap to the development of private firms.

If a wealth tax and income tax together have a combined marginal rate equivalent to more than 100 per cent of income then there is a strong incentive for the taxpayer, not only to stop saving, but to dis-save. In these circumstances the most that saving can do is to reduce the rate at which his wealth declines. A $2\frac{1}{2}$ per cent rate of wealth tax is equivalent to a 50 per cent rate of income tax at a 5 per cent rate of return on capital; and equivalent to a 25 per cent rate of income tax at a 10 per cent rate of return on capital. Thus, suppose the marginal rate of income tax for a particular taxpayer is 70 per cent and his marginal rate of wealth tax is $2\frac{1}{2}$ per cent. At a 5 per cent yield the combined marginal rate on his property income would be 120 per cent. The incentive to dis-save can then be seen most clearly if we imagine that such a taxpayer received a legacy of £2,000 and invested it at 5 per cent to yield £100 p.a. income. In the first year the tax would then be £120 (£50 wealth tax plus £70 income tax) i.e. £20 more than the income. Over succeeding years the whole of the income and of the capital would gradually be taxed away if the taxpayer did not consume it. The incentive to dis-save in these circumstances must surely be strong.

The other economic dangers from a wealth tax of this kind are that it is likely to prevent the building up of a private business as rapidly as would otherwise occur, or indeed, restrict it to a certain maximum size, depending on the threshold and rates. We are, of course, talking about firms which are unincorporated or which are closely owned; once a firm has attained the size at which it can go public and its shares are readily saleable in the market, then a personal wealth tax may have little or no effect on the business as such. A wealth tax affects a business when the business assets are not in this readily disposable form and constitute a high proportion of the total assets of the owners. But it is just this sort of firm amongst which the rapid growth firms are to be found, and a wealth tax would inhibit that growth and might, indeed, prevent the firm ever attaining a size at which it could go public. How serious the difficulty is obviously depends on the weight of the wealth tax in relation to other taxes, but there is no doubt that there is some level of wealth tax which would undermine the mixed economy as we know it today. A similar problem exists with agriculture; over 50 per cent of farms are in individual ownership and they are especially vulnerable to a wealth tax because of the high capital value of land relative to income yield. The imposition of a wealth tax without special concessions would carry a serious danger of farm fragmentation, leading to inefficiency. There is little doubt that an additive wealth tax raises in an acute form the conflict between a desire for equality and efficiency.

Wealth Tax Proposals for the United Kingdom

Since the early 1960s the Labour Party, encouraged by the T.U.C., has toyed with the idea of a wealth tax. The party literature and the T.U.C. economic reviews stressed the case for a wealth tax to reduce inequality of wealth. The Labour Party included the proposal for a wealth tax in its February 1974 Election Manifesto and in his first budget Chancellor Denis Healey committed the party to one. However, he undertook that before it was introduced there would be a Green Paper to act as a discussion document so that the possibilities should be thoroughly aired and further that the Green Paper might be considered by a Select Committee of the House of Commons who could take evidence from a wide range of sources.

The Green Paper duly appeared in the summer of 1974 and a Select Committee was set up at the end of that year which took evidence during 1975 and reported in November 1975. The Select Committee was unable to agree on a majority report but published five different reports. These were a draft prepared by the Chairman of the Committee, Mr. Douglas Jay; the same draft as amended by the Committee but ultimately rejected by it; a draft report presented by the Liberal member, Mr. John Pardoe; a draft by the Conservatives in the name of Mr. Maurice Macmillan; and a fifth report submitted by Dr. Jeremy Bray, a Labour member. Whilst the absence of two Labour members abroad in the final stages of the Committee may have been the immediate cause of the failure to produce an agreed report, the differences between the reports are most instructive. Essentially they spring from different philosophies about the objectives a wealth tax should serve.

The objectives of the wealth tax were set out in a somewhat confused way in the Green Paper, but two purposes were envisaged, namely equity and a reduction in inequality, though it was not clear whether the equality objective was what we have called a radical or a limited one. Beyond stating a commitment to a wealth tax, the Green Paper left almost everything else open. Two wealth tax scales were included, but it was stressed that the scales and the threshold (set at £100,000) were for illustrative purposes only. It was suggested that the investment income surcharge might be allowed as an offset to wealth tax and that there might be some sort of ceiling provision; there was also a hint of a possible reduction in income tax. The Select Committee Chairman's draft report made equity the main objective of the tax but also wished it to contribute in a limited way to a reduction in inequality. The details were in line with that objective, including a wealth tax scale somewhat less than that of the lower of the two scales contained in the Green Paper and with provision for a number of other concessions. The Conservatives' report was almost wholly concerned with equity and proposed a low proportional wealth tax with substantial reductions in other taxes. The Liberal report accepted equity as the main purpose and wished the wealth tax to make a limited contribution to reducing inequality; its distinctive feature, however, was the proposal to use a heavy wealth tax as a means of making big reductions in income tax to stimulate effort and enterprise—an efficiency objective. Finally Dr. Bray's report was concerned essentially with reducing inequality and proposed the adoption of the heavier of the two wealth tax scales in the Green Paper with little or nothing by way of special concession.

It is noteworthy that all the reports, except that of Dr. Bray which received the least support in the Committee, saw equity (or horizontal equity) rather than a reduction in inequality as the main objective of a wealth tax. It is in line with this objective that these reports all proposed, in contradiction to the Green Paper, which was illogical on this point, that the threshold of a wealth tax ought to be relatively low, say £30,000, in order that the tax could replace completely the investment income surcharge. Further, the main reports had in common the proposal to give much more substantial concessions to private business and agriculture than were suggested in the original Green Paper.

In the event, in December 1975, the Chancellor announced that as the Select Committee had taken longer over their work than the government had hoped he did not feel able to carry out his original intention to introduce a wealth tax in the current session of Parliament. Despite pressure from the Trade Unions he kept to this view. He may have been influenced by the weak parliamentary position of the government and by the unpropitious economic climate. However, a wealth tax remained a Labour Party commitment. It was reiterated in the Party Manifesto for the 1979 election and was also part of Labour's Programme in the 1983 election. Since then, however, the commitment has been allowed to lapse.

Capital Gains Tax

Arguments For and Against Taxation of Gains

The arguments of equity, equality and efficiency all apply to some extent to capital gains taxes. Capital gains are an addition to spending power, add to taxable capacity and hence, on grounds of equity, should be taxed, especially if converting income to capital gains is a device for avoiding income tax. Gains accrue mainly to the rich; they can only accrue to property owners and, amongst property owners, the wealthiest tend to hold a larger proportion of their assets in forms which benefit from gains. Thus, a capital gains tax can contribute to a reduction in inequality in the distribution of wealth. Finally, the efficiency argument: without a capital gains tax there is investment distortion—a bias in favour of assets which yield capital growth rather than taxable income, including the holding of wealth in "non-productive" forms like antiques, stamps, pictures, which are expected to appreciate.

The question which arises, however, is whether the benefits are outweighed by the disadvantages. In practice, like an annual wealth tax, the benefits turn out to be less substantial than might have been expected and the disadvantages are serious. As always with capital taxes the big problem is administration. A capital gains tax requires two valuations for each asset because tax is levied on the difference in value. Despite the attempt to minimise valuation difficulties by the use of a realisation rather than an accrual basis, the problem remains formidable, giving rise both to inequities and to high operating costs.

As the Royal Commission (majority report)* warned: "A tax on capital gains . . . cannot be expected to prove a tax of simple structure or one that would be free from a number of arbitrary solutions of its various problems."

Capital gains tax not only has relatively high administrative costs to the Revenue authorities; there are also very high compliance costs for the taxpayer. The conclusion from a survey of accountants

---

*Final Report of the Royal Commission on the Taxation of Profits and Income, Cmnd. 9474, 1955.

and the tax departments of banks on compliance costs, carried out in the spring of 1971 in the United Kingdom, was that "capital gains tax emerged as pre-eminently the tax with high compliance costs: complicated, confusing and with horizontal inequities".* Since then there have been some simplifications in the United Kingdom capital gains tax but also new complications associated with indexation.

The contribution of a capital gains tax to reducing inequality is limited because, for administrative reasons, gains taxes in practice are always levied on a realisation rather than an accruals basis; but a fully progressive tax is hardly possible with a realisation basis, because realisation of assets is often "bunched" in time, and where bunching occurred, if the tax were progressive, more tax would be paid than if realisation had been spread more evenly over the years. Hence, to avoid this inequity, a capital gains tax needs to be proportional or only mildly progressive. But the sacrifice of progression means abandoning the more generally accepted criterion of ability to pay and makes the capital gains tax a weak instrument for diminishing inequalities in the distribution of wealth.

In practice, also, capital gains taxes invariably generate some inefficiencies; in particular a capital gains tax may reduce the mobility of capital. There is a danger that funds remain "locked-in" to particular investments because the owners seek to avoid paying capital gains tax by not realising the gain. This feature is accentuated if death is not treated as a "deemed" realisation for capital gains tax purposes, for then, if the owner retains the ownership of those assets until he dies, no gains tax is payable. If the tax restricts the movement of funds in this way, new and expanding firms may find fund-raising in the market more difficult.

Let us turn now to the history of capital gains taxes in the United Kingdom, which illustrates many of these features.

---

*C. T. Sandford, *Hidden Costs of Taxation*, Institute for Fiscal Studies, 1973, p. 145. For a full account of the compliance costs of capital gains tax in the U.K. at that time, see Chapter 7.

U.K. Capital Gains Taxes

Although the first capital gains tax by that name in the United Kingdom dates only from 1962, attempts to tax capital gains of a sort, in land, especially increases in value resulting from community development, go back to the land taxes of Lloyd George's famous 1909 budget. After the introduction of general capital gains taxes, taxes on development gains in land continued in the form of the betterment levy 1967–70, and more recently, the development gains tax and the development land tax (both now abolished). But it would be outside the scope of this book to examine the special features of development charges; we shall concentrate on the taxation of capital gains in general.

The short-term gains tax of 1962 (as outlined in Chapter 6) treated certain short-term gains as income for tax purposes. The 1965 legislation introduced a long-term gains tax and modified the short-term gains tax of 3 years earlier, so that gains on assets acquired and realised within 1 year were assessed to income tax; all gains on assets held for over 1 year were treated as long term. Long-term gains were charged at 30 per cent, with provision for a lower rate for taxpayers with small incomes by which, in effect, a proportion of the net gain was charged to income tax and surtax if this benefited the taxpayer. Losses were allowable where gains would be chargeable and could be carried forward. Various assets were exempt from tax, notably one residence, savings certificates, premium bonds, life insurance policies, chattels under £2,000, and capital receipts not derived from assets, e.g. football pool winnings. Charities and approved superannuation funds were exempt. Capital losses could be offset against gains and unrelieved losses carried forward.

For purposes of capital gains tax a husband and wife were treated as one unit.

Capital gains of companies were treated as income and charged to corporation tax, but a gain on a physical asset could be "rolled over" by a business and, provided the proceeds were reinvested within a year in another physical asset, no gains tax was payable.

Inevitably, for practical reasons, gains were taxed on a realisation (not accrued) basis; hence a valuation was required on acquisition (or budget day 1965 for assets acquired before then) and no disposal. But disposal did not mean only sale; as originally introduced death and gifts were treated as disposals, but gifts totalling less than £100 per donor were annually exempt and, on death, the first £5,000 of gains was exempted. A retirement relief for family businesses also exempted £5,000 of gains.

Since 1965 nearly every Finance Act has been partly taken up with amendments to the tax. The main changes of principle have been the following:

(1) *Exemption provisions.* In 1968 a general exemption provision was introduced where chargeable gains did not exceed £50 per year. The amount and form of this exemption has changed over time. Following the introduction of individual income taxation in 1990–91 (see above p. 187) the married couple are no longer treated as the unit for capital gains tax and in 1991–92 the exemption was £5,500 of gains per individual per annum.

Other exemptions have also been raised. The retirement relief has been frequently increased and the age at which it can be claimed reduced to 55. The figure below which individual chattels are exempt was £3,000, with a marginal relief in 1991–92.

In 1969 the range of securities exempted from capital gains tax was extended to cover all those issued or guaranteed by the British government. In 1984 the exemption was extended to corporate bonds.

(2) *Abolition of short-term gains tax.* In 1971 the short-term gains tax was completely abolished, gains realised within a year henceforward being subject to the long-term gains tax. This represented a considerable simplification and removed the inequity by which gains on assets held for 364 days might be subject to a much higher charge than gains on assets held for 366 days; but it completely severed any link between capital gains tax and income tax until such a link was re-introduced in 1988 (below).

(3) *Changes in deemed realisation provisions.* Also in 1971 the Conservative Government abolished the provision by which death counted as a deemed realisation under the tax, leaving the estate duty valuation as the acquisition value in the hands of the heirs; parallel with this provision went the abolition of the charge to capital gains tax every 15 years on discretionary trusts. Ceasing to treat death as a deemed disposal effected a considerable simplification; but it accentuated the lock-in effect of capital gains tax and could be held to be inequitable. At the time, the Labour Party spokesman on Treasury affairs pledged his Party to re-introduce the provision; but when Labour came to power in 1974 they did not do so.

One of the arguments used to justify the change was that capital left at death had been subject to a double charge: capital gains tax and estate duty. When, therefore capital transfer tax, with its taxation of lifetime gifts replaced estate duty (see below) the treatment by which gifts counted as a realisation was somewhat anomalous. Despite the lower scale for gifts, under capital transfer tax, the combined capital gains tax and capital transfer tax on a lifetime gift might exceed the tax payable on a similar amount left at death. This situation was changed in 1980 when a rollover relief was introduced for gifts between individuals. A gift would not be subject to gains tax unless and until disposed of by the recipient, at which time the gain would be calculated on the acquisition value of the donor, but any capital transfer tax paid at the time of the gift would be allowed as a deduction against the gain. (After Inheritance Tax replaced capital transfer tax in 1986, gifts between individuals were exempt from death duty unless made within seven years before death.)

(4) *Indexation for inflation.* For some years criticism had been directed against the failure to provide any inflation-proofing in the capital gains tax. Gains were assessed on increases in money values; if money values rose more rapidly than the real value of the assets taxed, a gains tax, in effect, became a wealth tax.

After a departmental review of this issue, in his 1976 budget Mr. Healey declined to index the tax but improved the exemption limit. He argued that insulation against inflation could not logically be confined to capital gains tax payers; if they enjoyed it, in principle inflation proofing ought to be extended to holders of building society and savings bank deposits. But, he said, "We cannot afford to go down this road." His successor, Sir Geoffrey Howe did not have these inhibitions. In 1982 he provided for the indexation of the acquisition price of assets provided they had been held for more than one year. The acquisition price is up-rated by the rise in the retail price index. The provision was not retrospective and applied only to price rises after March 1982. The up-rating cannot be used to turn a gain into a loss.

These restrictions meant that the indexation was a very partial measure. Moreover, because it was the original acquisition costs that was indexed, not the total value as at March 1982, a future tax charge on inflationary gains would still arise in respect of many assets held before that date.

(5) *A new base and new rates, 1988.* In 1988 Mr. Lawson, Sir Geoffrey's successor, removed the inflation anomaly by the radical measure of changing the capital gains tax base line from 1965 to 1982. No gains on assets held before April 6, 1982, are chargeable. At the same time capital gains became subject to the individual's top marginal rate of income tax, which, as a result of the income tax cuts in 1988 (see p. 141) meant either 25 or 40 per cent.

Whilst these have been the main changes there have been many others narrower in their impact; they include a more favourable treatment of gains in authorised unit trusts; the exemption of gifts to charities; the inclusion of the first letting of a non-residual building as an occasion of charge; the extension to capital gains tax of the capital transfer tax arrangements for agricultural land and historic houses; and the extension of facilities for payments by instalments.

Assessment of Capital Gains Tax

From the start, save for the short-term gains tax abolished in 1971, capital gains were treated more favourably than other forms of income. Despite the alignment of rates in 1988, that continues to be the case. Capital gains enjoy a substantial annual exemption, separate from the income tax threshold and, like the latter, indexed. Capital gains tax can be completely avoided on assets retained until death. Capital gains enjoy full indexation, which is a much more favourable treatment than is meted out to the income tax payer the value of whose savings deposits has been eroded by inflation. Investing for capital gains remains a significant way of avoiding income tax.

Death Duties

Death duties have notable advantages over other forms of capital tax. Duty is levied at a time when transfer of ownership is inevitable; we can expect that the accumulator of wealth will suffer less loss of satisfaction from the prospect that his wealth will be taxed at his death than if he had paid the tax during his life; and that (given generous treatment of widows and dependent children) the beneficiaries from the estate, whose legacies are reduced by tax, will not miss what they never had. There is a particular moral justification for taxing inherited wealth in that the inheritors have usually done nothing by their own efforts to merit the legacies. Moreover, the particular problem of capital taxes is reduced to manageable size because only a small proportion (under 2 per cent in the United Kingdom) of total property has to be valued for death duty purposes in any one year, and that at a time when an inventory of the property is required anyway to carry out the will of the deceased or the laws of intestacy.

On the other hand, because death duties are often very heavy (much heavier than annual wealth taxes) standards of administration and valuation need to be very high if serious inequity is to be avoided and reliefs are necessary to prevent hardship, for example, when property values fall markedly between the date of death and the disposal of assets to meet death duty.

The usual arguments of equity, efficiency and equality apply. A death duty is less suitable than a wealth tax as a supplement to income tax but it does at least ensure that, in the long run, the taxable capacity embodied in wealth is tapped by the Revenue. On efficiency grounds a death duty has much to commend it; it is only likely to be a disincentive to effort, enterprise or saving if the object of these activities is a desire to bequeath. Further, as inherited wealth is almost certainly the greatest single cause of inequality in both incomes and capital in our community,* effective death duties are essential for a policy of promoting equality.

Estate Duty versus Inheritance Tax

A strong case can therefore be presented for making a death duty the core of any system of capital or wealth taxation. But what sort of death duty? As we indicated at the beginning of this chapter, in principle there are two main categories with variants: estate duty and inheritance tax (or legacy duty). Under estate duty tax is levied on the aggregate value of the property left by the deceased regardless of its destination. Under inheritance tax duty is levied on the legacies regardless of the size of estate from which they came. The inheritance tax may be progressive in relation to each individual legacy; or progressive on a cumulative basis on legacies received over a period of years or a lifetime; or progression may take into account not only the size of the legacy but the prior wealth of the beneficiary.

Both estate duty and inheritance tax may be linked to gift taxes which may be more or less closely integrated with the death duty. Thus the capital transfer tax, as introduced into the United Kingdom in 1974, provided for a donor gift tax, the rate of tax on each taxable gift being determined by the total of such gifts, the lifetime total of gifts being aggregated to determine the rate of duty on the estate left at death. However, under the U.K. tax, gifts and property left at death were not treated identically; the rate of tax on lifetime

*For an indication of the importance of inheritance on the distribution of wealth, see C. D. Harbury and D. M. W. N. Hitchens, *Inheritance and Wealth Inequality in Britain*, George Allen & Unwin, 1979.

gifts was lower than on transfers at death. An accessions tax is the form of inheritance tax corresponding to the capital transfer tax. An accessions tax would be levied cumulatively on the recipient of gifts and legacies, the rate of tax on any one gift or inheritance being determined by the total received by way of inheritances or gifts.

Let us begin by comparing the simple version of estate duty and inheritance tax. The relative merits and defects of these two taxes are a matter both of historical and of recent controversy in the United Kingdom. The main arguments used in favour of estate duty are that it is easier to administer and a better revenue yielder than inheritance tax.

Even the simplest form of inheritance tax would require an "account" for each beneficiary from an estate, compared with a single account for each estate under estate duty; so administrative costs would necessarily be higher.

Estate duty is a better revenue yielder than inheritance tax in the sense that, if the same scale of progressive rates was applied to estates and to inheritances the yield of the estate duty would be higher. Only if an estate was left to one heir would the inheritance tax yield the same revenue as estate duty; in all other cases the yield would be less. Let us illustrate by reference to past rates of estate duty in the United Kingdom. Ignoring special concessions, the rates of estate duty which applied between 1949 and 1969 in the United Kingdom were 80 per cent on an estate of £1 million and 50 per cent on an estate of £100,000.* Let us assume the same rates for an inheritance tax. Then under estate duty, from an estate of £1,000,000, £800,000 goes to the Exchequer. Under inheritance tax the yield depends on the disposition of the property. If all was left to one heir his pre-tax legacy would be £1,000,000 and 80 per cent (£800,000) would go in tax as with estate duty. If, however, the estate was left in parcels of £100,000 each to ten people, then under inheritance tax the rate on each bequest would be 50 per cent, making a total revenue of only £500,000. However, there is no *need* for the rates to be the same. Inheritance tax rates could be calculated which would realise the same yield as estate duty, but the

*During this period the rates of estate duty were by totality and not by brackets; i.e. they were average and not marginal rates.

tax payment would be differently distributed; sole beneficiaries from an estate would pay more than under estate duty, whilst beneficiaries from an estate widely dispersed would pay less. Nevertheless, if the inheritance tax provided a bigger impetus to diffusion of wealth than estate duty, this feature must always tend to reduce the yield of inheritance tax as compared with estate duty.

It is, indeed, one of the main advantages of inheritance tax that it might be more effective in dispersing property—that it might be a better instrument to promote equality in wealth holding. An inheritance tax provides an incentive to wealth holders to spread their wealth more widely, because, by so doing, they reduce the amount of tax paid on it; but whether many would do so is an open question and we know insufficient of the psychology of millionaires to be able to answer it. More important, it is large inheritances rather than large estates which perpetuate inequality and by taxing large legacies more than small the inheritance tax is striking at the heart of the problem of inequality of wealth.

Another advantage of inheritance tax is that it is basically more equitable and sensible. As long as death duties were very low it was possible for wealthy men to insure against them so that they could pass on their estate intact to their heirs; then the incidence of tax was on the estate owner. But with high levels of death duties only owners of small estates can save enough of their income to meet death duty liabilities on their estate (including the insurance policy). The formal incidence of tax is on the heirs. Under inheritance tax this is recognised and payment related to benefit received. Estate duty, on the other hand, to quote Winston Churchill, is an assertion of "the vicious principle of taxing property instead of persons"; an attempt "to tax the dead instead of the living."*

Further, because the inheritance tax relates to the beneficiaries and not, like estate duty, simply to the total property left at death, inheritance tax offers more scope for adjusting tax according to the circumstances of the beneficiary in ways which accord with prevailing notions of equity. A common feature of inheritance taxes is

*Winston S. Churchill, *Lord Randolph Churchill*, 1906, chapters 15 and 16.

different scales of duty for different degrees of relationship, with the successors in the direct line paying at lower rates than successors in the indirect line or strangers in blood. Such differentiation, however, whilst it may help to sustain the family unit, may cut across the objective of reducing inequality. Another possible provision under inheritance tax is special exemptions to the minor children of a deceased parent; thus the Swedish inheritance tax allows an exemption for each year by which the child's age falls short of majority. Such sophisticated provisions are very difficult or impossible under estate duty. Also it is simpler to integrate a gifts tax with an inheritance tax than with estate duty—gifts and legacies can be treated precisely on a par.

Incidence of Death Duty

As we have already indicated, the formal incidence of death duty is on the heirs who are deprived of property they would otherwise have had. What of the effective incidence? We need to look at the effects on the supply of the factors of production in general—on effort, enterprise and saving—and to distinguish between the incentives of the accumulator of the property and of the inheritor. We also need to examine the position of the private business, including agriculture.

Effect on the Supply of the Factors of Production

We should expect death duty to have less effect on the effort and enterprise of the accumulator than an income tax of equivalent yield, for death duty, unlike income tax, does not prevent a man from *himself* enjoying the full fruits of labour or risk taking. Enterprise and effort will only be affected by death duty considerations if the person concerned wished to save at least a part of the income so acquired for his heirs; the effect on enterprise and effort can therefore be subsumed under the effect on saving. Will death duty significantly affect the incentive to save?

Much saving is undertaken with no thought of bequests in mind; people accumulate property for a variety of reasons—future security and enjoyment; the power that wealth confers; inertia—the sheer inability to spend their wealth; the desire to manage a large business; the posthumous glory of dying rich; and many others which are unaffected by death duty considerations. Nevertheless the desire to bequeath is a motive which may grow in importance with the age of the property owner when the other motives have been realised or gone by the board. And it is older people who hold most accumulations of wealth, and who may be induced by the tax not only to cease saving but to spend out of capital. A death duty does not *necessarily* discourage saving; a property owner seeking to leave his heirs a particular sum might be encouraged to save *more* to achieve his object despite the duty: but if marginal rates were very high it would seem more likely that he would give up the unequal contest, stop saving from income and perhaps spend from capital.

The effect on the prospective heir may provide some offset to the disincentive effects on the property owner. The tax reduces the expectations and the actual inheritance of the heir and may thus stimulate him to work and save.

Apart from the effects on the incentive to save of property accumulator and heirs, where the net effect, which influences the long run rate of capital accumulation, is not clear, the main consequence of a heavy death duty is a transfer of assets from the private to the public sector. The property accumulator does not have to make any provision to meet death duty liability, and the inheritor is likely to regard the post-tax inheritance as his capital and make no attempt to meet the tax, in whole or in part, by economies in consumption. Thus high death duties are likely to be paid almost wholly from capital; this does not, of course, mean that capital is physically destroyed. It means that payment of death duty is met by a sale of assets and the state applies the revenue to its capital account to reduce its borrowing requirement. Because death duties are largely not met by a reduction in demand on current output they do little or nothing to release resources for government purposes. Essentially death duties are concerned with the structure of property ownership in the community—with ownership as between the public and private sectors and also between individuals and families within the private sector. This realisation should help to clarify the purpose a death duty should serve and the form of tax most suitable for that purpose.

Effect on the Private Business

Our general or macro analysis of the effective incidence of death duty needs to be supplemented by partial or micro analysis. A death duty may have particular effects on certain forms of economic activity, i.e. the private business, whether in industry, commerce or agriculture. The large public joint stock company is unlikely to be affected by death duties. The death of a major shareholder will not affect the company's activities if the shares are readily marketable. But a private business owned by one man, a partnership or a private company may face serious problems.

Consider a family business of moderate size (say upwards of £200,000) of which the chairman, who was also the majority shareholder, dies. It is probable that the available non-trade assets of the deceased would be insufficient to meet death duty liabilities. Other members of the family might be able to buy the shares, but possibly only at the cost of a substantial loan on the security of the business. A new interest might have to be sought, perhaps on unfavourable terms to the family, either in the form of a large new shareholder from outside the family or, more drastically, a complete takeover by another company. Not only may death duty affect the private firm at the time of a shareholder's death in the way we have described, but it generates anticipatory action—in the form of earlier transfer of ownership to younger people (if there is no gift tax or if gift tax rates are lower than death rates), the acquisition of liquid assets by the business, or the seeking of outside interest or takeovers in anticipation of death duties. If the company is large enough it may decide to reduce the impact of death duties by "going public".

Clearly not all these results would necessarily be detrimental to the efficient use of resources, for example, transfer to younger people or take-over by a holding company which supplied up-to-date management methods, could be just what the family business needed at that juncture. The Bolton Committee feared that the existence of heavy death duties was a major disincentive to the founder of a business enterprise as he approached retirement;* but other research has cast doubt on this view.† We are really very ignorant about how important a motive for entrepreneurs is the desire to pass on a business to the next generation.

Agriculture has been, and remains, the family business par excellence, with even the private company making little headway. Because of the high capitalisation of agriculture, in the form of land, and because agricultural land prices may be affected by a variety of factors unconnected with the return obtainable from its use in agriculture, the owner-occupier of even a modest-sized farm is liable to come within the scope of heavy rates of death duty.

How far a death duty has detrimental effects on the efficiency of the private business, including agriculture, depends amongst other things on the weight and form of the tax; the existence or otherwise of special concessions to private businesses; the trend of agricultural land prices; and the evolution of specialist institutions in the capital market to provide finance for firms caught or liable to be caught in a death duty net. To some of those matters we shall return in the next section in the context of the United Kingdom death duties.

Death Duties in the United Kingdom

From 1894 to 1974 the main, and from 1949 the sole, death duty in the United Kingdom was estate duty. It deserves a special place in our fiscal history as the first *consistently* progressive tax. It was introduced by Sir William Harcourt at rates rising from 1 per cent to 8 per cent—described by contemporaries as "enormously high". By 1914 the maximum rate had risen to 20 per cent, by 1919 to 40, by 1939 to 60, and by 1949 to 80. These rates were calculated on the totality of the estate—i.e. a single rate was charged on the whole estate. In 1969 Mr. Roy Jenkins, as Chancellor, replaced the system of progression by totality (sometimes referred to as the "slab" basis) by progression by brackets (sometimes called the "slice" scale).

---

*Report of the Committee of Inquiry on Small Firms, Cmnd. 4811, November 1971, pp. 224–229.
†Jonathan Boswell, *The Rise and Decline of Small Firms,* Allen & Unwin, 1972, chapter 5.

The intention of the change was to leave effective rates much as before; the maximum rate on the slice scale became 85 per cent, with a ceiling provision that limited the total amount that could be taken in tax to 80 per cent. Inflation makes the same nominal rates of duty annually more burdensome; partly to allow for past inflation, Mr. Anthony Barber, in 1972, introduced a new and lower scale (with a maximum of 75 per cent), raised the threshold of the tax and provided for a special £15,000 exemption for property left to a surviving spouse. This remained the scale until the abolition of the duty.

The concern of governments for the effects of estate duty on agriculture and the private business was shown by a series of reliefs. An agricultural concession was first introduced in 1925 and from 1949 took the form of a 45 per cent reduction of duty on the agricultural value of agricultural land. A similar concession for the industrial premises, plant and machinery of a sole trader or a closely-owned unquoted company was allowed in 1954. Provisions by which estate duty payments on real estate (land and buildings) could be made in instalments over a period of years had existed from the inception of the tax; latterly they were extended to unincorporated business and to shares of closely-owned unquoted companies.

Criticism of Estate Duty

In the 1960s and 1970s estate duty was subject to an increasing volume of criticism on two issues of principle: its avoidability and the form of the tax. Let us look at these points in more detail.

Estate duty was widely referred to as "the voluntary tax" because of the ease with which it could be avoided. Many methods were available. Thus estate duty could be reduced by the "death bed" purchase of agricultural land to take advantage of the agricultural relief. One of the more sophisticated avoidance methods was the setting up of a discretionary trust — a trust under which the trustees have discretion to make payments to any of a large number of possible beneficiaries, with the result that a "beneficial interest" only passed (and hence death duty was only payable) on the death of the next but last of the possible beneficiaries.* Above all, there was the loophole that gifts, as such, were not subject to tax. From the inception of estate duty there was a provision by which gifts made within a certain period before death were aggregated with the estate and charged to estate duty and this so-called gifts *inter vivos* period had been extended to 7 years in 1968. But provided people gave their property away early enough, death duty could be entirely avoided. Wealth holders who did not wish to become dependent on children or grandchildren but yet wished to pass on much of their wealth intact could secure their independence by buying an annuity and avoid estate duty by giving the remainder of their estate away and living for 7 years thereafter.

In failing to have a general gift tax to support its death duty the United Kingdom was almost unique amongst the "mixed" economies. At the same time the rates of death duty in the United Kingdom were outstandingly high. The combination of easy avoidability and high rates gave the maximum encouragement to avoidance. Undoubtedly much avoidance took place,† but nonetheless death duties in the United Kingdom, expressed as a proportion of G.N.P., yielded more revenue than perhaps any other country obtained from death duties and gift taxes combined.‡ Thus the prime objection to the avoidability of estate duty was not loss of revenue to the government, but the fact that the gains from avoidance were not evenly spread; the system conflicted with the principle both of equity and of equality.

Responsibility for taking action to avoid estate duty rested on one person, but the consequences were felt by others: thus those with parents who were mean, lethargic or took a sanguine view of their life expectation suffered, compared with those whose parents were generous, active and realistic about their life expectation. The heirs of the owners of property which lent itself most readily to gifts or to being put in trust benefited compared with the heirs to property not

*Chancellor Roy Jenkins attempted to tighten up on discretionary trusts in 1969, but his measures were only of limited effectiveness.

†E. G. Horsman, The Avoidance of Estate Duty by Gifts *Inter Vivos*: Some Quantitative Evidence, *The Economic Journal*, September 1975.

‡*Taxation of Capital on Death: A Possible Inheritance Tax in Place of Estate Duty*, Cmnd. 4930, March 1972, p. 11.

so easily disposed of by gift or trust. In general the rich were most likely to be able to take advantage of avoidance opportunities; they could afford the best advice, could give without impairing their living standards and, especially if they had inherited property, were most likely to be in a position to give early, so increasing the chances of avoiding duty. Finally, the gifts *inter vivos* provision was particularly inequitable in the case of premature death. Two wealth owners might make gifts at the same age; one survived the requisite period and no duty was paid; the other died within 7 years and the gifts were taxed. Yet equity would have suggested that any discrimination ought to have been the other way round, the earlier death justifying more generous treatment because of the likelihood that the heirs to the shorter-lived would have been more dependent on him.

The second objection to estate duty was the one we have already discussed—that by imposing tax on the property left by the deceased irrespective of its destination, estate duty put the emphasis the wrong way round and that a variant of the inheritance tax would be both more equitable and more favourable to a reduction in inequality. Amongst academic writers in particular, opinion was growing in favour of an accessions tax, or something like it.*

Proposals for Reform and Capital Transfer Tax

The first official moves towards a possible major reform occurred when Mr. Barber was Chancellor of the Exchequer. In March, 1972 a Green Paper was issued as a basis for discussion: *Taxation of Capital on Death: A Possible Inheritance Tax in Place of Estate Duty*, Cmnd. 4930. As the title implies it concentrated on the second issue, the form of death duty. It was a document which committed the government only to sounding out views. Although the Green Paper recognised that "all the possibilities will need to be discussed" its

---

*For example, J. E. Meade, *Efficiency, Equality and The Ownership of Property*, Allen & Unwin, 1964; *The Economist*, Taxing Britain's Wealth, 15 and 22 January 1966; Oliver Stutchbury, *The Case for Capital Taxes*, Fabian Tract 388, December 1968; C. T. Sandford, *Taxing Personal Wealth*, Allen & Unwin, 1971; A. B. Atkinson, *Unequal Shares, Wealth in Britain*, Allen Lane, The Penguin Press, 1972.

attitude to a full accessions tax was unpropitious. The document stated that: "administratively it would represent a most formidable task because it would involve keeping a record over a lifetime for every person who might at some time receive an inheritance above any *de minimis* limit that might be prescribed". The practical possibilities were considered to be a simple inheritance tax or one in which legacies received over a 10-year period might be aggregated. The most surprising omission from the Green Paper was any consideration of a possible gift tax; it was apparently envisaged that if an inheritance tax was introduced it would be accompanied by a gifts *inter vivos* provision similar to that under estate duty. The Inland Revenue received evidence about the replacement of an estate duty by inheritance tax, but before the Chancellor announced his decision on it the Conservatives had lost power.

The new Labour Chancellor, Mr. Denis Healey, lost no time in declaring his policy on death duties. In his first budget, March 1974, as part of "A determined attack on the maldistribution of wealth in Britain", he proposed a lifetime gifts tax, as he put it to "mesh in" with estate duty. A White Paper* published in August 1974 gave further details and a second Finance Bill, in the autumn of 1974, enacted the new capital transfer tax. The tax came into force for lifetime transfers as from March 26, 1974 (the budget day of its announcement) and replaced estate duty on transfers at death as from March 13, 1975 (when the Bill became law).

Originally, as set out in the White Paper and in the Finance Bill, rates of tax on *inter vivos* gifts were to be the same as those at death. However, in the Committee stage of the Finance Bill the government changed its mind and introduced a lower rate for lifetime transfers: the lifetime rates were made half the rates at death on estates of up to £100,000, but thereafter they rose more rapidly so that the marginal rates were the same at £300,000. The capital transfer tax was cumulative. Taxable gifts were added to each other in determining the rate of tax on any one gift and these were added to the estate left at death to determine the tax on that.

Capital transfer tax as introduced, carried an annual exemption

Capital Transfer Tax, Cmnd. 5705, August 1974.

of the first £100 of gifts to any one recipient and over and above that the exemption of £1,000 per donor per annum. In addition, the first £15,000 of transfers carried a nil rate, so that, in effect, there was a lifetime exemption of £15,000. Another notable feature of the tax was the complete exemption of transfers between husband and wife, whether during lifetime or at death.

The problem posed by discretionary trusts was to be dealt with by a periodic charge on the capital of the trust. The tax included a concession to agriculture but restricted to "full-time working farmers" and with a limit of £250,000 or 1,000 acres. In the 1975 Finance Act this took the form of a preferential valuation for agricultural land, using a rental formula instead of open market value. The tax did not originally contain any reliefs for the private business, except that the lower scale for lifetime gifts was justified as an encouragement to the owners to transfer farms and businesses to the next generation, thus reducing the chances of "gerontocracy".

As introduced the rates of tax (on a "slice" scale), rose from a zero rate on the first £15,000 to a marginal rate at death of 50 per cent on £100,000 and 75 per cent on estates over £2 million. Free transfer between husband and wife meant that, apart from the annual exemption, ordinary gifts out of income and gifts in consideration of a marriage (which benefited from an exemption) a married couple were able to pass on £30,000 to a child tax free.

Changes in Capital Transfer Tax

When introduced capital transfer tax was strongly attacked for its severity. In fact the rates were lower than those of the estate duty it superseded (where the marginal rate was 60 per cent on an estate of £100,000 and the top rate of 75 per cent related to an estate of £500,000). The free transfer between husband and wife was also an important new easement in capital transfer tax. On the other hand, lifetime gifts were taxed for the first time as such; and, unlike estate duty, capital transfer tax was cumulative; the rate of tax on any lifetime gift and on the estate at death was determined by reference to the total of taxable gifts previously made.

Mr. Healey indicated that he expected the yield from death

duties and gift tax to fall slightly at first, compared with what it would have been under estate duty, but then to pick up as the cumulative provisions came into their own. The general taxation of lifetime gifts and the periodic charge on discretionary trusts under capital transfer tax seemed to deal adequately with the two major forms of estate duty avoidance.

In the event, first, under Mr. Healey himself, still more under Sir Geoffrey Howe, the tax was successively watered down—or, as the Tories put it, its teeth were drawn. In his 1976 budget Mr. Healey altered the form of agricultural relief for working farmers to a 50 per cent reduction in valuation of land and buildings for transfer tax purposes. In 1975 he allowed businesses the option to pay tax in interest free instalments over 8 years (a very valuable relief in inflationary times) and in 1976 he introduced a new relief by which a transfer related to a private business would attract tax on only 70 per cent of its value; this figure was reduced to 50 per cent in most cases from October 1977. Also in the 1976 budget Mr. Healey increased the annual exemption for gifts to £2,000. He likewise eased the tax burden on works of art and historic houses. In 1978 he increased the zero rate band by £10,000 to £25,000 and raised the starting point of each taxable band correspondingly. Further the periodic charge on discretionary trusts was postponed instead of taking effect immediately, as had been intended.

When Sir Geoffrey Howe became Chancellor he initiated a review of the tax by Lord Cockfield, Minister of State at the Treasury. Subsequently almost every budget saw new concessions and reliefs. Thresholds were raised, exemptions increased, relief extended to agricultural landlords (at first a 20 per cent rebate, then increased to 30 per cent) tax rates reduced and the period of cumulation reduced from lifetime to 10 years.

Mr. Lawson and Inheritance Tax

As with capital gains tax, Mr. Lawson continued in the same direction as his predecessor but with larger strides. In his first Budget, in 1984, he cut the rates (from a top rate of 75 per cent to 60 per cent) and reduced the scale for lifetime gifts. The most dramatic and radical changes, however, came in 1986 and 1988. In 1986 the Chancellor abolished the provision for the taxation of lifetime gifts between individuals (extended in the following year to gifts to trusts where there was an interest in possession) reverting to a gifts *inter vivos* provision. Such gifts were taxable only if made within 7 years before death, the rate of tax increasing from 20 per cent of the death rate for deaths in the 6–7th year to 100 per cent of the death rate for gifts in the 3 years prior to death. As the tax was now, virtually, a death duty only, its designation of capital transfer tax doubtless seemed inappropriate. Yet he presumably did not wish to appear to be reverting to the old maligned estate duty. Flouting established usage, he therefore designated what was left behind of the capital transfer tax "Inheritance Tax". In 1987 he simplified the rate structure and raised the threshold substantially and then, in 1988, he abolished all the rates except that at 40 per cent. Table 9.1 contrasts the structure and rates when Mr. Lawson came to the Exchequer in 1983, with that after his 1988 Budget.

The threshold of Inheritance Tax is indexed and, in 1991–92

TABLE 9.1
Changes in Death Duty Structure and Rates 1984 to 1988

Band of Chargeable Value	1983–84 Capital Transfer Tax Rate on Death	1983–84 Capital Transfer Tax Lifetime Rate	1988–89 Inheritance Tax Rate on Death	1988–89 Inheritance Tax Lifetime Rate
£000	%	%	%	%
0–60	NIL	NIL	NIL	Not
60–80	30	15	NIL	chargeable
80–110	35	17½	NIL	if gifts
110–140	40	20	40	between
140–175	45	22½	40	individuals
175–220	50	25	40	or into a
220–270	55	30	40	trust with
270–700	60	35	40	beneficial
700–1,350	65	40	40	interest,
1,350–2,650	70	45	40	unless within
Over 2,650	75	50	40	7 years before death

stood at £140,000. Gifts to charities, political parties or for "national purposes" enjoy complete exemption except to foreign donees. There is conditional exemption for national heritage assets.

Assessment of Inheritance Tax

Whatever Mr. Lawson chooses to call the death duty he left behind him when he quit the Exchequer, his "Inheritance Tax" is very much an estate duty with nearly all the deficiencies of the former estate duty plus some of its own.

As we argued earlier, the estate duty (i.e. donor-based) form of death duty is both less equitable and less geared to reducing inequality in the distribution of wealth than is a genuine inheritance (donee-based) tax.

The elimination of the lifetime gifts component (except for the gifts *inter vivos* provision) means that the simplest form of tax avoidance lies wide open—and the one of which the rich are best equipped to take advantage. With free transfer between husband and wife at 1991–92 thresholds, £280,000 can be passed from parents to children every 7 years with no tax payable—and that apart from the annual exemption (currently £3,000) and other exemptions like wedding gifts.

The *inter vivos* provision is itself a particularly unsavoury, if not to say iniquitous, feature of the "Inheritance Tax" as it was of the old estate duty. It constitutes a "lottery on life", a "dice with death"—a state-created gamble in which the loser is not the gambler but his unfortunate heirs; and often those who lose because of it are those whose parents have died young, and whose needs are likely to be greatest.

Again, quite apart from their inequity, it must be doubted whether the reliefs for agriculture and the private business really benefit the economy as distinct from the existing owners of the relieved assets. Tax reliefs become "capitalised", that is to say they become reflected in the price of the asset so as to equalise (or nearly so) the return to different types of investment. Thus the relief to agricultural landlords raises the price of agricultural land, as does the larger relief (now without upper limit) to full-time working farmers—which makes it particularly difficult for farm managers to become owners.

The new dimension which Mr. Lawson has added to the former estate duty is its lack of progression. Formally a death duty at a single rate above a threshold is progressive because the larger the estate the smaller its tax free proportion and therefore the higher the average rate of tax paid on it. But clearly, with a single rate, the degree of progression is limited. Moreover, for many wealthy people it will be entirely counteracted by the concessions to agriculture and the private business. Currently (1991–92) there is a 50 per cent reduction in the value for transfers of agricultural land and buildings owned and occupied by the transferor and in the value for transfer of a sole proprietor's business or a partner's interest in a partnership or a controlling shareholding; and a 30 per cent reduction for let agricultural land and for minority shareholdings and certain other business assets (subject to qualifications). Effectively the rate of tax on such assets is reduced from 40 to 20 per cent (where the relief is 50 per cent) or 28 per cent (where the relief is 30 per cent). It is in the estates of the richest that such assets figure most prominently. Quite apart from the scope of the rich to reduce their Inheritance Tax bill by gifts and other avoidance devices, it is probable that the effective incidence of Mr. Lawson's tax is regressive at the upper end: that the proportion of the estate taken in tax rises at first as the estate increases but then falls for the larger estates containing substantial relieved assets.

For most of this century death duties have been regarded, by Chancellors of the Exchequer of whatever party, as taxes to reduce inequalities in the distribution of wealth—or at least to put some limit on wealth accumulation. Mr. Lawson's Inheritance Tax, with its single rate, reliefs and loopholes, fails to fulfil that purpose. It strikes the author as somewhat odd that Mrs. Thatcher and Mr. Lawson, who put such stress on the enterprise culture, should have been so generous to large inheritors. The enterprise ethic surely implies that people should be rewarded according to their contributions to society: that the entrepeneur who produces a new gadget which delights or benefits millions should be entitled to keep most of the million pounds of profit that he makes. It seems entirely contrary to that philosophy that those who have received millions of pounds by inheritance, with no corresponding contribution, should keep as large or an even larger, proportion of it.

Postscript

In the 1992 Budget, confirmed by the result of the General Election, the Chancellor, Mr. Lamont, further increased the relief on business property (including agriculture) raising the 50 per cent relief to 100 per cent and the 30 per cent relief to 50 per cent and extending it to shares quoted on the Unlisted Securities Market. The threshold of Inheritance Tax was raised to £150,000 and the annual exemption for capital gains tax to £5,800.

CHAPTER 10

Local Government Expenditure and Income

Why Local Government?

In a federal state, governmental functions are necessarily shared between the individual states or provinces on the one hand and the central federal authority on the other. When a federation is formed hitherto independent or autonomous states agree to unite for some purposes and retain their autonomy for others, and this division of powers is written into the constitution.

In a unitary state like the United Kingdom (and in respect of local government within the states of a federation) the position is different; regional and local governments derive their powers and functions from the central government which could at any time, by the ordinary process of legislation, change the powers of local authorities or abolish them altogether. Why then have local authorities in a unitary state?

The answer is partly political, partly economic. In a democracy local government provides a local centre of political interest and activity; it is a training ground for national politicians; and local grievances can often be dealt with locally instead of occupying the time of national statesmen. Also it may be more *efficient* for local matters to be dealt with in the light of local circumstances and local needs by people who are accountable on the spot; and the separation of function between central and local government may prevent the growth of a top-heavy bureaucracy. Further, genuine local autonomy provides the opportunity for innovation and experimentation; fresh minds and different points of view can be brought to bear on problems; subsequently experiments successful in one area may be extended to others.

The picture is complex. There are some functions of government which, on political grounds, are essentially the province of the central government, like foreign affairs and defence. There are others where the over-riding demand for national uniformity leaves no scope for local discretion, e.g. the rules and levels of the main social security benefits. There are other governmental functions which need to be run on a large, perhaps national, scale if they are to be economically run, such as the administration of income tax. In services where there is scope for local discretion, and which therefore are appropriate to delegate to local government, economic and political desiderata may conflict, for the technically optimum size of unit for a service may cover too large an area to generate local political interest, moreover the optimum size of different services is difficult to assess, will vary between services and will alter over time with changes in technology.

Further, no system of local government will be determined solely by reference to general economic and political desiderata. Special factors will come into play, such as the influence of history, tradition, ethnic groupings, local, regional and sub-national loyalties. Where local authorities are set up with discretionary powers, some measure of central control over, or intervention in, their activities will take place. The central government's concern with overall management of the economy (see Chapter 12) may require it to retain powers to ensure that total local government spending is in line with national economic policy. Governments may feel under an obligation to ensure minimum standards in certain services. In some aspects of services uniformity of treatment may be considered essential. Interventions may also be necessary in the form of grant aid to allow for externalities arising from certain services and to secure some regional redistribution of income. Besides those cogent reasons for central government control over local government, in practice ministers may intervene for more narrowly party political ends and be unwilling to tolerate local plans which conflict with the national objectives they have set themselves (e.g. the establishment of comprehensive secondary education).

Although in recent years local government expenditure in the United Kingdom has been growing more rapidly than central government spending, the proportion of total government expenditure by local authorities is substantially less than in the first decade of the 20th century (see Table 2.3). This relative decline is partly a product of the centralisation fostered by two world wars and the large nationally administered system of social security payments; it is also partly a reflection of a national desire for uniformity of treatment in particular services. But there is also no doubt that, over the years, functions have been taken from local authorities or never given to them because they were considered too small in both resources and territorial area to carry them out effectively or because they simply were not trusted by the government in power. Not only that, perhaps more serious for local democracy has been the tightening of central control, so that local autonomy has been sapped and local authorities are in danger of being regarded simply as offices of Whitehall.

Reorganisation of local government areas seems to have done nothing to reverse the trend to increased central control. It is not our purpose to examine the politics of local government, but some brief description of the present organisation of local government is essential to an understanding of the fiscal implications.

The Structure of Local Government in the United Kingdom

Local government in Great Britain was reorganised by Acts in 1965 (for London) and 1972 and 1973. Acts of 1985 and 1986 abolished the six metropolitan counties and the Greater London Council respectively. The present system is thus a mixture of single and two tier authorities. The main divisions now are as follows:

(1) Metropolitan districts in England (36);
(2) Non-metropolitan counties (47) and districts (333) in England and Wales;
(3) Regions and Island Authorities (12) and districts (53) in Scotland;
(4) The City of London and the London boroughs (32).

Besides these local government units the country is covered by a network of regional economic planning councils of appointed members; but they have purely advisory functions and are of no fiscal significance. The question of a more significant devolution to Scotland and Wales periodically raises its head, but there is little immediate prospect of its implementation.

Local Government Expenditure

Local government is big business. In 1990, on current and capital account together, local government collectively spent over £61 billion, serviced a capital debt of some £53 billion and employed over 2¼ million persons. Local authorities, individually, are amongst the biggest landlords and landowners in the country.

Table 10.1 sets out the main items of local government current expenditure in 1964, 1974 and 1990. The items included in the table are all those totalling 2 per cent or more of local government current expenditure in any of the three years. The particular years are chosen so as to give the decade leading up to the Layfield Committee (set up in June 1974) which is something of a watershed, and the latest figures available at the time of writing. The items are divided into spending on goods and services on the one hand and transfers and subsidies on the other. Perhaps the outstanding feature is the dominance of education in the local authority current account. If scholarships and grants to students are included, education accounts for nearly 40 per cent of current total spending and a still larger proportion of expenditure on goods and services (exhaustive expenditure). The next largest item after education is debt interest at between 10 and 22 per cent in the years we have chosen.

Table 10.2 shows local authority expenditure on capital account for the same years and all items are included which account for 6 per cent or more of expenditure on capital account (which is substantially smaller than the total of current account spending). Housing is the biggest single item in the two earlier years and would still be in 1990 except for the offsetting item of receipts from sales of houses. Capital grants to the personal sector are also mainly for

TABLE 10.1
Local Authority Expenditure on Current Account, 1964, 1974, 1990

Main items	1964 £ million	1964 Percentage of total current expenditure	1974 £ million	1974 Percentage of total current expenditure	1990 £ million	1990 Percentage of total current expenditure
Goods and Services						
Roads and public lighting	179	7.1	432	4.6	2,120	3.9
Sewage and refuse disposal	122	4.8	231	2.5	1,850	3.4
Parks, pleasure grounds etc.	46	1.8	161	1.7	2,153	3.9
Police	174	6.9	627	6.7	5,046	9.2
Fire services	43	1.7	154	1.7	1,130	2.1
Education	937	37.1	3,083	33.2	18,780	34.4
NHS and personal social services	175	6.9	650	7.0	5,028	9.2
School meals and milk	77	3.0	264	2.8	—	—
General administration	56	2.2	189	2.0	1,987	3.6
Other*	147	5.7	852	9.1	4,543	8.3
Transfers and Subsidies						
Rent rebates and allowances	—	—	—	—	4,522	8.3
Scholarships, grants to universities etc.	74	2.9	241	2.6	1,541	2.8
Debt interest						
to central government	125	4.9 ⎫ 17.6	670	7.2 ⎫ 22.0	4,622	8.5 ⎫ 9.7
to other creditors	320	12.7 ⎭	1,376	14.8 ⎭	682	1.2 ⎭
Other	51	2.0	362	3.9	644	1.2
Total Current Expenditure	2,526	100.0	9,292	100.0	54,648	100.0

* Including allowances for non-trading capital consumption of £383m in 1974 and £2,070m in 1990. — Means negligible; no separate figures recorded in National Accounts.

Source: National Income and Expenditure 1964–74, table 50; *United Kingdom National Accounts, 1991*, table 8.2.

Notes: Items are included in the table if comprising 2 or more per cent of current expenditure in any of the three years. Percentage columns do not always add up exactly due to rounding.

Because of changes in composition and designation, figures for some items are not precisely comparable over time.

TABLE 10.2

Local Authority Expenditure on Capital Account, 1964, 1974, 1990

Main items	1964		1974		1990	
	£ million	Percentage of total capital expenditure	£ million	Percentage of total capital expenditure	£ million	Percentage of total capital expenditure
General public services	—	—	—	—	617	8.9
Roads and public lighting	105	9.3	327	9.0	1,500	21.5
Housing†	495	43.7	1,693	46.4	1,273	18.3
Sewerage and refuse disposal	74	6.5	136	3.7	221	3.2
Education	180	15.9	525	14.4	1,041	15.0
Recreational and cultural affairs	23	2.0	71	1.9	600	8.6
Capital Grants to personal sector	20	1.8	196	5.4	804	11.5
Other*	235	20.8	697	19.1	907	13.0
Total Capital Expenditure	1,132	100.0	3,645	100.0	6,963	100.0

* Excluding net lending to private sector.
† Net of receipts from sales: £4,364 in 1990.
Source: National Income and Expenditure, 1964–74, table 51; *United Kingdom National Accounts* 1991, table 8.3.
Notes: Items are included in the table if comprising 6 or more per cent of capital expenditure in any of the three years. Because of changes in composition and designation, figures for some items are not precisely comparable over time; in particular the designation "General public services" did not appear in earlier national accounts. Percentage columns do not always add up exactly due to rounding.

housing. Next in importance to housing on capital account come education and roads.

It is instructive to compare the relationship between the totals of current and capital expenditure respectively. In 1964 capital expenditure was running at a level equal to 45 per cent of current expenditure; in 1974 the figure was 39 per cent; in 1990 it was down to 13 per cent (or 21 per cent excluding receipts from house sales) and it had fallen substantially below that in the early 1980s. Successive governments, seeking to reduce local government spending found it easier to cut capital than current spending.

Growth in Local Government Spending

Taking current and capital spending together, the figures show a big growth in local government spending in money terms; but, of course, because of the fall in the value of money, that statement tells us very little. We can obtain a much better idea of what has been happening by comparing local government spending with G.N.P. In 1964 local government expenditure was about $12\frac{1}{2}$ per cent of G.N.P. at factor cost. It then rose steadily to nearly 16 per cent by 1970, fell back a little, but then rose to a peak in 1975 at $17\frac{1}{2}$ per cent of G.N.P.—an increase as a proportion of G.N.P. of 40 per cent. As G.N.P. itself rose over this period by some 27 per cent, the growth of local government spending in real terms was much more than 40 per cent. Over the latter part of this period, the rise in local government spending was much faster than the rise in central government spending. This is the background to the appointment of the Layfield Committee (below). Since 1975, local authority spending has been pulled back from its peak (to 13 per cent of G.N.P. in 1990) and has also fallen as a percentage of central government spending since the peak of the mid-1970s.

Like central government spending, the spending of local government is characterised by the "relative price effect" (see above p. 41) i.e. that prices in the public sector tend to rise more rapidly than prices in the private sector.

Local Government Revenue

Revenue from local authority current expenditure in Great Britain can be grouped under three broad heads: grants-in-aid from central government, local rates together with the community charge and income which is basically fees from services provided—trading profits, rent, interest and miscellaneous charges—of which the largest component is council house rents. Table 10.3 shows the relative importance of these three components.

We have included in the table a year intermediate between 1974 and 1990 in order to show changes in the proportions of rate income and grant income which otherwise would not be revealed. At the beginning of the 1960s rates and grants contributed about equally to local government current revenue. By 1964 grant income was moving ahead of rate income. By 1974 the ratio was 61:39. By 1982 it had fallen back markedly to 57:43 from a peak in 1976 of 68:32. The 1990 figures show the restoration of the pre 1976 trend, with a ratio of grants to local taxes of 73:27. This ratio reflects big increases in grants as the government has sought to temper the burden and reduce the unpopularity of the community charge; and, to a lesser extent it also reflects the significant amount of uncollected community charge.

Apart from current surplus which is usually the biggest component, capital receipts are mainly derived from central government grants (amounting to £2039 million in 1990) with any balance derived from borrowing.

Let us now say something more about the two major sources of local government revenue—grants and rates.

Grants-in-Aid

Grants shift some of the incidence of local authority expenditure from the local taxpayer to the national taxpayer; they thus broaden the basis of local government finance. There is a sense in which grants from central government are necessary because Westminster retains to itself virtually all forms of taxation except one, the local rate or the community charge or its successor. (Although the non-

TABLE 10.3
Local Authority Revenue Current Account

Categories	1964		1974		1982		1990	
	£ million	per cent	£ million	per cent	£ million	per cent	£ million	per cent
Grants—General	900	31.5	4,177	42.4	12,768	37.7	26,833	45.1
Specific	259	9.1	561	5.7	3,322	9.8	11,255	18.9
Total	1,159	40.6	4,738	48.1	16,090	47.5	38,088	64.0
Rates and community charge*	1,096	38.4	3,089	31.3	12,098	35.6	13,937	23.4
Trading surplus, rent, interest etc.	602	21.1	2,028	20.6	5,646	16.7	7,504†	12.6
Total	2,857	100.0	9,855	100.0	33,834	100.0	59,529	100.0

* Community charge replaced domestic rates in Scotland, from April 1989 and in England and Wales from April 1990.
† Includes £2070 million imputed charge for consumption of non-trading capital.
Source: Table 50, *National Income and Expenditure, 1964–74* and table 8.2 *United Kingdom National Accounts,* 1991.
Note: Percentage columns do not always add up exactly due to rounding.

domestic rate continues alongside the community charge, it is no longer under the control of local authorities.) Indeed the Layfield Committee, in its Report of 1976, asserted that, since 1967, when the general grant was revised and renamed the Rate Support Grant, "the main determinants of the size of the grant have been the government's view of the desired level of local expenditure and the acceptable increase in the level of rates". But, even if local authorities were not restricted to one form of taxation, there would still be a case for supplementing local revenue with grants from the central government.

Purposes of Grants

With one important argument for grants we are already familiar in other forms—a particular application of the social and private costs problem, the spillover or externality effect. Part of the expenditure of local authorities will give rise to benefits to the community as a whole over and above the benefits to local residents. The most obvious example is expenditure on roads; motorways and major trunk roads are constructed and financed directly by the Department of the Environment, but even the roads which it is the responsibility of local authorities to build and maintain will be continuously used by people from outside the local area. Necessary expenditure on roads will fall unevenly on local authorities; central government financial assistance is partly a way of establishing and maintaining an adequate standard for the national communication network but also it is a matter of equity. A less clear cut example is education expenditure; if education carries the kind of social benefits which we considered in Chapter 4, which accrue nationally rather than locally, then it is appropriate that national sources should supplement local revenue to provide for education expenditure.

Another important motive behind grants is redistributive: an equalisation function. The central government has provided grant aid varying in amount between authorities to try to allow for the differing needs for expenditure between authorities and their differing resources. The higher the ratio of need to resources of a particular local authority, the more grant aid it should receive. This purpose underlies the development of "general", "block" or "formula" grants since 1929.

Finally, grants are a means by which central government can seek to impose national policy on local authorities. This may take a number of forms. Thus by means of grants the central government can stimulate particular kinds of expenditure by local authorities and at the same time control standards and, where necessary, ensure something like the equality of provision of certain services which public opinion requires. Where central government imposes an increased expenditure on local authorities or reduces their income, additional grant aid is appropriate. Thus the revenue loss from the de-rating of agriculture in 1929, intended to assist a depressed industry, had to be made good. More recently the rate rebate scheme and the 1967 relief for the domestic ratepayer were deliberate government policies to prevent a regressive tax falling too severely on those with small incomes and large families; additional grant-in-aid was appropriate in order to compensate for loss of rate revenue.

The most significant interventions of this kind relate to the government's macro-economic policy — its attempt to control the level of activity and the rate of inflation by budgetary and monetary policy (see Chapter 12). Most recently the attempt to use grants to enforce national policy on local authorities has taken a more extreme form. Mrs. Thatcher's government has sought to reduce local authority spending as part of its overall policy of ridding inflationary pressures from the system and reducing the size of the public sector. Simply to reduce the total grant aid to local authorities was not considered adequate for this purpose, for many local authorities could make good the reduction by increasing the local tax. Hence the Local Government Planning and Land Act, 1980, introduced a system of penalties whereby grant could be withheld from authorities which exceeded target levels of spending specified by the government.

Grants fall into two broad categories; the specific grant and the general grant. The specific grant relates grant aid to a particular service; it can take a number of forms, but the most common has been to make the grant a percentage of approved expenditure i.e. a matching grant. The general grant, on the other hand, can be used by local authorities towards the cost of any service. The trend of the past two decades has been markedly towards general grants. In principle the specific matching grant is more effective for the purpose of stimulating the development of a particular service. But such grants have the disadvantage, from the Treasury's point of view, that they are "open ended"; the cost to the national Exchequer depends on the enterprise or extravagance of individual authorities. Specific non-matching (or lump sum) grants, on the other hand, provide no incentive for the local authority to spend its own money on the service. The general grant is not open ended; its amount can be determined in advance. In principle it gives more discretion to local authorities and is therefore favourable to local autonomy; in practice, however, even before the changes in 1980, local authorities complained that since the introduction and extension of general grants, the tightening of central control in other ways (e.g. by legislation, audit, approval of schemes) had left them with little real autonomy.

The Rate Support Grant and Subsequent Changes

As Table 10.3 indicates, in recent years the general grant has assumed overwhelming importance within the grant provision and we concentrate on that.

Before 1980 the aggregate Exchequer grant was fixed each year by the government, after consultation with the local authorities, as a proportion of what was known as "relevant expenditure", which was broadly current expenditure net of receipts of fees and charges. There were no statutory rules or other formal criteria for determining the total of grants. From the total so fixed was deducted certain "specific" and "supplementary" grants, leaving the general grant known as the Rate Support Grant (R.S.G.).

The R.S.G. had three components which determined the distribution amongst local authorities. The smallest component was the domestic element, ·introduced to reduce the rate levy on domestic property compared with non-domestic. The other two components were the resources element and the needs element. The resources element in the R.S.G. aimed to increase the resources of the poorer authorities to bring them up to a national standard. Each year the government set a national standard rateable value per head of population. A local authority whose rateable value per head of population was less than this standard received a sum based on its "local deficiency in rateable value". This was equal to its population multiplied by the difference between the national standard and its rateable value per head. The resources element was calculated by applying the local rate poundage to the local deficiency in rateable value. In effect, the government acted as a ratepayer to make up the deficiency in local rate yield. A minority of authorities did not receive the resources element because their rateable value per head was above the national standard. Amongst those who did receive it, the resources element ensured that the same local rate poundage, with its associated grant, would raise the same revenue per head of population.

The objective of the needs element in the R.S.G. was to compensate for differences between authorities in what they needed to spend per head of population. A complicated formula, annually prescribed by the government, determined what each authority would get. The formula was based on an analysis of past expenditure and took account of indicators of expenditure needs, such as the age distribution of the population and road mileage. The larger the proportion of children of school age the higher education costs would tend to be, whilst the costs of some of the personal social services would vary with the numbers of the elderly. Road mileage affected costs such as road maintenance and refuse collection.

The basis of the calculation of both the resources and the needs element has been the subject of criticism. Rateable value is an imperfect measure of resources, whilst the concept of needs is imprecise, and the formula used is very complicated. One senior civil servant informally described the R.S.G. allocation as "all very much higher mathematics tempered by political expediency".

In 1980 came a new method of assessing needs and resources. The Secretary of State assessed the expenditure needed to enable each authority to provide a standard level of service and sought to tailor the grant to it. Any authority spending above that level had to pay an increased proportion itself. It also suffered the penalty of a reduction in grant which was more than proportional to its over-spend. The design of this so-called unitary grant was based on the dubious assumption that the government (or, more accurately, government officials) could determine, accurately and objectively, the cost of providing services at a given standard to any authority.

In 1990 came a further change, consequent on the introduction into England and Wales of the community charge together with the uniform business rate (see below). The community charge, levied on virtually all adults over 18, meant that differences of rateable value between authorities in respect of domestic rates were no longer relevant, whilst the "nationalising" of business rates had the same effect for non-domestic property. So the uniform or block grant was replaced by a revenue support grant broadly in line with the old needs element in the R.S.G. although the factors which determined its level for each authority had changed.

In 1991 to reduce the burden of the community charge, which the government considered to be "unsustainably high" (*Financial Statement and Budget Report 1991–92*), the government introduced a new grant called the Community Charge Grant to reimburse authorities for the gross cost of reducing charges in 1991–92 by £140 at an estimated cost of £5.6 billion. The funds to finance the new grant were found by increasing the standard rate of V.A.T. from 15 per cent to 17½ per cent.

Local Rates

Although local domestic rates were replaced by the community charge in Scotland in 1989 and in England and Wales in 1990, the community charge is itself due for abolition and both the Conservatives and the Labour Party have promised a replacement which, like the local rate, will be a form of property tax. Moreover, the non-domestic rate remains in place even though a local authority no longer has control over its level. It is therefore appropriate to examine, in some detail, the rating system as it existed pre 1989/90 and assess its merits and defects; then to follow through the debate on the reform of local government finance; to assess the arguments for and against the community charge and the changes in non-domestic rates; and finally to indicate briefly the nature of the taxes the Conservative and Labour parties respectively have proposed as replacement for the community charge.

Rates were an outlay tax on the use of real estate (land and buildings) and thus were partly a tax on the use of house room and partly a tax on a factor of production. The basis of the tax was the "rateable value". In principle the rateable value was the annual letting value of the property with the tenant responsible for internal repairs, maintenance and insurance. In practice, because of subsidised council rents, rent control and the decline of the private rented sector, adequate market rental evidence has been lacking; consequently the "rateable value" became an assessed annual value, which bore little relationship to a market value, particularly where inflation has been high and because valuations have been infrequent. Rates were formally payable by the occupier, although often paid with the rent.

Rates were levied at so much per £ of rateable value (e.g. 75p in the £). Agricultural property (except dwelling houses) was exempt; charities in general were 50 per cent exempt, churches completely exempt. Until 1963 industrial and transport property had enjoyed a 50 per cent de-rating and shops, offices and public buildings 20 per cent, but in that year they were re-rated. From then until the domestic relief was introduced in the Rate Support Grant in 1967, nearly equal amounts of local revenue had come from domestic and non-domestic rates.

Opposition to Rates

All taxes were unpopular, but there was a particular outcry against rates from the later 1960s. Whilst most of the opposition was to domestic rates, with the depression of the early 1980s rates in industry and commerce came in for increasing attack. It was the vocal opposition to rates which prompted various features of central government policy like the introduction of domestic relief in 1967, the growth of grants to take the pressure off rates as local spending grew, the setting up of the Layfield Committee in 1974 and an electoral promise by the Conservative Party to abolish domestic rates.

Let us look at the arguments against rates.

Arguments Against Rates

Many of the arguments against rates apply particularly to either domestic or non-domestic rates, but two apply to both.

Subject to arbitrary assessment. The method by which rates are assessed is open to objection. To be fair, valuations need to be frequent, but regular valuations at frequent intervals are expensive and in practice valuations have only taken place after unduly long intervals, consequently resulting in sharp adjustments when revaluations have taken place. Moreover, relative rate burdens depend on the relative valuations of different types of property; there is an element of arbitrariness in valuation; different officers may value the same property differently because the valuation process is less than scientific. This can lead to inequity between taxpayers.

This objection has particular force when the existence of rent controls and rent subsidisation has removed any genuine open market for rentals, which is the theoretical basis for rating values.

Rates lack buoyancy. Rates have not the automatic "expandability" of income tax revenue, which automatically rises as incomes increase without any change in rates of tax. But rate revenue is not inexpandable in any fundamental sense; an increase in the rate in the pound tends to bring a proportionate revenue increase. The point is that rates *have* to be increased in order to get a revenue increase. Only to a limited extent is an increase in the income of the community reflected in an increase in rateable value; and rate revenue does not automatically and regularly rise with inflation. (Conversely, if there were to be a general fall in prices the real income from rates would rise.) Thus there is a psychological and political barrier to obtaining increased revenue from rates, which is heightened by inflation. Not everyone would regard this feature of rates as a disadvantage; it has the effect of increasing the perceptibility to the local electorate of the actions of local authorities.

Non-Domestic Rates

Uncertain and probably regressive incidence. As we pointed out in Chapter 8, the effective incidence of taxes on factors of production is particularly difficult to determine, so that their use makes it harder for a government to pursue meaningful social and economic objectives in its tax policy. Whilst the ability of a business to pass rates forward into prices will depend on a variety of factors including the state of the economy and the degree of competition it faces with its products, at least a proportion of rates are likely to be so passed on especially in the short run.* A study by Mair,† used input-output analysis to determine the element of rates in the prices of different goods and Family Expenditure Survey data to determine the purchases of households in different income groups. On the assumption that the whole of rates was passed forward into prices he concluded that non-domestic rates were regressive in relation to household income. As a proportion of income, the non-domestic rates shifted on to the lowest income group was almost twice that of the highest income group.

Discouragement and distortion of investment. Non-domestic rates are a discouragement to investment in buildings for commercial and industrial purposes and a deterrent to modernisation. Moreover there are important differential effects. Some business sectors are hit much more than others because of the nature of their capital requirements; heavy industry, public utilities and retail distribution are amongst those most affected. Moreover the rate burden may vary considerably as between one area and another (e.g. in 1978–9

---

*For a summary of the complex factors affecting the effective incidence of non-domestic rates, see C. T. Sandford, *The Case for the Abolition of Non-Domestic Rates*, National Federation of Self Employed and Small Businesses Ltd., chapter 3, 1981.

†D. Mair, The Incidence of Non-Domestic Rates, in R. Jackman (ed.) *The Impact of Rates on Industry and Commerce*, C.E.S. Policy Series No. 5, Centre for Environmental Studies, 1978.

the rate poundage was 72.8 in Leeds and 115.3p in Manchester although this may have been moderated by differences in the level of valuation in the two cities). Thus investment patterns and locations are distorted and our efficiency criterion is infringed.

Detrimental to the balance of payments. Unlike V.A.T., there is no rebate for the element of rates entering into export prices, nor is a corresponding tax added to import prices; hence non-domestic rates are detrimental to the balance of payments. This point is the more significant in that *O.E.C.D. Revenue Statistics* show the burden of property taxes in the United Kingdom (measured as a percentage of G.N.P.) higher than that of any of the other twenty-four O.E.C.D. countries.

Particularly onerous for new firms. Rates, unlike income tax or corporation profits tax have to be paid whether the firm is making a profit or not. They therefore hit particularly hard at time of depression in an industry or in the economy as a whole; and they particularly deter new firms where it is to be expected that it will take several years before the business will make profits.

Miscellaneous disadvantages to business. Finally there are a number of miscellaneous features which make rates particularly disadvantageous to businesses. Before the uniform business rate introduced in 1990 they were less predictable than most other costs, depending in part on local and national political considerations. In any one year they might be quite out of line with the general increase in costs and prices; rate increases of over 40 per cent were not unknown in particular localities in recent years. Further, rates are a form of cost on which, especially in the short run, it is very difficult, if not impossible, for an existing business to economise.

Domestic Rates

Regressive between households. The regressiveness of rates was established very clearly by the *Report of the (Allen) Committee of Inquiry into the Impact of Rates on Households.** The 1965 report showed that, of the

*Cmnd. 2582, 1965.

household sample surveyed in England and Wales, the lowest income group (with an income of £312) paid 8.1 per cent of the household income in rates; the percentage fell as household income increased so that for the largest incomes it was under 2 per cent (1.8 per cent for incomes of £1,560 and over). Not only that, the burden of rates fell heaviest on a group of retired poor and might also be particularly onerous on the larger family. The Allen Committee further considered that one in seven families had incomes low enough to suffer some "hardship" from the payment of rates and over 7 per cent "serious hardship". Rates clearly infringed our criterion of ability to pay.

Regressive between areas. Rates are regressive as between local government areas. To maintain the same standard of efficiency a poorer area (with lower rateable value per head) needs to levy higher rates per £, than a richer area; moreover in a poorer area the need for some of the local authority services, especially welfare services, will be greater.

An inadvisable tax on house-room. Domestic rates are a tax on the use of house-room and as such they suffer from the general disadvantages of outlay taxes (see Chapter 8); they impose a loss of satisfaction on the taxpayer over and above the gain to the Exchequer; and they tend to restrict the supply of house-room (probably by reducing the size and quality of houses rather than the number). Moreover, housing in some form is a necessity which successive governments have considered it their duty to "subsidise" in one way or another (e.g. by council house subsidies, rent control and income tax concessions). It can be regarded as an extension of this objection that rates are a tax on improvements; if a householder extends his property or improves it by increasing the amenities, he raises its rateable value.

Not paid by all local residents. It is argued that the rating base is too narrow; that adults who are non-householders do not pay rates although they benefit from local government services.

Criteria for Local Taxes

Not all these arguments can be accepted at their face value; moreover, before these arguments against rates, both non-domestic and domestic, are allowed to prevail, we need to remind ourselves that rates are a local tax, that there are particular needs a local tax must meet and that, for all their deficiencies, rates may meet these needs better than the alternatives.

Ideally a local tax should meet a number of requirements, some are desirable but not essential, others are of fundamental importance.

(1) The tax base should be widely and fairly evenly dispersed throughout the country so that the tax can provide significant revenue in every locality.

(2) A local tax should meet certain administrative requirements, it should be economical to administer on a small scale and difficult to evade.

(3) A local tax must be localised within the jurisdiction of the taxing authority, i.e. the tax base must not be something which is readily transferable across local authority boundaries. (E.g. a whisky tax would make a poor local tax, because if the tax was lower in one authority than in a neighbouring one, people living in the "dear" area could readily buy their whisky in the "cheap" area and carry it back home.)

(4) Because a local authority is likely to have only one or two sources of local taxation, these need to be able to generate a high and reliable yield.

(5) A local tax should not accentuate local disparities of wealth—it must not encourage the rich in poor areas to move to rich areas so that the poor areas get poorer and the rich, richer. This consideration constitutes a powerful argument against a markedly progressive local income tax.

(6) It is desirable but not essential for the tax to be reserved for local use, i.e. not a tax which central government also levies.

(7) It is important that the tax should be perceptible; people should know when they are paying a local tax.

(8) The seventh criteria links with the eighth, which is of the utmost importance; a local tax should promote local accountability and therefore responsibility in decision-making by local authorities. This principle was enunciated by the Report of the Layfield Committee, which we examine more fully below.

Measured against these criteria the domestic rate comes out very well. The tax base is widely and fairly evenly dispersed, requirement (1); it meets the administrative requirements (2); it is effectively localised (3); and generates a high and stable yield (4); it does not exaggerate local disparities of wealth (5); it is reserved for local use (6); it is perceptible (7) and promotes accountability because ratepayers are also voters (8). Moreover several of the significant disadvantages of rates can be, indeed to some extent have been, overcome by other means. Thus the existence of rate rebates modified the regressiveness of rates between households. Layfield discovered that, taking these reliefs into account, domestic rates were progressive up to levels of £40 per week, roughly proportional to income between £40 and £60 and regressive at higher incomes (1976 values). Similarly, the R.S.G. is intended to offset the regressiveness of rates as between rich and poor areas. Moreover there are counter-arguments to some of the arguments put against rates. Thus, to say that only the householder pays rates when all adults benefit from local services ignores the contribution which spouses and other adults make to household expenses and hence indirectly to rates. The argument for exempting house-room as a "necessity" can be countered by the view that house-room is unduly favoured by income tax concessions and zero rating under V.A.T.; that this leads to over-investment in housing; and that tax neutrality would be brought nearer, and economic efficiency promoted, by a local domestic property tax. Further, the local rate has the positive and unusual merit for a widespread high revenue tax that its compliance costs are very low (see Table 5.1).

What of the non-domestic rate? It meets the first six criteria quite well, though not as well as the domestic rate on requirements (1) and (5); non-domestic properties are probably less evenly dispersed across the country than domestic and because rates will be much more significant in the costs of some businesses than of households, rates may well lead to some relocation to the detriment of poor areas. On the fundamental criteria, (7) and (8), however, the non-domestic rate fails completely. The effective incidence of the non-domestic rate is far from perceptible; e.g. consumers are unaware of the rates they pay in the prices of the goods and services they buy. Above all, the non-domestic rate does nothing to promote local accountability. Business, as such, has no vote. In so far as extra revenue could be squeezed from the non-domestic ratepayers there was little or no electoral penalty. Thus, in the Inner London Borough of Camden, in 1980–81, 80 per cent of the total rate revenue was raised from non-domestic ratepayers. The "democratic control" which Layfield required was notably absent.

It may, however, be argued, that it is only right that business should contribute to local revenue. Some services, like sewage and waste removal, street paving and lighting, benefit all ratepayers including industrial ratepayers; it is therefore appropriate that some local tax should be paid by industrial and commercial concerns; moreover, in a very rough and ready way, there is some correspondence between the size and frontage of a building and the amount of these benefits received. Similarly police services help to provide security for industrial and commercial buildings (in the same sort of way as a night watchman) just as they help to protect private property.

However, this argument does not apply to the biggest items of local authority expenditure, education and housing.* Moreover, with the other services we listed, the correspondence between payment and benefit is very haphazard. There is a case for allowing non-domestic rate payers to pay directly for the services they use by way of an economic charge rather than to require them to pay a

---

*It has been calculated that, in 1986, approximately 15 per cent of the benefits of local authority services was received by the business sector. (R. Jackman, Paying for Local Government: an Appraisal of the British Government's Proposals for Non-domestic Rates, *Government and Policy*, Vol. 5, No. 1.)

tax irrespective of whether or how much benefit of service they derive.

Reform of Local Taxation

The past 20 years have seen an almost continuous debate on local government finance centering on the form of local taxation.

The re-organisation of the structure of local government in the 1960s and early 1970s was carried out without any fundamental reconsideration of methods of local government finance. The Conservative government published a Green Paper on *The Future Shape of Local Government Finance* (Cmnd. 4741) in July 1971, but it did little beyond surveying the scene and drawing attention to the difficulties of introducing any new major source of local government revenue. However, concern continued to grow and, in June 1974, the Labour Government set up the Committee of Inquiry on Local Government Finance (chaired by Sir Frank Layfield, Q.C.) "To review the whole system of local government finance in England, Scotland and Wales and to make recommendations". The Committee's report, published in May 1976* is far more comprehensive than the succession of official documents which followed it, and its diagnosis and recommendations retain their relevance; hence it merits careful consideration.

Findings and Recommendations of the Layfield Report

The Commiteee concluded that there was "no coherent system" of local government finance. They found a confusion of responsibility and lack of accountability; they defined accountability as meaning, primarily, that "whoever is responsible for deciding to spend more or less money in providing a service is also responsible for deciding whether to raise more or less in taxation". The main recommendations of the Report are concerned with the establishment of "a financial system based on a clear identification of responsibility for expenditure and for the taxation to finance it". The Report posed a

---

*Local Government Finance, Cmnd. 6453, May 1976.

choice: to move to a more explicit system of central government control or to one of much more local control.

A move towards greater government control would mean an increasing share of local expenditure financed by grants, with the government deciding how much each local authority would spend and for what purposes. This would be a major new administrative task.

The alternative would be to strengthen local accountability and reverse the trend towards increased government control. Councils would be responsible to their electorates for both the expenditure incurred and the revenue they raised; a much larger proportion of revenue than at present would be raised locally. The government would intervene only on essential issues of national policy. In the interests of managing the economy the government would have to retain some measure of control over the total of local authorities' spending, but without seeking to influence local authorities' preferences over the development of individual services.

Implementing this second option would require new sources of local finance and the Committee recommended the introduction of a local income tax (L.I.T.) to be levied by non-metropolitan counties, metropolitan districts and Scottish regions.

Whilst the Committee stressed that the choice was for the community and the government to make, it revealed a "strongly held view" for the second alternative as "the only way to sustain a vital local democracy" and "thereby make councillors more directly accountable to local electorates for their taxation and expenditure decisions". The cost of administering the local income tax, the Committee considered, would be justified to achieve this purpose.

Whichever choice was adopted they recommended that the local rating system should remain but be used to finance a smaller proportion of local expenditure. The Committee considered that local rates met most of the requirements of a local tax well. But they considered that certain changes should be made of which the major were:

(1) Capital values to replace rental values as the basis for assessing domestic property;

(2) A widening of the tax base—to include agricultural land and buildings;

(3) Payment of rates by monthly instalments for all ratepayers;

(4) More frequent and regular revaluations.

On grants, they approved the block grant, but stressed the need for stability and certainty in grant distribution. They encouraged a search for better ways of measuring needs (including a "unit cost" approach) and better ways of measuring the wealth or taxable capacity of an area than by rateable value per head. In order to achieve local accountability the Report stressed that local tax rates from year to year should closely parallel expenditure policies—a requirement necessitating stability in income from grants. Layfield also proposed that the "needs" and "resources" elements of the R.S.G. might be fused into a new "unitary" grant.

The most disappointing feature of the Layfield Report was the minimum space it devoted to the subject of non-domestic rates and its failure to propose a radical change in view of the failure of non-domestic rates to reflect the principle of local accountability, which the Committee made the keynote of its Report. Professor George Jones, one of the members of the Layfield Committee, had this to say on the subject in a subsequent paper.*

A study of the Layfield Committee . . . provides an intriguing irony. Although set up in 1974 in response to outcries about huge increases in domestic rates, it never came near to recommending their abolition or even their substantial replacement with another tax. Indeed it proposed that they be retained and, further, that in addition to this unpopular tax there should be a new unpopular tax, local income tax—a prospect of little attraction to most politicians. The Layfield Committee, however, came nearer to proposing the abolition of non-domestic rates as a local tax, and here is another irony. Most of the evidence it received about rating concerned domestic rating and its dominant theme was critical, whereas it received little evidence about non-domestic rating, and most of that, although deploring high local govern-

*G. Jones, Some Post Layfield Reflections about Non-Domestic Rating on Commercial and Industrial Properties, in R. Jackman (ed.), op. cit. 1978.

ment expenditure and high rates in general, accepted it as a valid local tax. There was no significant attack on it as such even from organisations representing non-domestic ratepayers. Doubts about the validity of non-domestic rates arose in the minds of some members as the Committee probed into the system of local taxation. Having considered the appropriate principles of taxation and their application in practice, some members came to the conclusion that non-domestic rates were unsuitable for local taxation and should not be included in any desirable new arrangements. But this opinion, not backed by any strong support from outside the Committee and emerging at a late stage of the Committee's work, was never able to win over a majority of the members. The proposition looked too way out and too radical.

It was only with the onset of economic depression in the later 1970s and early 1980s that a move from business gathered force for the abolition of the non-domestic rate on industry and commerce.

Labour Government's Response to Layfield

In the wake of the Layfield Report the Labour Government published a "preliminary response" in the form of a Green Paper* as the basis for continuing consultation. The Government did not accept that a choice must be made between increased central control and finance, or more autonomous local government based on new sources of local finance and they rejected a local income tax. By the time of the election of a Conservative Government, no major changes had taken place.

Conservative Government and Reform of Local Finance

The Conservatives came into office in 1979 having promised to abolish the domestic rate but with little idea of what to put in its place. The furthest the Conservatives got towards implementing their promise on domestic rates in their first term was to issue a Green Paper, *Alternatives to Domestic Rates*, Cmnd. 8449, December

Local Government Finance, Cmnd. 6813, 1977.

1981 in which were considered, in some detail, the three taxes regarded as feasible alternatives to rates: local sales tax, local income tax and a poll tax. The Green Paper did not set out any firm proposals but examined some of the implications of these possibilities, individually and in combination with each other and with a much lighter local rate. None of these alternative tax possibilities were free from serious difficulties. By the time of the 1983 General Election the Conservatives had decided not to adopt any of the alternatives to rates but rather to "legislate to curb excessive and irresponsible rate increases by high spending councils and to provide a general scheme for limitation of rate increases for all local authorities, to be used if necessary" (Conservative Manifesto, 1983).

In 1985 a revaluation of domestic and non-domestic properties in Scotland had led to a major redistribution of the rate burden and a storm of protest. The Government was concerned that the same, or worse, might happen in England and Wales, where revaluation was even more overdue. Moreover, its attempts to control local spending had not been very successful. Its revived interest in reforming the financial arrangements for local authorities led to another Green Paper, *Paying for Local Government* (Cmnd. 9714), in 1986, in which it set out, for discussion, its proposed reforms. With some minor modifications these became law, for implementation in 1989 (the community charge in Scotland) and 1990. The major elements were:

(1) The replacement of domestic rates in England, Wales and Scotland (but not Northern Ireland) by a community charge.

(2) Provisions by which the non-domestic rate was set nationally instead of locally; rateable values were reassessed; and the revenues distributed to each local authority according to the size of its adult population.

(3) The restructuring of the grant system (as discussed above) consequent upon the other changes.

The Community Charge

The community charge is a locally determined poll tax levied on virtually all adults over the age of 18. Measured against our specific criteria for a local tax, a poll tax comes out well on many counts: clearly it is a tax base widely and evenly dispersed; it has the potential for a high and stable yield; it certainly does not exaggerate local disparities of wealth; it is reserved for local use; it is very perceptible and promotes local accountability. Like rates it has low taxpayer compliance costs. However, it falls down on administrative requirements and the tax base is more mobile across boundaries than real property.

Let us examine more closely its alleged advantages and disadvantages compared with local domestic rates.

The community charge was said to be fairer than the domestic rate in the sense that it would secure a close relationship between benefit and tax. All adults use local services but only about half of them paid rates. With the community charge all adults pay. The argument is not wholly convincing. Spouses with no income of their own no more paid the community charge than they had paid rates. Any earning adults would normally make a contribution to household expenses including rates. Moreover, to treat the community charge as a payment for benefit implies that all adults received equal benefits from local services. But this is very far from true. The largest proportion of local authority expenditure is on education which benefits the 5–18 year olds who don't pay the community charge; if educating their children is treated as a benefit to the parents, then it must be stated that such parents are only a proportion of the local adult population.

The second argument in favour of the community charge and that stressed by the Government was that it would promote perceptibility and accountability. As a result of block lump sum grants and the uniform business rate, extra spending would fall entirely on local taxpayers. Moreover, the maximum rebate permitted under the community charge was not 100 per cent, as had formerly applied to rates, but 80 per cent—so that extra spending meant a charge on *all* adults. However, whilst undoubtedly promoting accountability, block grants, uniform business rates and exemptions limited to 80 per cent had nothing to do with the community charge as such; they could equally well have been applied in respect of domestic rates.

The features of the community charge *per se* which were held to promote accountability were the fact that each adult received a poll tax demand and so was made more aware of local spending; and that each adult had to pay. But, we are back to the counter arguments rehearsed above. Spouses without income do not pay anyway and other adults would usually have paid indirectly. It is possible that the more direct payment may increase knowledge and accountability and that local electors may therefore more readily use their votes to punish spendthrift councils, but this argument for preferring the community charge to domestic rates does not appear very strong.

The disadvantages of the community charge as compared with rates are two-fold.

First, the administrative costs of the community charge are much higher than those of domestic rates, and inherently so, not just because of start-up costs. This is partly because community charge demands have to go to, and tax has to be collected from, roughly twice as many people. However, this is not the whole story. Not only the original registration process, but also keeping the register up-to-date is costly and complex. In some authorities the annual turnover on the register is as high as 50 per cent. Because, unlike a home which (apart from caravans and boats) is immobile and readily visible, the base is a highly mobile individual, evasion is much higher and non-payment a much more serious problem.

Secondly, the community charge, a poll tax, is much more regressive than domestic rates. We have argued that a local tax needs to be proportional or mildly regressive to avoid movements of population which accentuate local disparities of wealth, but a poll tax is excessively regressive. Whilst, as with rates, the regressivity can be tempered at the lower end of the scale by rebates, at the upper end the regressivity is pronounced and widely seen as bitterly unfair. Under rates the rich did, by and large, pay substantially more tax than the poor, if not proportionately more. Under the poll tax the rich man in his castle pays the same as the poor man in his cottage.

There is a counter-argument that (as we pointed out in Chapter 4) an individual tax should not be condemned for regressiveness; what matters is the overall progression of the tax system and indeed the tax and expenditure system have to be taken together. The regressivity of rates can be offset by progressivity elsewhere in the tax system. To this there are two responses.

The community charge is the only local tax; if there are to be significant differences in local tax levels, only to a limited extent can the regressiveness of the local tax be offset by progressive national taxes. Secondly, the context in which the community charge has been introduced is one in which, as we have seen above, (and also in Chapter 11) the notional tax system has been made much less progressive.

The introduction of the community charge was accompanied by transitional provisions aimed at reducing the impact of the changes and restricting the extent of loss of both individuals and local authorities. However, the difficulties of the transition were accentuated because of a rise in the average level of taxation, itself increased by non payment of poll tax. In the event, authorities in the north and north-west suffered and the majority of households found themselves paying more, whilst a minority of high income earners paid significantly less.

The community charge continued to be a subject of acute controversy and a major cause of unpopularity for the Conservative Government. At the end of 1990, Mrs. Thatcher was replaced as Prime Minister by Mr. Major. A review was conducted by Mr. Heseltine as the new Secretary of State for the Environment, following which the Government announced that the community charge would be dropped to be replaced after the General Election by a so-called Council Tax. In the meantime the Chancellor of the Exchequer sought to reduce the remaining community charge bills by the special grant we have already described.

The National Non-Domestic (or Uniform Business) Rate

The introduction of a uniform national non-domestic rate poundage with regular quinquennial revaluations removed some of the disadvantages of non-domestic rates: it stopped the distortion of investment between areas as a result of different levels of rate; it removed the possibility of serious inequities from an out-of-date valuation base; and it removed much of the unpredictability of rate increases and the possibility that businesses might be "milked" by a spendthrift local council. However, it left unmet the other objections to the non-domestic rate which we listed above. The changes converted the non-domestic rates from a local tax to a hypothecated national tax i.e. a national tax where the revenue is earmarked for a particular purpose. It removed, so to speak, any pretence that non-domestic rates were a meaningful local tax. It can be strongly argued that, given the disadvantages of business rates—a tax on a factor of production, with no refund for exports and distorting investment as between businesses with different real capital requirements, it would be better to abolish the non-domestic rate. Compensatory revenue could be provided partly from an increase in V.A.T. (or a widening of the V.A.T. base) and partly by charging businesses directly for the local services which they use.

The Future of Local Taxation

The community charge seems set to remain the local tax at least until 1993. The Conservative victory at the General Election in 1992 means that the community charge is due to be replaced by a new tax, to be called the "Council Tax", which is a domestic property tax which also takes some account of the number in the household. Whilst many of the details are as yet unclear, the principles would appear to be that the liability for tax would fall on the occupier of the property, as with the rates, and each household would be sent one bill. Properties would be allocated into bands (of which there would be eight) on the basis of capital values, and, within a band, all properties would pay the same. There would be a 25 per cent discount for single adult households. The bands are so arranged that the tax, whilst much less regressive than the community charge, falls less heavily on those with high value houses than the local rate.* The intention would be to raise as much revenue from the council tax as the community charge in 1991–92.

The Labour Party, for its part, is proposed a return to a modified system of domestic rates, but using a number of indicators, not just rental value, to reflect the capital value.

The Liberal Democrats, for their part, proposed to replace the community charge by a local income tax.

The period since the beginning of the 1960s has seen the ratio of grants to taxes in local government fall and then rise again to new heights. At the same time the non-domestic rate has effectively ceased to be a local tax, so that the proportion of their revenue which local authorities themselves control is now less than ever. At the same time, especially by its rate-capping and then charge-capping, the Conservative Government has further increased central control of local authorities. The alternatives which the Layfield Committee set forth appear as a starker choice than ever before. If there is to be genuine local government additional sources of local revenue must be found over and above any property tax. This conclusion leads inevitably to a local income tax. If the two main parties remain implacably opposed to introducing one, then possibly revenue-sharing of a uniform national income tax base, as is operated in Germany, might be an acceptable solution; but it would still leave local authorities in effective control of only a minority of their income.

*For a perceptive critique of the proposals for the council tax, see J. Hills and H. Sutherland, *Banding, Tilting, Gearing, Gaining and Losing: An Anatomy of the Proposed Council Tax*, July 1991, Suntory Toyota International Centre for Economics and Related Disciplines, London School of Economics.

CHAPTER 11

Taxation, Public Expenditure and the Distribution of Personal Income and Wealth

In the introduction to this book (p. xi) we pointed out that government expenditure and taxation, whether by deliberate policy or not, affected the distribution of income and wealth; an examination of these distributional effects is the object of this chapter.

The distribution of income and wealth are closely linked. One of the biggest causes of inequality in incomes is the inequality of wealth from which income is derived. Conversely inequalities of income provide opportunities for different rates of saving and so promote inequalities of capital or personal wealth. This inter-relationship should be borne in mind throughout the chapter.

A problem common to a consideration of both the distribution of income and of wealth is the inadequacy of the statistical data. The Royal Commission on the Distribution of Income and Wealth 1974–79, effected some improvements and there have been further refinements since, but deficiencies remain. The deficiency of the data has two main consequences: we shall have to spend much time in setting out sources and characteristics of the data so that its limitations can be properly appreciated; secondly, the conclusions that we draw from the figures cannot be as definite as we should wish.

Income Distribution and the Effect of Taxes and Benefits

The interdependence of the manifold prices and incomes in the economic system means that almost any government policy measure will have some influence on the distribution of incomes, but the influence of some measures is bigger and more direct than that of others.

A policy which widens educational or training opportunities may be expected to reduce earned income inequalities by increasing the supply of skilled relatively to unskilled labour. Government policy directed against monopoly—whether of a corporation, a trade union or a professional association—may be expected to benefit consumer incomes relatively to producer incomes. Rent control increases the income of tenants relatively to landlords. And monetary policy, requiring changes in interest rates, has its effect on rentier and shareholder incomes.

Our concern, however, is to concentrate primarily on income distribution as affected by budgetary measures, viz. government expenditure and taxation (including the effect of tax reliefs). We shall start by looking at the distribution of income before and after the effect of income taxes; we shall then move on to try to take into account the effects of other taxes as well, and of that part of government expenditure the benefits of which can be allocated to individuals or households.

A Conceptual Problem—the Life Cycle of Income

The usual procedure for analysing the distribution of income is to take the income figures for a particular year and see how much income in that year is received by people in different income classes. From this we usually proceed to calculate concentration ratios—i.e. what percentage of income is held by the top 1 per cent of income receivers, the top 5 per cent, the top 10 per cent and so on. The distribution of income for 1 year, so compiled, can then be compared with other years.

Such a procedure, however, suffers from a basic limitation. The picture in the statistics is static; a snapshot at a point of time. As such it may show bigger inequalities than if we were able to compare the incomes of the same people for a period longer than 1 year. If we were to take several years together the effect would be to iron out some short-term fluctuations. More important still, if we were to compare lifetime earnings we might find a very substantial diminution in inequality. For many people an earnings "profile" would show earnings starting low, rising gradually during working life to a peak and then falling before or at retirement. The static picture might show A at the start of his working life and B at the peak with very different incomes, when their aggregate lifetime incomes might be identical.* University students would regard themselves as part of today's poor, yet on a basis of aggregate lifetime earnings they would be in the top 10 per cent or so of income receivers. A pattern of lifetime earnings that varies significantly with age also raises the possibility that income distribution may appear more or less unequal because of changes in the age composition of the population (and for that matter the sex composition too). Thus, during the 1960s, in which Britain had a larger proportion of young people in the labour force (from the birth-rate bulge which reached its peak in 1947) and also a growing proportion of old people, inequalities on the basis of a static comparison may have appeared bigger than they would on the basis of a lifetime's comparison. We have a long way to go before we shall have statistics which enable us to make these more sophisticated, but more meaningful, comparisons.

The Statistical Sources—Their Limitations and Differences

The basic data available on income distribution are derived from two main sources: Inland Revenue statistics (from which are derived the figures for a Survey of Personal Incomes compiled annually) and the annual Family Expenditure Survey.

The fundamental weakness of the figures is that neither of the two basic sources was designed with the object of providing a comprehensive incomes survey. The Inland Revenue figures are a by-

---

*To make an accurate comparison we would, of course, have to allow for price changes and compare the *present* value of lifetime earnings (see the calculations on the rate of return to education, Chapter 4).

product of tax administration. The Family Expenditure Survey is a sample survey of expenditure patterns intended primarily for the compilation of the Retail Price Index. The data from these two sources differ in two major respects, apart from other limitations: in coverage and in relation to the income unit.

(1) *Coverage.* The Inland Revenue figures are as comprehensive as legal sanction can make them with the exception that they omit all incomes not subject to income tax. The Family Expenditure Survey is a voluntary survey of a sample of some 7,000 households. The degree of accuracy is not as high as the Inland Revenue data and it is particularly inadequate on the higher incomes, where the numbers included are very small and the information itself may be more suspect.

(2) *The Unit.* Inland Revenue figures are based on the income tax unit—which treated husband and wife as one until 1990–91, so that, for example, a married couple each with an income of £3,000 would appear in the figures as one income of £6,000. The Family Expenditure Survey (F.E.S.) data are based on the household unit. Information is collected about the income of individual members of the household but is presented as combined household incomes. A household, for F.E.S. purposes, is defined as one person living alone or a group of people living at the same address having meals prepared together and with common housekeeping. In general, household income comes out on average at about 12½ per cent more than tax unit income.

As we have seen, neither source publishes individual incomes. If we could compile the figures for individuals, with husband and wife treated separately, it seems likely, on the basis of some calculations by Professor A. R. Prest and Dr. T. Stark* that the resulting picture would be one of less income inequality.

In our first analysis we employ the Inland Revenue data to explore the effect of income tax on the distribution of personal

---

*Some Aspects of Income Distribution in the U.K. Since World War II, *The Manchester School*, September 1967.

income. Then we use the F.E.S. data in an attempt to look more comprehensively at the effects of taxes and benefits on real income.

The Distribution of Income before and after Income Tax

The implications of the basic limitation of the Inland Revenue data—that they only cover income which is taxable—need to be explored rather more fully. Besides incomes below the tax threshold, other items which should or might be classed as income are excluded. Thus, child benefit and interest on certain national savings instruments are excluded. Education scholarships and grants are tax free. Certain fringe benefits, like the subsidy on canteen meals, luncheon vouchers and miners' concessionary coal (or its cash equivalent) are untaxed, whilst other "perks" like the private use of the firm's car are taxed on less than the benefit to the recipient. Employees' national insurance contributions and super-annuation contributions are taken into account, but not employers' national insurance contributions, though it could be argued that these are properly regarded as part of the employee's income. Capital gains are not treated as income. Other omissions result from evasion by non-disclosure or understatement. Certain incomes are not known to the local tax office e.g. employees' superannuation contributions and some investment income taxed at source. The Inland Revenue currently makes an estimate for these using other sources, but warns that the margin of error may be large (see *Inland Revenue Statistics 1990*, p. 25). Finally there is a limitation in the figures resulting from changes in the tax threshold, which reduce comparability from one year to the next.

Table 11.1 is based on Inland Revenue data with the deficiencies to which we have already referred. It shows how income is distributed, before and after tax, amongst the 21.2 million tax units included in the survey for 1988–89. In both distributions in the table the tax units are ranked according to their distribution before tax (e.g. if the effect of income tax was to move some "tax units" from the top 10 per cent to the 11–20 per cent bracket, they nonetheless still appear in the top 10 per cent in the after tax

TABLE 11.1

Distribution of Income Before and After Income Tax U.K., 1988–89

	Tax units			
	Income before income tax		Income after income tax	
Percentile groups	Percentage of income	Average income (£)	Percentage of income	Average income (£)
Top 1%	7.4	100,500	6.0	68,700
2– 5%	11.4	38,700	10.6	30,000
6–10%	9.9	27,000	9.7	22,200
Top 10%	28.7	39,000	26.3	30,000
11–20%	15.2	20,600	15.3	17,400
21–30%	12.1	16,400	12.3	14,000
31–40%	10.1	13,700	10.4	11,800
41–50%	8.6	11,600	8.9	10,100
51–60%	7.3	9,000	7.6	8,600
61–70%	6.2	8,400	6.5	7,400
71–80%	5.1	6,900	5.4	6,100
81–90%	4.0	5,500	4.4	5,000
Bottom 10%	2.7	3,700	3.1	3,500

Source: Data, provided to the author by Inland Revenue Statistics Division, based on the Survey of Personal Incomes.

bracket). In other words, the before and after tax comparison, in each band, is of the same people.

The figures show income tax significantly reducing the income share of the top 10 per cent, especially of the top 1 per cent. Their share falls from 7.4 per cent to 6.0 per cent of a much smaller total. The average income of the top 1 per cent falls from £100,500 to £68,700 as a result of income tax, a reduction of £31,800. The whole of the rest of the income distribution, below the top 10 per cent, increases its share, with the biggest increase in the bottom 10 per cent.

The ratios are interesting. Overall the pre-tax average of the top 10 per cent was 10.6 times that of the bottom 10 per cent. This ratio was reduced to 8.6 as a result of income tax—which still suggests a considerable degree of inequality. Perhaps a more telling statistic is that the total income of the top 10 per cent after income tax was almost as large as that of the bottom 50 per cent. Until we know more of the composition of the tax units (e.g. the bottom 10 per cent might be mainly single young people, whilst the top 10 per cent might be mainly married couples both earning) we cannot draw any firm conclusions. In any case, what is important for income distribution is the effect of tax and expenditure taken as a whole. Our next section examines this topic. Before we leave the income tax figures, however, it is useful to get some historical perspective. Although there are difficulties in the longer comparisons because of changes in coverage it is clear that there was a considerable decline in the concentration of income at the top of the scale post war, but an increase in concentration in the past decade. In 1949 the top 10 per cent received about 33 per cent of total income before tax; by 1979–80 this was down to about 25. The corresponding post tax figures are 27 and 23. However, the figures for 1988–89, in Table 11.1, show a reversal of the trend, with a pre-tax percentage of 29 and a post-tax percentage of 26.

The Effects of Taxes and Benefits on Household Income

The data for an attempt at a more comprehensive look at the effect of tax and public expenditure on income distribution comes almost wholly from the Family Expenditure Surveys, which have been conducted since 1957. The F.E.S. currently covers a sample of some 7,000 households. The response rate in 1988 was 71 per cent. It is recognised that there is a non-response bias, with under representation of the highest income receivers, the elderly and the self-employed, but no attempt is made to correct it. The survey collects information on the composition of each household and the income, direct tax and expenditure of household members. When the sample is broken down into income groups and different family sizes the numbers may be quite small and hence there is a danger of the expenditure results being affected by one or two unrepresentative purchases, which, in any case, mainly relate to a period of only two weeks. As is usual in this kind of survey there is an under-reporting of the amount spent on alcoholic drink, tobacco, confectionery, ice cream and soft drinks, and the figures have been stepped up to make them consistent with total sales.

The attempt to measure the effect of taxes and expenditure on income distribution, using F.E.S. data, is made annually and published in *Economic Trends*. Before considering some actual figures it will be useful to outline the stages in the process, each of which raises problems of a practical or/and conceptual nature. Using ORIGINAL INCOME as a starting point, state cash benefits are added to obtain GROSS INCOME. The deduction of direct tax from gross income gives DISPOSABLE INCOME. From disposable income taxes on expenditure are deducted and the value of benefits in kind added to give FINAL INCOME.

Original income is family income before the addition of benefits or the deduction of tax. It comprises mainly (99 per cent) income from earnings, investment income and occupational pensions. But it is not a very meaningful concept. It is certainly not identical to the income the family would have had in the absence of all government taxation and spending. Take state retirement pensioners, for example. If, during their working lives, they had not expected to receive a state pension on retirement nor had been required to pay taxes and national insurance contributions, they would have had both the incentive and the means to provide for a private income in retirement. Indeed, by virtue of contributions, many would claim that they have paid for (at least a part of) their own pensions.

The addition of state provided cash benefits (like pensions, child benefit, income support, rent rebates, sickness and unemployment pay) to original income to obtain gross income raises no very serious problems and the coverage of cash benefits is fairly comprehensive. To obtain disposable income from gross income, income tax, employees' national insurance contributions the national insurance contributions of the self-employed and (for 1988, the latest year for which data is available at the time of writing) domestic rates are deducted. No account is taken of capital taxes or of corporation tax. Employers' national insurance contributions, once treated as though they were part of the taxed income of the employee, are currently regarded as being fully passed on into prices and treated as an intermediate tax on expenditure.

The treatment of indirect taxes, or taxes on outlay, as the first stage towards final income, has been subject to criticism. Taxes on final goods and services, V.A.T., tobacco tax, duties on alcoholic drinks, oil tax paid by final consumers, car tax and vehicle excise duty, are all assumed to be passed on 100 per cent in prices; no consideration is given to the possibility that they might be partly borne by profits, wages or rent or a combination of these factor incomes. Intermediate goods and services are those purchased by industry and the tax on them is included in respect of goods entering final consumption. Then it is assumed to be passed on 100 per cent. As well as employers' national insurance contributions, the taxes covered include non-domestic rates, vehicle excise duties and oil duties on industry and commerce.

The biggest problems arise with the allocation of benefits in kind. First, only a proportion of total expenditure is allocated—the main benefits in kind which are included are state education, school meals, milk and other welfare foods, National Health Service, housing subsidy, travel subsidies. The omitted items fall into four broad categories: defence and costs of administration; roads, research and aid to industry; environmental services, e.g. refuse collection, museums, parks and fire services; and capital expenditure on social services, e.g. school and hospital building.

Within the services included, the allocation of benefits in kind is on a standard or "fixed" basis. Thus, in education the benefit of state education is taken to be the average net cost per child to public authorities under each of the main categories of education establishment. Similarly benefits from the National Health Service (except maternity services which are separately allocated) are assumed to be the same for all persons in each of eight age/sex categories.

In principle it would be better to take the value placed on these various services by the recipient rather than the average cost to the state; but this is hardly possible. However, to value the output at the cost of the input does imply that if, say, teachers have a salary increase the value of educational services to the community goes up; and, what is patently untrue, that the value of the benefit derived by the community is always equal to the cost.

Overall approximately 70 per cent of government revenue is currently allocated to households and just over 50 per cent of expenditure. The large proportion unallocated is a serious disadvantage; moreover the differing degree of allocation of taxation and expenditure means that there is an imbalance so that any "break even" point (where a household exactly gets back in benefits what it pays in taxes) is not very meaningful.

As a refinement in analysing the data, in 1990 (in respect of the 1987 results) the concept of equivalisation was introduced: i.e. household income was adjusted to allow for household size and composition. (A married couple is treated as 1.00, a single adult as 0.61 and children as different fractions according to age e.g. 5–7 year olds as 0.21. To obtain the household equivalent income, the total of the household unit according to the scale, is divided into the total household income.)

Let us turn now to some actual figures. Table 11.2 summarises the data for 1988. The figures show considerable inequality across the income ranges. Thus the average original income of the top 20 per cent of households was 24 times that of the bottom 20 per cent. But, as we have indicated, original income is an unsatisfactory concept. The differences in gross income are much less marked but still substantial, the top 20 per cent being 6.7 times the average of the bottom 20 per cent. After direct taxes have been deducted the ratio falls to 6.1 per cent and after allowing for indirect taxes and non cash benefits it falls to 4.3 per cent.

Clearly the household composition is very significant in explaining the differences. The top 20 per cent has (equal with the next highest 20 per cent) the highest proportion of economically active people, it also has the lowest number of people in full time education and the lowest number of retired persons. Conversely the lowest 20 per cent (equal with the next lowest) has the largest number of retired persons; it also has the lowest number of economically active and is in line with the average of all households for the numbers of children and those in full time education.

A vertical comparison within each household income group throws additional light on the picture. The final income of the bottom 20 per cent is four times that of their original income and some 8 per cent above their gross income. The top 20 per cent show a final income of 88 per cent of original income and 76 per cent of gross income.

Table 11.2b brings out the percentage changes to each household group resulting from taxes and benefits. Taking the two tables (11.2a and 11.2b) together it is clear that cash benefits both absolutely and relatively go strongly in favour of the poor. To a rather less extent benefits in kind also favour the poor. When we turn to taxes the position is rather different. It should be remembered that direct taxes in this context consist of income tax, the national insurance contributions of employees and the self-employed and local domestic rates (before allowance for rate rebates which are treated as an addition to cash benefits). The tables show that, whilst the better off pay substantially more in direct taxes than the poorer, the progression in the tax system is very limited, especially amongst the three upper quintiles. With indirect taxation the appropriate base is disposable income rather than gross income; and here, although the absolute amount of tax paid rises with income, the pattern is one of marked regressiveness. We cannot directly add the percentages of direct and indirect tax (and we must remember that no allowance is made in the figures for rate rebates) but it would appear that, at best, the United Kingdom tax system is proportional in its incidence over most of its range rather than progressive, with the top 20 per cent paying a smaller proportion of their income in tax than the rest. Redistribution takes place through benefits rather than through taxes.

The F.E.S. data provides some useful guidelines to the formal incidence of individual taxes. Thus V.A.T. emerges as progressive over the first two ranges of income and thereafter roughly proportional. Domestic rates would be strongly regressive if, at the lower end of the income scale, this regressiveness were not tempered by rate debates. Tobacco duty is regressive over most of the income ranges as are intermediate taxes. The duty on oils is progressive except for the top 20 per cent of the income distribution. Beer tax and the duty on wines and spirits tend to figure as a smaller proportion of the budgets of the bottom 20 per cent of income receivers, but thereafter are more or less proportional.

Overall the analysis of household income shows a redistribution of real income flowing in various ways—from the richer to the poorer, from the working to the retired and from those without

TABLE 11.2a

Redistribution of Household Income through Taxes and Benefits, 1988

	Groups of households ranked by equivalent disposable income					All households
	Bottom 20%	2nd 20%	3rd 20%	4th 20%	Top 20%	
Average per household (£ p.a.) *						
Original income	1,210	4,440	10,750	16,260	29,170	12,360
plus cash benefits	3,210	2,800	1,760	1,080	720	1,910
Gross income	4,430	7,240	12,500	17,340	29,880	14,280
less direct taxes (see text)	670	1,220	2,450	3,790	6,690	2,960
Disposable income	3,760	6,020	10,050	13,540	23,190	11,310
less indirect taxes	1,080	1,470	2,410	2,900	3,710	2,320
Post tax income	2,680	4,540	7,650	10,640	19,480	9,000
plus benefits in kind	2,120	2,020	2,060	1,720	1,220	1,830
Final income	4,800	6,570	9,700	12,360	20,700	10,830
Average per household (number)						
Children†	0.6	0.6	0.8	0.6	0.4	0.6
Adults	1.6	1.7	2.1	2.1	2.0	1.9
Persons	2.2	2.3	2.9	2.7	2.4	2.5
People in full-time education	0.5	0.5	0.6	0.5	0.3	0.5
Economically active people	0.3	0.7	1.4	1.7	1.7	1.2
Retired people	0.7	0.7	0.4	0.2	0.1	0.4
Ratios						
Final divided by original income	3.97	1.48	0.90	0.76	0.71	0.88
Final divided by gross income	1.08	0.91	0.78	0.71	0.69	0.76

* The table shows unequivalised income to the nearest £10. Equivalised income has only been used in the ranking process to produce the quintile groups.

† Defined as persons aged under 16, or aged between 16 and 18, unmarried and receiving non advanced further education.

Source: Economic Trends, March 1991.

TABLE 11.2b
Redistribution of Household Income through Taxes and Benefits, 1988

	Groups of households ranked by equivalent disposable income					All households
	Bottom 20%	2nd 20%	3rd 20%	4th 20%	Top 20%	
Benefits in cash as % of original income	265.3	63.1	16.4	6.6	2.5	15.4
Benefits in cash as % of gross income	72.5	16.9	14.1	6.2	2.4	13.4
Direct taxes as % of gross income	15.1	16.9	19.6	21.9	22.3	20.7
Indirect taxes as % of disposable income	28.7	24.4	24.0	21.4	16.0	20.5
Benefits in kind as % of original income	175.2	45.5	19.2	10.6	4.2	14.8
Benefits in kind as % of gross income	47.9	27.9	16.5	9.9	4.1	12.8

Notes and source as Table 11.2a.

children to those with. Whilst these broad conclusions are not open to serious question, the deficiencies of the methodology, in particular the large unallocated taxation and expenditure, cast doubts on the extent of the redistribution. The authors of a recent paper* have attempted to allocate all taxes and expenditure for the year 1971. They employ several alternative assumptions about tax incidence. They allocate the cost of administering welfare services to the recipients of welfare. They allocate expenditure on pure public goods, like defence and law and order, in several alternative ways each with its own rationale—(1) on a per capita basis, which assumes all benefit equally; (2) on an income basis—assuming benefit is proportional to income; (3) on the basis on income from property (including private pension rights) which reflects the view that the propertied obtain more benefit because they have more to be protected. The upshot of their calculations is that, whichever allocation mechanisms are used, when all taxes and a larger proportion of expenditure are allocated, the net effect is to reduce the "pro-poor" redistribution, as compared with the more limited allocation undertaken by the Central Statistical Office and published in *Economic Trends*.

Changes in the Distribution of Household Income, 1977–88

The *Economic Trends* article for March 1991 also gives a comparison of household incomes and the effects of taxes and benefits for the years 1977–88, re-worked using the new methodology of equivalisation, to obtain figures sufficiently consistent to indicate clearly the trends in income distribution. A selection of the data is given in Table 11.3. It shows that the distribution of household income has become markedly more unequal during the period. On all the measures of income the percentage share of total income of the top 20 per cent has increased whilst the share of all the other quintile groups has fallen, with the one exception of the second highest group where the share of equivalised disposable income has

*Michael O'Higgins and Patricia Ruggles, The Distribution of Public Expenditure and Taxes among Households in the United Kingdom, *Review of Income and Wealth*, September 1981.

TABLE 11.3

Percentage Shares of Household Income, ranked by Equivalent Disposable Income, 1977, 1983 and 1988

	1977	1983	1988
Equivalised original income			
Bottom 20%	3.6	3.0	1.9
2nd 20%	10	8	7
3rd 20%	18	17	16
4th 20%	26	26	25
Top 20%	43	47	50
All households	100	100	100
Equivalised gross income			
Bottom 20%	8.9	8.5	7.1
2nd 20%	13	12	11
3rd 20%	18	17	16
4th 20%	24	23	23
Top 20%	37	39	43
All households	100	100	100
Equivalised disposable income			
Bottom 20%	9.7	9.3	7.6
2nd 20%	14	13	11
3rd 20%	18	17	16
4th 20%	23	23	23
Top 20%	36	38	42
All households	100	100	100
Equivalised post-tax income			
Bottom 20%	9.4	9.0	6.9
2nd 20%	14	13	11
3rd 20%	17	17	16
4th 20%	23	22	22
Top 20%	37	39	44
All households	100	100	100

Source: Economic Trends, March 1991.

remained the same. Thus, the share of equivalised original income of the bottom 20 per cent fell from 3.6 per cent in 1977 to 1.9 per cent in 1988 whilst the share of the top 20 per cent rose from 43 to 50. Similarly, the share of post-tax income of the bottom 20 per cent fell from 9.4 per cent to 6.9 per cent over these 11 years whilst the share of the top 20 per cent rose from 37 per cent to 44 per cent.

The ratios of the highest and lowest quintiles tell the same story. In 1977 the top quintile group received approximately 12 times the equivalised original income of the bottom group; in 1988 the corresponding figure was 26 times; the ratio for equivalised gross income has increased from 4.2 to 6.1; for equivalised disposable income from 3.7 to 5.5; and for equivalised post-tax income from 3.9 to 6.4. There was no change in the percentage share of household income of the top 20 per cent, on any of these measures, between 1977 and 1979. The big increase in inequality has been the outcome of the Conservative years in government. As the analysis relates to calendar years, the full effect of the reduction to 40 per cent of the top rate of income tax in the 1988 Budget, has yet to appear in the figures. Nor has the community charge, which is more regressive than the domestic rates, yet had its effect. Nor the introduction of individual taxation which especially benefited the wealthier couples.

The Distribution of Wealth

Just as various government policy measures may influence income distribution, similarly a large number of different measures may affect the distribution of personal capital or wealth. A government may promote wealth-holding by encouraging home ownership in various ways, by offering tax relief, like Tax Exempt Special Savings Accounts (T.E.S.S.A.s) for small savers, or encouraging equity shareholding by schemes like Personal Equity Plans (P.E.P.s) and employee share-holding. At the same time it may seek to reduce inequalities of wealth by heavy taxation of large wealth-holdings, indirectly by taxing income from property more heavily than "earned" income, or directly by a wealth tax, capital gains tax, death duties or a combination of the three. Heavy income taxation limits the scope to accumulate capital. A government may also resort to an occasional small capital levy, such as the "special contribution" of Sir Stafford Cripps in 1948 and the similar special levy on investment income imposed by Chancellor Jenkins in 1968 which, together with income tax and surtax, amounted for the one year to more than 100 per cent of the highest property incomes.

As capital taxes Britain currently has the so-called Inheritance Tax as a descendant of capital transfer tax and estate duty and, if it be counted as a capital tax rather than an income tax, the capital gains tax. We should certainly anticipate that, despite avoidance, the former estate duty, with very high maximum rates for over a generation, would have significantly influenced the distribution of wealth.

The Basis of the Statistics

The basic source for data on the distribution of wealth is information collected by the Inland Revenue as a by-product of the administration of (in the past) estate duty and capital transfer tax and (currently) Inheritance Tax. The principle behind the Inland Revenue calculations of the distribution of personal wealth is that, in any year, the estates of those who die are taken as representative of the whole of the sex and age-group to which the deceased belonged. To convert the sample of estates in any age–sex group into the whole of the estates for that group, the number of estates and the total property in each range is multiplied by the reciprocal of an appropriate mortality rate for that age–sex group. Thus, to give a somewhat over-simplified example: suppose that in a particular year four estates in the range of £100,000–£200,000, totalling £550,000, owned by women aged 85–86, became liable to death duty. If the mortality rates for that year for women of that age were 1 in 5, then it is assumed that in the population as a whole there are 20 estates owned by women 85–86 of a size between £100,000 and £200,000 totalling £2,750,000 in all. On the basis of the estates which come liable to duty for the year in question the calculations are carried out for both sexes, and for all age groups; the aggregate of the numbers of estate and value of property in each range then gives the distribution of wealth.

Statistical and Conceptual Problems

By now the reader will not be surprised to learn that the statistics are less than perfect for our purpose. There are difficulties relating to the completeness and accuracy of the data, and there are conceptual problems. The statistical difficulties are of three main kinds.

Sampling errors. The method used to "gross up" the figures of the estates of those dying to obtain an estimate of the wealth distribution of the living gives rise to sampling errors; for example, the total number of very large estates is small and those large estates falling liable to death duty in any one year may not be representative; in particular large estates possessed by those dying young may be unrepresentative for their age and sex group (for which the mortality rates are low and therefore the reciprocals, used as multipliers, are high). As Professor Atkinson vividly put it: "A wealthy young man crashing his sports car could add one thousand to the estimate of the number of people with wealth over £200,000." Another problem is that of choosing the most suitable mortality rate—when these rates are affected by a number of social and economic factors.

Omissions. The information collected by the Estate Duty/Capital Taxes Office only includes estates reported for death duty purposes: it excludes deaths where no property has been left or where the amount was small or of a kind where transfer can take place without a "grant of representation". In addition, if the estate is below a certain figure (£70,000 in 1987 and 1988) detailed accounts are not required by the Inland Revenue. Accounts are requested for a small sample of these "excepted" estates and the estimates are based on these accounts but the information may not be as good as that for the non-excepted estates. The information derived from death duty data only covers about one-third of all estates (including the excepted estates) but a very much larger proportion of the total wealth. Other assets not covered by death duty data include certain settled property and assets held in discretionary trusts.

Valuations. The valuation of some assets recorded at the death of the owner is unrealistic as a measure of value to the living. The value of life assurance at death is a maturity value plus any bonuses, whereas to the living their life assurance has a much lower value. Other examples are housing values—where values at the lower end of a possible range are likely to be used and also where a discount is allowed on the valuation of jointly owned property; and consumer durables, valued at a second-hand realisable value. In both these cases the value to the living would be more than the value at death.

Besides these statistical difficulties there are others of a more conceptual nature. Thus the unit for estate duty or capital transfer tax purposes is the individual; a family unit might be more meaningful in analysing the distribution of wealth. Secondly, as with the pictures of income distribution, what we get from this method is a snapshot of the distribution of wealth at a point in time. Many people will be shown as possessing little wealth who 20 years later may be quite large wealth holders. In other words there is a life cycle of saving and some part of the inequality in the distribution of wealth at a point of time simply reflects the differences of wealth associated with differences of age. Thirdly, there is the problem of what to include within personal wealth. It can be argued that private pension rights should be included and the argument is particularly strong where it is possible to realise a capital sum in exchange for part of those rights. More difficult is the problem of *state* pensions. A person contributing to a state retirement pension will not need to save as much for his retirement and the state pension can therefore be regarded as an equivalent addition to his wealth. On the other hand, a state pension right is not an asset which he is able to realise for a capital sum. More doubtfully still, it is sometimes argued that we should add to personal wealth a sum to allow for the benefits of the National Health Service and other state insurance benefits, and indeed that we ought to include a value to the council house dweller which represents the advantage he possesses from his council house tenure at subsidised rents. A further problem which has exercised the minds of some economists is whether we ought not to count as wealth the capitalised value of an individual's future earning power.

The conceptual and the statistical difficulties come together on some of these issues. Thus, if it is decided that the value of pension rights should be included as wealth, the problem of an appropriate valuation has to be faced—which rests on assumptions about life expectations, future earnings and future interest rates and about how the value of pension rights should be distributed across the population. Although the government actuary has produced values for both occupational and state pension rights (see Table 11.5, below) the calculations inevitably involve a degree of arbitrariness.

Some of the conceptual problems will never be resolved satisfactorily; but with the encouragement of the Royal Commission on the Distribution of Income and Wealth, considerable progress has been made in supplementing and making good the deficiencies in the statistics derived from death duty accounts principally by using data from other sources which has been used to build up a national personal sector balance sheet.

The current procedure followed by Inland Revenue in preparing estimates of the distribution of wealth is to start with a sample of estates from the death duty data in each year of death and gross it up to give the total value of estates reported. Wealth multipliers — derived from appropriate death rates — are then applied to provide estimates of the wealth of all the members of the adult population who would have been liable to submit accounts had they died. About six hundred different multipliers are applied each year, to take account of sex, age, marital status, country (within the United Kingdom) and whether or not the individual was living in an owner-occupied dwelling. The data are then adjusted to bring the death values of assets to values appropriate to the living. Finally imputed asset values are added to cover the excluded individuals so that the whole adult population is represented. Whilst the exercise calls for judgement on a number of issues, sensitivity analysis (i.e. calculations to see how much difference is made by alternative methods and assumptions) applied to a number of the methods used has indicated the general robustness of the figures.* Since then the Inland Revenue has undertaken further refinements.†

The Inland Revenue started to make estimates of the distribution of wealth in 1962. Using the current methodology they have been

*See A. B. Atkinson and A. J. Harrison, *The Distribution of Personal Wealth in Britain*, Cambridge University Press, 1977.
†For a full account of the current Inland Revenue methodology and full details of the adjustments and the reconciliation with the personal sector balance sheet, see Estimates of the Distribution of Personal Wealth, *Economic Trends*, H.M.S.O., October 1990.

TABLE 11.4

Trends in Distribution of Personal Wealth since 1976
Percentage shares of Estimated Personal Marketable Wealth of Total
Population of United Kingdom aged 18 and over

	1976 per cent	1980 per cent	1984 per cent	1988[1] per cent
Most wealthy 1 per cent	21	19	18	17
Most wealthy 2 per cent	27	25	24	25
Most wealthy 5 per cent	38	36	35	38
Most wealthy 10 per cent	50	50	48	53
Most wealthy 25 per cent	71	73	71	75
Most wealthy 50 per cent	92	91	91	94
Least wealthy 50 per cent	8	9	9	6

[1]Provisional.
Source: Economic Trends, October 1990.

able to re-work the estimates for the years from and including 1976, but not earlier because the data was not available. Comparison of the pre 1976 figures with the later ones is hazardous.

Table 11.4 concentrates on marketable personal wealth (omitting any value for occupational and state pensions) and is confined to years since 1976 for a consistent series. It shows that the top 1 per cent of wealth holders owned around one-fifth of marketable wealth over this period and the top 10 per cent of wealth owners around a half. The bottom half of the population owns only a few per cent. The table reveals a decline in the share of the most wealthy 1 per cent between 1976 and 1988 but this is partly made good by the next wealthiest 1 per cent and the share of the top 5 per cent is the same in 1988 as in 1976. The most wealthy 25 per cent of the population have increased their share. The share of the least wealthy 75 per cent has therefore fallen from 29 to 25 per cent; that of the least wealthy 50 per cent has fallen from 8 to 6 per cent.

The outstanding feature of Table 11.5 is the difference which is made to the figures by the inclusion of pension rights, especially state pension rights. When all pension rights are included the share of the top 1 per cent in 1988 falls from 17 to 10 per cent and the top 10 per cent from 53 to 36 per cent. The effect on the least wealthy

TABLE 11.5

Concentration of Personal Wealth in 1988[1] on Various Assumptions

Percentage Shares of Estimated Personal Wealth of Total Population of United Kingdom aged 18 and over

	Marketable wealth (excluding all pension rights)	Wealth including occupational pension rights	Wealth including occupational and state pension rights
Most wealthy 1 per cent	17	13	10
Most wealthy 2 per cent	25	19	15
Most wealthy 5 per cent	38	31	24
Most wealthy 10 per cent	53	44	36
Most wealthy 25 per cent	75	67–72	58–61
Most wealthy 50 per cent	94	89–93	82–87
Least wealthy 50 per cent	6	7–11	13–18

[1]Provisional.

Source: Inland Revenue Statistics 1990.

half of the population is also very marked, rising from 6 to between 13 and 18 per cent. The third column in Table 11.5 presents a picture of much less inequality than the first column.

Twentieth-Century Changes in the Distribution of Wealth

Several attempts have been made to estimate the changes in the distribution of wealth from early in the twentieth century. One of the most recent* looks at the period 1923–81. Like the Inland Revenue estimates for later years, these estimates are based on the estate duty method, but, in order to obtain a series as consistent as possible, they do not incorporate all the recent refinements introduced by Inland Revenue. The most important differences are that the mortality multipliers used are adjusted for social class (not owner-occupation); the total adult population is defined by

*A. B. Atkinson, J. R. F. Gordon and A. Harrison, Trends in the Shares of Top Wealth Holders in Britain, 1923–81, *Oxford Bulletin of Economics and Statistics*, Vol. 51, No. 3, August 1989.

TABLE 11.6
Shares in Marketable Personal Wealth in Great Britain[1] 1923–81

	1923	1938	1960	1971	1981
Top 1%	60.9	55.0	34.4	28.8	22.5
Top 5%	82.0	77.2	60.0	53.0	46.0
Top 10%	89.1	85.4	72.1	68.3	62.8
Top 20%	94.2	91.6	83.6	84.8	79.9
Bottom 80%	5.8	7.4	16.4	15.2	20.1

[1]Figures for 1923 relate to England and Wales only.
Source: A. B. Atkinson *et al.*, ibid.

reference to an age threshold reduced linearly from 23 in 1923 to 18 in 1973 and thereafter maintained at 18; no adjustments are made for settled property missing from estate duty data, for the value of pension rights or for the over-valuation of life policies. From 1923 until 1938, data was only available for England and Wales; thereafter data relates to Great Britain. (Data for Northern Ireland only became available from 1974 and is not included in the figures.) Data for a selection of years is given in Table 11.6.

The figures show a major decline in the share of the top one per cent of wealth holders. Interestingly, however, the share of the top 4 per cent below the top one per cent remains remarkably constant: in 1923 it was 21.1 per cent, in 1981 it was 23.5 per cent. Although over the period as a whole the bottom 80 per cent significantly increased their share (by 14.3 percentage points) the main beneficiaries of the big decline in the share of the top one per cent were those in the 6th to 20th percentile whose share rose by 21.7 percentage points from 12.2 to 33.9.

Why Has Inequality Declined?

Whilst there is no doubt about the decline in inequality in the statistical sense, there is scope for different interpretations of the causes of the decline and how meaningful it may be. The most obvious causes would appear to be the growing affluence of a wide section of the population, the increase in what Atkinson *et al.* call "popular wealth", defined as the value of consumer durables and owner-occupied housing, together with the effect of progressive taxation, especially estate duty. But other factors have been at work, one of which is the increased ownership of property by women, often in the form of joint ownership with their husbands. Further, one feature reflected in the estate duty statistics has been the increase in the proportion of wealth held by younger people; and evidence of the growth of gifts *inter vivos* over this period* suggests that some of the decline in inequality results from gifts from parents to children and grandchildren to avoid estate duty.

These last two features are not what many people would normally understand by a decline in inequality; these forms of redistribution of wealth reveal the inadequacy of using the individual as our "unit" rather than the family.

There has also been another factor potently at work during the century—changes in relative prices. As Professor Revell suggested in 1965, the decline in the price of land in the twenties reduced the degree of concentration of wealth; paradoxically, however, the increase in the price of land and real property in post-war years has also tended to reduce concentration because of the growth in the numbers of owner-occupiers of houses and farms, who have secured much of the benefit. Similarly changes in the price of ordinary shares, the personal holdings of which tend to be heavily concentrated in the hands of the wealthiest, can have a very significant effect; thus a decline in the wealth of top wealth holders between 1971 and 1976 owed much to the fall in share prices over that period. Fluctuations in the stock market, such as the dramatic fall in share prices in October 1987, can also bring about variations in the pattern of wealth ownership from year to year.

A New Face to Inequality?

We have pointed out the continued decline in concentration of wealth amongst top wealth holders without any substantial increase

---

*See, for example, C. T. Sandford, *Taxing Personal Wealth*, Allen & Unwin, 1971, pp. 84–88 and appendix B; and E. G. Horsman, The Avoidance of Estate Duty by Gifts *Inter Vivos*: Some Quantitative Evidence, *The Economic Journal*, September 1975.

in the share of the least wealthy half of the population since at least the middle 1970s and it could well be that inequality in the United Kingdom has a new face. Since the Second World War and especially in the early 1970s and much of the 1980s the value of house property soared and rose much more than prices in general. The Royal Commission on the Distribution of Income and Wealth estimated that private housing constituted some 40 per cent of personal marketable wealth. The new face of inequality could well be, not between the richest 1 or 5 or 10 per cent of the population and the rest, but between the half of families fortunate enough to own houses at a time of inflation and the other 50 per cent who have not enjoyed that good fortune. Inflation can be a more powerful instrument than taxation in changing the distribution of wealth.

On the other hand we should not assume that the trend to reduced concentration of wealth at the top will continue or indeed is irreversible; nor should we discount the effects of taxation. As we showed in Chapter 9, the Inheritance tax, with its single rate of 40 per cent and its scope for tax free gifts and other loopholes particularly favours the richest. It is by no means unlikely that, if the 1988 rates of income tax, or rates not much higher, continue and if Inheritance tax retains its present form for some years, we shall see a move back towards the older form of inequality—the concentration of wealth at the top.

CHAPTER 12

Regulation of the Economy Through Budgetary Policy

By "budgetary" or "fiscal" policy we mean changes in government income or expenditure designed to affect the level of activity in the economy as a whole. The prime aim of such a policy is to maintain a high level of employment without inflation. It is often referred to as "stabilisation" policy, though this term may mislead in that it may erroneously suggest that the objective is nil economic growth. Following developments in economic theory, associated particularly with John Maynard Keynes, which analysed the cause of unemployment and suggested remedies a government could adopt, it was accepted that whether a budget was to be balanced, in deficit, or in surplus, should be determined by the needs of the economy as a whole and not by narrow accounting considerations. In Britain the white paper on Employment Policy, 1944, agreed by all three major political parties, acknowledged that a government should be responsible for maintaining a "high and stable level of employment". This responsibility was to be carried out by budgetary policy and also monetary policy (which is concerned with the quantity of money and the rate of interest).

Until the later 1970s the emphasis of the policy-makers in Britain in pursuing stabilisation policy was on budgetary or fiscal policy. Thereafter there developed and still is much controversy amongst economists about the appropriateness and effectiveness of fiscal policy especially in dealing with inflation, and about the role of monetary policy. Our prime concern in this book is government income and expenditure, and we shall not enter into the technicalities of monetary policy; but we shall seek to give an appreciation of the criticisms of budgetary policy as it has been pursued since the Second World War and also some understanding of the views of the "monetarists" and the current emphasis on supply side factors. But we start by presenting what has been the post-war orthodoxy on budgetary policy prefaced by the orthodox Keynesian view of the theory of employment.

Keynesian Employment Theory

Causes of Unemployment

We can distinguish several causes of unemployment. Characteristic of underdeveloped countries is unemployment resulting from a lack of complementary resources (tools, raw materials, machines) necessary to keep wage-earners at work; but this source of unemployment is rare in technically advanced industrial countries like Britain, occurring only temporarily when bad weather holds up coal supplies and electricity cuts close factories, or when strikes prevent the delivery of components and workers on the assembly line become temporarily redundant.

Unemployment more frequently arises in advanced countries because of structural features and more particularly structural changes in the economy. There may be unemployment associated with a "casual" labour scheme, say in the docks, and seasonal unemployment, for example where an area is particularly dependent on tourism, or in the construction industry during the worst winter weather. More serious, unemployment may arise because of changes in demand for goods, either in the home or the export market, resulting from changes in tastes or technology, such as the superseding, wholly or partly, of one form of heat and power by other forms which can be generated more cheaply. In the U.K. these factors tend to generate regional unemployment. Governments can help with these problems by, for example, decasualisation, and by ensuring that those who are rendered unemployed by technical change have redundancy payments, retraining opportunities and reasonable living standards during their period without work; but these types of unemployment do not call for any general measures of budgetary policy except to stop unemployment which starts in one industry (say because of a change in export demand) from spreading, or possibly to keep up demand for a particular product if the reduction is believed to be temporary.

It is the third kind of unemployment which is potentially the most lethal for advanced countries and with which budgetary policy is primarily concerned—general unemployment resulting from insufficiency and instability of effective demand. Let us examine this at more length.

Employers employ workers because they expect that third parties (consumers) will be willing to pay for the goods the workers help to produce. In other words the "demand for labour" (the number of workers employers will require at any given wage rate) depends on the effective demand for the goods and services the workers produce. When we speak of "effective demand" we are emphasising the point that demand is not the same as desire or need; demand is desire *backed up by purchasing power*. A starving man has a desire and a need for bread but he has no demand for it if he has no money with which to buy it.

Our explanation so far has applied only to workers employed in producing consumption goods and services—goods purchased to meet family needs directly. There are also other goods, "investment" goods, machinery, factories, raw materials, which are not purchased directly by consumers but are bought by producers to assist in the process of producing consumer goods. The level of employment in these industries (e.g. machine tools or textile machinery) depends on the demand from producers for these investment goods.

Nor have we yet mentioned the government, which determines employment in defence industries and many social services directly by the amount it spends on (its demand for) these products. Government demand can conveniently be divided into consumption demand (for current goods and services) and investment demand (e.g. schools, roads, hospitals) for goods which will help to provide services in the future. Also the government adds to the potential private demand of pensioners, the unemployed, and large families when it distributes to them benefits in cash but, at the same time, it reduces potential private demand by its taxation.

For the moment we have ignored export demand; that apart, we can say that the level of employment depends on aggregate effective demand (or expenditure) which can be divided into private consumption demand, private investment demand and government consumption and investment demand $(C+I+G)$.

For the moment let us regard G as an independent "constant" and concentrate on $C+I$. What factors determine C, the demand for goods and services for consumption purposes? Clearly the most important element is the level of aggregate incomes in the community, together with the proportion of total incomes spent on consumption goods (rather than saved)—a relationship which Keynes called the propensity to consume. Investment demand (I) depends on employers' expectations of the likely profitability of new equipment, which rests on a balancing of expected future returns against cost, in which a crucial consideration is the current demand for consumption goods and services; if consumption demand is high and expected to remain high employers are more likely to buy new machines and seek to extend their premises. I will also be affected by the price of new machines, the rate of interest—which is a cost of borrowing to buy investment goods and new inventions which increase the prospect of profit by offering cheaper methods of production or superior products.

Given the level of government expenditure, $C+I$ determine the level of employment. If $C+I$ together create sufficient demand to maintain a high level of employment, as is well. But if the combined demand is insufficient, unemployment will result.

Starting from an equilibrium position with a high level of employment, supposing demand for investment goods fell, then unless there was a corresponding rise in C total demand for goods and services of all kinds would have fallen, less people would be needed to make them and unemployment would result.

Earlier economists held the view that the rate of interest would ensure a "full employment" equilibrium; if investment demand fell, less money would be borrowed, interest rates would fall and this would encourage investment demand. Moreover, the classical economists assumed that if interest rates fell people would save less, i.e. spend more on consumption goods, and hence the fall in investment demand would be compensated by a rise in consumption demand. Keynes demonstrated that a fall in interest rates did not have the effect of inducing people to consume more;* rather, when investment demand fell, those who became unemployed in investment goods industries had less income with which to buy consumption goods and services so that the demand for consumption goods also feel, further income reduction took place, which in turn made investment less attractive so that income and employment fell further.

Again, supposing that from an initial equilibrium position of high employment people wished to save a larger proportion of their incomes; a decision to save more means a reduction in demand for consumption goods and services (C); without an offsetting increase in I, unemployment would result; but a main determiner of I is C; the lower C is the lower is I likely to be; so I is more likely to fall than to rise, and unemployment develop. Without a corresponding increase in I the attempt to save more results not in more saving but in less income and hence in more unemployment.

The "multiplier" effect of decreases (or increases) in income (and employment) is clear from this analysis; say investment declines and as a result unemployment occurs; then the unemployed have less income and can spend loss on consumption goods and services; fewer workers are needed to produce the consumption goods and unemployment occurs in industries making consumption goods; thus total income falls further and there is a further decline in consumption demand and a further increase in unemployment. Conversely, if we start from a position of unemployment and there is an increase in I leading to higher incomes and more employment in the investment goods industries, then part of this increased income will be spent on consumption goods which will generate further income and employment. The income multiplier is defined as the total change in income as a result of an initial change of one unit. Its extent will depend on the proportion of the incremental

*Those familiar with Keynesian analysis will appreciate that lower interest rates led to an increased holding of money for the "speculative" motive rather than increased consumption.

change in the community's income which is saved. If the whole of the incremental increase in income from increased investment was saved, then the multiplier would be one; the total increase in income would equal the initial increase. The smaller the proportion of any increase in income saved (i.e. the larger the proportion spent on consumption goods and services) the bigger will be the multiplier, but it will always be finite unless the whole of incremental increases in income are consumed.* The employment multiplier can be similarly defined as the total increase in employment resulting from an initial increase. If the employment of one extra man on an investment project leads to the employment of two extra men in consumption goods industries, then the employment multiplier is 3. The income (or, more strictly, the money income) multiplier and the employment multiplier move in step as long as there is substantial unemployment; but as employment expands then some of the money income increase assumes the form of higher prices, and the nearer that we approach to 100 per cent employment the more prices rise and the less is the employment increase following any given income increase.

The content of *I* deserves more attention; *I* has generally been regarded as the volatile factor creating instability in the economy. Investment demand is composed of a replacement demand and an expansion demand. Past instabilities may result in a bunching of replacement demands which are also affected by technical obsolescence. Moreover, new demand for investment may lead to disproportionate fluctuations. Suppose, for example, that 100 machines were required to produce 100,000 goods for consumption (i.e. a ratio of 1:1,000) and that the machines had a life of 10 years. Then, if the demand for goods and replacement had been steady in the past , 10 new machines would be required each year for replacement. Suppose that the demand for the products increased 10 per cent to 110,000: then a further 10 machines would be needed to meet this new demand; in that year, then, the demand for the

---

*For those used to the terminology it can be said that in a self-contained economy the numerical value of the multiplier is the reciprocal of the marginal propensity to save (M.P.S.). Where there is international trade, the marginal propensity to import reduces the value of the multiplier on domestic incomes in exactly the same way as the M.P.S.

machines would increase 100 per cent (10 to 20). This relationship between the increased demand for consumption goods and the inducement to invest in the capital needed to produce them is known as the "accelerator". The effect of the accelerator is very much modified in practice by the existence of stocks of goods, by utilisation of spare capacity, by working machines longer hours and giving them a longer life by additional maintenance and repair. But the instability of I is an important fact of economic life.

Together the multiplier and the accelerator go a long way to explain the instability in the economic system which, before the Second World War, was characterised by the "trade cycle". Experience showed, as we pointed out in Chapter 1, that without government intervention the level of activity and employment in the economy fluctuated within wide limits; and Keynes explained how the price which was supposed to secure a high employment equilibrium (the rate of interest) failed to do so.

Let us now bring back the government into the picture. The diagram (Fig. 12.1) summarises the foregoing argument on the

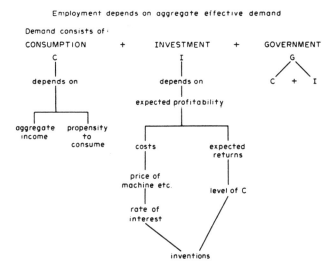

Fig. 12.1. Main determinants of employment.

determinants of employment in sufficient detail for us to be able to see the measures open to the government if there is a threat of general unemployment resulting from deficiency in effective demand. Clearly in these circumstances the government should increase effective demand, which it could do by increasing its own demand for consumption goods and services (without reducing private demand), increasing its investment demand (without reducing private demand), encouraging private investment (for example, by lowering interest rates or subsidising new investment) or increasing private consumption (for example, by lowering taxes and thus increasing aggregate net incomes). Before we examine in detail these various measures, however, we must take account of two complicating factors: the relationship between unemployment and inflation and between the internal price and income level and the external balance of payments.

Inflation

If general unemployment is a situation of deficiency in aggregate demand, leading to a downward pressure on output, employment and prices, inflation is a situation when the pressure on prices is all upward. In the traditional Keynesian analysis this upward pressure on prices arises because aggregate demand is in excess of aggregate supply at the current price level and supply cannot be readily increased because resources are already being highly utilised (i.e. there is a high level of employment and little spare capacity in equipment). In these circumstances, unless some countervailing action is taken by the government, prices will rise. Rising prices should not be regarded as synonymous with inflation but as a symptom of it. Price rises can be checked by controls, but this does not rid the system of inflation, which shows itself in other ways, e.g. adulteration of goods, scarcities and black markets.

To illustrate the relationship between employment and the price level let us suppose that, from a low level of income and employment, the government stimulates effective demand by some or all of the various methods indicated and that, as employment and income rise, the stimulus to effective demand is continued. At first the increases of demand will bring more people into employment; firms can expand output with little or no increase in unit costs; incomes and output can expand without any price increases. But as the process continues supply ceases to be able to keep up with demand and prices start to rise; moreover, bottlenecks will occur in the supply of particular raw materials or skilled labour, existing equipment will be worked at a level above its optimum and the quality of new labour taken into employment will decline, so that even if wage-rates were to remain unchanged unit costs would tend to rise. Thus the continued pressure of demand pulls up prices. If wage-rates also increase without corresponding increases in productivity then the demand inflation is reinforced by cost inflation. Price rises bring about a redistribution of real income in the community which may bear no relationship to social justice. People on fixed incomes suffer most and the value of savings held in monetary form is reduced. Inflation may also have serious repercussions on the balance of payments.

The Balance of Payments

The level of income, employment and prices within a country bears a crucial relationship to its balance of payments—the statement of all payments made by residents in a country to non-residents and by non-residents to residents over a period of time. The balance of payments on current account, which is the aspect of international payments mainly affected by budgetary policy, covers payments for imports and exports of goods and services (like shipping and tourism); it also includes interest payments on international loans.

We can illustrate the relationship between the internal levels of employment, income and prices and the balance of payments by considering two situations: first the effect of a slump in another country, say the U.S.A., on a second country, say Britain. Second the effect on a country's balance of payments (say Britain) of a degree of inflation larger than that of its competitors.

Effect of a slump in U.S.A. on Britain. If the U.S.A. suffered a major slump this would affect Britain in several ways. British exports would fall; Americans would have lower incomes and hence could afford fewer imports; further, because of the slump, American prices would have fallen so that Americans would tend to undercut British exporters not only in the American home market but also in third markets in which British and America were competitors. At the same time British imports from America would tend to increase because of their relative cheapness. These developments would have two effects; first, unemployment in British export industries and in British industries whose products had been displaced by American goods in the home market. Second, a British balance of payments deficit on current account and a drain on Britain's liquid assets, viz. gold and reserve holdings of other countries' currencies.

To reduce the unemployment and prevent it spreading (by the multiplier effect) the government should stimulate effective demand. But to do so accentuates the balance of payments deficit; if the government took no action against unemployment the payments deficit would be mitigated because, as unemployment grew at home, so incomes would decline and Britons could afford fewer imports; also prices would tend to fall and our goods become competitive with American goods. There are various possible ways in which we could maintain employment. Thus, if we had, or could acquire, sufficient liquid assets, we could simply ride out the deficit until the Americans had restored their employment levels (and our action would enable them to return more quickly to a high level of employment); if we were operating with a "fixed" exchange rate we could adjust it downwards (devalue) to offset the change in American price levels compared with our own or, if we were working within a regime of flexible exchange rates we could simply allow the rate to fall; or we could impose a series of import restrictions or/and export subsidies. But none of these solutions is free from difficulty; it is clear that a conflict may develop between the domestic needs of the economy and the external balance. (Similarly if a country was seeking to maintain the external value of its currency at an artificially high level, then it could do this by keeping down its own prices and incomes, but the cost would be measured in terms of unemployment and sacrificed growth.)

Inflation and the balance of payments. If a country allows more inflation than its competitors then, assuming a fixed exchange rate, its balance of payments on current account will deteriorate. Imports will grow because of high incomes in the home market, because imports are cheaper relatively to home-produced goods and because importers are likely to offer better delivery dates. Exports will fall because producers will be attracted by the relatively easy profits of the home market, price rises will have made exports more difficult to sell, potential overseas purchasers may be discouraged by lengthy delivery dates and because the economy has no slack to enable any new opportunities (e.g. for producing and exporting new products) to be taken up. In these circumstances the country which has allowed the inflation must cut back demand, income and employment to get its price and income levels back into line; devalue its currency; or impose a series of import restrictions and export subsidies.

Methods of Budgetary Policy

We are now in a position to examine more closely the methods of budgetary policy as it has been practised in the United Kingdom for most of the post-war period. The general principle was that government made regular short-term forecasts; it estimated for the next year or 18 months the main components of demand; its own expenditures, private consumption, private investment and exports. If, in the light of its forecasts, total demand appeared insufficient to maintain employment then the government would take action to stimulate demand through budgetary policy possibly supported by monetary policy and alterations in hire purchase regulations. Conversely, if the forecasts suggested an excess demand, then the government would take measures to curb demand and so check inflation.

Methods against Unemployment

In determining the method or methods to be adopted several criteria should be borne in mind. First the speed with which the measure will act; methods of forecasting are imperfect and statistics of output and employment are always inevitably slightly out of date, so that it is important to adopt measures which act quickly once the policy has been decided. Second, the extent to which the measures can be directed to a particular region of the country, e.g. to deal with unemployment resulting from an export recession in a regionally concentrated industry. Third, the value of the things which are produced; for example, the government might increase demand by stock-piling uniforms for the Armed Forces which might not be used for many years if at all; this would be better than doing nothing, but worse than increasing demand for things people really wanted, which would, for example, be achieved by a tax reduction which left people free to spend additional net income on what they pleased. Fourth, it may need to take account of any possible adverse effects on the balance of payments, and it might seek to stimulate demand especially for products for which there was a low propensity to import. Finally, in determining its measures the government should consider the importance of investment relatively to consumption; e.g. emphasis on stimulating investment would be more likely to promote future economic growth. Britain has been applying a smaller proportion of its G.N.P. to investment than most other advanced industrial countries, so that a stimulus to investment may be a particularly attractive option.

Government investment. Early emphasis on government measures to promote employment tended to be concentrated on "public works". Private investment was seen to fluctuate considerably and it was suggested that public investment might fluctuate in a counter-cyclical manner; that it should rise when private investment fell and vice versa. Government investment does have the advantage that it can be directed to a particular area, but there are many difficulties about trying to adjust it frequently and rapidly. If action was to be speedy there would have to be a series of measures kept on hand, all ready to put into operation when the slump threatened; yet if the measures were really wanted, there would be considerable difficulties in holding them up. Again, public investment is heavily concentrated on the construction and civil engineering industries—

hospitals, schools, roads; fluctuations in public investment would mean major expansions and contractions in these industries. The view of the Plowden Committee (outlined in Chapter 3) for forward planning and stability in government expenditure applies especially to investment expenditure where a "stop–go" policy can be very wasteful (e.g. by the disbanding of construction teams; and by the loss of economies of scale as well as imperfections in overall design where major building projects, like universities, are conceived and built piecemeal instead of according to a single overall plan).

Government consumption expenditure. Increased government consumption expenditure may take either of two forms: expenditure on goods and services or cash benefits. Neither offers much scope as a flexible weapon of budgetary policy. Salaries of civil servants, teachers or doctors could hardly be increased or decreased according to the needs of employment policy; it might be possible to bring forward an improvement to a service in time of depression (e.g. the raising of the school-leaving age) or postpone it if inflationary trends predominated in the economy, but such developments need careful planning and preparation and are usually live political issues, so that there are practical and political difficulties about advancing or retarding them. Where improvements in social services have been postponed in Britain since the war there has been no clear intention to determine the date of introduction according to the level of activity in the economy; rather, postponements (like that of the raising of the school leaving age in the aftermath of the 1967 devaluation) have been *ad hoc* reactions to crises. Similarly cash benefits such as pensions and family allowances could not be used for stimulating or contracting demand: they could be increased quickly in time of depression but would be very difficult to reduce subsequently.

Of the measures we have discussed only increased government expenditure on goods and services could, to a limited extent, be directed to a particular area (e.g. by increased employment of office workers in town A rather than town B). The Regional Employment Premium (1967–1977) was a form of wage subsidy limited to manufacturing industry in development areas; its purpose, however, was less to cope with short-term fluctuations in employment than to create a sounder basis for regional economies. More generally a temporary employment subsidy applied nationally, reductions in national insurance contributions or in the rates of a payroll tax, could be used to promote employment.

Encourage private investment. A government can encourage private investment by a monetary policy of low interest rates; or by a budgetary policy of investment subsidies. Subsidising investment does not yield speedy results, but has the advantage that it promotes long-term economic growth and can to some extent be applied to particular industries or areas. The various forms of U.K. policy to encourage investment were outlined in Chapter 7 (pp. 180–183). On the whole these measures have been aimed at higher levels of long-run investment and at promoting investment in development areas rather than at offering an investment stimulus as part of stabilisation policy; but they have on occasion been used for stabilisation purposes, notably in calendar years 1967 and 1968 when the rates of investment grants were increased for a strictly limited period to try to arrest the downturn in investment (and employment) in 1966. Besides such general measures, increasingly in the 1970s *ad hoc* measures have been used to shore up ailing firms and enable them to re-equip. Whilst these have involved government expenditure, often on a very large scale, they do not really fit into the picture of budgetary policy based on short-term economic forecasts.

Stimulate private consumption. The government can stimulate consumption by reducing taxes, thus increasing net personal incomes. The extra goods produced are what people want and reductions in outlay taxes can take effect quickly; income tax changes take rather longer to become effective as new code sheets have to be prepared. Only to a limited extent can tax reductions be directed to a particular industry or area; if there is an excise duty on a commodity or group of commodities the demand for which has temporarily fallen the tax could be reduced, but this practice carries dangers: if people expect that a drop in sales will be followed by tax reductions purchasers may hold off the market in anticipation of the reduction and minor fluctuations in demand and output may be accentuated. The most important taxes—income tax, V.A.T., alcoholic drinks, petrol, tobacco— could not be directed to any particular region; local rates could be reduced in particular areas (and grants-in-aid given) but only limited results could be achieved by juggling with rates and there would be obvious political complications.

Another possible way of stimulating consumption demand would be not by less taxation in total, but by different taxation; rearranging taxes so that they fall more heavily on the savers in the economy and less leavily on the spenders—in other words increasing the community's propensity to consume from a given net income. This means, in practice, reducing tax on the poor and increasing it on the rich. Faced by a threat of general unemployment a government is unlikely to rely solely on this method, but it is likely to take account of effects on the consumption function when deciding which taxes to reduce.

Whilst tax changes are one of the most useful media for implementing employment policy, frequent changes create inequities and uncertainty, lead to attempts to anticipate changes and make rational consumer and producer planning more difficult.

The various measures discussed can be used singly or in combination. All are likely to involve a budget deficit, which can be met by borrowing from the public or the banks (new money creation). If, as is not unlikely (see pp. 315–317) the policy is associated with a balance of payments deficit, there will be an addition of both the internal and external national debt. In so far as the policy is successful in generating employment, additional taxable incomes will be generated which will restrict the budget deficit and hence the rise in internal debt.

Measures against Inflation

Against inflation precisely the same policies apply in reverse, for demand must be restricted; the criteria, appropriately restated, retain relevance: speed of action; ability to direct to a particular part of the country; that things cut out should have as low a value and as high an import content as possible; that investment should be spared the axe in the interests of long-term growth. Inflation can be met by reducing government investment, cutting government current expenditure, discouraging private investment or cutting consumption by higher taxes or by taxes which fall *more* heavily on the spenders (the poor) and less heavily on the savers (the rich). The disadvantages and limitations of the various methods the reader can spell out for himself from what has already been said.

So far we have simply presented what has been, for most of the period since the Second World War, the orthodox view of budgetary policy. Let us now consider how it has worked out in practice and what limitations have come to be recognised; and examine the increasing volume of criticism to which the post-war orthodoxy has been subjected and the current change of emphasis.

Assessment of Budgetary Policy in U.K.

In terms both of the degree of success of the policy and of the nature of the criticisms, we must distinguish two periods: from the end of the war to the late 1960s; and from the later 1960s to 1991 (the time of writing). During the first period the policy enjoyed a measure of success and the criticisms were concerned with improving and supplementing policy rather than changing its basic nature. In the later period the policy appeared to fail and some of the criticisms were fundamental, questioning its whole basis.

The Second World War to the Late 1960s

During this period, measured in terms of employment levels the policy appeared to be very successful; only for relatively short periods did unemployment rise above 2 per cent of the insured population. This compares very favourably with other industrial countries during the same period and is in marked contrast with British experience inter-war when, after the boom following the First World War, unemployment never fell below 10 per cent until preparations for the Second World War were well advanced, and at its worst was over 20 per cent of the insured population. The figures before and after the Second World War are not precisely comparable because the insured population inter-war was a smaller proportion of the working population and covered the occupations most vulnerable to unemployment; nevertheless the change was enormous and the benefit correspondingly large.

The less favourable side of the coin is that the period saw a continuous rise in prices, averaging about 4 per cent per annum. Between the devaluation of 1949 and the devaluation 1967, retail prices almost doubled. If Britain's employment record was better than most industrial countries her inflation was worse.

The price rises undoubtedly had serious social consequences. Pensions and more especially family allowances lagged behind price increases and people with fixed or relatively fixed money incomes suffered serious reductions in living standards. Not only did fixed income receivers lose because of the big decline in the real value of their income; if their savings had been in a savings bank or in government securities the real value of their capital fell too. To take the extreme instance, anyone who, in 1947, bought Consols or Treasury 2½ per cent bonds (which are irredeemable) found the real value of the income halved by 1968 and the real value of the capital reduced by more than four-fifths (in 1968 a £100, 2½ per cent, Treasury bond would only fetch £35 in the market and this £35 would buy only half what it would have bought in 1947).

Also inflation played a significant part in the recurrent balance of payments crises which plagued the British economy every few years and failure to curb inflation was the root cause of the two devaluations.

Moreover the rate of economic growth of the British economy, whilst good by historical standards, was poor when compared with most other Western "mixed" economies. One of the main reasons for this relatively poor performance was felt to be the so-called "stop–go" policy, with the stops necessitated by the balance of payments crises.

Thus it was not surprising that dissatisfaction with budgetary policy emerged. On several grounds it was suggested that budgetary policy, at any rate as hitherto conceived, suffered from significant limitations and required supplementation. The criticisms can be grouped under four main heads.

(1) *Imperfect techniques and policy implementation.* The tools available for budgetary policy-making are deficient. Statistical data take time to collect and are therefore always to some extent out of date; the statistics, usually a by-product of administration, often do not measure precisely what the economist would wish to measure; thus the indicators on which forecasts are based are faulty. Forecasting itself is necessarily imperfect—economic relationships vary over time; people do not always react in the same way to similar situations; and many non-economic factors influence the economy. The United Kingdom's economy is heavily dependent on movements in foreign trade and world prices, which are particularly difficult to predict. Political decisions exercise an influence; foreign wars or crises affect the international economy whilst a General Election at home may encourage a Chancellor to take a sanguine view of the state of the British economy. Often the decision about whether or when to stimulate or reduce demand is finely balanced. Policy measures take time to implement and to become effective. Thus, for example, unemployment usually continues to rise for some time after the upturn in output from a recession, because the initial increases in demand are partly met from stocks and also because the first stages of an upturn are often associated with big increases in productivity as equipment is used at levels near to optimum. If, at this point, a government stimulates demand, by cutting taxes or increasing government expenditure, the danger is that the measures only take effect after the recession is over and so serve to fuel the next boom. Some economists,* indeed, held that during this period policy was de-stabilising rather than stabilising.

(2) *Annual surveys insufficient.* Two rather different arguments were presented to suggest the inadequacy of budgetary policy conceived as an annual survey of adjustments required to secure full utilisation of resources for the following year. The first argument, that annual changes of policy instruments were insufficiently frequent, follows logically from the deficiencies inherent in the policy-making process which we have just outlined. Because of the imperfections of

*Most notably, J. C. R. Dow, *The Management of the British Economy 1945–60*, C.U.P., Students' edition, 1970.

the statistical indicators, once it is clear that a certain action is required, it should be taken with all speed without waiting for the next budget; moreover, in principle, frequent adjustments should mean smaller and finer adjustments, whilst infrequent changes are apt to be large and abrupt. The later years of this period therefore witnessed more frequent adjustments in revenue and expenditure associated with "mini-budgets" partway through the year. One measure was specifically introduced in 1961 to give inter-budget flexibility, the so-called "regulator", by which purchase tax and excise duties could be varied by up to 10 per cent of existing rates,* without prior recourse to Parliament. The regulator was used on a number of occasions.

The other line of criticism of the annual budgetary survey was that a year was too short a period in which to review the economy — that if a longer horizon was taken it might improve Britain's rate of growth; industrialists would be more inclined to make, and stick to, longer term investment plans and not allow short-term fluctuations to divert them from trend. In other words, short-term forecasting for budgetary policy should be supplemented by medium-term forecasting and fiscal planning should be accompanied by indicative planning. Hence the setting-up of the National Economic Development Council (N.E.D.C.) in 1961 and the experiments with indicative planning through the 1960s which reached their high-water mark in the ill-fated National Plan for 1964–70.†

(3) *Budgetary policy inadequate for regional economic problems.* If unemployment were high all over the country, then a general stimulus to demand through budgetary policy appeared to be the appropriate remedy. But regional variations in unemployment created a dilemma: whilst demand might need to be restrained in the Midlands, in the North or Wales the need might be expansion; or to put it another way, the restrictions on demand necessary to prevent the Midlands and the South-east from "over-heating" added to an already unduly high level of unemployment in Northern Ireland,

---

*This means that a 10 per cent purchase tax could be increased to 11 per cent (not 20 per cent). When purchase tax was abolished, a similar provision was included in V.A.T.
†For an account of indicative planning, see C. T. Sandford, *National Economic Planning*, Heinemann Educational Books, 2nd ed., 1976.

the Highlands of Scotland, South Wales and Devon and Cornwall. We have already mentioned the difficulty of directing budgetary measures to particular areas. Consequently resort was made to extra-budgetary measures, such as the negative compulsion of requiring certificates for industrial or office development, which could be withheld unless the development was in an area of relatively high unemployment; and to measures which were in the broadest sense budgetary, i.e. concerned with government revenue and expenditure, but which were adopted outside the framework of the annual budget—notably the Regional Employment Premium (R.E.P.), which was a form of wage subsidy to manufacturing industry in development areas.

(4) *Unsatisfactory to deal with inflation, especially cost inflation.* The orthodox argument in this period had been that inflation could be counteracted by tax increases which "mop-up" the excess demand or purchasing power; reducing people's incomes by higher income tax or what people can buy for the same monetary expenditure by additional outlay taxes, checks the pressure of demand on resources.

Two arguments have been advanced which cast doubt on the effectiveness of increased taxation to reduce inflation. The first is that the increased taxes cut not consumption but saving;* hence higher taxes have no direct effect on the demand for goods and services. The argument can be presented in a more sophisticated form as follows: one of the main determinants of the propensity to consume is *previous* income; once people get used to a particular level of consumption, should income then fall their consumption expenditure will tend to continue at its earlier level. (This would suggest that, to be effective, additional taxation to restrict excess demand needs to be levied on those who save little or nothing.)

The second argument really embraces the first: that for a variety of reasons higher taxes will not, in the long run, check inflation. Whilst some short-term benefit may be gained, the attempt to cure inflation by high taxation is self-defeating. Thus it is argued that

---

*For example, Sir John Hicks, *After the Boom*, Occasional Paper 11, Institute of Economic Affairs, 1966.

high taxes reduce the supply of the factors of production and hence the rate of economic growth; whether the tax increases are on income or outlay they generate cost inflation by stimulating wage increases and causing executives to seek a level of remuneration which offsets the tax; and that high taxation, especially high profits tax, makes employers less resistant to wage and salary demands and generally careless about increases in other costs (e.g. expense accounts). The most notable exponent of this thesis was Mr. Colin Clark* who further argued that "in rather a subtle manner, the existence of a high level of taxation alters the whole climate of politics: politicians tend to lose their capacity to resist pressures, whether governmental or private, leading to cost increases, in the more or less unconscious knowledge that a rise in prices will lower the real value of all fixed charges on the budget and in that way lighten their burden", Mr. Clark cited empirical evidence from a number of countries, both inter-war and post-war, to support his argument that, where taxation exceeds 25 per cent of net national income at factor cost, forces are set in motion which result, not immediately, but within a few years, in a general rise in costs and prices. Whilst few economists would be prepared to be as precise as Mr. Clark about the exact danger level, or accept all the details of his arguments, many economists would claim that his thesis contains a substantial element of truth.

But even if higher taxes were effective in reducing demand, there remained the most serious criticism—their inappropriateness to deal with inflation which was cost rather than demand generated The largest element in cost is wages. It is *possible* to check pressure for wage increases by reducing demand for goods and services, which in turn reduces demand for labour; but, given the existence of a strong trade union movement, inflation might only be checked by these means at the cost of a high level of unemployment, much unused capacity and substantial loss of output, not to mention industrial unrest and human misery.

The problem can be expressed in a somewhat different way—viz. the difficulty of reconciling full employment, stable prices and free

*C. Clark, *Taxmanship*, Hobart Paper 26, Institute of Economic Affairs, 1964.

collective bargaining. It is possible to have two of these, but very difficult to succeed in having all three. Suppose, for example, that there is full employment and free collective bargaining. Then a high level of demand is tending to pull up prices; at the same time there is a strong tendency for wages to rise. On the one hand trade unions are in a strong position to demand wage increases. The tendency of prices and profits to rise provides a "moral" argument; the low unemployment means that few union members feel insecure in their job and hence a large proportion of members are concerned with wage-rates rather than getting or keeping jobs; union funds are high (able to sustain a strike if necessary) because members are in employment. Moreover, the existence of traditional differentials between workers of different grades and occupations tends to keep wages in line; if one group of workers obtains a rise, this is an argument to support the claim of another group. On the other hand when employment is high employers' resistance to wage demands will be low; with high demand and probably high profits employers will not want to strike on their hands, especially if, as is likely in these circumstances, stocks are low; moreover to say that employment is high is another way of saying that labour is scarce and some employers may be pleased to grant wage increases in the hope of attracting additional workers. Hence the combination of full employment and free collective bargaining generates price increases.

This problem underlies the various attempts in this period to secure an effective prices and incomes policy. Such policies were attempts to hold inflation in check at a lower cost in terms of unemployment. They consisted of extra-budgetary measures to check wage increases, which involved some degree of restriction on the freedom of trade unions and which, in this period, culminated in the statutory incomes policy introduced by the Labour government in 1966.

The late 1960s to 1991

The decade of the 1960s ended with a new phenomenon which did not fit into the post-war orthodoxy—rising prices accompanied by rising unemployment; and the period 1970 to 1991 has been marked by levels of unemployment and rates of price increase far higher than anything in the previous period.

The increase in the retail price index averaged 8 per cent in 1970–73; the annual rate rose to 16 per cent in 1974 and to a peak of 24 per cent in 1975. It then fell to a little over 8 per cent in 1978 but rose again, after Sir Geoffrey Howe's first budget (see above p. 209) and the implementation of the Clegg Commission pay awards in the public sector, to reach 18 per cent in 1980. Thereafter it steadily fell and stood at 6 per cent at the end of 1982. It continued its downward trend and in June 1986 it stood at 2.5 per cent, the lowest annual rate since 1967. Meanwhile, from 600,000 in 1970 the level of unemployment rose at the beginning of the 1970s, fell in 1973 and 1974, before resuming an upward movement which continued almost without interruption to well into 1983 to reach the horrifying level of 3.2 million or more than 11 per cent of the workforce. After 1979 there was a substantial fall in gross domestic product, with the heaviest reduction being in manufacturing industry. Meantime the balance of payments moved into heavy deficit in 1973 and subsequently the exchange rate was allowed to float.

G.D.P. started to grow again in 1982 and then followed a period of sustained growth to the end of the decade and a big boom in the housing market. But unemployment remained above 3 million until well into 1987; it started to decline from the autumn of 1986 and thereafter fell steadily to a level of 1.6 million (5.6 per cent of the labour force) in March 1991.

By then the trouble had switched again to inflation, which, having remained below 5 per cent until mid 1988 began thereafter to rise so that, by the autumn of 1990, the annual rate had reached a peak of 10.9 per cent. Unemployment started to rise again from March 1990, well before inflation peaked; by August 1991 it had reached 2.4 million, 8.5 per cent of the work force and the rise looked set to continue for many months with the total approaching, or again exceeding, the 3 million mark. Prices were brought down again quickly from their peak of 10.9 per cent, doubtless helped by the United Kingdom's entry into the Exchange Rate Mechanism (E.R.M.) in October 1990, and by the autumn of 1991 were down to

4 per cent. Meanwhile, as the unemployment figures suggest, there had been another severe recession and a huge balance of payments deficit. As 1991 nears its end, there are some signs of recovery.

In assessing the record we should recognise that these have been years of instability in the international economy with other countries also suffering from record levels of inflation and unemployment, though some, like W. Germany, weathered the storm better than the United Kingdom. The international economy was rocked by a huge boom in world commodity prices between the end of 1972 and early 1974, crowned by a four-fold increase in the price of oil after the Israeli–Arab war of October 1973. The adverse movement in the terms of trade (the volume of exports required to obtain a unit of imports) was the equivalent of a reduction of some 5 per cent of the U.K. gross national product—a massive change which necessarily had major repercussions on the economy. The price of oil again doubled between 1979 and 1980, but by then Britain was itself an oil producer so that the effects were rather different on her than on other non-oil producing western nations. In the later 1980s the Stock Exchange slump of October 1987 revived memories of the 1929 crash and raised the spectre of a major world depression and led many countries, including the United Kingdom, to take reflating action, expanding credit and drastically cutting interest rates. In the event these measures not only proved unnecessary but fuelled the inflationary boom. Before long interest rates were raised as rapidly as they had previously fallen, damaging industry and leaving many new houseowners with high mortgages in dire straits, especially if they found themselves in the ranks of the unemployed.

Some would see the bad record of those years as a product of these abnormal international features; of the attempts of unions to maintain real wages in the face of falling terms of trade and slow economic growth (with the public sector pre-empting almost all the additional output becoming available); of inflationary expectations, which, once they take hold, generate more inflation; and of errors in forecasting and budgetary policy. For such, the orthodox budgetary methods, more skilfully pursued and supplemented by new and improved incomes policies, remain the way to salvation. But others have presented more fundamental criticisms of the whole post-war approach and we must briefly consider them here; the most important of these have been the "monetarists".

The Monetarist School has gained the most adherents in recent years including the Conservative government under Mrs. Thatcher. Monetarists argue that, in pursuing the kind of fiscal policies which we have outlined, the importance of "money" has been underestimated, if not ignored. Where monetary policy has been used, the tendency has been to concentrate on changes in interest rates (especially Bank Rate), whereas the key monetary variable is the money supply (cash and bank current and deposit accounts). The money supply depends crucially on the way in which budgetary deficits are financed. Broadly speaking, if the government can finance its deficit by borrowing from the public, there is no increase in the money supply; but if the deficit is financed by borrowing from the Bank of England, the result is a monetary expansion. One difficulty is that financing a large budget deficit by borrowing from the public might only be possible at the cost of a substantial rise in interest rates. As governments are reluctant to see large increases in interest rates—which put up their debt charges, raise the cost of house-purchase and discourage investment—they are the more likely to permit an increase in the money supply to take place.

If the money supply increases at a greater rate than gross national product, inflation will follow; there is a lag of about 12–18 months before changes in the money supply affect employment, and perhaps 18 months to 2 years before they exert their effects on prices. Monetarists put much emphasis on price expectations as perpetuating and increasing inflation; once the expectation of inflation gets hold, people will take expected price increases into account in their economic bargains of all kinds, and this will make inflation all the more difficult to control.

Monetarists consider that there is what Professor Milton Friedman (the most famous of the American monetarists) calls a "natural" rate of unemployment, what Mr. Sam Brittan* refers to as a "minimum sustainable" rate of unemployment and what has

---

*Second Thoughts on Full Employment, The Centre for Policy Studies, 1975.

also been called a non-accelerating inflation rate of unemployment or N.A.I.R.U. This rate is determined by conditions in the labour market such as the mobility of labour, knowledge of job opportunities, relationship between income in work and income out of work. Any attempt to fix an employment target which involves unemployment levels below this rate will generate inflation and, in the long run, more unemployment, although it will be possible to push unemployment below the N.A.I.R.U. in the short-run.

With exceptions, monetarists put little faith in incomes policies to control inflation. Some accept the possibility that an incomes policy may help to break inflationary expectations and that it may be useful as an interim measure whilst the supply of money is adjusted to what is required; beyond that, many monetarists consider incomes policy irrelevant. They argue that trade unions do not "cause" inflation; it is the increase in the money supply which does that. But what constitute "causes" and what are "conditions" of inflation is to some extent a matter of terminology. Economists generally would agree that if trade unions push for higher wages inflation can be stopped if the government refuses to increase the money supply: credit would be restricted, stock exchange prices would fall, investment would decline, unemployment would ensue and this would check the inflation. But if a government, wishing to avoid these detrimental consequences, allowed the money supply to increase following a round of wage increases, it is a matter of argument whether the "cause" of the inflation is militant trade unionism or the rise in the money supply.

The strength of the monetarists' case is the detailed empirical work they have undertaken to show the correlations between changes in the money supply and changes in employment and price levels. Yet, in a sense, it reveals their weakness too, for the monetarists' analysis rests on time lags which are difficult to predict and complex inter-relationships between income, employment, inflation and the balance of payments, the processes involved in which are, as Professor D. E. W. Laidler, an eminent British monetarist, puts it, "only crudely understood".*

*Memorandum to the Expenditure Committee, reproduced in the *Ninth Report of the Expenditure Committee, Session 1974*, H.C. 328, 1974.

Moreover experience has shown that the money supply is not only difficult to control in practice but even difficult to define.

The Future of Budgetary Policy

The debate on the control of the economy by fiscal policy continues; there is no unanimity amongst economists about how far the orthodox post war policy should be changed; about the value of incomes policy; about the validity of much of monetarism.*

A new consensus is unlikely to emerge at all quickly. But some general conclusions can be tentatively drawn about the future of budgetary policy.

First, there is no question that governments can and should exercise control over the economy by taxation and public expenditure. The question is how actively? Even the Conservative governments which have heavily emphasised monetary policy and interest rate changes allow for budget deficits to appear in time of unemployment; they do not seek to offset the "automatic stabilisers" by which fiscal drag increases government revenue in time of inflation whilst when there is unemployment revenue drops whilst expenditure rises on unemployment benefits and income support.

Second, in all camps there is a disillusionment with the outcome where policy-makers make frequent adjustments to the economic system and a widespread belief that the economy would function more effectively if certain general guidelines were followed, whether these were monetary guidelines (e.g. X per cent increase in the money supply per annum) or budgetary guidelines (e.g. a balanced budget on average of the cycle from boom to recession) Budgetary "fine tuning" is out.

Third, there is no doubt that the monetarists have established the point that "money matters", even if many economists are far from going the whole way with them. The size and finance of a budget deficit and changes in the money supply are matters of concern now

*For a classification of economists' attitudes to monetarism and a fascinating debate on the whole subject see *Monetary Policy, Third Report from the Treasury and Civil Service Committee 1980–81*, H.C. 163, 1981.

in Britain—to economists, the public and the Chancellor—in a way which they were not a decade or two ago.

Fourth, it is now widely recognised that the time horizons of fiscal policy need to be longer than the 12 or 18 months of traditional budgetary forecasting. Whether we were talking of changes in the money supply, taxation, or public expenditure, the effects take longer to work through than 12 or 18 months; the longer-term consequences of these policy measures need to be more thoroughly considered.

Fifth, it seems likely that the balance of policy objectives has shifted as a result of the experience of inflation of the 1970s. Control of inflation has risen in importance as a policy objective compared with the reduction of unemployment. In the future, target levels of unemployment are likely to be set higher than hitherto. This is not only because of the monetarists' insistence on the dangers of exceeding the "minimum sustainable" rate of unemployment. Orthodox budgetary economists have for long held that governments were too ambitious in their employment targets.

Finally, and most importantly, there is a new emphasis on supply side measures for dealing with unemployment and inflation. The experience of the 1970s and 1980s has demonstrated that, after big shocks to the world economic system, like the oil crises or the crash of the stock markets, prices and employment do not quickly revert to former levels. A recent comprehensive study,* drawing widely on international experience, outlines the policy measures that can be taken to lower unemployment without creating inflation—or, in other words, to lower the N.A.I.R.U. The authors' researches demonstrated that unemployment was highest in countries with *unconditional* unemployment benefits for very long or indefinite periods, because the unemployed become less active in looking for work, or unwilling to take jobs outside their own field. They showed that once workers had been unemployed for long periods, their chances of obtaining work were much reduced; moreover this kind of unemployment had little effect in restraining wage pressures in the labour market. Hence they recommend that the right to *uncondi-*

*Richard Layard, Stephen Nickell and Richard Jackman, *Unemployment, Macroeconomic Performance and the Labour Market*, Oxford University Press, 1991.

tional unemployment benefit should be limited; but that there should be a temporary employment and right to work programme, to which those whose benefit has run out are entitled by law. Help should be concentrated on the long-term unemployed or those at risk of long-term unemployment. Better and more intensively manned placement services, on the Swedish model, should be provided and more selective and intensive high quality re-training programmes. To discusss the measures and their other recommendations in detail would be outside the scope of this book. The relevance to our topic is summed up by the following quotation from this study: "The aim of manpower policy is to improve the supply side of the economy, on the assumption that this is the main limiting factor, not aggregate demand" (p. 64).

This diagnosis and the policy measures proposed would meet with widespread acceptance by economists. This is not to deny the importance of budgetary policy; it is to suggest that it will play a much less important role in the future than it played in the 30 years or so following the Second World War.

CHAPTER 13

Inflation and Taxation

The earlier chapters of this book contain numerous references to the effect of inflation on tax incidence and the tax system; but the importance of inflation is such as to justify a separate chapter to pull the references together and to provide a more systematic treatment and analysis.

The relationship between inflation and taxation goes in both directions. Taxation may both help to generate inflation and, indeed to cure it. We deal with these matters particularly in Chapter 12. In this chapter we are concerned with the effect of inflation on the taxpayer and the tax system, and what may, or should, be done about it. We begin by analysing the effects of inflation on the main categories of tax—income, capital gains, wealth and wealth transfer and outlay taxes. We look at the particular problems inflation poses for the measurement and taxation of business profits. Finally we examine the general arguments for and against the inflation-proofing of the tax system and briefly review the record of U.K. governments.

Personal Income Tax and Capital Taxes

Let us start by examining the effects of inflation on the incidence of income tax on the assumption that the government takes no counter-vailing action and consider a taxpayer whose money income rises in line with prices. He will find himself paying more tax on the same real income because (1) the value of personal and other allowances remains fixed in money terms and so falls in real terms—in other words the starting point of tax is reduced in real terms. (2) With a progressive income tax not only the starting point of taxable income but also the starting point of each higher rate bracket falls in real terms and hence the taxpayer may well find himself moving into higher brackets. Thus, as a result of inflation, the taxpayer pays tax on a larger proportion of his income and may also find himself paying at a higher marginal rate.

The additional tax revenue which accrues to the government through the effect of inflation in this way is known as "fiscal drag". The obvious way of remedying this situation is to link allowances and thresholds (including rate bands) to an index of retail prices, so that allowances are automatically increased and rate bands widened in proportion to the price rise. A good case can be made for excluding certain price increases from the index used. Price increases resulting from rises in outlay taxes might be excluded, so as not to frustrate government policy for reducing demand by this means. Also prices reflecting changes in the terms of trade (rises in import prices relatively to export prices) might be excluded; such price rises imply a reduction in the real value of the United Kingdom's national income to which personal incomes must adjust. On the other hand, it is obviously more convenient to use the ordinary "cost of living" or retail price index and to do so would be more readily understood. In any case it is not feasible to adjust allowances and rate bands more frequently than once in twelve or at best once in six months. Hence there remains a lag generating some fiscal drag and also ensuring that price changes which, for the good reasons mentioned, the government does not wish to offset are not corrected for in the income tax for up to twelve months.

Adopting bracket indexation in this way would go far towards meeting the problems caused by inflation in relation to earned income. But there is a more difficult problem with investment income. Essentially it is that inflation changes the tax base: it causes income from capital, as defined for tax purposes, to diverge from the economic definition of income. To the economist income is the sum available for consumption over a period of time whilst maintaining capital intact. Suppose that there is a 10 per cent rate of inflation, that a man is receiving 12 per cent interest on a savings bank deposit and that his marginal rate of income tax is 50 per cent. At the end of the year he will be taxed £6 on every £100 deposit. But he needed £10 of the interest to maintain his capital. His real income was therefore only £2 and he should have been taxed only £1. Indeed, if the rate of inflation exceeded the rate of interest, he would be paying income tax on negative real income.

It is more difficult to adjust for this effect of inflation. If a person retains the same investments throughout the tax year then, to calculate taxable income, the figure of capital at the beginning of the year could be increased by the rate of inflation and deducted from the capital sum plus interest at the end of the year. With fluctuating balances an interest formula could be applied.

Interest income over a period could be used as the proxy measure of the nominal balance. The interest receipt could be multiplied by the fraction by which the rate of interest exceeded the rate of inflation. Thus suppose that interest receipts were £100; that the average interest over the period was 10 per cent; and that the rate of inflation was 8 per cent. Then taxable real income would be £20 arrived at as follows:

$$£100 \times \frac{(10-8)}{(10)} = £20.$$

Clearly there are considerable administrative problems in trying to apply a capital-income adjustment of this kind. In particular in computing taxable income it would hardly be possible to give an inflation adjustment for the decline in value of cash balances held in the home or for non-interest-bearing current accounts. But the complications do not end there. The logical implication of treating only real interest as an addition to taxable income is that, where the taxpayer is allowed to offset interest payments against tax, the allowance should be restricted to the component of real interest. This would have the consequence that, in years when the rate of inflation was higher than the rate of interest, mortgage interest relief for owner occupiers would be negative. In other words there would have been a net addition to their tax bill!

Governments have not unnaturally fought shy of capital-income adjustments. An alternative and more practical approach would be to widen the use of index-linking in loan markets, so that interest rates were offered on a real basis—like the so-called "Granny Bond" in the United Kingdom, whose purchasers are offered a rate of return equal to the rate of inflation plus a few per cent extra. Securities offered on this basis could be taxed only on the extra.

If these are the most important effects of inflation on the incidence of income tax they are not the only ones. Vito Tanzi, in an excellent book on the subject,* has pointed out the significance of inflation on collection lags. There is always some lag between when income is earned and when the tax payment is made. With P.A.Y.E. it is short, but with the income of the self-employed and some investment income not collected at source it could be long. The higher the rate of inflation, the lower the real tax payment arising from any given lag. Further, there is often an element of discretion about the timing of some tax payments and inflation encourages postponement, such postponement merging into tax evasion. Tanzi points out that where inflation is very high and a substantial proportion of tax payments are heavily lagged, there can even be a negative fiscal drag from income tax.

The remedy for this kind of effect of inflation lies in administrative practice—the minimisation of lags, with heavy interest penalties for delays.

The effects of inflation on capital taxes are similar to those on the taxation of earned income. With a progressive death duty, gifts tax or annual wealth tax, the real value of any allowances is reduced, the threshold points are lowered and the tax brackets narrowed. A larger proportion of a taxpayer's assets become subject to tax and he may be pushed into a higher marginal rate bracket. If the tax is a heavy one, such as a capital transfer tax, falling on the individual only at irregular intervals, there is more likelihood of serious inequity than with income tax. The problem can be met by indexing allowances and thresholds, as with income tax, though the use of a retail price index may be less appropriate.

If a wealth transfer tax (like capital transfer tax or an accessions tax) is cumulative, so that the rate of tax on any one gift depends on the total of previous gifts, indexation should not only relate to the

---

*Vito Tanzi, *Inflation and the Personal Income Tax: An International Perspective*, Cambridge University Press, 1980.

exemption levels and brackets, but should include previous gifts, so as to determine their real value at the time a new gift is being made.

With a capital gains tax bracket indexation (raising any thresholds and widening any rate bands) is also necessary, but is not enough to inflation-proof the tax. It is necessary to ensure that tax is levied on the real gain and not the money gain. In effect, inflation turns a capital gains tax into a wealth tax, sometimes with very high rates. To take a simple example. An asset is bought for £100 and sold a year later for £120. Let us assume that during that year, prices also rose 20 per cent. Then there would have been no real gain or loss. Without an inflation allowance, gains tax would be charged on £20. At the rate of 30 per cent, tax would be £6. This would have been equivalent to a wealth tax of 5 per cent (£6 on £120).

Inflation-proofing a capital gains tax can be done by indexing the acquisition price so that, when an asset is realised, the gain is calculated by subtracting from the disposal value the acquisition value increased by the percentage rise in an approved index, e.g. the index of retail prices. The index, like the retail price index, could be published monthly.

Taxes on Outlay or Expenditure

Inflation raises fewer problems in relation to taxes on outlay or expenditure than in relation to income taxes. *Ad valorem* outlay taxes, like V.A.T, rise in proportion to the rise in the price of the products on which they are imposed and thus tend to adjust to the rate of inflation automatically. Excise duties, however, are often specific (see p. 187). In the absence of counter-action, assuming the prices of the products on which the excise duties are levied have reflected the general rate of inflation, the post tax price falls somewhat in real terms; the rate of tax falls in real terms; and there is a falling off in revenue—a fiscal drag in reverse. These effects can be remedied by indexation—by raising the excise duties period- ically in proportion to the rate of inflation. Where, as with V.A.T., there is an exemption threshold, that can be "bracket-indexed". It might be useful to remind ourselves at this point that one of the advantages of a direct expenditure tax (pp. 125–28) over an income tax is that bracket indexation is all that is required to counter the principal effects of inflation. No capital-income adjustment is called for.

Taxes on Business Income

In principle, and in the absence of inflation or any special investment incentives, the profits of a company are arrived at on the basis of historical cost accounting. The aim is to reach a genuine figure for the company's income which is the difference between the revenue from the sale of its products over a period, and the costs incurred in order to obtain that revenue. With fixed assets, which can be expected to last over a number of years, a proportion only of the cost of the asset can appropriately be charged against the income of any one year. Hence a depreciation allowance is provided for on the basis that, by the time the asset wears out, the sum of the annual allowances will be equal to the original cost. The depreciation allowance is intended to cover both wear and tear and obsolescence. Because there is an element of subjectivity in determining annual depreciation allowances, for tax purposes the rate of depreciation for assets of different kinds is laid down by the tax authorities, in what are, necessarily, somewhat arbitrary rules.

Another consideration in determining taxable profit is the level of stocks. If stocks of materials and work in progress were increased over a period and the whole of the cost of the materials and of the additional work in progress were charged against the income from the sales of the period, it would reduce profits by costs which had not been incurred in generating the income of the period. Hence any increase in the value of stocks has to be added in when computing taxable profits.

Inflation plays havoc with these arrangements. In the absence of inflation adjustments, depreciation allowances on the historical cost of fixed assets are inadequate. When an asset reaches the end of its life, the sum of the depreciation allowances is insufficient for replacement. Real profits are less than nominal profits and, in effect, the real capital of the firm is being eaten away.

Similarly with stocks; if their value rises simply as a result of price increases taxable profits rise although the real value of the stocks has remained the same. In addition, inflation reduces the real value of any monetary working capital held in the business. On all these counts the firm is being subject to profits tax on a sum in excess of its real profits.

There is one partial offset. Interest payments on debenture stock are treated as a cost. If there is an unanticipated inflation, then, because interest payments are fixed in money terms, the real costs of this loan finance are reduced.

The whole question of how to inflation-proof business income for tax purposes is bound up with the exceedingly complex issue of inflation-accounting generally. In the United Kingdom in January 1974 an Inflation Accounting Committee (known as the Sandilands Committee) was set up to consider methods of allowing for price changes in accounting and to make recommendations. It reported in September 1975. Broadly, the Committee recommended the rejection of the historical basis of accounting and its replacement by cost figures which reflected the current value of assets (known as Current Cost Accounting or C.C.A.). After many years of debate and consultation, in March 1980, the accountancy profession introduced a statement of standard accounting practice (S S A P 16) on the applications of C.C.A., setting out the adjustments necessary to arrive at current cost operating profit. Such adjustments could be the basis of an inflation-proof tax regime, though there are considerable complications and possible alternative procedures;* and, as we have previously seen, the whole question of depreciation allowances is inextricably linked with that of investment incentives.

The simplest part of inflation-proofing corporation tax is to bracket index any threshold or thresholds, such as those which, in the United Kingdom, relate to the reduced rate of corporation tax.

---

*For details, see the government's Green Paper, *Corporation Tax*, Cmnd. 8456, January 1982.

Policy on Inflation-Proofing

Arguments and Counter-Arguments

Why inflation-proof the tax system anyway? The reasons should be fairly clear from what we have said on the effects of inflation on taxpayers, but it is worth restating them concisely. First, without inflation-proofing, fiscal drag would be likely to increase the overall tax take. Of course, a government can reduce taxes to offset the fiscal drag, but, with revenue in its hands without the odium of having to raise tax rates, it may well yield to the pressures to spend. No less important is the effect on the distribution of the tax burden. Inflation does not mean all paying more in proportion. With income tax those with the most allowances, those on the margin of higher rates and those who pay tax promptly are the ones who lose most. Likewise there is a redistribution of the tax burden between payers of different kinds of taxes because inflation causes unplanned switches in the balance of taxation. Thus income tax grows in revenue importance while excise duties decline. If, to start with, the balance of tax between taxpayers and between groups of taxes reflected considered policy, inflation plays havoc with it. As Allen and Savage* write: "If the distribution of the tax burden is to be changed, it seems preferable to make specific alterations to the schedule of rates and allowances rather than let inflation produce rather unpredictable results." Again, a failure to inflation-proof business taxation may have serious effects on business investment or cause grave liquidity problems for industry.

Various arguments have been used against indexing the tax system. It is held that it would reduce the automatic stabilising effect of the system; thus, if there is inflation, fiscal drag automatically helps to counteract it by cutting demand. But, even with indexing, there would still be some short-term stabilising effect because of an irreducible element of time lag. Further, the reduction in "take-home pay" resulting from fiscal drag in times of inflation

*R. I. G. Allen and D. Savage, Indexing Personal Income Taxation, from *Indexing for Inflation*, Thelma Liesner and Mervyn A. King (eds.) IFS/Heinemann Educational Books, 1975.

might stimulate wage demands, and give an impetus to cost inflation which would be avoided by indexing. Another objection is the partial nature of the adjustment—the argument which Mr. Healey used of capital gains tax (p. 231)—that whilst some injustices could be easily rectified others would remain and perhaps become more glaring (e.g. the indexing of capital gains tax would not help those with real losses on savings bank deposits). Again, the further one moves to remedy inequities, the larger become the administrative and compliance costs. Finally there is the politician's concern that indexing taxation will be seen as acceptance of defeat in the "battle" to control inflation and thereby help to generate inflationary expectations and hence inflation itself. As a counter to this argument it can be maintained that, if people have more confidence that inflation will not result in arbitrary additions to their tax burdens, they are likely to be more moderate in their wage demands.

There is one argument against inflation-proofing which is really beside the point—the view that it restricts the Chancellor's discretion. When we talk, say, of indexing income tax allowances and brackets, we do not mean that the Chancellor is constitutionally debarred from modifying them. When the budget comes round he can repudiate the indexation in a particular year if he wishes. The point is that the starting point for his changes is the indexed allowances and brackets. If he fails to raise allowances or widen brackets by the extent of the price rise he must be explicit about it. If he is raising allowances by 10 per cent when the rate of inflation is 12 per cent, he must present his measures as a 2 per cent reduction not as a generous 10 per cent increase. The Chancellor's discretion is unfettered, but his actions are made transparent.

Policy in the United Kingdom

As we described in Chapter 12, from the end of the 1960s to 1982 the average rate of inflation was several times that of the previous post-war period and at the peak, throughout 1975, prices were between 20 and 30 per cent higher than a year previously. No attempt was made to index any aspect of the tax system until 1977.

Before then any offsetting measures rested on the Chancellor's whim and, although some changes were made, particularly in income tax allowances, their extent fell considerably short of what was required to negate the effects of inflation on the tax system. The results were predictable. To take the case of income tax, those with most allowances fared badly—and, as family support at that time partly took the form of child tax allowances, those with large families lost out; because of the peculiar structure of the U.K. income tax with its wide basic rate, there was an arbitrary effect depending on the taxpayer's position on the scale. Those doing badly were people who had been just below the starting rate of tax and who were brought into the tax net by inflation; those at the lower levels of the basic rate band whose average tax rate rose markedly; and those with taxable incomes just below the level at which higher rate commenced or on the lower rungs of higher rate tax, who found themselves whisked upwards to higher marginal rates.

On business the most marked effect was the liquidity crisis of 1974–75 leading to the hurried introduction of the stock relief scheme as a temporary measure.

The balance of taxation altered significantly as between direct (or income and capital taxation) on the one hand and indirect (or, more accurately, outlay taxes) on the other. In particular, over the 10 years 1966–67 to 1976–77 the proportion of total tax revenue raised from specific excise duties fell from 30 to 19 per cent. Apart from a possible failure on the part of Chancellors fully to appreciate what was happening, there was doubtless a reluctance to raise these duties in line with inflation because of the effect on the incomes policies which characterised many of these years.

The measures which have been taken since 1977, together with the provisions for capital allowances which existed before, have been described elsewhere in the text in considering the individual taxes. Whilst Mr. Healey, as Chancellor, was moved reluctantly along the path of indexation by the Rooker-Wise amendment (p. 145), Sir Geoffrey Howe marched down it more boldly and willingly. The United Kingdom now has indexation of the main personal allowances and the income tax brackets. The threshold and brackets of inheritance tax are indexed and also the acquisition price of capital gains tax. Excise duties are annually revalorised more or less as a matter of course.

The position today (1991) is much better than it was in the early 1970s when inflation rates started to accelerate. But there remain important gaps in inflation-proofing. The difficult problem of the indexation of capital-income has been largely ignored. More seriously perhaps, the abolition of 100 per cent capital allowances and the withdrawal of stock relief have left business dangerously exposed to inflation in the absence of agreed procedures of inflation accounting.

CHAPTER 14

International Perspective and the European Community

Taxation has many international ramifications. There are problems of location and jurisdiction. If a citizen of the United Kingdom earns some income by temporarily working abroad, should that income be subject to U.K. income tax, to the foreign income tax, to neither or to both? Should a capital tax, like wealth tax or death duties, apply to the world-wide property of the residents of a country, or should the place in which the property is situated determine the tax jurisdiction? How should one treat, for tax purposes, the profits of multi-national companies? Such profits may be earned in one country, paid out as dividends in another, or passed unobtrusively between countries by transfer pricing—the purchase of goods or materials by one branch of the company from another—at artificial prices in order to minimise tax payments.

Subtle legal distinctions abound in this area, such as those between "residence", "ordinary residence" and "domicile". A complicated network of agreements affecting tax arrangements between countries has grown up. The problems raised by these international arrangements are both complex and detailed and to consider them would take us well beyond the scope of an introductory textbook on public finance. All we shall do here is to record their existence and to note that the way the issues are resolved has implications both for the equity and efficiency of the tax system.

However, we shall explore two questions of international significance of a more general nature. We shall seek to discover how the U.K. tax system stands in relation to other countries with similar economies; in particular how heavily is the United Kingdom taxed by comparison with others? Secondly, we shall look at some of the tax implications of U.K. membership of the E.C.

International Comparisons of Taxation

It used to be a widely-held view that the United Kingdom was the most heavily taxed country. This view probably arose from the fact that, before 1979, our top rates of income tax (at 83 per cent on earned income and 98 per cent on investment income) were the highest in the Western world. But this is no more an accurate measure of the overall level of taxation than the corresponding view that, because our top rate of income tax is now amongst the lowest (at 40 per cent) we are now at the bottom of the league. Terms like "weight" or "heaviness" or "burden" of taxation are not free from ambiguity; but one measure of the overall weight of tax is to express total tax revenues as a percentage of national output.

The Organisation for Economic Cooperation and Development (O.E.C.D.) annually publishes figures for the 24 O.E.C.D. member countries expressing taxation as a percentage of G.D.P. at market prices. As we discussed in Chapter 2 with reference to government expenditure, a better denominator might be the factor cost measure of national output, so as to avoid the distortions arising from the differing proportions of outlay taxes and subsidies which enter into market prices in different countries. However, international organisations have agreed on market prices as easier to calculate, so we must accept that measure, whilst being aware of its potentially distorting effects. If G.D.P. at factor cost were used as the denominator, all the percentages would be higher.

Table 14.1 shows figures for 15 of the 24 O.E.C.D. member countries—leaving out the smaller or least developed to make a more manageable and meaningful comparison. The year 1965 is the first year for which the O.E.C.D. collected and published these figures, so we have taken that as our starting point. We have then looked at the figures for 1975 and 1985, i.e. at intervals of a decade, and added the most recent figures available. The order of countries is their ranking for tax levels in the most recent year, 1989.

TABLE 14.1
Total Tax Revenue (including Social Security Contributions) as a Percentage of G.D.P. at Market Prices

Country	1989	1985	1975	1965
Sweden	56.1	50.4	43.6	35.2
Netherlands	46.0	44.9	43.7	33.2
Norway	45.5	47.6	44.9	33.3
Belgium	44.3	47.6	41.8	31.2
France	43.8	44.5	36.9	34.5
Austria	41.0	43.1	38.6	34.7
Finland	38.1	37.0	35.1	29.5
Germany (Fed. Republic)	38.1	38.0	35.7	31.6
Italy	37.8	34.4	26.2	25.5
United Kingdom	36.5	37.9	35.5	30.4
Canada	35.3	33.1	32.4	25.4
Switzerland	31.8	32.0	29.6	20.7
Japan	30.6	27.6	20.9	18.3
Australia	30.1	00.0	27.6	23.2
United States	30.1	29.2	29.0	25.9

Source: Revenue Statistics of OECD Member Countries, 1965–1990, O.E.C.D., Paris, 1991.

Before discussing the outcome we need to comment on certain general features.

First, a matter of definition. The taxes included in the figures are for both central and local government. Social security contributions are included because they are a compulsory levy and also because countries contribute to national insurance funds to varying extents from general taxation; thus to exclude them would generate an additional element of arbitrariness.

Secondly, as may be divined from what we said in Chapter 2, because the demarcation line between income and expenditure is adjustable, comparisons may be misleading; essentially the same outcome can be obtained from different levels of taxation associated with different administrative arrangements. Thus countries which (like Sweden) raise taxes to pay child benefits in cash will, other things being equal, have higher tax levels than those countries giving child benefits as tax allowances. Similarly, investment incentives may be by means of a grant or a tax relief. Thus the comparisons should be regarded as giving only a broad indication of the relative importance of taxation in different countries.

The first point which stands out in the comparison is that, for every country, there has been a very significant increase in taxation over the last 25 years. Even though several countries managed modest reductions between 1985 and 1989, in all cases the 1989 level is substantially higher than that of 1965.

The United Kingdom at 10th out of 15 is just below the half way mark in the table. In fact in the three previous years listed, the United Kingdom was, in each year, exactly half way down the table at 8th position. The lower position of the United Kingdom in 1989 arises from the reversal of the previous upward trend. In fact the reversal is rather larger than the figures in the table indicate, because the peak year was 1982 when the percentage of tax revenue to G.D.P. at market prices stood at 39.1. Although there has been this reduction from the peak, it is remarkable that the percentage in 1989 is higher than that of 1979, the date the Conservative Government came to power, when the percentage was 32.6.

The big reductions in rates of income tax in the past decade have been offset by the increases in social security contributions and in V.A.T.

Harmonisation in the European Community

Diversity of Tax Practice and Philosophy

Table 14.1 shows some diversity amongst E.C. countries in overall weight of taxation from 36 per cent in the United Kingdom to 46 per cent in the Netherlands. The inclusion in the comparison of the smaller and less developed E.C. countries accentuates the comparison; thus, in 1989, the percentage of total tax revenue to G.D.P. at market prices in Greece was 33. But total tax burden is only one aspect of their diversity: individual E.C. countries differ markedly in the ratio of direct to indirect taxation; in the proportion of "tax" taken in social security contributions; in the "form" of taxes, notably the differing structures of corporation tax; in tax philosophy, such as how far the tax system should be used to reduce inequalities in the distribution of income and wealth; and in tax morality.

Thus, to point up a few of the differences by some examples. The United Kingdom (in 1989) got 39 per cent of total tax revenue from taxes on personal and corporate income, against 17 per cent in France and 60 per cent in Denmark. Conversely, the United Kingdom raised 18 per cent from social security contributions against 44 per cent in France and 2 per cent in Denmark. On the outlay tax front, whereas France, Italy, Germany and the United Kingdom raised between 25 and 32 per cent of their revenue from taxes on goods and services, Greece and Portugal each raised 45 per cent. Within these outlay tax totals there are considerable divergencies. We shall shortly be looking at the divergencies in rates of V.A.T., but as a matter of principle the United Kingdom insists on zero rating for foodstuffs (and other "essentials" such as children's shoes and clothes and fuel other than hydrocarbon oils) whereas most E.C. countries are content to tax these items, but at a reduced rate. In excise duties, likewise, the differences are wide, with the more northern countries—Denmark, the United Kingdom and Ireland —having much heavier taxes on alcoholic drinks and tobacco than the southern countries like Greece, Italy and Portugal.

Objectives and Progress of Tax Harmonisation

The objective which has predominated in E.C. thinking about tax harmonisation has been commercial, although, as we shall see later, other objectives have emerged. The economic philosophy of the E.C., enshrined in the Treaty of Rome, is the promotion of the economic growth of its members by removing obstacles to competition, promoting the free movement of goods and factors of production and thus helping to bring about the optimum location of industry. This philosophy implies, in particular, the harmonisation of sales taxes, which affect the movement of goods, and of corporation tax, which affects the movement of capital. Current thinking in the Commission is to leave personal income tax entirely to the discretion of member states, to leave wide scope for them to pursue different welfare policies and levels of expenditure, and also not to consider wealth transfer taxes as subjects of tax harmonisation, at least for a very long time to come.

It was natural that harmonisation policy should start with a general sales tax. Abolishing customs duties between E.C. countries lost some of its point if taxes on goods differed between countries, so that people could buy in the low tax and carry goods to the high tax member country. Moreover differing tax rates on the same products amongst member states required the imposition of different taxes at the borders, which precluded the possibility of abolishing "fiscal frontiers" between E.C. members. Thus the first move towards harmonisation was agreement on the form of a general sales tax.

Following the Neumark Report of 1962,* a value-added tax was accepted as the general sales tax to be adopted in the E.C. Apart from any general advantages which may be claimed for V.A.T. (see above, p. 202) it was attractive to the strongest of the E.C. countries. France already had a V.A.T.; although it stopped short of the retail stage, few administrative changes would be necessary for France if V.A.T. became the E.C. sales tax. Germany also had a general sales tax (in the form of a "cascade" or "gross" turnover tax) which lent itself readily to adaptation into a V.A.T.; moreover, the Germans were thinking of making the change to a V.A.T. anyway. Their cascade turnover tax (which, like V.A.T., taxed outputs when products changed hands at all stages of the productive process but, unlike V.A.T., did not allow for the deduction of input tax) imposed more tax the larger the number of stages of production and thus created a distortion in favour of vertical integration (the merging of firms at different stages of production). The self-checking mechanism of V.A.T. (see p. 207) may also particularly have recommended V.A.T. to some E.C. countries in preference to a retail sales tax.

Three stages can be distinguished in the harmonisation process: form, coverage or structure, and rates. What progress has been made in harmonising V.A.T.? Two Directives in 1967 required member countries to adopt V.A.T. in place of existing general sales taxes and for all new members, the United Kingdom, Denmark and

---

*The E.E.C. Reports on Tax Harmonisation: Report of the Fiscal and Financial Committee, International Bureau of Fiscal Documentation, Amsterdam, 1963.

TABLE 14.2
Rates of V.A.T. in E.C. Countries, 1989

	Reduced rates	Standard rates	Luxury rates
Belgium	6 and 17	19	25 and 33
Denmark	—	22	—
Germany (Fed. Republic)	7	14	—
France	2.1 and 5.5	18.6	25[1]
Greece	6	16	36
Ireland[2]	5.2 and 10	25	—
Italy	4 and 9	19	38
Luxembourg	3 and 6	12	—
Netherlands	6	18.5	—
Portugal[2]	8	19	30
Spain	6	12	33
United Kingdom[2]	—	15[3]	—

[1]From 1 January, 1990.
[2]Also have substantial zero-rating.
[3]Increased to 17.5 in 1991.

Ireland in the 1970s and Greece, Portugal and Spain in the 1980s, the adoption of V.A.T. in place of existing general sales taxes has been a condition of entry.

The first stage of harmonisation of a general sales tax—the acceptance and introduction of a V.A.T. by member states—was followed, after a gap, by the second. The Sixth Directive, adopted by the Council in 1977 and which came into force January 1, 1979, provided for a common coverage or base of V.A.T.

The question of rates has proved more difficult. Table 14.2 indicates the differences in V.A.T. rates which existed in 1989. In fact the E.C. thinking about harmonisation of V.A.T. rates has been changing. Neumark originally envisaged completely uniform rates and the Commission were considering two rates, a normal or standard rate and a reduced rate. Recognising the difficulties which a move to completely uniform rates would create for some countries with rates and rate structures very different from the average, the Commission began to think of a band of rates, rather than identical rates, as a more realistic proposition compatible with E.C. objectives. Thus a band of 12–18 per cent (representing a 3 per cent range around 15 per cent) was considered, with a similar band of reduced rates. The accession of the United Kingdom to the Community created a further complication and illustrates the problems raised by the different fiscal traditions of member states; as part of its renegotiation the United Kingdom government "made it clear that any agreement on harmonisation of the tax base must include a provision for zero-rating".*

The agreement to establish a single market by the end of 1992 gave an added urgency to the negotiations on harmonisation—or, as it became known—approximation. In August 1987 the Commission brought forward a series of proposals to enable border checks to be removed and for approximating V.A.T. rates. They reiterated the proposal that there should be only two rates, a standard rate and a reduced rate with individual countries allowed to choose within a band of 14–20 per cent standard and 4–9 per cent reduced. The Commission proposed that V.A.T. should be levied on intra community trade by the exporting country. Thus a British exporter to Germany would charge the German importer the United Kingdom rate of V.A.T. and the German importer would reclaim that, along with V.A.T. on his other inputs, from the German revenue authorities. In the technical jargon, this constituted moving from a destination to an origin principle in the levy of V.A.T. on intra community trade. Goods to countries outside the Community would remain zero rated. Because this switch would mean the reallocation of V.A.T. revenues within the Community (net importing countries would lose revenue and net exporting countries gain) it was also proposed that a clearing house should be set up which would effect the necessary adjustments to ensure that the consuming countries gained the benefit of the revenue.

These proposals ran into much opposition—on the revenue effects on some countries from approximating rates (e.g. Denmark would be a very heavy loser of revenue); on the complications of the clearing house; on the proposed rate structure, with the United Kingdom, for example, insisting on retaining zero rates; on whether the permitted bands were so wide as to lead to trade distortion; and on the principle of whether it was necessary to specify bands at all.

*Membership of the European Community, Report on Renegotiation, Cmnd. 6003, H.M.S.O., March 1975.

It was pointed out that it could be left to the market to bring about approximation as long as minimum rates were specified. Any country which chose to set rates significantly above the minimum should be free to do so, but it would face the consequences of a possible loss of trade. The existence of a minimum rate would serve to prevent competitive undercutting.

It is important to realise that, as long as trade takes place between registered traders, differences in V.A.T. rates between member countries do not distort trade. Registered traders, whether they have imported the goods or not, always sell them at the V.A.T. rates of the country in which they are selling. It is only in respect of purchases by members of the public and other non-registered traders that distortion may arise from differences in rates.

In the light of these considerations the Commission was forced to think again. The outcome has been a political agreement, reached in June 1991, by which, by January 1st 1993, there will be a minimum 15 per cent standard rate and two reduced rates around 5 per cent. "Luxury" rates of V.A.T. will disappear. Countries (the United Kingdom, Ireland and Portugal) currently applying zero rates to certain necessities will be allowed to continue to do so. Special arrangements are being made in respect of car purchases and mail sales.

On the administrative side, agreement had already been reached at the end of 1990 for an interim measure, to last for a considerable number of years (at least to 1997), which would allow the abolition of frontier controls. As now, exports to other E.C. countries would be zero rated, but, instead of V.A.T. being imposed by the importing country at the frontier, the importer would pay the V.A.T. along with his periodic V.A.T. returns. Businesses would be required to provide V.A.T. authorities every quarter with a list of the V.A.T. numbers of their customers in other member states, plus the total value of trade with each of them. Special arrangements were also agreed to combat V.A.T. fraud.

Progress with V.A.T. has proceeded much further than with other taxes and we will only briefly look at them.

It has been agreed that excise duties will be confined to beer, wine, spirits, tobacco and petrol. Agreement on the form of tobacco tax—a mixed system of specific duty (per 1,000 cigarettes) and an *ad valorem* component had been reached and implemented before the initiative to complete the internal market by end 1992. The Commission made a series of proposals in July 1987 to approximate excise duties but had to revise them fundamentally, in October 1990, to provide for a minimum rate for each category of product and a non-obligatory target rate. Political agreement has been reached on the method of operating excise duties, without frontier controls, by means of inter-linked bonded warehouses, so that tax is only paid at the retail stage. Legally binding minimum rates have so far been agreed on several items, but not (at the time of writing) on all.

Least progress has been made in respect of corporation tax.* The latest move (at the end of 1990) was a decision by the Commission to set up a special committee of experts to report within one year on the need for harmonisation of E.C. member states' company tax systems.

Changing Objectives and Reconsideration

The process of harmonisation in no way resembles a steady progress to a predetermined goal, but rather a somewhat stumbling compromise towards several goals. There is an almost continual process of rethinking. The initial emphasis of tax harmonisation was almost entirely commercial, but new objectives have emerged; the constraints imposed by the situation of member states have come to be more fully appreciated; and the development of other E.C. policies have revealed other needs.

Originally contributions by member states to the Community budget had been based on a formula. But it was agreed that the Community budget should be derived from its "own resources" and would include sums corresponding to up to a small percentage of V.A.T. If contributions were to be fairly apportioned amongst member states, then a uniform tax base was required, but this would not exclude the possibility of zero-rated goods, which would

*For a consideration of the main issues, see M. Devereux and M. Pearson, Harmonising Corporate Taxes in Europe, *Fiscal Studies*, Vol. 11, No. 1, Feb. 1990.

constitute part of the tax base. It was this new objective which provided the impetus for the Sixth Directive providing for a common V.A.T. base (above).

Other motivations are evident from the latest proposals of the Commission on excise duties where they have proposed high duties on alcohol and tobacco on health grounds. The recent proposal for an E.C. energy tax is motivated by environmental considerations. The establishment of the Exchange Rate Mechanism (E.R.M.) and moves towards Economic and Monetary Union (E.M.U.) raise further issues. The United Kingdom's membership of E.R.M. helps to keep inflation under control but restricts the scope to allow the exchange rate to fall to increase U.K. competitiveness. The object of E.M.U. is a common currency, and thus fixed exchange rates between members. Were this to come about, members would have completely lost control of one of the tools for managing the economy, and protecting their national balance of payments. In such circumstances provisions which allowed member states to vary their own rates of V.A.T. and excise duties within certain limits would seem to be more important for controlling their economies.

Professor Douglas Dosser has argued convincingly* for some further re-orientation of Community thinking on tax harmonisation to take these considerations into account. He argues that personal income tax and social security contributions should be retained as member state taxes and corporation tax, V.A.T. and excise duties should be treated wholly or in part as Community taxes. The structure of all these Community taxes should be harmonised so that contributions to the European budget based on them would be equitable between members. He would wish to see corporation tax levied at an equal rate throughout the Community and forming the basis of European budgetary finance; but he would prefer V.A.T. and excise duties to differ in overall rates, within wide bands and at national discretion, over and above a small, basic Community rate. This, Dosser believes, would offer a workable compromise. It would promote integration and unification whilst at the same time provid-

*Douglas Dosser, Tax Harmonisation in the European Community, *The Three Banks Review*, June 1973, and *British Taxation and the Common Market*, Charles Knight, 1973, especially chapter 7.

ing a large potential income for a European budget and leaving considerable fiscal flexibility to member states. Further, it would minimise the costs of change and allow for national diversity in policies towards welfare benefits and income redistribution.

One thing is certain. Progress towards tax harmonisation will not be rapid.

CHAPTER 15

Reappraisal and Reform

In this final chapter we attempt to draw together some of the threads and suggest conclusions that emerge from our study of government expenditure and revenue. To many of the problems raised we do not presume to offer precise, definite or final answers. Our purpose is to highlight the main issues; to ask the questions rather than provide the answers; but at the same time, where possible, to suggest directions along which solutions might usefully be sought. The chapter is directed in particular to current problems of government revenue and expenditure in the United Kingdom, but many of these problems have their counterparts in other Western economies.

We start by considering the level of government expenditure and the problems it raises. We go on to examine some possible changes in the methods of financing public expenditure: we look at tax reforms and then at a possible approach to financing welfare expenditure including, most notably, the linking of welfare and taxation, especially the tax credit proposals of the Conservative Government of 1970–74. Finally we examine methods of improving decision-making in relation to taxation and public spending.

How Much Government Expenditure?

We have seen, in Chapter 2, the extraordinary peace-time growth of public spending since the early 1960s, a growth especially marked in the period 1964–68 and 1973–75. We also saw that, despite their unmistakable intentions, the Conservative governments since 1979 failed to reverse that growth to any great extent. The influences making for increased public spending are very strong: the relative price effect; the growth in the proportion of public sector goods generating concrete personal benefits and hence strong support amongst consumers; the growth in numbers employed in the public sector, dependent for income and conditions of work on public spending; perhaps, above all, the tendency of civil servants and politicians to press for increased spending. Bigger budgets mean more power, better promotion prospects and possibly higher salaries for civil servants and ministerial heads of departments; but their motives for public spending are not necessarily self interested, for it is natural for senior civil servants and ministers, immersed in their departmental work, to equate the national good with more spending on "their" service, be it education, health, maintaining the nation's defences or whatever. The Treasury's armoury for resisting these manifold pressures has not proved very effective.

A high and growing level of public expenditure, more particularly the taxation required to release resources for public use, presents serious problems. Inflation is more difficult to hold in check; effort, saving and enterprise may be discouraged; evasion and avoidance are stimulated; the costs of raising additional revenue may rise disproportionately. Since 1979 we have seen big cuts in the top rates of income tax and reductions in the standard rate but the overall tax burden on the middle to low income groups has not been reduced.

But how much public spending should there be? To use the term of Professor J. K. Galbraith, where does the "social balance" (the "right" relationship between the private and public sectors of the economy) lie?

The basic problem of allocating resources between the public and private sectors of the economy springs from the characteristic of publicly provided goods that, unlike private goods purchased in the market, there is no direct relationship between benefit and cost; hence there is no relatively clear-cut determination of how much should be allocated to each service and hence to the whole public sector.

Furthermore the question "How much?" cannot be separated from the question "Of what kind?"

There is some level of public spending on goods and services (exhaustive expenditure) which would signal the effective end of the mixed economy as we know it. Such a situation might be reached if public spending was 60 per cent of G.N.P. If that consisted wholly of exhaustive expenditure, then the composition of well over half of output would be directly determined by the state and much of the remainder indirectly determined by it. However, if half of state spending at that level was transfer payments, the recipients of which were free to determine how they spent their transfer incomes, the position would be very different.

Again, the question "How much?" is linked with "How efficient?" Attitudes to public spending rightly vary according to the views taken of the efficiency of government provision compared with private. Our consideration of the control of public spending in Chapter 3 suggested that there had been significant progress in recent years, especially through the F.M.I. and the National Audit Office; but much remains to be done. Major changes have been made in education and the health service intended to improve efficiency and consumers' choice, but there are doubts as to their suitability and effectiveness and it is too early to make a judgement.

An important issue in considering the question "How much public expenditure?" is the adequacy and appropriateness of the tax system which sustains it. The more equitable the tax system is perceived to be and the less it distorts economic choices, the more easily can public expenditure be sustained. This brings us to a consideration of possible tax reforms. But we should remind ourselves of the conflict between the various "principles" of taxation, which we discussed in Chapter 5. With possible reforms we often face a "trade off" situation. A gain in simplicity may only be attainable at the cost of some sacrifice in equity; or a reduction in inequality is offset by a loss of efficiency. Even if we can quantify some of the consequences of prospective changes, and many defy precise measurement either from their very nature or our imperfect tools, what constitutes an improvement is often a matter of judgement.

Tax Reform

Let us start with a series of fairly modest reforms which ought not to be too difficult to attain, which could be implemented piece-meal and could meet particular needs. The proposals are put forward in concise form partly for reasons of space, but mainly because, in large measure, the arguments to support them can be drawn from earlier chapters.

Income Tax and National Insurance Contributions

One major conclusion to emerge from the Meade Report on *The Structure and Reform of Direct Taxation* was that the present so-called income tax in the United Kingdom is really a hybrid. So many forms of saving have been granted full or partial tax relief—super-annuation payments, mortgage interest, insurance premiums—that the "income tax" is half way to an expenditure tax. As we saw in Chapter 6 an expenditure tax is an attractive proposition. If the prospect of a full-blooded switch to a direct expenditure tax is too daunting for the tax authorities, to widen further the range of tax exempt savings would take us nearer to the expenditure base and might reduce the investment distortion of the present system. The alternative would be to back track towards a genuine income tax and reduce the area of relief for savings. In fact Conservative Chancellors have followed neither route consistently. Mr. Nigel Lawson, as Chancellor, specifically repudiated the idea of a direct expenditure tax and cut back on the tax concessions on insurance premiums on new life policies as well as holding constant in money terms the mortgage interest relief. But then he and his successors introduced new forms of savings relief like P.E.P.s and T.E.S.S.A.s. There has been little principle in the approach and the United Kingdom income tax remains a rather indefensible hybrid.

An attractive proposal to improve both the horizontal and vertical equity of the income tax is a switch from tax allowances to tax credits. We shall say more below about the Conservative tax credit scheme. This proposal is more modest. A tax credit is a direct offset to tax liability, whereas an allowance is an offset to taxable income. A credit could be separate from the tax bill, paid by a separate agency, or it could simply be deducted from the gross tax bill. The particular merit of a credit is that the benefit to tax payers is the same irrespective of their tax rate; whereas a tax allowance benefits tax payers according to their marginal tax rate. Such a switch would also make possible the elimination of an objectionable feature of the present system of taxing income. In Chapter 6 we noted the existence of a regressive kink towards the top of the basic rate band where employees' national insurance contributions end. A sensible plan would be to integrate income tax and N.I. contributions to eliminate the kink by bringing together the upper limit of N.I. contributions and the start of higher rate tax. This cannot be done under a system of tax allowances because there is no uniform relationship between them. Taxable income starts at different income levels for different taxpayers because of their differing allowances. With tax credits the whole of income would be taxable (but the tax bill would be reduced by the credits). There would then be no problem of integrating N.I. with income tax in the manner proposed to eliminate the kink.

Indeed, there is much to be said, anyway, for making the employees' N.I. contribution a simple additional proportional *tranche* to the income tax. By so doing N.I. would become proportional instead of regressive and firms' compliance costs for collecting it would be reduced. It is often maintained that people pay N.I. contributions more readily than income tax because they associate the N.I. payment with specific benefits. The evidence for this assertion is lacking; but, if desired, the link could be retained. A specific rate of tax, on top of ordinary income tax, could be designated the social security tax; and it could be varied separately from the rates of income tax. However, the two would be collected as one and, unlike the present employees' N.I. contribution, the social security tax would be proportional across all income. Such a change would do something towards restoring the progressiveness of the tax system overall, which we saw (Chapters 6 and 11) was so conspicuously lacking at the upper end since the massive reductions in top income tax rates and the switches to V.A.T. The extent of the growth in income inequality during the past decade is to many (including the author) a matter of acute concern.

A major change in income tax which has been under consideration in Inland Revenue and government circles intermittently is a change in method of income tax administration from revenue assessment to self-assessment. The authors of the major study of the subject* produce arguments which constitute at least a prima facie case for the change. Self-assessment would be associated with the abolition of *cumulative* P.A.Y.E., a system of great ingenuity but one which has tended to bind the United Kingdom to a uniquely wide basic rate band. The main merits of the change would be a reduction in administrative costs; an increased flexibility in marginal tax rates making possible a smoother progression in the income tax; and the scope for introducing a local income tax, on the same base, at a much lower administrative cost than the alternative ways hitherto proposed. This would much improve the prospect of obtaining more genuine local autonomy with accountability. The snag about self-assessment is the inevitable increase in income tax compliance costs.

The appropriate tax unit for income tax, as we saw in Chapter 6, poses a difficult problem because of changing economic and social conditions and the inevitable clash between the principle of equal treatment for individuals and the recognition that ability to pay is related to the overall financial circumstances of the family. The author can only express his own value judgement, which is that he supports the move to a system of mandatory independent taxation implemented in 1990–91. This system better reflects modern social attitudes than the dependency principle, which underlay the former tax treatment of husband and wife. What he is much less happy about is the retention of the former married man's allowance redesignated the married couples' allowance. The logic of independent taxation is that an allowance for marriage should go. It would have been much better to abolish it and use the savings to finance a home responsibility payment which could be introduced to cover circumstances in which wives (or, for that matter,

*N. A. Barr, S. R. James and A. R. Prest, *Self-Assessment for Income Tax*, Heinemann Educational Books, 1977.

husbands or single persons) needed to stay at home to look after young children or dependent relatives. However, it might be unreasonable and unrealistic to expect older women, who had not worked for years, to be able to make good the loss of benefit by going out to work. They grew up in an economic and social climate when dependency on a husband was the reality. Thus it might have been wise and just to have a tapered cut-off related to age by which, say, husbands with wives at present over fifty could continue to claim the married man's allowance until their wife became eligible for a state retirement pension. Those whose wives were below the designated age would never receive it.

The home responsibility payment could be made taxable; in practice tax would only be paid by those with substantial income from other sources, because it would be more than offset by the personal allowance. It would thus serve to counteract some of the tax advantage that Mr. Lawson's reform brought to married couples with substantial investment income.

In the event Mr. Lawson's reform makes it much more difficult to move away from a marriage allowance than if it has been accomplished as part of the overall reform. One easy but very slow method would be to leave it unchanged in money terms (as Mr. Lamont did in the 1991 Budget) thus allowing it to fall in value and gradually wither away. But funds would then have to be found from elsewhere for the home responsibility allowance. Taxing child benefit might be one way. Non-working mothers without considerable other income would not pay the tax because they could offset it against otherwise unused personal allowances.

Inheritance Tax and Accessions Tax

As we saw in Chapter 9, a donor-based tax, like the United Kingdom's so-called Inheritance Tax, is not the most suitable tax for reducing inequalities of wealth; in its present form it is a particularly feeble instrument for that purpose. A government wishing to pursue that objective would do well to switch to an accessions tax, which taxes recipients of gifts and legacies rather than donors. An accessions tax is likely to promote equality in wealth holding more than a donor-based tax and no less effectively than an annual wealth tax, without the same risk of detrimental economic effects and with less administrative problems. It would be somewhat more expensive to administer than the inheritance tax.* The Liberal Party for long favoured this form of death duty and the same presumably goes for the Liberal Democrats. The Labour Party now also seems to be supporting a change to a donee-based tax to judge from recent statements from the Shadow Chancellor.

Value Added Tax

Two reforms might be considered for V.A.T., one concerning its rate structure, the other its administration.

The United Kingdom V.A.T. is characterised by a wide range of zero rating and exemptions as a result of which something like 40 per cent of consumption expenditure does not bear tax (or, in the case of exemptions, only minimal tax in so far as input tax is passed on in the price). This creates distortions in consumption and production patterns and increases compliance costs. The main justification for the zero-rating is to leave "essentials" like food, fuel and children's clothes free of tax; and also to leave certain "merit goods", like books and newspapers, tax free. There are major difficulties in defining both "essentials" and "merit goods". Food includes caviar as well as bread; and books include pornography as well as the bible. The case for zero-rating caviar and pornography is not obvious. As for children's clothes, the differentiation has to be by size, with the result that small adults get the benefit and big children (who most need the benefit because they have grown fastest) don't.

Apart from such anomalies, however, it is true that the poor spend a larger proportion of their income on the zero rated goods than the better off. Consequently, as a result of zero rating, over the lower range of incomes V.A.T. is actually progressive.

However, whilst the poor may spend a larger proportion of their income on food and children's clothes, the absolute amount they

---

*See C. T. Sandford, J. R. M. Willis and D. J. Ironside, *An Accessions Tax*, I.F.S. 1973, for a full discussion of an accessions tax, including its likely administrative cost.

spend on these items is much less than the rich. A study undertaken for the Irish Commission on Taxation showed that the top income decile spent four times as much on food as the bottom decile and twenty times as much on clothes. (The poorest tend to buy all their clothes second-hand.) There is no reason to think that the figures in the United Kingdom would be very different. Thus the principal beneficiaries of zero rating in absolute terms are the wealthy.

All this makes a strong case for removing zero rating and compensating or, better still, over-compensating the less well off by increased social security payments and child benefits and raising the income tax threshold. It would have the effect of reducing inequalities in disposable and final income.

On the side of "administration" the biggest defect of V.A.T. is the heavy compliance costs which fall on small firms and the competitive disadvantage under which this places them.

The most promising move to reduce this disadvantage would seem to be for the United Kingdom to adopt the practice of several European countries and introduce differential payment periods. The majority of traders would remain on a three-months collection and payment period as at present. The smaller firms could be allowed to make annual returns.* The largest could be put on a monthly return basis. There would be a saving of compliance costs for the many small firms and some increase for the large firms — but with their computerised systems the additional cost to the large firms would be small. More significant, the shorter payment periods for the large firms would reduce their cash flow benefit from V.A.T. whilst that of the smallest firms would be increased. Thus, on account of both compliance costs and cash flow benefit the small firms would gain relatively to the large and the state-imposed competitive disadvantage small firms at present suffer would be alleviated. All this would be achieved at no cost to the Exchequer; instead the Exchequer would benefit from a once-and-for-all gain. So much more revenue comes from the few large firms than the many small that there would be a net speeding-up of payments into the Exchequer. This would, of course, be at the expense of the large

---

*Small firms are at present allowed to do this, but on rather onerous terms of payment on account which remove any cash flow benefit. The option has been little used.

firms' liquidity. However, hitherto many of them have been in the happy position that their cash flow benefit exceeded their compliance costs.

Tax Changes to Improve the Environment

In Chapter 5 we indicated that one of the principles of taxation was efficiency in the allocation of resources, or minimum price distortion of production and consumption. However, we also recognised that there are existing distortions in the system which give rise to social costs over and above private costs, i.e. where the costs to the community are not taken into account by private producers or consumers. Thus, where there are industries creating pollution in one form or another, in the absence of government action the polluting industry is over-expanded compared with its size if the price took account of all the costs. In such a situation there is a strong case for using taxes to bring price more into line with social cost.

One such measure has already been introduced into the United Kingdom through the differential tax on leaded and unleaded petrol, but there is a case for increasing the differential to give more incentive for consumers to use cleaner petrol. Other worthwhile possibilities are tax incentives for the manufacturers to introduce catalytic converters in cars. Catalytic converters can remove a significant proportion of the pollutants from burning petrol—in particular hydrocarbons, carbon monoxide and nitrogen oxide. One method of encouraging catalytic converters would be to have a differential car tax; currently in the United Kingdom all cars carry a 10 per cent car tax in addition to V.A.T. This tax could be set lower for cars with catalytic converters compared with those without so that it paid the manufacturers to produce them and the consumer to buy them.

Similarly, small cars with low petrol consumption create less pollution than large "gas guzzling" cars. A differential vehicle excise duty and a differentiation in company car taxation could encourage the use of small cars and benefit the environment.

Ways in which taxation can improve the environment are likely to become increasingly important in the future; much research is taking place in this area and is likely to produce practicable possibilities that are not confined to cars.

Radical Reform—Proposals of the Irish Tax Commission

Comprehensive tax reform is the dream of the academic tax reformer and the nightmare of the tax administrator. Administrators who have to keep the revenue rolling in, and the politicians whose horizons are restricted to the next election, tend to view comprehensive tax change with disfavour. That is why we began this section with a series of possible tax reforms which were modest and could be implemented piece-meal. But where a system, like that of the United Kingdom, has grown somewhat haphazardly over the years, and because of the interactions and links between taxes, it is difficult to achieve satisfactory reform which falls short of the comprehensive. Hence we conclude this section with proposals for a radical and comprehensive reform of direct taxes in which the main elements essentially hang together. The proposals were published in July 1982 by the Irish Tax Commission.*

The Irish tax system is sufficiently similar to that of the United Kingdom for the main recommendations to be equally applicable here. Indeed, the Commission's proposals incorporate into an integrated system some of the suggestions we have already considered.

The basic proposal of the Commission is the adoption of a comprehensive income tax. They consider that the income tax base should be widened to include capital gains, gifts and legacies. At the same time most of the existing tax allowances should go, with personal allowances being replaced by tax credits. With such a wide base the rate of tax can be kept low and they propose that it should be a flat rate. Full inflation-proofing of the income tax is proposed, including a capital-income adjustment.

The Commission recommended that the social security payments of both employers and employees should be replaced by an additional *tranche* of income tax levied on all income as redefined for tax

*First Report of the Commission on Taxation: Direct Taxation, Dublin, July 1982.

purposes. For reasons we discussed earlier, the Commission proposed that the social security tax should be distinguished from income tax and a separate social security fund retained.

Corporation tax, they considered, should be charged at the same rate as income tax and the tax on dividends fully imputed; in other words tax on distributed profits would simply amount to income tax collected at source.

If income tax is imposed at a flat rate how is progression to be introduced into the system? The answer is partly by means of public expenditure; partly by the use of tax credits instead of allowances; partly by ridding the system of the regressiveness in social security contributions; but also by the introduction of a direct expenditure tax imposed on the top 5 or 10 per cent of spenders. The Commission also recommend a single rate of V.A.T. on a wide base.

The Commission made no judgement on whether or not the state should use taxation to reduce inequality of wealth holding. However, if that should be an objective of government policy, they recommend an accessions tax rather than an annual wealth tax as the appropriate instrument.

The Commission has preserved a fine balance amongst the conflicting objectives of equity, simplicity and efficiency. To adopt a single rate of income tax with minimum reliefs in relation to a comprehensive tax base and apply the same rate to corporation tax is a major simplification. The simplification is taken further by a social security tax which uses the same base. At the same time efficiency is promoted because the choice of form of business organisation and decisions on form of investment are not distorted by tax considerations. Also the scope for tax avoidance by means of switches between "income" sources is drastically reduced, if not fully eliminated. Full inflation-proofing of the tax system and the introduction of a progressive expenditure tax are complications, but in the interests of horizontal and vertical equity the Commission could do no less. The proposals give sufficient flexibility to allow for detailed adjustments in accordance with the political philosophies of different governments.

It has to be said that Irish governments have shown little inclination to implement the Commission's recommendations save in minor ways. The U.K. government could do far worse than take their recommendations on board.

Alternative Approaches to Welfare Expenditure

Reforms of the kind we have discussed would probably enable more revenue to be raised from the tax system for welfare expenditure or other purposes without the shoe pinching quite as much. In this section we look at other approaches to welfare expenditure; the first is concerned with the introduction of more private money for welfare spending; the second two are concerned with methods which link taxation and welfare expenditure.

User Charges

An obvious method of raising funds for state provision of welfare services is by increased user charges. Some user charges (with exemptions for particular categories of persons, like children and retired persons) are already largely accepted, such as charges for prescriptions, dental treatment and spectacles. Another example of how the cost can be placed more on the beneficiary is the finance of higher education partly by loans rather than grants as the government has recently done. Mr. Douglas Houghton, for 9 months in 1966 Minister Without Portfolio with responsibility for co-ordinating social policy on pensions, health and the education services, made the novel proposal that *extra* resources for the health service should be found from increased user charges, but these should not be flat rate charges; they should be graduated by means of national income assessments through the income tax coding system.*

Nor need increases in user charges be restricted to the social services. The Layfield Committee pointed out the tendency for the proportion of expenditure of local authorities met from fees and charges to fall (from 10 per cent of rate fund expenditure in 1969–70 to 7 per cent in 1973–74) and revealed the existence of a wide range of approaches to charging. They recommended a review of charging

---

*Douglas Houghton, *Paying for the Social Services*, Institute of Economic Affairs, 1967.

policies for local services. As we saw in Chapter 10, there is a particular case for abolishing or reducing business rates and charging businesses for the services provided by local authorities.

Negative Income Tax/Tax Credit Schemes

Over the years various schemes have been put forward to provide income support for the poorer members of the community based on the principles of linking social security payments with income tax.* Using the income tax mechanism was seen to have several positive advantages. It provided a form of means-testing which was impersonal, more or less universal and more widely acceptable than separate means tests for welfare benefits. It was likely to secure a high "take-up" — there would be no stigma attached to it. If income tax allowances were converted into credits, the full benefit would go to those who currently only partially benefit because their income is too low for them to pay tax. In addition linking the two systems might enable a number of individual benefits to be replaced and offer significant administrative economies.

In recent years the need for action to co-ordinate welfare benefits with each other and with the tax system has become more urgent because of the phenomenon of the "poverty trap" (see p. 149).

The proposal to link tax and welfare payments which came nearest to being enacted, and is still a possibility for the future, is the Tax Credit Scheme of the Conservative Government of 1970–74, which the Conservatives were committed to implement if they had won the 1974 election. The scheme was first presented in the form of a Green Paper† in October 1972 and also reported on by a Select Committee of the House of Commons. It proposed a partial merger of the income tax and social security systems with the dual purpose of improving income support for poor people and reforming the whole system of personal tax collection. This was to be brought about through the introduction of a new form of credit which would replace personal tax allowances, including the then existing child

---

*See Cedric Sandford, Chris Pond and Robert Walker (eds.), *Taxation and Social Policy*, especially chapters 11 and 12.
†*Proposals for a Tax Credit System*, Cmnd. 5116, October 1972.

tax allowances, family allowances (paid to the mother through the Post Office for second and subsequent children) and the family income supplement (F.I.S.). The Green Paper used the following illustrative figures for the credits: £4 for a single person, £6 for a married man and for the one parent family and £2 for a child. Subject to the qualifications below, the credits were to be paid to those in work through their employer; to occupational pensioners through the employer; and to people drawing national insurance benefits (e.g. sickness or retirement) or temporarily unemployed, through the Department of Health and Social Security and the Department of Employment respectively. The Green Paper left open the question whether the child credit should be paid through the employer (generally to the father) or through the Post Office (like family allowances) to the mother, but the government accepted the recommendation of the Select Committee to pay through the Post Office.

Each individual in the scheme would receive a notification of his credit entitlement which he would give to his employer or other paying authority. The employer would deduct tax from all income at the basic rate (then 30 per cent); then against this tax employers would set the amount of credit to which the taxpayer was entitled. If the credit exceeded the tax the difference would be paid to the individual; if tax exceeded credit the difference would stand as a tax deduction. Table 15.1 gives some examples of the way this would work.

TABLE 15.1
Illustrations of the Operation of the Tax Credit Proposals

	Weekly pay £	Less tax at 30 per cent £	Plus credit £	Pay after tax and credit £
Single person	10	3	4	11
	25	7.50	4	21.50
	50	15	4	39
Married with two children	10	3	10	17
	25	7.50	10	27.50
	50	15	10	45

It will be seen that the credits performed two functions: like the present income tax allowances they would graduate income tax broadly according to family circumstances; to the extent that credits exceeded tax, unlike the present tax allowances, they would automatically provide a weekly income supplement.

Various other proposals made possible the elimination of most of the remaining tax allowances (e.g. instead of a tax allowance on mortgage interest or insurance premiums the taxpayer would pay a smaller sum to building societies or insurance companies and the government would compensate them). Any allowances that remained would have to be claimed after the end of the income tax year. Higher rate tax would also be paid in arrears. The deduction of tax at basic rate from the whole income of all those in the scheme meant that unemployment pay and sickness benefits, which then escaped taxation simply because of administrative difficulties, could easily be taxed; and the simplifications, including the elimination of the cumulative element in P.A.Y.E., would have substantially reduced administrative costs to the Inland Revenue and compliance costs to employers.

Whilst the scheme would cover all employed persons earning (in 1972) above £8 per week, all main national insurance beneficiaries and most occupational pensioners, it excluded the self-employed and those with under £8 per week other than pensioners. The self-employed were omitted because it was only possible to calculate their tax liabilities after the end of the tax year when their accounts were completed, and it was not considered feasible to pay credits each week with no tax offset. Those with under £8 per week were excluded because to have helped them sufficiently to take them off supplementary benefit would have meant raising tax credit levels to everyone, and this would have been too costly. The Green Paper expressed the hope that means might be found to enable these groups to be incorporated in the scheme later.

The Green Paper claimed: "The tax-credit scheme cannot of itself offer a complete solution to all the problems of poverty. But to those within it, and this includes the great majority of people at work and everyone in receipt of the main national insurance benefits, it offers the prospect of a system of family support which would be easier to understand than the present one, which would provide its benefit largely automatically and which, being integrated with the tax system, would extend the benefit of tax allowances to people who have insufficient income to pay tax. By doing so it would relieve hundreds of thousands of pensioners from the need to claim supplementary benefit. It would also bring significant increases in income to a further three or four million pensioners who already have some margin, but not a great one, above the supplementary benefit level, and would similarly prove of great help to hard-pressed families of working age—especially those with children—many of whom cannot be helped effectively through F.I.S. and other means-tested schemes. Some means-testing—and the flexibility which only means-testing can secure—would remain, but its role in the social services as a whole would be reduced. These are substantial gains, for which the government hope the tax-credit scheme will be widely seen as a welcome new departure."*

To the critics this over-stated the case. They pointed to the limited coverage of the scheme and the many means-tested benefits that would remain. They were also concerned that no satisfactory explanation appeared in the Green Paper of where the £1,300 million net cost of the scheme (on the basis of the illustrative figures) would be found. Yet this was vital to assessing its effects on income distribution. Linked with this point was the fact that much of the benefit of the scheme would, on the basis of the illustrative figures, go to those not in poverty. Moreover, the critics did not consider the scheme sufficiently flexible to make it possible to direct help sufficiently to those most in need.†

A majority of the members of the Select Committee recommended the adoption of the scheme with amendments, but two minority reports by Labour members criticised the scheme on the grounds we have outlined. In his first budget speech Mr. Healey stressed the "serious drawbacks of the tax credit scheme proposed by the previous administration", but went on to add that "we have not taken any decision against the principle of a negative income tax".

---

*Paragraph 115, Cmnd. 5116.
†A. B. Atkinson, *The Tax Credit Scheme and the Redistribution of Income*, IFS, September 1973.

The Labour Government of 1974–79 never endorsed the tax credit scheme, but it did implement a measure with some of the characteristics of the tax credit scheme on a limited scale, i.e. the replacement of the income tax child allowances by improved family allowances including payments to the first as well as subsequent children, made through the Post Office.

A Negative Wealth Tax or National Bounty

An idea which has long appealed to the author might be called a negative wealth tax (or national bounty), although it is not precisely on a par with the negative income tax. The proposal is that at a particular time in his life each person residing and born in this country should receive from the state a lump sum payment of, say, £4,000. Whilst this might normally be paid at age 21, as a coming of age bonus, the sum could be obtainable, in whole or in part, for approved purposes (e.g. to pay for higher education) at an earlier age, but not younger than 18.

The proposal has a number of attractions. In general our welfare and social services provide income benefits, yet some needs can better be met by the provision of "capital" benefits. Thus the bonus would provide the security of a small nest egg and complement at the lower end what death duties may do at the upper end to diminish inequalities of wealth. The bounty would meet a particular welfare need—that of the young couple setting up house; many couples can meet annual mortgage payments on a house but lack a deposit; a £4,000 dowry would give a combined sum of £8,000 for setting up house. Again, the scheme is fairer than existing social service expenditure to the less-well-endowed intellectually. Currently the intellectual *élite* gain the benefits of state subsidisation in the later stages of secondary and in higher education as a result of which they derive personal benefits from subsequent high earnings. This scheme would benefit all; the intellectual high-fliers could use the bounty towards the cost of higher education, but would have to supplement it with loans, not grants; the bounty would also provide opportunities for the less intellectual, e.g. helping to set them up in a small business. The scheme is also fairer between the sexes than current welfare expenditure, in which expenditure on higher education predominantly benefits men.

There are two obvious objections to the negative wealth tax or national bounty. The first is cost, which at £4,000 per person would be of the order of £3,600 million per annum; the second is irresponsible use of the bounty. A substantial part of the cost could be met by ending, for those eligible for the bounty, some income benefits, namely the special mortgage relief scheme and income tax concessions on mortgage interest; and substitution of education loans for grants. But the whole cost would not need to be met by taxation; insofar as bonuses were saved they would not be a drain on current resources. This is where there could be a match up with capital taxation, like death duties, which does not release current resources to the government. Further, should an accessions tax be adopted, the bounty should count as a gift within the terms of the tax and hence those who had already received capital sums would pay tax on the bounty and on subsequent capital receipts more tax would be paid than otherwise.

Some irresponsible use of the bounty, after age 21, must be accepted. People only become responsible when given responsibility. The bounty would not need to be paid in cash but could be placed in a bank account on behalf of the beneficiary, say half in national savings certificates and half in unit trust certificates; thus the temptation to use it for a spending spree would be reduced.

The transition to the scheme would also raise problems. If introduced for the 21-year-olds of 1992, those attaining that age the year before would naturally feel deprived. Transitional provisions for phasing would be necessary, e.g. for those who had missed the endowment, the retention for a considerable period of the benefits which were replaced for those who received it.

Reforming Policy-making Procedures

Reforming the content of taxation or of welfare provision does not exhaust the area of reform. We need to ensure, as far as we may, that the mechanism for future changes is appropriate; that the policy-making procedures in relation to both taxation and public expenditure are the best we can devise.

A number of suggestions can be made to improve the tax policy-making process.* To start with a firm commitment to more open government would help. In the 1960s and 1970s considerable progress has been made in this regard—the use of Green Papers and other consultative documents and of Select Committees of the House of Commons became regular practice; but it is not yet invariable practice. Thus when capital transfer tax was introduced there was no Green Paper, and the review of the tax ordered by Sir Geoffrey Howe was largely carried out behind closed doors. Moreover, whilst there has been a flood of Green Papers and consultative documents since 1979 (e.g. on corporation tax, on the taxation of husband and wife and on local taxation) the ensuing reforms often seemed to bear little relationship to the Green Paper proposals. The use of Select Committees has been completely dropped—yet a thorough investigation of the community charge proposal by a Select Committee before it was introduced might well have avoided the fiasco that ensued. Consultation must be genuine and full.

The party stage is crucial in relation to new taxes For example, capital gains tax, wealth tax and capital transfer tax were all commitments of the Labour Party prior to assuming office. Unfortunately the evidence suggests that little detailed work was done on them in Opposition and, at any rate with capital gains tax and capital transfer tax, they were rushed into legislation with inadequate consideration. The Conservatives in recent years have given fuller consideration whilst in Opposition to the new taxes they had in mind, like V.A.T.; but they have rushed into commitments to abolish taxes—notably S.E.T., capital transfer tax and local domestic rates—before they were clear on what to put in their place. Neither procedure makes for good tax policy. Unfortunately there is no mechanism to ensure that politicians eschew the rash commitment.

At the departmental stage there is much to be said for a tax

*For a full consideration of this topic see Ann Robinson and Cedric Sandford, *Tax Policy-Making in the United Kingdom*, Heinemann Educational Books, 1983.

equivalent to P.E.S.C.—a committee, with representatives from the revenue and other appropriate departments, chaired by a senior Treasury official. Such a committee would be in a position to look ahead in the light of anticipated revenue needs; to examine the likely effects of alternative taxes, and to place proposals for new taxes into the context of the present and likely future tax system.

One function of such a committee would be to prepare a tax-expenditure budget. As we have pointed out in Chapter 4, the United Kingdom published, in the annual Public Expenditure White Papers and continues to publish in its successor documents, a list of direct tax reliefs and their estimated cost to the Exchequer. But good policy-making requires more than this. The tax expenditures need to be put alongside explicit expenditures in their appropriate programmes, e.g. the cost of mortgage interest relief presented as part of the housing expenditure programme. And the distributional effects of tax expenditures should be explored. A number of countries, including the U.S.A. and Canada, have gone farther along this path than the United Kingdom.

Ends and Means

Regardless of personal philosophy, measures such as we have just outlined to promote more meaningful communal choice should be welcomed. Of the possible reforms in taxation and welfare expenditure this will not be true; people will differ on grounds of principle and of philosophy. How far do we *want* to try to mitigate inequalities of income and of capital through taxation? How far, in welfare expenditure, do we want public provision and how far private? Should the emphasis of welfare expenditure be on cash (or vouchers) or in kind? How far should the balance of state welfare expenditure be tilted from universal to selective provision? Should "capital" benefits partially replace "income" benefits?

Those with the more individualistic philosophy in so far as they wish to mitigate inequalities will seek to do so through income and wealth redistribution rather than by provision in kind and will incline to methods emphasising private rather than public provision, individual and family responsibility rather than "state" responsibility. The negative income and capital taxes might appeal more readily to them. "Collectivists", on the other hand, tend to be suspicious of negative income and negative wealth tax; and seek universal state education, health provision and pensions as providing a more congenial social milieu and a less class-ridden society.

Our concern in this book is not to judge between the two approaches but to seek to bring out some of the implications and thus help to distinguish between means and ends and, where possible, give some indication of the cost of pursuing particular ends. The dividing line between the two groups is not as clear cut as we have suggested. Indeed, there has been a reaction against the more extreme forms of collectivism. Nevertheless, the issues are fundamental. The tax and welfare reforms adopted (or allowed to pass by default) will profoundly influence the nature of our society.

Postscript

In the 1992 Budget the car tax (referred to on p. 368) was reduced to 5 per cent.

Selected Bibliography

The following is a short selection of publications regarded as particularly useful for understanding the topics considered in this book.

ALLAN, C. M. *The Theory of Taxation*, Penguin Modern Economics, 1971.

ATKINSON, A. B., GORDON, J. P. F. and HARRISON, A. Trends in the Shares of Top Wealthholders in Britain, 1923–81, *Oxford Bulletin of Economics and Statistics*, Vol. 51, No. 2, August 1989.

BARR, N. A., JAMES, S. R. and PREST, A. R. *Self Assessment for Income Tax*, Heinemann Education Books, 1977.

BECKER, G. S. *Human Capital. A Theoretical and Empirical Analysis with special reference to Education*, Princeton, 1964.

BLAUG, M. *An Introduction to the Economics of Education*, Penguin, 1972.

BLUM, W. J. and KALVEN, H. *The Uneasy Case for Progressive Taxation*, University of Chicago Press, 1953.

BREAK, G. F. Effects of Taxation on Incentives, *British Tax Review*, June 1957.

BRITTAN, S. *Second Thoughts on Full Employment*, The Centre for Policy Studies, 1975.

BROWN, C. V. and DAWSON, D. A. *Personal Taxation Incentives and Tax Reform*, P.E.P., 1969.

BROWN, C. V. *Taxation and the Incentive to Work*, Oxford University Press, 1980.

BROWN, C. V. and JACKSON, P. M. *Public Sector Economics*, 4th edition, Blackwell, Oxford 1990.

BROWN, C. V. and SANDFORD, C. T. *Taxes and Incentives: The Effects of the Cuts in Higher Rate Income Tax*, Economic Study No. 7, Institute for Public Policy Research, 1991.

CULLIS, J. G. and WEST, P. A. *The Economics of Health*, Martin Robertson, 1979.

DEVEREUX, M. and PEARSON, M. *Corporate Tax Harmonisation and Economic Efficiency*, Institute for Fiscal Studies, Report Series No. 35, 1989.

DEVEREUX, M. and PEARSON, M. Harmonising Corporate Taxes in Europe *Fiscal Studies*, Vol. 11, No. 1, February 1990.

DILNOT, A. and WEBB, S. Reforming National Insurance Contributions: A Progress Report, *Fiscal Studies*, Vol. 10, No. 2, May 1989.

FIELDS, D. B. and STANBURY, W. T. Incentives, Disincentives and the Income Tax, Further Empirical Evidence, *Public Finance*, No. 3, 1970.

HICKS, U. K. The Terminology and Methods of Tax Analysis, *Economic Journal*, March 1946.

HILLS, J. *Changing Tax*, C.P.A.G., London 1988.

HILLS, J. and SUTHERLAND, H. *Banding, Tilting, Gearing, Gaining and Losing: An Anatomy of the Proposed Council Tax*, Welfare State Programme, Suntory-Toyota International Centre for Economics and Related Disciplines, July 1991.

HOCKLEY, G. C. *Monetary Policy and Public Finance*, Routledge & Kegan Paul, latest edition.

HOUGHTON, R. W. (ed.), *Public Finance*, Penguin Modern Economic Readings, 1970.

JAMES, S. and NOBES, C. *The Economics of Taxation*, Philip Allen, latest edition.

KALDOR, N. *Expenditure Tax*, Allen & Unwin, 1955.

KAY, J. A. and KING, M. A. *The British Tax System*, Oxford University Press, latest edition.

KIND, P., ROSSER, R. and WILLIAMS, A. *Valuation of Life: Some Psychometric Evidence* in *The Value of Life and Safety*, ed. M. W. Jones-Lee, North Holland 1982.

LAYARD, R., NICKELL, S. and JACKMAN, R. *Unemployment: Macroeconomic Performance and the Labour Market*, Oxford University Press, 1991.

LEES, D. The Economics of Health Services, *Lloyds Bank Review*, April 1960.

LIESNER, T. and KING, M. A. (eds.), *Indexing for Inflation*, Institute for Fiscal Studies, 1975.

LIKIERMAN, A. and TAYLOR, A. *Government's New Departmental Reports: Challenges and Potential Problems*, ACCA Research Report 19, 1990.

LIKIERMAN, A. and TAYLOR, A. *The Government's First Departmental Reports*, ACCA Research Report 24, 1991.

MCGUIRE, A., FENN, P. and MAYHEW, K. (eds.) *Providing Health Care: the Economics of Alternative Systems of Delivery*, Oxford University Press, 1991.

MEADE REPORT—*The Structure and Reform of Direct Taxation*, Report of a Committee chaired by Professor J. E. Meade, Institute for Fiscal Studies/George Allen & Unwin, 1978.

PEACOCK, A. T. The Political Economy of Social Welfare, *The Three Banks Review*, December 1964.

PEACOCK, A. T. and WISEMAN, J. *The Growth of Public Expenditure in the United Kingdom*, 2nd ed., Allen & Unwin, 1967.

PESTON, M. On the Nature and Extent of the Public Sector, *The Three Banks Review*, September 1903.

PESTON, M. *Public Goods and the Public Sector*, 1972.

PETERS, G. H. *Cost Benefit Analysis and Public Expenditure*, Eaton Paper 8, Institute of Economic Affairs, 3rd ed., 1973.

PIACHAUD, D. and WEDDELL, J. M. The Economics of Treating Varicose Veins, *International Journal of Epidemiology*, Vol. 3, No. 1, 1972.

PLIATZKY, L. *Getting and Spending*, Basil Blackwell, 1982.

PREST, A. R. and BARR, N. A. *Public Finance in Theory and Practice*, Weidenfeld & Nicolson, latest edition.

RIDGE, M. and SMITH, S. *Local Taxation: The Options and the Arguments*, Institute for Fiscal Studies, Report Series No. 38, 1991.

ROBERTSON, D. J. and PEACOCK, A. T. *Public Expenditure Appraisal and Control*, Oliver & Boyd, 1963.

ROBINSON, A. and SANDFORD, C. T. *Tax Policy-Making in the United Kingdom*, Heinemann Educational Books, 1983.

ROBINSON, B. and STARK, G. The Tax Treatment of Marriage: What has the Chancellor Really Achieved? *Fiscal Studies*, Vol. 9, No. 2, May 1988.

SANDFORD, C. T. *Taxing Personal Wealth*, Allen & Unwin, 1971.

SANDFORD, C. T. *Hidden Costs of Taxation*, Institute for Fiscal Studies, 1973.

SANDFORD, C. T., WILLIS, J. R. M. and IRONSIDE, D. J. *An Accessions Tax*, Institute for Fiscal Studies, 1973.

SANDFORD, C. T., WILLIS, J. R. M. and IRONSIDE, D. J. *An Annual Wealth Tax*, Institute for Fiscal Studies, 1975.

SANDFORD, C. T. *The Case for the Abolition of Non-Domestic Rates*, National Federation of the Self-Employed and Small Businesses Limited, 1981.

SANDFORD, C. T., GODWIN, M. R., HARDWICK, P. J. W. and BUTTERWORTH, I. *Costs and Benefits of VAT*, Heinemann Educational Books, 1981.

SANDFORD, C. T. and ROBINSON, A. Indirect Taxation: Back to the Drawing Board, *Accountancy*, August 1988.

SANDFORD, C. T., GODWIN, M. R. and HARDWICK, P. J. W. *Administrative and Compliance Costs of Taxation*, Fiscal Publications, Bath 1989.

TANZI, V. *Inflation and the Personal Income Tax: An International Perspective*, Cambridge University Press, 1980.

VEVERKA, J. Growth of Public Expenditure in the U.K. since 1790, *Scottish Journal of Political Economy*, Vol. 10, No. 1, 1963.

WEST, E. G. *Education and the State*, Institute of Economic Affairs, 1965.

WHITTINGTON, G. *Company Taxation and Dividends*, Institute for Fiscal Studies, Lecture Series No. 1, 1974.

WILLIAMS, A. The Economics of Coronary Artery Bypass Grafting, *British Medical Journal*, 3 August 1985.

WOODHALL, M. *Student Loans: Lessons from Recent International Experience*, Policy Studies Institute, 1982.

Official Publications

Royal Commission on the Taxation of Profits and Income, Second Report, Cmnd. 9105, 1954, and *Final Report*, Cmnd. 9474, 1955.

Control of Public Expenditure, Cmnd. 1432, 1961 (the Plowden Report).

Output Budgeting for the Department of Education and Science, Education Planning Paper No. 1, H.M.S.O., 1970.

Value Added Tax, N.E.D.O., H.M.S.O., 1971.

Value Added Tax, Cmnd. 4929, 1972.

Taxation of Capital on Death: A Possible Inheritance Tax in Place of Estate Duty, Cmnd. 4930, 1972.

Reform of Corporation Tax, Cmnd. 4955, 1972.

Proposals for a Tax Credit System, Cmnd. 5116, 1972.

Select Committee on Tax Credit, H.C. 341-1, 1973.

Wealth Tax, Cmnd. 5704, 1974.

Ninth Report of the Expenditure Committee, Session 1974, Public Expenditure, Inflation and the Balance of Payments, H.C. 328, 1974.

Select Committee on a Wealth Tax, Volume I: Report and Proceedings of the Committee, H.C. 696-1, 1975.

Local Government Finance, Cmnd. 6453, 1976 (the Layfield Report).

The Taxation of Husband and Wife, Cmnd. 8093, 1980.

Alternatives to Domestic Rates, Cmnd. 8449, 1981.

Corporation Tax, Cmnd. 8456, 1982.

The Incidence of Taxes and Social Service Benefits (published annually in *Economic Trends*).

First Report of the Commission on Taxation: Direct Taxation, (Irish Tax Commission), 1982.

Report of the Committee on Enforcement Powers of the Revenue Departments, H.M.S.O., 1983 (the Keith Report).

Paying for Local Government, Cmnd. 9714, H.M.S.O., 1986.

The Reform of Personal Taxation, Cmnd. 9956, H.M.S.O., 1986.

Financial Reporting to Parliament, Report by the Comptroller and Auditor-General, National Audit Office, H.C. 576, H.M.S.O., 1986.

Financing and Delivering Health Care. A Comparative Analysis of O.E.C.D. Countries, O.E.C.D., Paris 1987.

Taxing Consumption, O.E.C.D., Paris 1988.

Taxation of Net Wealth, Capital Transfers and Capital Gains of Individuals, O.E.C.D., Paris 1988.

Top Up Loans for Students, Cmnd. 520, H.M.S.O., November 1988.

Working for Patients, Cmnd. 555, H.M.S.O., London 1989.

Estimate of the Distribution of Personal Wealth, *Economic Trends*, H.M.S.O., October 1990.

Inland Revenue Statistics 1990, H.M.S.O., 1990.

Financial Reporting to Parliament, Cmnd. 918, H.M.S.O., 1990.

Financial Statistics, No. 347, H.M.S.O., March 1991.

Revenue Statistics of OECD Member Countries, 1965–1990, O.E.C.D., Paris 1991.

United Kingdom National Accounts, the CSO Blue Book, H.M.S.O., 1991 edition.

Helping the Nation to Spend Wisely, National Audit Office (undated).

Royal Commission on the Distribution of Income and Wealth, Reports Nos. 1–8.

Index